The Cotonou Agreement:

A User's Guide

 COMMONWEALTH SECRETARIAT

Published by the Economic Affairs Division
of the Commonwealth Secretariat

Commonwealth Secretariat
Marlborough House
Pall Mall
London SW1Y 5HX
United Kingdom

Designed and published by the Commonwealth Secretariat
Printed and bound in the UK by The Charlesworth Group, Wakefield.

Wherever possible, the Commonwealth Secretariat uses paper sourced
from sustainable forests or from sources that minimise a destructive
impact on the environment.

ISBN 0-85092-789-7

Price: £18.99

Web site: http//www.thecommonwealth.org

Contents

Putting the Cotonou Agreement in Context

The Cotonou Agreement is an international agreement covering development assistance, trade and political relations between the 15 members of the European Union (EU) and the 79 members of the African Caribbean and Pacific (ACP) Group. While formal relations with individual groupings of ACP countries can be traced back to 1963, it was only in 1975 with the signing of the Georgetown Agreement that the ACP Group formally came into being, as the basis for the negotiation of a comprehensive trade, development assistance and political partnership arrangement with the EU. These negotiations gave rise in 1975 to the first Lomé Convention between an EU of nine member states and an ACP Group consisting of 46 countries.

Under Lomé I, primacy in the Agreement was given to trade co-operation, co-operation on commodities and industrial co-operation, with an extensive chapter on financial and technical co-operation. Since 1975 the ACP-EU co-operation framework has evolved considerably in terms of the nature and range of co-operation instruments available, the focus of co-operation activities and the geographical coverage of the Agreement.

Lomé I saw the establishment of a basic framework for financial and technical co-operation consisting of three main types of instruments: programmable instruments, non-programmable instruments and loan instruments. The non-programmable STABEX instrument, designed to financially assist countries facing unforeseen declines in agricultural export earnings, was a major innovation at the time.

Over successive Lomé Conventions the product coverage of the scheme was greatly extended and under Lomé II it was supplemented by a similar scheme – SYSMIN – for mineral-dependent ACP economies. While existing instruments were elaborated and further instruments added under Lomé III (aid to refugees and returnees) and Lomé IV (a structural adjustment support facility), the basic structure and philosophy of aid instruments remained constant until

2000. Programmable aid was made available at national and regional levels to support long-term development co-operation activities. Non-programmable assistance was made available to assist countries in dealing with unforeseen eventualities (man-made or natural disasters, or sharp declines in commodity prices), while loan financing was offered in support of large-scale public and private sector investments.

However, the signing of the Cotonou Agreement brought about a radical change in the structure of financial and technical co-operation instruments. Part 2 of this **User's Guide** explores this and it constitutes the main body of the *Guide*.

Similarly, the basic framework for trade relations established under the first Lomé Convention, while repeatedly elaborated and developed, has remained constant, based as it is on the extension by the EU of non-reciprocal trade preferences to the ACP Group. The extent of the preferential access granted to ACP countries has been constantly enlarged over the course of successive Lomé Conventions. But in successive Lomé Conventions the principle of duty-free access has been constrained by qualifications arising from the application of the EU's Common Agricultural Policy (CAP), the application of the rules of origin and the existence of safeguard provisions which allow the EU to withdraw certain preferences should these threaten to disrupt EU markets.

However, the signing of the Cotonou Agreement lays the basis for a fundamental transformation of the basis for ACP-EU trade relations by setting out a timetable for the negotiations of successor arrangements which will transform the current arrangements from a non-reciprocal preferential trade arrangement into a reciprocal preferential trade arrangement. Part 3 of this *Guide* explores this evolution and the impending transformation of the basis of ACP-EU trade relations.

In the political sphere, ACP-EU relations have evolved since 1975. For many years emphasis was placed on the political neutrality of the Lomé arrangement. Indeed, in 1980 the European Commission's in-house magazine *The Courier* identified one of the four fundamentals of the Lomé policy as being:

> *... one contract binding two regional groups, excluding and manipulation or discrimination inspired by unilateral assessments of the partners sovereign choice of economic systems, political regimes and development models. This means non-alignment and respect for national and cultural individuality ...*[1]

In more recent years increased emphasis has been placed on the political basis of the relationship, culminating under the Cotonou Agreement in the establishment of the 'essential element' and 'fundamental element' provisions, which explicitly deal with the political underpinnings of the partnership. While this was the culmination of the evolution of the political basis of the relationship throughout the 1990s, it does mark a formal change. Part 4 of the *Guide* explores this development.

Geographically, the scope of ACP-EU co-operation has expanded considerably. In 1975 the ACP consisted of six Caribbean, three Pacific and 37 African countries. It now consists of 16 Caribbean, 15 Pacific and 48 African countries. Altogether 77 ACP states are signatories of the Cotonou Agreement;[2] by 2005 some 25 EU member states will also be signatories. Thus the Cotonou Agreement brings together more than 100 countries in an integrated trade, development assistance and political co-operation relationship. Not surprisingly, the provisions of the Agreement are complex. The basic text, which has been simplified, consists of 100 articles (compared to 369 under the Lomé Convention), taking up over 55 pages (compared to 98 pages for the Lomé IV Convention). However, the basic Cotonou Agreement is supplemented by six annexes (one of which, Annex V, contains, in addition to its three main chapters, three protocols, each of which itself has numerous annexes), three protocols and 53 declarations, most of which are joint declarations but some of which are solely EU or ACP declarations. In their entirety these annexes, protocols to annexes, annexes to protocols to annexes, stand-alone protocols and declarations stretch to over 191 pages. This makes the Cotonou Agreement as a whole a complex document to find one's way through.

It is this complexity which has given rise to the need for a ***User's Guide***.

The Geographical Distribution of ACP Signatories

	Africa	Caribbean	Pacific	Total ACP
Lomé I	37	6	3	46
Lomé II	42	9	7	58
Lomé III	45	13	8	66
Lomé IV (1)	45	15	8	68
Lomé IV (2)	47	15	8	70
Cotonou Agreement	48	15	14	77

Notes

1   *The Courier ACP-EEC*, No. 58, Special Issue, November 1979, p. 27.

2   Cuba and East Timor are members of the ACP Group but are not yet signatories of the Cotonou Agreement. South Africa is a member of the ACP Group and a signatory of the Cotonou Agreement, but does not benefit from the trade or financial and technical co-operation provisions.

The Purpose of the *User's Guide*

This **User's Guide** should be seen against the background of efforts to simplify the basic text of the ACP-EU co-operation agreement. As a consequence of these efforts, detailed provisions essential to the implementation of ACP-EU co-operation activities have often been relegated to annexes and protocols (and even annexes to protocols) or have been left for elaboration to internal guidelines and memoranda by the implementing agencies concerned (the European Commission or, in the case of the Investment Facility, the European Investment Bank (EIB)). This has given rise to a simple question and answer guide to the various aspects of ACP-EU co-operation. The **Guide** is divided into four main parts.

Part 1 provides a general introduction to the structure of the Cotonou Agreement and explains where its various provisions can be found.

Part 2 takes a more detailed look at the financial and technical co-operation arrangements established under the Cotonou Agreement. This constitutes the main body of the text and is divided into 12 sections. It begins with an **overview** of the financial framework for ACP-EU co-operation, which looks at the objectives of the Agreement, the financial package made available, the changes since Lomé IV and the types of aid available

It then looks at how co-operation with ACP countries at the **national** level is planned and implemented, examining how funds are allocated, how a Country Support Strategy (CSS) is drawn up and how a national indicative programme (NIP) is established.

This is followed by a similar section on ACP-EU **regional co-operation**, which looks at how regional funds are allocated, how regional funds are pro-grammed and how pan-ACP regional programmes are established. It also looks at the scope for non-state actor involvement in regional co-operation programmes.

The nature and structure of the newly established **Investment Facility** is then reviewed, with an attempt being made to explain not only what financial packages are potentially available, but also how to access them.

In the following two sections consideration is given to the operation of the two joint institutions established within the framework of ACP-EU co-operation, the **Technical Centre for Agricultural and Rural Co-operation** (CTA) and the **Centre for the Development of Enterprise** (CDE). These sections look at the objectives of these institutions, the level of funds available, how the institutions work, the different types of programmes supported and how to become a beneficiary of these various support programmes.

In the light of the introduction of the 'rolling programming' concept (with its 'use it or lose it' dimension) detailed consideration is given to how the process of reviewing the implementation of co-operation activities is organised. The aims of the review process, how the process is structured, and the intended outcome of the various stages of the review process are all examined. Particular attention is given to this issue since under the Cotonou Agreement the review process has a direct bearing on the level of financial assistance which will ultimately be made available to each country and region.

In the next two sections consideration is given to the role of **non-state actors** and the **private sector**. The *Guide* reviews the basic provisions on the involvement of non-state actors and the private sector, their roles in the programming process and the implementation of co-operation activities. In the case of non-state actors it looks at the role the EU Delegate should play in fostering non-state actors' engagement with the ACP-EU co-operation process and the criteria which have been established to guide non-state actor involvement. Given the increased emphasis on non-state actor involvement, the *Guide* also reviews the experience of non-state actor engagement with the ACP-EU co-operation process to date. With regard to the private sector, it reviews the ACP-EU instruments of co-operation likely to be of most interest to the private sector, highlighting in particular the benefits which can be gained by ACP companies from the tendering preferences extended under the Agreement.

The final three sections of this part of the *User's Guide* deal with procedures for **project submission**, **administrative structures** and the **implementation of co-operation activities**. Detailed questions of implementation are not addressed, since this would require a detailed consideration of the operation of the relatively new **Europeaid** structure, which is only now beginning to overcome its initial institutional teething troubles.

Part 3 of the *User's Guide* looks at **trade arrangements** under the Cotonou Agreement. This part is divided into three sections. The first section provides an **overview** of the Cotonou trade provisions: what they cover; their main objectives; where the various provisions can be found; and the institutional arrangements for trade co-operation. The second section looks at **current market access arrangements**. This reviews the scope of the market access arrangements; the special treatment accorded agricultural products; the rules of origin applied under the ACP-EU trade regime; the administrative arrangements applied to the movement of goods under the trade arrangement; the safeguard clause; commitments made on trade in services and commitments entered into in trade-related areas. The third section looks at the provisions for **future ACP-EU trade arrangements**. This covers a review of the debates around the ACP experience of non-reciprocal trade preferences; what the Agreement says on future trade arrangements; and the link between World Trade Organisation (WTO) rules and future ACP-EU trade arrangements.

Part 4 of the *User's Guide* deals with **political relations** under the Agreement. These questions are dealt with in a single section. The areas covered include: the scope of political dialogue; the basic principles underpinning the ACP-EU relationship; the commitments entered into through endorsement of these principles; the procedures for invoking the 'suspension clause'; the provisions for dealing with corruption; the mechanisms for institutionalised political dialogue; commitments made on peace building, conflict prevention and conflict resolution; the link between political dialogue and performance-based aid allocations; the commitments made on migration; and the provisions for consultations on coherence issues.

The main body of the *Guide* is supplemented by 29 annexes which provide more detailed information on the issues raised in the main text. For easy access, each annex is mentioned on the page where the first reference is made to the information it contains.

The overall purpose of the *Guide* is to provide through 149 simple questions easily accessible information on what is possible under the Cotonou Agreement.

The ultimate aim is to create a better understanding of the Agreement, so as to maximise the benefits which people in ACP countries gain from it.

The Commonwealth Secretariat's role in the production of this guide needs to be seen in the context of the fact that half of the member states of the ACP Group are also members of the Commonwealth.

Part 1

The Structure of the Cotonou Agreement

1.1 A Breakdown of the Basic Provisions

The Cotonou Agreement is divided into six parts dealing with:

- general provisions;
- institutional arrangements;
- co-operation strategies;
- development finance;
- special provisions for least developed, landlocked and island ACP countries;
- **final provisions**, which cover a range of issues linked to the entry into force, implementation and suspension of the Agreement.

Part 1, **General Provisions**, has two titles.

Title I deals with the **objectives of co-operation**, the **principles** intended to guide co-operation activities and the **actors** involved in co-operation activities.

Title II deals with the **political relationship** which underpins ACP-EU co-operation. This includes:

- the scope of political dialogue;
- the 'essential elements', violation of which can lead to a suspension of application of the provisions of the Agreement;
- 'fundamental elements', which signatories are expected to promote respect for;
- commitments on peace building and conflict prevention;
- commitments on the promotion of policy coherence;
- commitments dealing with the issue of migration.

Part 2, **Institutional Arrangements**, sets out the various joint institutions whose task it is to give concrete expression to the political dialogue process. These include:

- the ACP-EU Council of Ministers;
- the ACP-EU Committee of Ambassadors;

- the ACP-EU Joint Parliamentary Assembly.

Part 3, **Co-operation Strategies**, consists of two titles with eight major chapters.

Title I deals with **development strategies**. This title covers:

- the basis for the establishment of development strategies (principles, objectives and approaches);
- the various areas in which support can be extended, including
  - economic development
  - social and human development
  - regional co-operation and integration
  - thematic and cross-cutting issues, such as gender, the environment, institutional development and capacity building.

Title II deals with **economic and trade co-operation**. This title includes chapters on:

- objectives and principles;
- new trading arrangements, dealing with the basis for the establishment of a long-term framework for ACP-EU trade relations;
- the arrangements to be applied during the transition (until 2008);
- co-operation in international fora, including the WTO;
- co-operation on specific commodity issues;
- trade in services;
- trade-related areas;
- co-operation on fisheries agreements and food security.

Part 4 deals with **development finance**. It consists of four major titles setting out:

- objectives, principles and guidelines;
- the scope and nature of the development finance to be made available;
- guidelines for the utilisation of development assistance in different areas, including:
  - debt
  - structural adjustment
  - export earnings losses
  - support for specific sectoral policies
  - microprojects and decentralised co-operation

- humanitarian aid
- investment and private sector development
- technical co-operation;

- the procedures for the management of aid.

Part 6, **Final Provisions**, deals with a range of issues linked to the entry into force and implementation of the Agreement. These include:

- the relationship to other agreements;
- the territorial scope of the Agreement;
- the ratification procedures for the Agreement;
- provisions to allow accession of new member states;
- the duration of the Agreement;
- the provisions to be followed for its revision;
- the procedures to be followed for the suspension of a member state in violation of the 'essential element' provisions of the Agreement;
- dispute settlement provisions;
- a denunciation clause, to allow member states to withdraw from the Agreement should they so choose.

Making Sense of the Relevant Texts

The aim of the Cotonou Agreement was to simplify the basic agreement to make it more accessible and comprehensible to those who need to use it. While to a certain extent this has been achieved in the main body of the text, this is at the expense of *a complex set of annexes, protocols, declarations and annexes to protocols which are attached to the Agreement and which themselves form an integral part of the text.* These are supplemented by an *internal EU agreement on the financing of co-operation activities with ACP countries and detailed internal guidelines which the European Commission alone draws up and which form the basis for the actual implementation of co-operation activities under the Agreement.*

The *User's Guide* seeks to bring together the relevant data from each of these different sources under a series of simple headings so that users can find their way through what is otherwise a complex set of regulations and instructions. Where necessary, the data brought together under each of the simple headings are supplemented by annexes which contain the original texts, copies of key documents or more detailed summaries of the role of key institutional players.

1.2 The Annexes to the Cotonou Agreement

While the main body of the Cotonou Agreement has been simplified, this has been at the expense of the inclusion of extensive annexes, protocols, annexes to protocols and declarations.

The first three Annexes to the Cotonou Agreement deal with the financing of development co-operation activities.

Annex I sets out the finances to be made available under the Agreement for the implementation of the various co-operation activities.

Annex II elaborates on the terms and conditions for financing various operations, ranging from the Investment Facility, through the financing of micro-projects and small-scale operations to the provision of assistance with short-term fluctuations in export earnings. Other provisions included in this annex deal with capital movements, non-discrimination in the provision of services and investment protection.

Annex III deals with the financing of the activities of the **Centre for the Development of Enterprise** (CDE) and the **Technical Centre for Agricultural and Rural Co-operation** (CTA).

Annex IV elaborates on the implementation and management of long-term development co-operation activities, dealing in particular with:

- the **programming process** at national and regional levels;
- **project implementation**;
- the **tendering process**;
- **monitoring and evaluation**;
- the **role of different actors in the aid management process**.

Annex V elaborates on the **trade provisions applicable to ACP-EU trade until 2008**. This is the most extensive and complex of the annexes, extending in the version printed in the *Courier* to 131 pages. Annex V has three chapters, and five protocols, with no less than 23 Joint Declarations elaborating on these various provisions.

Protocol 1 of Annex V dealing with rules of origin has seven titles and 15 annexes and stretches to 111 tightly printed pages.

Annex VI provides a listing of those countries accorded special treatment as a result of their status as least developed, landlocked or island ACP countries.

In addition to these annexes, this section of the Agreement also contains three protocols, dealing with the **operating expenditures of joint institutions, privileges and immunities** and the **treatment to be accorded South Africa** as a result of its special status within the ACP Group.

The protocol on South Africa stipulates that:

- in trade matters, the terms of the EU-South Africa Trade, Development and Co-operation Agreement take precedence over the provisions of the Cotonou Agreement;

- South Africa shall participate fully in the political dialogue aspects of the Agreement;

- the provisions on co-operation strategies shall also apply to South Africa;

- the provisions on development financing and trade co-operation shall not apply to South Africa.

Also annexed to the Agreement are some 53 Declarations, most of which are Joint Declarations but some of which are Declarations solely by the EU or the ACP. The Declarations dealing with trade issues are listed in the box on the next page. The Declarations which do not deal with trade issues relate to a wide variety of issues including:

- **actors in the partnership;**

- **migration;**

- **the functioning of joint institutions;**

- **immunities and privileges;**

- **cultural heritage;**

- **copyright;**

- **outermost regions of the EU;**

- **accession;**

- **various aspects of development financing** (debt relief, programming, export revenue losses).

Declarations Dealing with Trade Relations

Declaration IX	Joint Declaration on Article 49(2) on trade and environment
Declaration X	ACP Declaration on trade and environment
Declaration XXII	Joint Declaration concerning agricultural products referred to in Article 1(2)(a) of Annex V
Declaration XXIV	Joint Declaration on rice
Declaration XXV	Joint Declaration on rum
Declaration XXVI	Joint Declaration on beef and veal
Declaration XXVII	Joint Declaration on the arrangements governing access to the markets of the French overseas departments for products originating in the ACP states referred to in Article 1(2) of Annex V
Declaration XXIX	Joint Declaration on products covered by the Common Agricultural Policy
Declaration XXX	Joint Declaration on Article 1 of Annex V
Declaration XXXI	Community Declaration on Article 5 (2)(a) of Annex V
Declaration XXXII	Joint Declaration on non-discrimination
Declaration XXXIII	Community Declaration on Article 8(3) of Annex V
Declaration XXIV	Joint Declaration on Article 12 of Annex V
Declaration XXV	Joint Declaration relating to Protocol 1 of Annex V
Declaration XXXVI	Joint Declaration relating to Protocol 1 of Annex V
Declaration XXXVII	Joint Declaration relating to Protocol 1 of Annex V on the origin of fishery products
Declaration XXXVIII	Community Declaration relating to Protocol 1 of Annex V on the extent of territorial waters
Declaration XXXIX	ACP Declaration relating to Protocol 1 of Annex V on the origin of fishery products
Declaration XL	Joint Declaration on the application of the value tolerance rule in the tuna sector

Declarations Dealing with Trade Relations (continued)

Part 2

Development Assistance under the Cotonou Agreement

2.1. Overview

> This overview seeks to situate aid to ACP countries made available under the Cotonou Agreement in the context of:
>
> - the objectives of the Cotonou Agreement;
> - the overall volume of aid resources to be made available;
> - the different instruments through which aid is made available;
> - the different forms in which aid made available through the European Development Fund (EDF) can be deployed.
>
> The overview closes by reviewing the conditions under which budgetary support can be made available in ACP countries and the scope for support for micro-projects.

What are the Stated Objectives of ACP-EU Co-operation under the Cotonou Agreement?

The Cotonou Agreement seeks to centre the ACP-EU co-operation process on the:

> *... human person, who is the main protagonist and beneficiary of development.*

The aim of EU aid is thus to support the efforts of ACP states to **reduce and eventually eradicate poverty in ways which are consistent with sustainable development and the gradual integration of ACP countries into the world economy.**[1] These objectives are meant to inform the development strategies adopted by ACP countries, while accommodating their diverse social, economic, cultural and political circumstances.

Part 1, Title I, Article 1

Under the Agreement emphasis is placed on:

- developing the private sector;
- increasing employment;
- improving access to productive resources;

- meeting basic needs;

- ensuring an equitable distribution of the benefits of growth and respecting the rights of the individual.

In this context, specific reference is made to **improving the functioning of both democratic societies and the market economy** and supporting the emergence of an **active and organised civil society**. Particular reference is made to **systematically taking account of gender issues in all areas**.

In implementing development co-operation activities emphasis is placed on:

- equality between the partners;

- promoting local ownership and wide participation in co-operation activities;

- ensuring predictable resource flows within a framework of dialogue and mutual obligations;

- ensuring that appropriate approaches are adopted consistent with the situation in each ACP country and region.

Thus, according to the provisions of the Agreement, development co-operation activities supported by the EU should be tailored to local needs, locally owned, actively involve ACP nationals, be based on a dialogue of equals and involve mutual obligations. Development co-operation should also be based on the predictable availability of resources.

In many respects the Cotonou Agreement sets extremely high standards for the local ownership of the aid deployment process.

Significantly, both parties, the EU and the ACP, commit themselves to taking:

Part 1, Title I, Article 3

... all appropriate measures ... to facilitate the attainment of the objectives of the Agreement

and to:

... refrain from any measures likely to jeopardise these objectives.

ACP-EU co-operation is underpinned by a shared commitment to a series of political principles set out in Article 9 which deals with 'essential elements' and the 'fundamental element'. These include:

- respect for all human rights and fundamental freedoms;

- promotion of democracy;

- the maintenance of the rule of law;

Article 9

- transparent and accountable governance.

All of these elements are seen as essential to sustainable development.

Respect for human rights, democracy and the rule law constitute **'essential elements'** of the partnership relationship, violation of which can lead to the suspension of co-operation activities. Good governance constitutes a **'fundamental element'**, violation of which can lead to the suspension of particular co-operation activities only under certain circumstances.

How Much Aid is Available under the Cotonou Agreement?

Under the ninth EDF, which finances co-operation under the Agreement, a total of Euro 15.2 billion is made available. This takes the form of both grants and loans. 74.3 per cent of this funding is in the form of grants; 25.7 per cent is in the form of loans. Euro 13.5 billion is drawn from grants from EU member states and Euro 1.7 billion is made available from the European Investment Bank's own resources.*

In addition, the European Commission intends to identify all the previously allocated aid funds which have not so far been used and add them to the funds available under the 9th EDF. In August 2001, the European Commission maintained that outstanding balances under previous EDFs totalled some Euro 9,900 million.

However, it is far from clear how this figure is derived. Tables in the August 2001 Commission communication show the following situation with regard to decisions (financing agreements signed), assigned funds (contracts signed) and payments (payments actually transferred) under the 6th, 7th and 8th EDFs.

Extrapolating from the tables below, the following picture emerges with reference to unspent funds. No decisions had been taken (i.e. no financing agreement had been signed) on a total of **Euro 6,090 million**. No contracts had been signed for the implementation of actual activities on funds totalling **Euro 12,271 million** (these funds had not yet been assigned). Payments still needed to be made on a total of **Euro 15,073 million**.

Thus, as of 1 January 2001 technically some **Euro 15,073,269,000** of EDF funds were unspent. However, **Euro 2,802,220,000** of these funds had already been committed in the form of legally binding contracts, while **Euro 8,982,804,000** had already been committed to the financing of specific project and programme activities and had moved beyond the first critical stage in the deployment of EDF resources.

---

*See Annex 1 of this *User's Guide* for the full text of the Financial Protocol to the Cotonou Agreement.

Situation as of 31 December 2000[1] (figures in Euro)

Appropriation[2]	
6th EDF	7,829,081,000
7th EDF	11,514,969,000
8th EDF	13,345,115,000
Decisions[3]	
6th EDF	7,496,083,000
7th EDF	10,754,495,000
8th EDF	8,348,082,000
Assigned Funds[4]	
6th EDF	7,258,510,000
7th EDF	9,363,127,000
8th EDF	3,796,288,000
Payments[5]	
6th EDF	7,136,123,000
7th EDF	8,499,377,000
8th EDF	1,980,296,000

Situation as of 31 December 2000 (figures in Euro 000)

	6th EDF	7th EDF	8th EDF	Total
No decisions taken	332,998	760,474	4,997,033	6,090,405
No implementation contracts yet signed	570,571	2,151,842	9,548,827	12,271,240
Money so far unspent	692,858	3,015,592	11,364,819	15,073,269

Above and beyond these aid funds, the European Commission is also intending to make available all development aid channelled to ACP countries through the EU budget within the same co-operation framework as EDF funds.

9th EDF funds could not legally be deployed until two-thirds of ACP and all EU member states' parliaments had ratified the Agreement. On 1 April 2003 the Cotonou Agreement entered into force following the ratification of the Agreement by all EU member states. From this date funds from the 9th EDF could legally be disbursed.

The Ninth EDF Funding Package
(Million Euro)

OVERALL AMOUNT	15,200
● Grants from EU member states	13,500
● EIB Own Resources	1,700

Of this Euro 13,500 million in grant aid:

● Euro 2,200 million is allocated to the Investment Facility;

● Euro 11,300 million is allocated to the Long-term Development Co-operation Facility.

Of the Euro 11,300 million allocated to the long-term development co-operation facility:

● Euro 1,300 million is allocated to Regional Co-operation and Integration;

● Euro 10,000 million is allocated to National Long-term Development Co-operation.

Of the 10,000 million Euro allocated to national long-term development co-operation:

● Euro 90 million is allocated to the CDE;

● Euro 70 million is allocated to the CTA;

● Euro 4 million is allocated to the Joint Assembly.

How is Aid Made Available under the Cotonou Agreement?

Development assistance is made available through two basic instruments and two joint institutions. The two basic instruments are a **long-term development co-operation facility** and an **investment facility**. The two joint institutions through which assistance is extended are the **Centre for the Development of Enterprise** and the **Centre for Technical Co-operation in Agriculture**.

Euro 11,300 million has been made available in grants from EU member states to finance development co-operation activities under the **Long-term Development Co-operation Facility**.

Under the **Investment Facility** a total of Euro 3.9 million has been made available. This consists of Euro 2.2 billion drawn from EU member states' grants and Euro 1.7 billion made available from the European Investment Bank's own resources.

Euro 90 million is made available to the CDE from the Long-term Development Co-operation Facility to:

Annex III,
Article 2.1

... support the implementation of private sector development strategies in the ACP countries by providing non-financial services to ACP companies and businesses and support to joint initiatives set up by economic operators of the Community and of the ACP states.

Article 3.1

The CDE's focus is on:

- facilitating ACP-EU business contacts;
- assisting with development of business support services;
- supporting investment promotion activities;
- promoting technology and know-how transfers on all aspects of business management.

Some Euro 70 million is allocated to the CTA from the long-term development co-operation facility. The CTA's mandate is to:

... strengthen policy and institutional capacity development and information and communication management capacities of ACP agricultural and rural development organisations.

The focus of the CTA's activities is the provision of information services in support of capacity building in ACP countries for:

Article 3.2

... research, training and innovations in the spheres of agricultural and rural development and extension, in order to promote agricultural development.

What Happens Now in the Case of Export Earnings Losses?

The earlier Lomé Convention STABEX and SYSMIN schemes, which provided support to agriculture and mineral-dependent economies facing export earnings losses, were discontinued as from 31 December 2000.

Under the Cotonou Agreement **additional allocations** will now be made available to any ACP country facing both a **worsening export earnings situation** and a **worsening public finance deficit**. Both trends in export earnings losses and trends in the public deficit will determine the eligibility of individual ACP countries for additional resources.

(i) **With respect to export earnings losses,** ACP countries will be considered eligible for additional aid where:

- a 10 per cent (2 per cent for least developed ACP countries) loss of export earnings from all goods exported is experienced compared to the average of the three first years of the preceding four-year period;

or

- where a 10 per cent (2 per cent for least developed ACP countries) loss of export earnings from the total of agricultural or mineral product exports is experienced compared to the average of the three first years of the preceding four-year period, and the country derives 40 per cent of total export revenues from either agricultural or mineral exports.

Annex II, Chapter 3, Article 9.1

(ii) **With regard to the trend in the public deficit,** ACP countries will be considered eligible for additional aid where there is:

- a 10 per cent (2 per cent for least developed ACP countries) worsening of the programmed public deficit for the year in question or the following year.

Where these **two criteria are met additional funds may be allocated**, which will then be deployed within the framework of the indicative programme. Part of the money may, however, be set aside for use in the affected sector. Under the Agreement no country may benefit from these provisions for more than four successive years.

What Happens Now in the Case of Emergency Assistance?

While provision is made for the extension of emergency assistance to ACP countries under the Cotonou Agreement, it is stipulated that **'only in exceptional circumstances'** will emergency assistance be financed from the EDF. Emergency assistance will generally be financed from the EU's annual budget.

Emergency assistance can be extended to ACP countries faced with:

... serious economic and social difficulties of an exceptional nature resulting from natural disasters, man-made crises such as wars and other conflicts or extraordinary circumstances having comparable effects.

Part 4, Title II, Chapter 6, Article 72.1

Such assistance will be extended:

... for as long as necessary to deal with the emergency needs resulting from these situations.

Part 4, Title II, Chapter 6, Article 72.2

According to the Agreement such assistance will be:

... granted exclusively according to the needs and interests of victims of disasters and in line with the principles of international humanitarian law ...

with no discrimination between the victims of disasters.

In addition an ACP state taking in refugees or returnees may be granted similar support in order to meet acute needs not covered by emergency assistance.

Article 72.3

Emergency assistance extended under the provisions of the Agreement aims to:

a) safeguard human lives in crises and immediate post-crisis situations brought about by natural disasters, conflict or war;

b) contribute to the financing and delivery of humanitarian aid and to the direct access to it of its intended beneficiaries by all logistical means available;

c) carry out short-term rehabilitation and reconstruction to enable the parts of the population affected to benefit once more from a minimum of socio-economic integration and, as soon as possible, create the conditions for a resumption of development on the basis of long-term objectives set by the ACP country concerned;

d) address the needs arising from the displacement of people (refugees, displaced persons and returnees) following natural or man-made disasters so as to meet, for as long as necessary, all the needs of refugees and displaced persons (wherever they may be) and facilitate action for their voluntary repatriation and re-integration in their country of origin; and

e) assist the ACP State in setting up disaster prevention and pre-paredness mechanisms, including prediction and early-warning systems, with a view to reducing the consequences of disasters.

Article 72.6

Humanitarian and emergency assistance support can be requested by:

- the ACP country affected by the crisis situation;

- the Commission;

- international organisations or local or international non-state organisations.

The procedures in place for the commitment and disbursement of emergency assistance are aimed at ensuring the rapid and effective mobilisation of assistance to meet immediate needs.

Under Article 73, provision is also made for assistance to post-emergency actions. This can involve assistance to:

Part 4, Title II, Chapter 6, Article 73

- ease the transition from the emergency phase to the development phase;

- promote the socio-economic reintegration of the parts of the population affected;

- remove as far as possible the causes of the crisis;

- strengthen institutions in formulating a sustainable development policy for the ACP country concerned.

What Happens Now in the Case of Structural Adjustment Support?

While the specific structural adjustment support facility has been discontinued, under the financial protocol the Cotonou Agreement continues to make provision for assistance to **'macroeconomic and sectoral reforms'**. Assistance for macroeconomic and sectoral reforms is to be made available following a joint assessment of:

Chapter 2, Article 67.1

> *... the reform measures being undertaken or contemplated either at the macroeconomic or sectoral level*

and is aimed at providing:

> *... an overall evaluation of the reform efforts.*

The Agreement stipulates that:

> *ACP states undertaking reform programmes that are acknowledged and supported at least by the principal multilateral donors, or that are agreed with such donors but not necessarily financially supported by them, shall be treated as having automatically satisfied the requirements for adjustment assistance.*

Article 67.4

Assistance may be extended in a:

> *... flexible manner and in the form of sectoral and general import programmes or budgetary support.*

Article 67.5

Under the Agreement considerable emphasis is placed on placing reform programmes in their regional context. Against this background Article 67 stipulates that structural adjustment support should seek to:

a) incorporate, from the beginning ... measures to encourage regional integration and take account of the consequences of trans-border adjustment;

b) support the harmonisation and co-ordination of macroeconomic and sectoral policies, including fiscal and customs areas, so as to fulfil the dual aim of regional integration and of structural reform at national level;

c) take account of the effects of net transitional costs of regional integration on budget revenue and balance of payments, either through general import programme or budgetary support.

What Types of Aid Can be Made Available under the Cotonou Agreement?

Article 61 of the Agreement sets out the different types of assistance that can be made available under the EDF. These include:

- funding for discrete projects;

- funding for sectoral programmes;

- sectoral or general import programme support either in the form of directly procured goods or an allocation of foreign exchange;

- budgetary support given either directly or indirectly to ACP governments;

- human and material support for the administration of projects and pro-grammes;

- credit lines;

- credit guarantees;

- equity participation in enterprises.

The type of assistance to be made available to individual ACP countries is determined by the ACP government during the programming process, in consultation with the EU, in the light of the Country Support Strategy.

Under What Conditions Can Budgetary Support be Made Available?

Direct budgetary support is extended to countries undertaking sector or macroeconomic reforms where there is:

- a transparent, accountable and effective system for the management of public expenditures;

Part 4, Title I, Chapter 2, Article 61.2

- a well-defined macroeconomic or sectoral policy supported by the main donors;

- open and transparent public procurement.

In addition, the Agreement allows budgetary assistance to gradually substitute for project assistance where clear sectoral policies are being pursued.

What Provisions are Made for Support to Micro-Projects under the Cotonou Agreement?

The Cotonou Agreement includes a commitment to extending support to micro-projects at local level which:

Chapter 5, Article 70

- have an economic and social impact on people's lives;

- meet a demonstrated and observed priority need;

- are undertaken at the initiative and with the active participation of the local community that will benefit from the activity.

Such micro-projects may be linked to activities in the focal sector or may be quite independent of the focal sector.

The contribution from the EDF to micro-project activities may not normally exceed three-quarters of the total costs. The remaining costs should be met by the local community concerned (either in cash or kind) or, in exceptional circumstances, through a financial contribution from the state or through the provision of equipment or services.

Multi-annual programmes are seen as the main vehicle for the deployment of financial assistance in support of micro-project activities. This establishes an overall financial framework within which support is extended through annual implementation plans.[6]

2.2 Co-operation with ACP Countries

This section looks at:

- criteria by which aid is allocated to individual ACP countries;

- the current allocations that have been made to individual ACP countries;

- the consultation process through which each ACP country decides on how it is going to spend the money allocated to it;

- the various stages of the process through which the use of aid allocated to each country is determined.

How is Cotonou Aid Allocated to Individual ACP Countries?

The initial allocations to ACP countries reflect both the current **needs** and past **performance** of the individual ACP country.

Annex IV,
Article 3.1

The assessment of the **needs** of individual ACP countries is based on:

- per capita income;

- population size;

- social indicators;

- level of indebtedness;

- concentration of dependence on export earnings;

- export earnings losses.

The assessment of an ACP country's performance is based on the country's:

- progress in implementing institutional reforms (including administrative, legal and policy reforms);

- performance in the use of aid resources allocated under previous Lomé Conventions;

- the effectiveness of the implementation of current Lomé aid operations;

- commitment to poverty alleviation or reduction;

- commitment to sustainable development measures;

- macroeconomic and sectoral performance.

Funds under the long-term development co-operation instrument are allocated to individual ACP countries in two parts, an **'A'** and **'B'** allocation.

The **'A'** allocation covers:

Annex IV, Article 3.2

... macroeconomic support, sectoral policies, programmes and projects in support of the focal and non-focal areas of Community assistance.

The **'B'** allocation covers:

... unforeseen needs such as emergency assistance where such support cannot be financed from the EU budget, contributions to internationally agreed debt relief initiatives and support to mitigate adverse effects of instability on export earnings.

How Much Aid is Allocated to Each ACP Country?

A total of Euro 7,120.8 million has been allocated under the 'A' envelope to 76 ACP countries.[7] This constitutes 71.2 per cent of the total amount of funding made available under the long-term development co-operation facility.[8] 'B' envelope allocations to the 65 ACP countries whose Country Support Strategies have been posted on the web to date total Euro 2000.2 million, or 20 per cent of the total amount allocated to the long-term development co-operation facility.

The 'A' and 'B' envelope country allocations (as of 30 April 2003) break down as set out in the following tables.

Aid Allocations at 30 April 2003

Country	'A' Allocation (Euro million)
Angola	117.0
Antigua	2.6
Bahamas	3.9
Barbados	6.5
Belize	7.8
Benin	208.0
Botswana	39.0
Burkina Faso	275.0
Burundi	115.0
Cameroon	159.0
Cape Verde	32.0
Central African Republic	86.0
Chad	202.0
Comores	20.0
Congo (Brazzaville)	43.0
Congo Democratic Republic	171.0
Cook Islands	2.0
Côte d'Ivoire	182.0
Djibouti	29.0
Dominican Republic	119.0
Dominica	3.7
Equatorial Guinea	13.0
Eritrea	88.0
Ethiopia	384.0
Fiji	21.0
Gabon	34.0
Gambia	37.0
Ghana	231.0
Grenada	3.5
Guinea	158.0
Guinea Bissau	62.0
Guyana	34.0
Haiti	180.0
Jamaica	73.0
Kenya	170.0
Kiribati	8.8
Lesotho	86.0
Liberia	74.0
Madagascar	267.0
Malawi	276.0
Mali	294.0

Aid Allocations at 30 April 2003 (continued)

Country	'A' Allocation (Euro million)
Marshall Islands	3.5
Mauritius	33.0
Mauritania	104.0
Micronesia	4.8
Mozambique	274.0
Namibia	48.0
Nauru	1.8
Niger	212.0
Nigeria	222.0
Niue	2.0
Palau	2.0
Papua New Guinea	81.0
Rwanda	124.0
Samoa	20.0
São Tomé & Príncipe	9.4
Senegal	178.0
Seychelles	3.9
Sierra Leone	144.0
Solomon Islands	6.7
Somalia	149.0
St Kitts	3.4
St Lucia	4.5
St Vincent	5.0
Sudan	135.0
Suriname	11.0
Swaziland	31.0
Tanzania	290.0
Togo	70.0
Tonga	3.7
Trinidad and Tobago	17.0
Tuvalu	3.3
Uganda	246.0
Vanuatu	12.0
Zambia	240.0
Zimbabwe	108.0
TOTAL	7,120.8

Aid Allocations at 30 April 2003

Country	'B' Allocation (Euro million)
Angola	29.0
Antigua	0.4
Bahamas	0.6
Belize	1.0
Benin	6.7
Botswana	52.0
Burkina Faso	76.0
Cameroon	71.0
Cape Verde	7.1
Central African Rep.	21.0
Chad	71.0
Comores	7.3
Congo (Brazzaville)	7.3
Cook Islands	0.6
Djibouti	5.8
Dominican Republic	57.0
Dominica	12.0
Equatorial Guinea	4.3
Eritrea	8.8
Ethiopia	153.7
Gabon	45.0
Gambia	14.0
Ghana	80.0
Grenada	3.9
Guinea	63.0
Guinea Bissau	19.0
Guyana	14.0
Jamaica	27.0
Kiribati	2.2
Lesotho	24.0
Madagascar	60.0
Malawi	69.0
Mali	81.0
Marshall Islands	1.1
Maurice	1.6
Mauritania	87.0
Micronesia	1.4
Mozambique	55.0
Namibia	43.0
Nauru	0.5
Niger	134.0

Aid Allocations at 30 April 2003 (continued)

Country	'B' Allocation (Euro million)
Nigeria	44.0
Niue	0.6
Palau	0.6
Papua New Guinea	85.0
Rwanda	62.0
Samoa	7.1
São Tomé & Príncipe	3.5
Seychelles	0.8
Solomon Islands	7.8
St Kitts	0.6
St Lucia	15.0
St Vincent	16.0
Sudan	20.0
Suriname	7.0
Swaziland	12.0
Tanzania	65.0
Tonga	2.0
Trinidad and Tobago	0.9
Tuvalu	0.7
Uganda	117.0
Vanuatu	3.3
Zambia	111.0
TOTAL	2003.2

How is it Decided What to Do with the Money?

Once each ACP government is informed of the allocation it is to receive under the long-term development co-operation facility, the next step is to determine how to use the money. This is known as the programming process.

The first stage of the programming process is the drawing up of the **Country Support Strategy**, which determines:

Annex IV, Chapter 1, Article 2

- where available assistance is to be used;

- the type of assistance to be made available;

- the most appropriate channels and agencies for the deployment of available assistance.

The aim of the Country Support Strategy is to set the broad policy framework within which EU assistance is to be made available. Indeed, the Country

Support Strategy is intended to provide the foundations on which the actual utilisation of EU assistance is determined through the programming dialogue.

The programming dialogue itself involves the **joint determination of how available funds are to be used**, with the ACP government being primarily responsible for drawing up the **National Indicative Programme**.

Under the Agreement the programming process has been extended in two significant respects. First, the programming process is to be opened up to include the participation of **non-state actors** in the programming dialogue. Second, the programming process is to include all EU resources destined for the ACP country concerned, including resources that have remained unutilised under previous Lomé Conventions and EU annual budget resources deployed in each ACP country.

What is the Programming Exercise?

Annex IV,
Chapter 1,
Article 4

The programming exercise is the process of consultation between the EU and individual ACP governments through which the utilisation of the money allocated to individual ACP countries is planned. The programming process determines:

- the **priority sectors for support**;

- the **type of assistance to be provided**;

- the **most appropriate agencies** for implementation of development co-operation activities.

Under earlier Lomé Conventions this dealt primarily with the multi-annual five year allocations made to all ACP countries and regions. Under the Cotonou Agreement it deals with the planned deployment of the 'A' and 'B' allocation to each ACP country within a **rolling programme of reviews of aid utilisation and performance**.

Under the Cotonou Agreement the programming process is meant to be a far more inclusive process with provision being made for the involvement of various non-state actors in the programming process.

Under the Agreement considerable emphasis has been placed on ensuring that the programming process deploys EU aid in line with both **national development priorities and objectives** and **EU development co-operation policy priorities and objectives**.

From the European Commission perspective six key features underpin the new approach to programming. These are:

- the primacy to be given to an ACP country's own policy agenda as the starting point for programming;

- the necessity of ensuring that all available EU aid in each country is deployed within a single comprehensive policy framework;

- the need to ensure greater complementarity between the deployment of EDF aid and the deployment of aid from EU member states and other donors;

- the importance, wherever possible, of adopting a sector-based approach to the deployment of EU aid;

- the importance of concentrating aid deployed in a focal sector or sectors;

- the need to ensure that aid programming and programme implementation is managed within a single logically coherent framework.[9]

The European Commission Perspective

From the European Commission perspective the two most important aspects of the new approach are the adoption of a **sectoral concentration** and, wherever possible, a **sector-wide approach**.

In the European Commission's view, sectoral concentration should mean that for medium to large national indicative programmes (over Euro 40 million) there should be no more than two focal sectors; for smaller programmes only one focal sector; and for programmes less than Euro 10 million only one project. Currently there are 40 ACP countries with 'A' allocations above Euro 40 million and 36 ACP countries with 'A' allocations below Euro 10 million.

Underpinning this desire to concentrate aid in a limited number of areas are concerns over **the management burden imposed by more dispersed programmes**. Linked to this, it is believed that the adoption of a **sector-wide approach**, in close consultation with other donors, should lead to the establishment of a coherent sectoral policy framework for the deployment of both local and external resources.

What is the Country Support Strategy?

The drawing up of the **Country Support Strategy** is the foundation of the programming of EU aid resources to individual ACP countries. The Country

Annex IV,
Chapter 1,
Article 2

Support Strategy is drawn up jointly by the ACP state and the EU, but should also involve *'consultations with a wide range of actors in the development process'*.

Each Country Support Strategy should be based on the needs and specific circumstances of the individual ACP state concerned. The Country Support Strategy is intended as an *'instrument to prioritise activities and to build local ownership of co-operation programmes'*.

Each Country Support Strategy should include the following standard elements:

a) *an analysis of the political, economic and social country context, constraints, capacities and prospects including an assessment of basic needs, such as income per capita, population size and social indicators, and vulnerability;*

b) *a detailed outline of the country's medium-term development strategy, clearly defined priorities and expected financing requirements;*

c) *an outline of relevant plans and actions of other donors present in the country, in particular including those of the EU Member States in their capacity as bilateral donors;*

d) *response strategies, detailing the specific contribution the EU can provide. These shall, to the extent possible, enable complementarity with operations financed by the ACP State itself and by other donors present in the country;*

e) *a definition of the nature and scope of the most appropriate support mechanisms to be applied in implementing the above strategies.*

While, under the Cotonou Agreement, the drawing up of the Country Support Strategy is a joint process, internally the European Commission sees **the EC Delegate and the Commission HQ staff playing a major role in drawing up the Country Support Strategy**. From the European Commission perspective, the EC Delegate, in preparing the Country Support Strategy, is expected to be familiar with the ACP country's policy agenda for the coming five years. The assumption is that each ACP government will already have established:

• a transparent and comprehensive budgetary process;

• a detailed and realistic revenue and expenditure plan;

• a prioritised long-term development strategy, with clear timeframes.

However, where this is not the case, the EC Delegate is expected to assist the

ACP authorities in compiling such a national development policy framework.

It is recognised by the European Commission that developing this country analysis is an intensive analytical exercise. In view of the very real human resource constraints facing the European Commission, considerable emphasis has been placed on close co-operation with other donors involved in similar exercises. As a consequence, wherever possible the EC Delegates have been encouraged to build on other planning processes initiated with the World Bank or IMF, particularly where Poverty Reduction Strategy Papers have been completed.

The EU believes that the outline assessment of the country's national development strategy and the analysis of the country situation should be **a realistic assessment of the country's situation** and not a political statement. As a consequence, the EU's country analysis is **not negotiated with the ACP government of the recipient country**. However, the recipient government is kept 'fully involved in the process' and is 'informed of the results'. Where the EU concludes that the ACP national government's agenda is unrealistic or is inconsistent with EU development co-operation policy objectives, then **EU co-operation activities may take place outside the policy agenda of the recipient ACP state**. However, this is most uncommon.

What is the National Indicative Programme?

On the basis of the indicative allocation ('A' envelope) and the objectives and priorities of the **Country Support Strategy**, each ACP government is then expected to draw up and submit a draft indicative programme. This draft indicative programme should contain:

Annex IV, Chapter 1, Article 4.1

- *the focal sector, sectors or areas on which support should be concentrated;*

- *the most appropriate measures and operations for attaining the objectives and targets in the focal sector, sectors or areas;*

- *the resources reserved for projects and programmes outside the focal sector(s) and/or the broad outlines of such activities, as well as an indication of the resources to be deployed for each of these elements;*

- *identification of eligible non-state actors and the resources allocated for non-state actors;*

- *proposals for regional projects and programmes;*

- *a reserve for insurance against possible claims and to cover cost increases and contingencies.*

This draft is then the subject of an exchange of views between the EU and ACP government, before the conclusion of a final indicative programme.

Annex IV, Chapter 1, Article 4.3

This final indicative programme should include:

- *specific and clearly identified operations, especially those that can be committed before the next review;*

- *a timetable for implementation and review of the indicative programme, including commitments and disbursements of resources;*

- *the parameters and criteria for the reviews.*

In line with the 'rolling programming' concept the national indicative programme should:

- identify concrete operations which are at an advanced stage of preparation and which warrant funding in the next two years;

- identify areas of activity to be developed over the following three years;

- link specific activities to available EU aid resources, from all instruments.

Once finalised, the indicative programme is annexed to the Country Support Strategy and forms an integral part of the document, which guides the deployment of EU aid in the following five years.

From the European Commission's perspective the NIP is intended to link **a blueprint for ongoing co-operation at the sectoral level** with a **source of funding** to be deployed within a specific timeframe. As such, the NIP work programme should be **entirely consistent with the Country Support Strategy, completely transparent, fully comprehensive and yet realistic.**

The indicative programme provides the basis for:

- regular ongoing dialogue between the EU Delegate and the National Authorising Officer (NAO);

- annual reporting on the progress of implementation of the agreed activities;

- the mid-term and final reviews which determine whether the 'high case', performance-related element of the indicative programme (the 'B' allocation) will actually be made available to individual ACP countries.

What is Rolling Programming?

Under the Cotonou Agreement a system of 'rolling programming' has been introduced. This involves the identification of specific activities to be financed in two-year blocs, within a five-year rolling programme of deployment of EU assistance. Each year the two-year planning horizon will move forward one year, with the possible modification of **areas of activity** and the **resources made available**. The nature and extent of these modifications will depend on the **annual evaluation of the country performance in effectively utilising available aid** in pursuit of **clearly articulated shared objectives**. Every two or two and a half years there will be a **strategic performance review**, which could lead to changes in both the **direction of the programme** and the **volume of aid made available**.

The significance of this system of 'rolling programming' is that it introduces a regular annual performance review, linked to mid-term and end-of-term performance reviews, on the basis of which **aid allocations to individual countries can be modified**.

This means that the new system introduces a clear **'use it or lose it' imperative to EDF aid**.

The Commission has stressed how the rationalisation of co-operation instruments and the ongoing nature of the programming dialogue will lead to greater **continuity**, **flexibility** and **transparency** in how EU-ACP co-operation activities are conducted.

However, there is a danger that the ongoing policy dialogue required in a process of rolling programming will **impose additional administrative burdens on ACP countries**. Under previous Lomé Conventions average commitment and disbursement rates for least developed ACP countries have tended to be **below those of non-least developed ACP countries**. If too rigorous performance criteria are applied to least developed countries within this new 'rolling programming' approach, this could create a situation **where least developed ACP countries are actually receiving proportionally less aid under the new arrangement than they received under the previous Lomé IV arrangement**. This is a danger that will need to be countered through the establishment of appropriate performance criteria, which take into account the widely differing capacities of ACP administrations to effectively absorb development assistance.

2.3 Co-operation with ACP Regions

This section looks at:

- the aims of programmes of support for regional co-operation;

- how much aid is allocated in support of regional co-operation programmes among ACP countries;

- how regional aid is allocated between ACP regions;

- the process of allocating assistance to pan-ACP regional co-operation activities;

- the programming process for the utilisation of regional aid;

- the scope for non-state actor involvement in regional co-operation activities.

What are the Aims of Regional Co-operation under the Cotonou Agreement?

Part 3, Title I,
Section 3,
Article 29

Article 30

Article 28

Support for co-operation with ACP regions under the Agreement now has a dual focus. On the one hand, there is support for **regional economic integration**, and on the other hand, support for **programmes of functional regional co-operation**. The overall aim of the regional co-operation provisions is to support ACP governments in their own efforts to promote regional integration and co-operation with the aims of:

- fostering the gradual integration of ACP economies into the world economy;

- accelerating economic co-operation and development;

- promoting the free movement of persons, goods, services, capital, labour and technology;

- accelerating economic diversification;

- promoting an expansion of trade.

The provisions dealing with the promotion of programmes of functional regional co-operation allow for the extension of assistance in support of projects and programmes in a wide range of areas, including:

- transport and communications;
- water and environmental management;
- health and education;
- research and technological development;
- disaster preparedness;
- controlling the arms trade;
- combating organised crime and illicit drugs;
- conflict prevention and resolution;
- protection of human rights and promotion of democracy.

Part 3, Title I, Section 3, Article 30

In terms of the deployment of regional co-operation funding, support for programmes of functional co-operation dominate, since such programmes are capable of absorbing (even if somewhat slowly) large volumes of development assistance. However, in terms of the evolution of EU support for ACP regions, growing emphasis is being placed on support to regional economic integration.

Article 7 of Annex IV to the Cotonou Agreement, which deals with 'Implementation and Management Procedures', states that:

Annex IV, Chapter 2, Article 7

> *... to the maximum extent possible, regional integration programmes should correspond to programmes of existing regional organisations with a mandate for economic integration.*

Indeed, under these provisions particular reference is made to providing 'specific support' to:

> *... groups of ACP States who are committed to negotiate economic partnership agreements with the EU.*

This is consistent with the EU's trade policy emphasis on regional integration and its belief that a regional approach provides the most appropriate framework for the negotiation of economic partnership agreements. This growing emphasis on support for regional economic integration is also reflected in the European Commission guidelines for the drawing up of Regional Strategy Papers.

How Much Aid is Allocated to ACP Regions?

Within the financing made available for long-term development co-operation, a special allocation has been set aside for support for regional co-operation. This regional envelope will initially consist of **Euro 1,300 million**. These funds will be used to support regional co-operation programmes (with a particular emphasis on support for regional economic integration) and pan-ACP programmes of assistance (contributions to the Global Fund for AIDS, TB and Malaria and the HIPC Initiative).

In the light of the range of pan-ACP programmes being financed from the regional allocation, funds are currently being re-allocated from the general reserve of the 9th EDF to the allocation for regional co-operation and integration.

How are Available Regional Funds Allocated?

At the beginning of the period of implementation of the Cotonou Agreement, each ACP region was given an indication of the volume of financial resources to be made available for the coming five-year period. The size of this allocation is based on:

Annex IV,
Chapter 2,
Article 9

... an estimate of need and the progress and prospects in the process of regional co-operation and integration.

The following allocations have been made to the various ACP regional groupings under the Agreement.

Region	Amount (Euro million)
Central Africa	55.0
East Africa*	223.0
West Africa	235.0
Southern Africa (SADC)	101.0
Caribbean	57.0
Pacific	29.0
Intra-ACP Co-operation	300.0
Reserve	300.0

*Under the Agreement this is referred to as the Eastern and Southern African region and includes COMESA, the East African Community, IGAD and the Indian Ocean Commission.

How are Funds Used for Pan-ACP Activities Deployed?

Requests for financing from funds held back for pan-ACP regional co-operation activities or co-operation which involves countries from different regions can be submitted by:

(a) *at least three mandated regional bodies or organisations belonging to different geographic regions or the National Authorising Officers of such regions; or*

Annex IV, Chapter 2, Article 13.2

(b) *the ACP Council of Ministers or, by specific delegation, the ACP Committee of Ambassadors; or*

(c) *international organisations carrying out operations that contribute to the objectives of regional co-operation and integration, subject to prior approval by the ACP Committee of Ambassadors.*

How are Regionally Allocated Funds Programmed?

The process of regional programming can be divided into two distinct types:

- where an established regional organisation is in place with a duly designated Regional Authorising Officer (RAO);

- where no established regional body is in place and there is no duly designated Regional Authorising Officer.

Where a duly designated Regional Authorising Officer is in place, the regional programming dialogue is conducted through the Regional Authorising Officer, who takes responsibility for co-ordinating the internal process of priority setting among the regional ACP countries concerned.

In certain regions of the ACP where long-standing regional co-operation organisations are in place (e.g. Southern Africa and the Caribbean), clear processes have been established for consultations on priority setting and the allocation of available regionally programmed EDF resources.

This tends to facilitate the process of priority setting and the allocation of available resources to specific activities. However, this process of internal consultation and compromise within ACP regional groupings can complicate the dialogue with the European Commission on regional priorities. Different departments of the Commission may wish to see their priorities reflected in specific regional programmes and this may not correspond to the priorities emerging in the ACP region following intra-regional consultations.

Where there is no duly designated Regional Authorising Officer, then the regional allocation is programmed in consultation with the National Authorising Officers of the countries concerned (e.g. the PALOP programme for regional co-operation among lusophone ACP countries).

The regional programming process consists of:

Annex IV,
Chapter 2,
Article 8.2

(a) preparation and development of a Regional Support Strategy (RSS) based on the region's own medium-term development objectives and strategies;

(b) a clear indication from the Community of the indicative resource allocation from which the region may benefit during the five year period as well as any other relevant information;

(c) preparation and adoption of a Regional Indicative Programme (RIP) for implementing the RSS;

(d) a review process covering the RSS, the RIP and the volume of resources allocated to each region.

The Regional Support strategy is drawn up by the Commission and duly mandated regional organisations in collaboration with the ACP states concerned.

What is a Regional Support Strategy?

According to Annex IV of the Cotonou Agreement, 'Implementation and Management Procedures', the aim of the Regional Support Strategy is to establish clear regional priorities. The Regional Support Strategy should include the following standard elements:

Article 8.3

(a) an analysis of the political, economic and social context of the region;

(b) an assessment of the process and prospects of regional economic integration and integration into the world economy;

(c) an outline of the regional strategies and priorities pursued and the expected financing requirements;

(d) an outline of the relevant activities of other external partners in regional co-operation;

(e) an outline of the specific EU contribution towards achievement of the goals for regional co-operation and integration, complementary insofar as possible to operations financed by the ACP States themselves and by other external partners, particularly the EU member states.

What is a Regional Indicative Programme?

The Regional Indicative Programme should set out:

(a) the focal sectors and themes of Community aid;

(b) the most appropriate measures and operations to achieve the objectives set for those sectors and themes;

(c) the projects and programmes enabling those objectives to be attained, insofar as they have been clearly identified as well as an indication of the resources to be deployed for each of these elements and a timetable for their implementation.

Annex IV,
Chapter 2,
Article 10.1

According to Annex IV:

the Regional Indicative Programmes shall be adopted by common agreement between the Community and the ACP States concerned.

Article 10.2

What is a Regional Strategy Paper?

While the Cotonou Agreement refers to the preparation of a **Regional Support Strategy**, as the basis for the programming process, the Internal Agreement between EU member states on the 'Financing and Administration of the Cotonou Agreement' and the Commission's own Programming Guidelines refer to the preparation of Regional Co-operation Strategies and Regional Strategy Papers respectively. The use of these different terms can cause confusion.

It appears as if the **Regional Strategy Papers**, which the European Commission refers to in its programming guidelines, consists of the **Regional Support Strategy** and the **Regional Indicative Programme**, together with an **executive summary** and the **EU Response Strategy**.

According to the Commission programming guidelines, the executive summary should at a minimum include:

- a summary of the main objectives;

- an outline of the major challenges facing the region in the medium term;

- the reasons for the choice of the focal sectors;

- the allocation of funds between focal and non-focal activities.

Programming
Guidelines Note
No. 9, Standards
Structure for
Regional Strategy
Papers in the
Framework of
the ACP-EC
Partnership
Agreement,
Brussels,
20 February 2002,
p. 2

The key additional element in the **Regional Strategy Paper**, however, compared to the scope of the Regional Support Strategy set out in the Cotonou Agreement, is the inclusion of the **EU Response Strategy**. In the European

Commission's view, the choice of sectors and activities to which 9th EDF resources should be directed should flow logically from:

- *EU policy objectives;*

- *the regional integration agenda;*

- *the analysis of the regional situation and the assessment of regional integration;*

- *lessons learned from past and ongoing EC experience;*

- *complementarity with interventions by other major donors and the region's own programmes;*

- *conclusions reached in the context of the 'policy mix/coherence analysis exercise;*

- *synergies and coherence with National Indicative Programmes;*

- *the indicative volume of funds available, including EIB support.*[10]

In the European Commission's view, given the context of the Cotonou Agreement:

... economic integration and trade support emerges as a natural focal sector in regional programming.

According to the European Commission:

The Regional Indicative Programme (RIP) will support regional economic integration initiatives, in particular it will contribute to the implementation of the region's own economic integration agenda.

Furthermore, according to the European Commission:

... it is expected that trade-related activities (notably those directly linked to the liberalisation process) represents at least 20% of the regional indicative allocation under the 9th EDF.

In the European Commission's view, this support may include flanking measures, including technical assistance; support for capacity building; harmonisation of tariffs; customs co-operation; trade facilitation; assistance related to transitional costs; budgetary support linked to trade liberalisation; and assistance to the private sector to fully benefit from liberalisation.

This reinforces the European Commission's emphasis that the *'hard core'* of the regional agenda should be regional economic integration and trade matters.[11]

There are a number of mandatory documents which should accompany the Regional Strategy Papers, namely:

- an intervention framework, containing both performance indicators and policy progress indicators which are specific, measurable, achievable, realistic and time-bound (SMART). In addition, mid-term and end-of-term targets should be indicated to allow for performance reviews;

- a chronogramme of activities;

- a timetable of indicative commitments and disbursements;

- a table of main ongoing projects and programmes financed by the Community;

- a donor matrix.[12]

Optional annexes that may be included can cover:

- a review of the economic and social context of the region;

- an assessment of regional policy and policy implementation in the focal sectors.

The European Commission is encouraging ACP regions to concentrate assistance in a limited number of focal sectors and to focus EU assistance in areas where the EU has a comparative advantage. Where support for functional regional co-operation programmes is sought, the European Commission is encouraging ACP regions to focus on areas where there is a clear added value to undertaking the activities at the regional level.

To facilitate the compilation of the Regional Strategy paper, the Commission has provided a number of standardised formats for the different sections of the regional strategy paper dealing with:

- General Provisions;

- The European Commission's Regional Co-operation Principles and Objectives;

- Presentation of the Indicative Programme.[13]

In the standardised framework for the presentation of the indicative programme, **Economic Integration and Trade Support** is specified as the first focal sector, while the second focal sector and non-focal sectors are left blank.

Who is Responsible for Drawing Up and Presenting Regional Programmes for Funding under the Cotonou Agreement?

Formally requests for financing under regional co-operation programmes need to be submitted by:

Annex IV,
Chapter 2,
Article 13

(a) a duly mandated regional body or organisation, or

(b) a duly mandated sub-regional body, organisation or an ACP State in the region concerned at the programming stage, provided that the operation is identified in the RIP.

However, who is actually responsible for the substantive work of preparing the financing proposal will vary depending on the nature of the project or programme. Generally, responsibility lies with the agency which will in fact be implementing the project. For example, if it is a regional road project, located in a specific ACP country, then the government department dealing with road transport is generally responsible for putting together the financing proposal. However, if it is a regionally co-ordinated study or training programme, the department of the regional organisation with sectoral responsibility for the activity may well take responsibility for the drawing up of the financing proposal.

What Scope is There for Non-state Actor Involvement in Regional Co-operation Programmes?

According to the Agreement, non-state actors should be consulted on the regional programming process *'where appropriate'*. The European Commission in its guidelines for regional programming envisages non-state actors having a role to play in a number of different dimensions of regional co-operation, ranging from economic and trade liberalisation through to conflict prevention and resolution.

In reality the extent to which non-state actors become involved in the development of regional co-operation strategies and the implementation of regional co-operation programmes varies greatly from region to region and from sector to sector. There are instances where non-state actors have played an active role in the development of regional strategies to combat HIV/AIDS. Equally, there are instances of artisanal fish workers' organisations seeking consultations with regional bodies on both the design of policy and programmes targeted at the artisanal fisheries sector.

The provisions of the Agreement on non-state actor involvement in regional co-operation programmes are thus permissive, while the actual level of involvement depends very much on the openness of regional structures to dialogue with and participation of non-state actors, and the capacities and interest of various non-state actors' organisations in engaging with regional policymakers and regional programme managers.

2.4 The Investment Facility

This section seeks to outline:

- the nature of the Investment Facility;

- the aims of the Investment Facility;

- the types of assistance available under the Investment Facility;

- the terms and conditions under which loans from the Investment Facility are extended;

- who is allowed to submit requests to the Investment Facility;

- the procedures for submitting a funding application to the Investment Facility;

- the information which should go into a funding request;

- the minimum size of funding request that the EIB will consider under the Investment Facility;

- the arrangements for extending assistance to small and medium-sized enterprises;

- the decision-making structures governing the Investment Facility.

What is the Investment Facility?

The **Investment Facility** is nominally a new vehicle for the extension of loans to enterprise and infrastructural development in ACP countries. The Investment Facility has been formally in place since June 2002. Following ratification by all EU member states, the Cotonou Agreement entered into force on 1 April 2003.

Euro 2,200 million will be made available from the grant allocations from EU member states under the 9th EDF, of which Euro 200 million will be made available for **interest rate subsidies** for selected projects financed both under the Investment Facility and from the EIB's own resources. The grant financed funds allocated to the Investment Facility will mainly be used to finance risk-sharing loan instruments. These funds will be deployed alongside Euro 1,700 million in loans drawn from the European Investment Bank's own resources.

The European Investment Bank is seeking to highlight the differences between the new Investment Facility and traditional EIB 'risk capital' and 'own resource' loan operations under the Lomé Convention. The Investment Facility can provide loans in a number of different forms, from conditional loans and participating loans, through various forms of subordinated loans, to quasi equity participation in a company which, under certain conditions, can be denominated in local currency.

The EIB stresses that it expects remuneration on the loans extended commensurate with the risks incurred. It highlights how the EIB will only take limited risk for certain types of loans denominated in US dollars or Euros, and will insist on adequate cover for even this limited risk in line with its basic statutes. This in part reflects the major change which has been introduced under the Cotonou Agreement, namely the establishment of the Investment Facility as a revolving fund, which should be self-financing.

Under Lomé III and Lomé IV, the EIB was mandated to allocate guaranteed amounts of 'risk capital' to ACP countries. Under Lomé IV bis, these guaranteed amounts became merely indicative. Under the Cotonou Agreement there will no longer be any country allocations (floors and ceilings) for loan financing. It is expected that the Investment Facility will be most active in those ACP countries where economic reforms and economic development are most advanced.

Funding from the Investment Facility will generally be provided on market-related terms and conditions so as to avoid distorting local capital markets. The aim is for funding from the Investment Facility to have a catalytic effect on local and foreign private investment. The Investment Facility can provide support to both private and commercially run public sector entities.

The Investment Facility can provide loans to activities in the following sectors:

- manufacturing;
- agro-processing;
- horticulture;
- mining;
- quarrying;
- transport;
- telecommunications;

- water supply and sewage;

- power generation and transmission;

- oil and gas development;

- tourism and related services.

Emphasis is also placed on extending loans in support of processes of privatisation in ACP countries.

What are the Aims of the Investment Facility?

Part 4, Title II,
Chapter 7,
Articles 74–78

The Investment Facility should be seen in the context of the provisions of the Cotonou Agreement on 'Investment and private sector development support'. These provisions recognise the importance of private sector investment to development co-operation and acknowledge the need to take steps to promote private investment. Under Article 76 reference is made to:

Article 76.1

... long-term financial resources, including risk capital, to assist in promoting growth in the private sector and help to mobilise domestic and foreign capital for this purpose.

Under the risk capital provisions, reference is made to providing equity and quasi equity investment, as well as guarantees:

... in support of domestic and foreign private investment.

Reference is also made to providing loans from the European Investment Bank's own resources. The terms and conditions for the provision of this financing are set out in Annex II of the Agreement.

The main purpose of the Investment Facility is to:

- directly finance enterprises;

- indirectly finance enterprises through local financial institutions;

- support privatisation processes;

- provide private infrastructure financing;

- support and build local financial and capital markets.[14]

Under the Investment Facility greater emphasis will be placed on supporting:

- private sector investment;

- revenue earning infrastructure in both the public and private sectors;

- financial sector development;

- catalytic lending to leverage other private finance.

The operation of the Investment Facility is to be monitored by a specially con-stituted **Investment Facility Committee**.

What Types of Financial Assistance are Available under the Investment Facility?

The Investment Facility offers loans and reimbursable financial assistance in a wide variety of forms. Under the Investment Facility funds may be used to provide risk capital in the form of:

- **equity participation**;

- **quasi capital assistance**;

- **guarantees** to cover political or other investment risks.

The quasi capital assistance may take the form of

- **conditional loans**;

- **participating loans**;

- **subordinated loans**.

Funds from the Investment Facility can also be used to provide **ordinary loans**.

Under What Terms and Conditions are Funds Made Available?

Loans extended in the form of quasi capital assistance from risk capital may take a variety of forms.

Conditional loans are linked to the fulfilment of certain conditions by the project, with repayments being waived if the conditions are not met. For example, a fixed interest rate of not more than 3 per cent may be charged, with a variable component also being charged related to the performance of the project.

For **participating loans**, servicing and duration of the loan is linked to the financial return on the project.

Subordinated loans are only repaid when all other claims have been settled.

In the case of subordinated loans the interest rate charged is market related.

Guarantees to cover political and other investment-related risks are provided at prices which reflect the risks insured.

Annex II,
Chapter 1,
Article 2

For **ordinary loans**, the interest charged consists of a reference rate applied by the EIB for comparable loans, with a mark-up determined by the EIB.

However, under special circumstances ordinary loans may be extended on concessional terms. This includes:

- for **infrastructure projects in least developed countries** or **post conflict countries** that are prerequisites for private sector development. In these cases a 3 per cent reduction on the interest rate charged on the loan is possible;

- for projects involving **restructuring operations linked to privatisation**. In these cases the interest rate subsidy is determined on a case by case basis but may not exceed 3 per cent and must never be less than 50 per cent of the reference rate;

- for projects with **substantial and clearly demonstrable social and environmental benefits**. In these cases the interest rate subsidy is determined on a case by case basis, but may not exceed 3 per cent and should never be less than 50 per cent of the reference rate.

The EIB likes to limit its use of interest rate subsidies so as not to disrupt the functioning of local financial markets. Often the interest rate subsidy is used to hedge against foreign exchange risks or is absorbed by the intermediate financial institution through the establishment of various business support services, rather than being passed on to the final beneficiary.

The terms applied to EIB 'Own Resource' loans are determined by the following criteria:

- the standard interest rate applied by the EIB;

- the characteristics of the project which affect the repayment period, which may not exceed 25 years;

- the construction period on the project which affects the grace period with reference to which repayments are set.

However, 'Own Resource' loans to public sector projects are eligible for an interest rate subsidy of 3 per cent, as are private sector projects in support of restructuring operations linked to privatisation and projects with clearly demonstrable social and environmental benefits. Interest rates, however, may never fall below 50 per cent of the reference rate.

Other forms of assistance which can be extended under the Investment Facility include:

- **Direct equity participation** by the Bank (on behalf of the EU) to strengthen the capital base of the company or ACP institution;

- **Indirect equity participation**, through intermediaries such as banks and other financial institutions, in ACP companies, especially small and medium-scale enterprises;

- **Financing of risk capital and venture capital funds**, which take stakes in small or medium-scale companies, especially start-up investments, but also existing firms which need capital injections to tackle modernisation or expansion;

- **Financing of 'joint ventures'** between European and ACP investors, usually by assisting the ACP partner in putting up its share of the capital;

- **Credit Lines to local banks**, generally for on-lending in domestic currency or provision of equity funding, with various forms of risk sharing;

- **'Apex' (financial sector) loans**; this channels funds through several banks, on a competitive basis, to fund small and medium-scale firms;

- **Support for privatisation purchase schemes and loan guarantee funds**.[15]

Terms and Conditions for EIB Own Resource Loans[16]

Term	Medium- to long-term (up to 20 years, occasionally more).
Grace	Dependent upon the running in time and implementation
Period	period of the project and the useful life of the installations. The moratorium (on principal payments) may typically be two years on an eight-year loan for an industrial project, with perhaps five years on a 20-year loan for a large infrastructure scheme.
Currency	The currency in which the loan is extended is the choice of the borrowers, but is normally a major convertible currency.
Repayment	Repayment is in the form of six monthly instalments, although other formulae can be negotiated on a case by case basis depending on the characteristics of the project
Interest	The interest rate is fixed at the date of signature of the
Rate	contract and reflects the EIB's high creditworthiness.
Interest	Provision is made for the extension of an interest rate subsidy
Subsidy	under specific conditions using funds made available by EU member states. The interest rate subsidy is used either to support expenditure by the borrower on environmental improvements, training programmes or other agreed items or, in certain cases, is passed on to the government in the form of budgetary support.
Security	A guarantee from an institution of high standing is required (first class bank or company) or, in the case of a public sector or mixed public/private sector project, government guarantees can be provided.
Ceilings	Loans can cover up to 50 per cent of project costs (although frequently it is much lower). There is no ceiling in absolute terms and no lower limit, although loans are not normally extended for amounts below Euro 1.5 million.

Who Can Submit Projects for Funding to the Investment Facility?

The EIB accepts projects submitted by both private and public project promoters, although an increased emphasis is now being given to support for private sector projects. One particular manifestation of this is the support extended by the EIB to enterprises undergoing privatisation.

Since 1989 projects funded by the EIB had initially been identified by:

- EIB staff on mission;
- EU delegations;
- other multilateral or bilateral financiers;
- government agencies;
- individual project promoters taking up direct contact.

The EIB aims to support local companies, in particular small and medium-sized enterprises, as well as projects put forward by foreign investors.

How Can Projects be Submitted for Funding to the Investment Facility?

Initial contacts with the EIB over a project can be quite informal, taking place by phone or fax.

However, subsequent processes of project appraisal are quite rigorous. In order to ensure the viability of the loans extended, all projects are subject to a rigorous internal process of appraisal by the EIB covering **economic, financial, technical and environmental viability**.

Considerable powers are delegated to desk officers under the EIB system for managing EDF funds. (A list of the contact details of the various EIB desk officers can be found in Annex 5.)

All projects funded by the EIB need to be approved by the government of the ACP country in which the project is located. While this appears an unnecessary bureaucratic process for projects which are increasingly intended to be private sector driven, the experience of the EIB has been that this rarely poses a problem. Nevertheless it remains a formal requirement for all projects being submitted under the Investment Facility and EIB Own Resource operations in ACP countries.

What Information Must Go into a Funding Request?

After the initial contact confirms the eligibility of the project for EIB funding, a project financing request must be prepared and submitted.

This financing request should include: **a description of the project** (nature, purpose, cost, working capital requirement, financial plan, timetable and expected return) and **information on the financial status of the promoter** (recent annual reports and financial statements).

More specifically, the following guidelines on the types of information to be included in a financing request have been set down by the EIB.[17]

(i) **General and legal information about the enterprises, its principal partners or promoters including:**

- documents showing the legal basis of the enterprise;
- audited financial statements;
- details of liabilities;
- dividend distribution policy.

(ii) **Technical data on the project** including:

- general purpose, justification and location;
- technical description;
- environmental impact assessment where relevant;
- engineering studies covering implementation issues;
- detailed cost estimates;
- operating costs;
- management and technical requirements.

(iii) **Economic data on the project** including:

- market data;
- production outlets;
- employment impact;
- the link to wider national development;
- the data used to calculate the economic rate of return.

(iv) **Financial data on the project** including:

- a breakdown of the projects operating and maintenance costs, depreciation and overheads;

- the financial plan for expenditures and revenues;
- estimates of working capital needs;
- the basis for the calculation of the internal rate of return;
- security and guarantees offered.

(For more details, see Annex 6 'Applying for EIB Funding'.)

How Big Must a Funding Request Be to Receive Direct Funding from the Investment Facility?

Normally, the EIB does not provide loans directly to enterprises below Euro 1.5 million. Given that only in exceptional circumstances will the EIB provide loans equivalent to more than 50 per cent of the costs of the project, normally the total project size needs to be in excess of Euro 3 million. Indeed, with the EIB normally providing loans equivalent to between 25 per cent and 30 per cent of the project cost, this implies an average project size of around Euro 4.5 million. Given the size of most ACP economies and the scale of small and medium-sized enterprises in the ACP, this is a relatively high minimum size for the provision of direct loans.

However, the EIB is willing to directly fund smaller projects where no global loan or 'Apex' facility is in existence if the project offers exceptional prospects.

How are Funds Made Available to Small and Medium-sized Enterprises?

Funds to small and medium-scale enterprises in ACP countries are largely made available though global loans administered through intermediate financial institutions or through 'Apex' facilities that allow a range of local financial institutions to make use of different forms of credit for on-lending.

Global loans can be used for:

- direct capital investment;
- assistance for feasibility studies;
- equity participation;
- conditional loans;
- subordinated loans.

The EIB estimates that using this system of global loans, around 25 per cent of EIB funding in the past five years has gone to small and medium-scale investments. The EIB hopes that its activities in support of small and medium-sized enterprises in ACP countries will increase under the Investment Facility.

The conditions under which small and medium-sized enterprises may draw down on these facilities depends on the terms of the individual global loan or 'Apex' agreement. Loans may be up to Euro 2 million, with interest rates being linked to prevailing market rates, with the repayment term being up to eight years.

In countries where no global loans or Apex operations have been established, for exceptionally promising projects the EIB will consider direct approaches for small-scale projects and deal with the project on a stand alone basis.

The experience of support to small and medium-sized enterprises through the provision of 'global loans' varies greatly in ACP countries. In some countries it has proved highly successful in promoting investment in the development of non-traditional exports (e.g. Zambian cut flowers).

The EIB also has a capacity to support parallel initiatives designed to enhance the capacity of the ACP private sector to take up funding from global loans (e.g. the provision of various business support services for project development).

What is an Intermediate Financial Institution?

An **Intermediate Financial Institution** is a commercial bank or local development finance institution with which the EIB co-operates in the provision of global loans for the financing of small and medium-scale investment projects. These commercial banks and development finance institutions then on-lend small amounts from the funds made available through the global loan to their own clients. These loans are extended on the basis of the local institutions' own credit judgement, acting in accordance with criteria agreed by the EIB when drawing up the global loan agreement.

The aim of the co-operation that the EIB builds up with Intermediate Financial Institutions is to draw on the local knowledge and manpower which the on-the-spot presence of these institutions provides in ACP countries. However, it is also seen as having an important role in developing local institutional capacity to extend effective assistance to the small and medium-sized enterprise sector.

The EIB also provides credit lines or other forms of financial support to micro-finance institutions and leasing companies.

(A comprehensive list of the ACP Intermediate Financial Institutions with which the EIB currently has dealings under the EDF can be found in Annex 7 'What Intermediate Financial Institutions Currently Manage EIB Global Loans?'.)

What Must Be Done to Move from a Funding Request to a Funding Decision?

Decision making with reference to funding requests submitted to the Investment Facility can be broken down according to the role of different institutional actors.

The first level of decision making is within the **ACP country** where the **endorsement of the ACP government** is required before any funding request can receive consideration. While this appears an unnecessary bureaucratic process it has rarely posed a problem. It is, however, a formal requirement for all projects.

Once approval has been received from the ACP government, a funding request may be submitted to the EIB. Such a request should ideally be forwarded to the EIB in the format set out in the EIB's guidelines. (These guidelines can be found in Annex 6 'Applying for EIB Funding'.) The second level of decision making is inside the **EIB** at the level of the **loan officer**. Under the EIB system, individual loan officers have considerable powers of decision making. It is the individual loan officer who decides whether a project is appropriate for consideration for funding under the Investment Facility and whether it should proceed to the stage of project appraisal.

The EIB encourages project promoters to take up early contact with the institution so that, where necessary, support can be given to the development of project requests for particularly attractive project proposals.

The appraisal process involves examination by the EIB of:

- the economic, financial and technical viability of the project;
- the management capacity of the promoter, in terms of their implementation and operational capabilities;
- the impact of the proposed project on the national economy (foreign exchange earnings, employment, etc);
- the environmental consequences of the project.

In undertaking the appraisal, the EIB uses its wide cross-sector technical, economic and financial knowledge and, where necessary, the knowledge of partner intermediate financial institutions with which it builds up working relationships.

The findings of these internal appraisals are then discussed with the project promoters.

Where a favourable appraisal is given, the EIB needs to secure the agreement of the European Commission. This can be seen as the third level of decision making. The European Commission is deemed to have given a favourable opinion if within two weeks of notification of the project it has not notified the EIB of an unfavourable opinion.

For all public sector or financial sector projects, the EIB has to obtain an opinion from the European Commission on the relevance of the project to the country co-operation strategy before taking a decision. The EIB's request for an opinion takes the form of a short memorandum outlining the objectives and rationale of the proposed operation and its relevance to the Country Strategy.

Where an Interest Rate Subsidy is being proposed then the agreement of both the **European Commission** and the opinion of the **Investment Facility Committee** must be sought.

In the areas where the Investment Facility Committee has been given responsibilities, the EIB may not proceed with a project request without a favourable opinion from the Investment Facility Committee. This can be seen as a fourth level of decision making. Where the Investment Facility Committee gives a negative opinion on a request to grant an interest rate subsidy, the EIB may still proceed with the loan, but without the benefit of the interest rate subsidy. The Investment Facility Committee must, however, be kept informed of any such decision.

Where no opinion of the Investment Facility Committee is required, the EIB takes its own decisions in line with the guidelines established by the Investment Facility Committee.

It should be noted that the project selection strategy varies from country to country to take into account the wider macroeconomic context. This is particularly the case for loans to the private sector.

What is the Investment Facility Committee?

The **Investment Facility Committee**[18] consists of representatives of EU member states and a representative of the European Commission. Each member state designates a representative and an alternate. Only the designated representative or alternate may vote in the Committee. The Chairperson of the Committee is elected by the members of the Committee and serves for two years. The Investment Facility Committee is serviced by the EIB.

Decisions of the Committee are taken by qualified majority with voting weighted on the same basis as in the EDF Committee. The Investment Facility Committee meets at least four times a year, although it can meet more frequently if so requested by the EIB.

The responsibilities of the Investment Facility Committee are twofold:

- to establish the guidelines and policy framework within which the Facility should operate in the light of the objectives of the Cotonou Agreement;

- to deliver opinions on proposals in certain specified areas.

The specific responsibilities in the sphere of policy include:

- approving and, where necessary, modifying operational guidelines for the Investment Facility;

- approving the investment strategies and business plans for the Investment Facility drawn up by the EIB;

- the establishment of performance indicators for the Investment Facility based on the objectives of the Cotonou Agreement;

- approval of the annual reports on the operation of the Investment Facility;

- approving general policy documents.

The specific responsibilities with regard to project proposals include:

- delivering opinions on proposals to grant interest rate subsidies, including on how the interest rate subsidy is to be used;

- delivering opinions on proposals on which the European Commission has given a negative opinion.

● How Long Does it Normally Take to Obtain a Decision on a Funding Request?

The EIB maintains that it tries to ensure that its decision-making processes are consistent with the tempo of business-driven initiatives. There are **accelerated procedures** for dealing with smaller scale projects.

Once a project request is received, the responsible EIB official will either:

- turn down the project because it is not deemed to be suitable for consideration;

- undertake a project appraisal and then turn down the project for clearly indicated reasons;

- place consideration of a project on hold while outstanding issues of concern within the project proposal are addressed in consultation with the promoter;

- process the application for funding.

It should be borne in mind that after appraisal, larger projects have to be subjected to the appropriate management board for approval.

The EIB sees its system as relatively rapid, efficient and cost-effective. However, there are no set timeframes within which funding decisions have to be taken.

2.5 The Technical Centre for Agricultural and Rural Co-operation

This section looks at the mandate, objectives and programmes of this joint ACP-EU institution. It provides an overview of:

- the mandate and objectives of the CTA;
- the size of CTA's budget;
- a description of how CTA works;
- a review of who the CTA works with;
- a review of current CTA programmes;
- how to become a beneficiary of various CTA programmes;
- how to become a CTA partner organisation;
- a review of CTA's current partner organisations;
- CTA's position on the involvement of non-state actors in ACP-EU co-operation activities.

What are the Main Objectives of CTA?

The mission of CTA, as set out in Annex III to the Cotonou Agreement, is 'to strengthen policy and institutional capacity development and information and communication management capacities of ACP agricultural and rural development organisations'. CTA will assist these organisations to develop and implement policies and programmes to reduce poverty, promote sustainable food security and preserve the natural resource base.

Annex III, Article 3.1

The principal functions of CTA is thus to develop, support and provide **information and communication services and products** in the sphere of agricultural and rural development and extension, to promote dialogue and information exchange between different and disparate bodies and professionals in ACP states.

CTA's activities take place at the local, national and regional levels and focus on the development of decentralised information and communication programmes. In any single intervention, CTA may work with governmental, inter-governmental or non-state actors in the implementation of information and communication activities depending on the perceived need.

On the basis of its 2001–2005 Strategic Plan, CTA has set itself two operational objectives, which are broken down into three operational programmes as indicated in the box opposite.

CTA's Objectives and Programme Areas

OBJECTIVE 1

To improve the availability of, and access to, appropriate relevant, adequate, accurate, timely and well-adapted information on priority information topics for ACP agricultural and rural development.

Programme 1: Information Products and Services (IPS)

- Increasing the availability of information

- Increasing the awareness of information sources

Programme 2: Communication Channels and Services

- Supporting an integrated use of communication channels

- Strengthening contacts and information exchange

OBJECTIVE 2

To improve information and communication management (ICM) capacity of ACP agricultural and rural development organisations.

Programme 3: Information and Communication Management, Skills and Systems

- Increasing human capacity to generate and manage agricultural information

- Increasing capacity to formulate and develop ICM strategies and models

How Big is CTA's Budget?

Under the financial protocol to the Cotonou Agreement, Euro 70 million is allocated to finance the activities of CTA for the five-year duration of the protocol.

The table below sets out CTA's total annual expenditures since 1997:

Annual Expenditures

Year	Euro
1997	9,818,000
1998	10,486,000
1999	11,645,000
2000	11,420,000
2001	12,140,000
2002	12,747,000

Sixty per cent of CTA's total budget goes on operational programmes, with 32 per cent going on staffing costs. Given the focus on information compilation, management and dissemination, all of which are skills intensive, this is a relatively small allocation to staffing costs. Some 8 per cent of the budget goes towards the running costs of CTA.

Breakdown of CTA Expenditures, 2002

	Euro	Percentage of total
Staffing Costs	4,438,000	31.5
Running Costs	1,142,000	8.1
Operational Programmes*	8,490,000	60.4
Total	14,070,000	100.0

*N.B. CTA aims to obtain an equal balance in the budgets of the three operational programmes.

How Does CTA Work?

In understanding how CTA works it is useful to make a distinction between:

- those services and products managed or provided directly from CTA headquarters (via its three operational departments);

- those activities and services provided through partners and intermediaries which CTA co-finances.

This second aspect of CTA's work has important capacity-building implications. It has developed extensively in response to the institutional changes which have taken place in the provision of support for agricultural and rural development throughout the ACP in the 1990s. The restructuring of extension services and the dismantling of marketing boards and agricultural parastatals have brought about dramatic changes in the institutional context in which CTA seeks to provide information services on agricultural and rural development issues. This has led to an increased emphasis on local capacity building and the extension of CTA services and products to a wider range of non-state actors involved in agricultural and rural development issues.

The objectives of CTA are pursued through activities in three programme areas:

- Information Products and Services;

- Communication Channels and Services;

- Information and Communication Management Skills and Systems.

The aim of the **Information Products and Services (IPS)** Programme is to increase awareness of information sources on critical topics in the facilitation of agricultural and rural development, and to increase the availability of such information to a wide range of stakeholders throughout the ACP.

Under this programme, greater use will be made of new information technologies. This is particularly the case for information services relevant to ACP agricultural policy issues. Complementary to this, greater emphasis is to be placed on publications dealing with policy issues and policy processes in priority areas.

The activities of IPS are described in more detail in the section 'What Programmes Does CTA Have Under Implementation?'.

The aim of the **Communication Channels and Services (CCS)** Programme is to strengthen contacts and systems for the exchange of information on critical topics and to support the integrated use of different vehicles and channels for communication of this information.

Under this programme, CTA essentially *'acts as a broker between organisations and between professionals working in the ACP agricultural and rural sectors, and as a platform for promoting dialogue and the exchange of information between ACP bodies and professionals.'*

While this programme seeks to make extensive use of information and communication technology, CTA promotes the use of conventional communication channels where access to ICT-based information services is limited and to integrate both forms of communication as much as possible.

This programme increasingly seeks to link up ACP nationals and institutions working on agricultural and rural development issues so as to enhance their capacity to use information services to participate effectively in key policy debates. The development of regional policy networks involving the public and private sector in debates around key issues of concern is accorded a particularly high priority.

More details of the activities of CCS are in the section 'What Programmes Does CTA Have Under Implementation?'.

The aim of the **Information and Communication Management Skills and Systems (ICMSS)** Programme is to increase the capacity of concerned stakeholders to formulate and develop information and communication management strategies and models, and to increase the human capacity of concerned stakeholders to generate and manage agricultural information.

The activities of ICMSS are structured around two main components:

- Information and communication management training;
- ICM support to partner organisations.

An increasingly important focus of this programme is on the development of market information systems and policy-making information support services.

The year 2003 has seen the addition of a further component to this programme, namely to increase the capacity of public and/or private organisations working in agricultural and rural development to formulate science and technology policies to develop the agricultural sector (see the section 'What Programmes Does CTA Have Under Implementation?' for more details on the specific activities).

The activities of each of these three operational programmes need to be seen within the framework of CTA's thematic approach. Themes of importance to ACP stakeholders are identified and each operational programme is required to develop co-ordinated and complementary activities around these themes in the light of their own areas of expertise and competence.

The themes which CTA covers on a regular basis relate to natural resource management, improvement in agricultural productivity, market-led development and agricultural policy (e.g. food security, trade and biotechnology). Among the cross-cutting themes which have been given increased prominence by CTA are information and communication technologies (ICTs), gender, youth and social capital.

All three operational programmes are supported by four common services, namely:

- **Planning and Corporate Services**, charged with, among other things, the systematic review of information and the development of methodologies for incorporating cross-cutting issues and special 'development policy' topics into CTA's three operational departments;

- **Administrative Services, Budget and Human Resource Development**, responsible for overseeing the management of budgeting and personnel issues;

- **Accounting Services and Financial Control**, which deals with all accounting and financial matters and ensures that the Centre's finances are managed in accordance with EDF regulations;

- the **Brussels Office**, charged with liaising with the EC and relevant organs of the ACP group and the EU.

With Whom Does CTA Work?

In considering the question of with whom CTA works, a distinction needs to be made between **those who benefit from the services CTA provides under its various programmes** (referred to as **'beneficiaries'**), and **those who participate in joint activities with the CTA** (known as **'partners'**). Many partnership relationships have emerged from the initial provision of CTA services. The aim is to progressively transform the nature of the CTA's relationship with beneficiaries into partnership relationships, although it is acknowledged that this cannot be achieved in all cases.

'Beneficiaries' are mainly individuals who attend CTA-supported training courses and workshops (they can be researchers, extension officers, documentalists, information service providers, radio programme producers, NGO leaders, trainers, network managers or representatives of community-based organisations) and institutions that receive CTA information services and products. 'Beneficiaries' are also groups which want to work with the CTA but which are unable to bring any financial or technical resources to the joint activities (e.g. consumer groups, youth groups or women's groups)

Partners range from research and training institutions, NGOs and documentation centres to policy networks and farmer organisations. Increasingly, partners are being selected from the NGO sector with the aim of increasing the range of ACP organisations capable of developing their own ICM strategies, and generating and managing information related to agricultural and rural development.

In this context CTA works with a wide range of state and non-state actors concerned with agricultural and rural development issues. Priority is accorded to developing partnerships with those organisations that work closest to farmers (including, of course, farmers' organisations). The next level of priority is working with public and private sector organisations involved in agricultural and rural development issues, including ministries, research institutes and networks, extension services, training institutions, rural radio and television broadcasting services, agricultural enterprises, chambers of commerce, trade unions and consumer groups.

In terms of specific categories which benefit from CTA's work, the CTA 'Strategic Plan and Framework for Action 2001–2005' identified the following **beneficiaries**:

- Government ministries;
- Policymakers;
- Researchers;
- Extension services;
- Rural broadcasters;
- Farmers' organisations;
- Exporters;
- Chambers of Commerce;
- Processors;
- Distributors;
- Women's groups;
- Youth associations;
- Trade unions;
- Consumer groups;
- Training institutions.[19]

Given its capacity constraints, CTA cannot work directly with all organisations involved in agricultural and rural development throughout the ACP; it has consequently developed general criteria for selecting CTA partners, namely:

- relevance of their work to the end beneficiaries (small-scale resource-poor farmers);
- the presence of women, the young and resource-poor farmers among potential beneficiaries;

- degree of complementarity with CTA activities;

- level of financial or technical contribution to the venture;

- the likely multiplier effect;

- ability to deliver services in a timely and effective manner;

- ability to sustain services after CTA's exit.[20]

What Programmes Does CTA Have under Implementation?

In looking at the various CTA programmes it should be borne in mind that CTA's work is increasingly focused around key themes, with complementary activities and synergies being developed between different programmes.

In this context, the **Information Products and Services Programme** is involved in five main areas of activity. These are:

- the publication of CTA's own reports in both print form and electronic form, as well as other electronic products including rural radio resource packs;

- co-publications with a range of collaborating organisations;

- a Publications Distribution Service;

- support to question and answer services (QAS) on agriculture and rural development issues;

- the Selective Dissemination of Information (SDI) to agricultural and rural development researchers.

The major CTA publication is the bi-monthly *Spore* magazine, which goes out in electronic and printed form in English, French and Portuguese, and has circulation figures of 21,000, 17,000 and 2,000 respectively. A survey of *Spore* readers in 2002 indicated a potential readership of over 1,000,000 people.

CTA's co-publishing activities cover a wide range of technical issues in agricultural and rural development (AGRIDOK series). Perhaps the most ambitious of CTA's co-publications was the seminal *Where There is No Vet*. Over 6,000 copies have been distributed in English and some 8,000 in French.

CTA's Publication Distribution Service has an extensive outreach, reaching a total of 29,916 subscribers in 2001, with over 10 per cent of these being new additions to CTA's client base. Of the new subscribers, one-third comprised farmers' organisations and co-operatives.

CTA's support to Question and Answer centres seeks to make a wide range of information on agricultural and rural development issues more easily available, with a growing emphasis on market information systems and essential texts on agricultural issues. Users of this service include researchers, lecturers, teachers, consultants, librarians, archivists, students, extension workers, policy-makers and planners, farmers and technicians. Areas covered by requests include: crop production, animal production, agricultural processing, markets and marketing, policy development, community education and various specific research topics.

More in-depth information support is provided to ACP researchers and practitioners in agricultural and rural development through the Selective Dissemination of Information service. This provides subscribers with bibliographical references and abstracts from major agricultural data bases. In 2002, there were 1,325 beneficiaries of this scheme in approximately 42 ACP countries. Additional in-depth assistance is extended through support for subscriptions to CD-Rom and internet databases. In 2002, 89 such subscriptions were paid, covering 40 countries.

The **Communication Channels and Services Programme** is involved in six main areas of activity. These are:

- supporting a range of regional networks dealing with agricultural and rural development issues;

- maintaining a number of Information and Communication Technology based activities, including the *Agritrade* website which focuses on issues in ACP-EU trade relations and a range of e-forums linked to the preparation of various conferences and seminars;

- organising and supporting study visits between ACP countries;

- organising CTA's own seminars;

- co-organising seminars with other institutions;

- supporting the participation of ACP nationals in agricultural and rural development seminars.

The **Information and Communication Management Skills and Systems Programme** is involved in four main areas of activity. These are:

- organising training on agricultural communication and information themes;

- supporting other specific thematic training courses;

- establishing partnership arrangements with public and non-state ACP organisations with the aim of increasing their capacity to generate agricultural information and develop their own information management policies and systems as well as communication tools;

- assisting national systems to develop science and technology strategies.

How Can One Become a Beneficiary of CTA's Publications Distribution Service?

CTA's **Publication Distribution Service** is subscription based. In order to become a subscriber you need to be a resident (or resident organisation) in an ACP country and to be involved in agriculture and rural development. Credit points are allocated on a yearly basis to subscribers, on the one hand, and to publications, on the other. Subscribers can then order publications up to their total credit point allocation.

If a subscriber exceeds their credit point allocation (or in the cases of individuals and organisations that are not eligible to receive CTA publications free of charge), individual publications may be purchased through a commercial distributor contracted by CTA. In addition to the direct distribution of publications, CTA also supports the establishment of commercial distribution channels for agricultural publications. It has established pilot partnerships with local book distributors and participates in international events concerned with agricultural issues.

Individuals and organisations in ACP countries can apply to become a beneficiary of CTA's Publications Distribution Service by filling in a standard application form, providing background information on the applicant, the nature of the work in which the applicant is involved, the institutional context and the subject areas of greatest interest.

The application is then reviewed, and if it is deemed eligible 'credit points' are granted, which can then be used to order CTA publications. Applications should be addressed to:

The Director, CTA, Post Box 380, 6700 AJ Wageningen, The Netherlands
E-mail: cta@cta.int
Website: www.cta.int

How Can One Become a Beneficiary of CTA Training Support?

Training support can be extended to individuals, to institutions for group training and for individual internships at centres of excellence. A standard application form is now available on the internet (see Annex 19). Information is requested on:

- the particulars of the course for which sponsorship is being sought;
- the individual and their current educational level;
- the institution and its major activities;
- the applicant's responsibilities and work experience;
- the applicant's level of computer literacy and language competence;
- the applicant's expectations of the course.

To be eligible to apply for training support the applicant must be an ACP national residing in an ACP country and be endorsed by an authorised officer of the applicant's organisation. Preference is given to suitably qualified female applicants.

Applications are judged on the basis of the following criteria:

- the relevance of the course to CTA goals;
- the consistency of the course with key CTA training themes, which include:
  - collection, analysis and dissemination of scientific information
  - production of extension materials
  - use of media (printed press, radio, television)
  - management of commercial information (market information systems, commercial and non-commercial regulations, etc.)
  - information management for agricultural systems analysis
  - use of new ICTs (websites and electronic networks, etc.)
  - Question and Answer Service management
  - management of agricultural policy networks;
- the duration of the course;
- the cost of the course;
- the venue of the course
- the institution providing the training.

Applications should be addressed to:

The Director, CTA. Post Box 380, 6700 AJ Wageningen. Netherlands
E-mail: cta@cta.int
Website: www.cta.int

How Can One Become a Beneficiary of CTA's Seminar Support Programme?

A standard application form for support under CTA's Seminar Support Programme is available on the internet (see Annex 8). The form requests:

- the personal contact details of the applicant;

- details of the organisation for which the applicant works;

- the applicant's work experience and skills level;

- the applicant's role at the conference and expectations of the conference;

- a description of the conference (title, venue, organiser, logistical arrangements);

- the identification of the major conference themes (up to three) of greatest interest from a list of over 53 categories divided into seven major headings (market-orientated production and trade, environment protection and natural resources management, agricultural socio-economic policies, animal production and health, crop production and protection, information and communication, and rural dynamics).

CTA support covers transportation and accommodation costs for a maximum of seven days. Applicants must be ACP nationals and must be drawn from one of CTA's target groups, while the conference must focus on one of CTA's priority themes. Particular priority is accorded to: policy formulation; food security; agricultural diversification; sustainable development; and natural resource protection. Priority is given to conferences organised in ACP or EU countries.

Applications should be received by CTA two months before the conference. Applications should be addressed to:

The Director, CTA, Post Box 380, 6700 AJ Wageningen, The Netherlands
E-mail: cta@cta.int
Website: www.cta.int

How Can One Become a CTA Partner Organisation?

There are two basic ways to become a partner in CTA programmes. The first way is to be approached by CTA, where programmes are under development or are being extended. The second way is for an organisation involved in agricultural and rural development issues to approach CTA in the light of the services and products CTA is seeking to make available.

Initial contact can be taken up with the head of the operational programme of greatest interest. Selection criteria have been developed in the main programme areas to try and ensure a more coherent approach to programme development. Simple application forms are available on CTA's website.

With the exception of requests relating to CTA's seminar support programme and co-publication programme, an extensive lead time is required in taking on new CTA partners. Proposals for partnership projects need to be received at least 11 to 15 months before the commencement of the partnership project.

The initial draft proposals formulated by the partner organisation in consultation with CTA need to be presented to CTA for review by CTA's Programmes Committee. Following this review, the project must be revised by the partner organisation. The revised project is then re-submitted to CTA's Finance Committee for approval.

The completion of this procedure allows financing for the partnership project to be incorporated into CTA's annual financial planning process. CTA's annual financial plan is then submitted to the ACP-EU Committee of Ambassadors (CTA's supervisory authority) for approval.

Partnership activities are then formalised into a contract.

CTA may finance activities of partners which form part of the project submitted. However, CTA does not currently finance the overhead costs of its partners.

Applications should be addressed to:

The Director, CTA, Post Box 380, 6700 AJ Wageningen, The Netherlands
E-mail: cta@cta.int
Website: www.cta.int

Who are CTA's Current Co-operating Partners?

Under the **Information and Communication Management Skills and Systems Programme**, CTA currently has some 35 national and local partnership projects under implementation. CTA co-operating partners embrace a wide range of organisations.

CTA's Current Co-operating Partners

CTA's current co-operating partners include:

- Fédération des Unions de Producteurs du Bénin (FUPRO) – Bénin;

- Fédération Nationale des Organisations Paysannes (FENOP) – Burkina Faso;

- Women Farmers Advancement Network (WOFAN) – Nigeria;

- Institut Africain pour le Développement Economique et Social – Centre Africain de Formation (INADES Formation) – Burkina Faso;

- Association villageoise pour le développement local (AVIDEL) – Burundi;

- Unité Nationale de Gestion et de Coordination/Ministère de l'Environnement (Cameroon);

- Centre National d'Appui à la Recherche (CNAR) Ministère de la Recherche (Chad);

- Kenya National Farmers Union (KNFU);

- International Institute of Tropical Agriculture/FOODNET;

- Agri Service Ethiopia (ASE);

- BIMTT (Bureau de Liaison des Centres de Formation Rurale) – Madagascar;

- Zambia National Farmers Union (ZNFU);

- Zimbabwe Farmers Union (ZFU);

- Africa Co-operative Action Trust (ACAT) – South Africa;

- Eastern Caribbean Agriculture Trading and Development Company (ECTAD) – St. Vincent and the Grenadines;

- Jamaica Agricultural Society (JAS);

- The Cook Island Ministry of Agriculture (CIMOA).

The activities covered under these partnership arrangements include:

- establishment of data collection systems;

- processing of this data and the establishment of databases;

- production of brochures, manuals, technical files and newsletters in local languages;

- establishment of village information and documentation centres;

- production of radio programmes and video and audio cassettes in local languages;

- meetings, workshops and seminars;

- development of websites and electronic discussion fora;

- local training courses for ICM methods and tools (see Annex 17).

CTA's Regional Partners

CTA's regional partners currently include:

- Association for Strengthening Agricultural Research in Eastern and Central Africa (ASARECA);

- Caribbean Agribusiness Marketing Intelligence and Development (CAMID) – Caribbean;

- Caribbean Agricultural Research and Development Institute (CARDI);

- Conference of Ministers of Agriculture/West and Central Africa (CMA-AOC);

- Eastern and Central Africa Programme for Agricultural Policy Analysis (ECAPAPA – ASARECA Network);

- Food, Agriculture and Natural Resources Policy Network (FANRPAN) (SADC);

- Inter-American Institute for Cooperation on Agriculture (IICA);

- Institute for Research, Extension and Training in Agriculture (IRETA) – Pacific;

- International Union for the Conservation of Nature (IUCN);

- Regional Agricultural Information Network (RAIN – ASARECA Network);

- Regional Economic Partnership Agreement (REPA) – West and Central Africa.

Under the **Communications Channels and Services Programme**, CTA has partnership arrangements with regional organisations and networks. The programmes under these arrangements consist of support to the management of agricultural information and communication, including networking around the following themes:

- agricultural policy;
- agricultural research;
- agricultural trade;
- natural resources management;
- regional information networking.

Under the Information Products and Services Programme CTA also has a special type of partnership relationship through the decentralisation of its agricultural and rural development Question and Answer Service Centres). CTA currently co-operates with six centres in decentralising CTA's QAS Service.

These six centres are:

- Agricultural Information for Development of Eastern Africa (AGRIDEA);
- Ghana Agricultural Information Service (GAINS);
- Centre d'Information et de Documentation Scientifique (CIDST) – Madagascar;
- Nigerian Agricultural Question and Answer Service (NAQAS);
- Programme for Agricultural Information Services (PRAIS) – Southern Africa.

What is CTA's Position on the Involvement of Non-state Actors?

Given that the Cotonou Agreement gives a high priority to the role of private sector organisations and is seeking to promote greater collaboration between public sector institutions and non-state actors, CTA is giving increased emphasis to working with farmers' associations, non-governmental organisations and other local and grassroots organisations involved in all aspects of agricultural and rural development.

2.6 The Centre for the Development of Enterprise

This section looks at the mandate, objectives and programmes of this joint ACP-EU institution. It provides an overview of:

- the mandate and objectives of the CDE;
- the size of the CDE budget;
- the structure of the CDE;
- the main focal sectors for CDE support;
- the geographical breakdown of past CDE co-operation activities;
- current CDE programmes under implementation;
- the types of support provided through CDE programmes;
- the level of funding provided by the CDE;
- how to apply for CDE assistance.

What are the Main Objectives of the CDE?

The objectives of the CDE are set out in Annex III of the Cotonou Agreement, **'Institutional Support, CDE and CTA'**. Article 2 of this annex declares the objectives of the CDE to be:

> *... to support the implementation of private sector development strategies in the ACP countries by providing non-financial services to ACP companies and businesses and support to joint initiatives set up by economic operators of the Community and of the ACP States.*

Annex III, Article 2

More specifically the CDE is mandated to:

- facilitate and promote business co-operation and partnerships between ACP and EU enterprises;

- assist in the development of qualified and competent national and regional business services providers;

- provide assistance for investment promotion activities;

- support initiatives which promote technology transfer and the transfer of know-how and best practices on business management;

- diffuse to ACP businesses information on **products standards** and **quality requirements** on external markets;

- provide information to European companies on business opportunities in ACP countries.

The CDE's activities are expected to be co-ordinated with and complementary to those undertaken by other private sector development initiatives in ACP countries.

Looking beyond the formal provisions of the Cotonou Agreement, under its new strategy the CDE is pursuing the following major themes:

- support to private sector development strategies;

- direct support to enterprises and capacity building for local service providers;

- support for SME development;

- development of sub-sector focused programmes;

- support for the establishment of business development services.

How Big is the CDE Budget?

Under the Cotonou Agreement Euro 90 million is allocated to CDE activities. The CDE seeks to work closely with other organisations supporting enterprise development. The organisations with which the CDE works include:

- the European Commission;

- the European Investment Bank;

- EU member states' development finance institutions;

- EU member states' national and provincial authorities;

- EU member states' business associations;

- international financial institutions;

- ACP regional institutions;

- ACP intermediate financial institutions;

- ACP sectoral associations and business chambers.

These collaborative links extend the resources available to the CDE by about 24 per cent, but mobilise substantially more resources for the projects which the CDE is involved in supporting.

A review of CDE activities in support of ACP private sector development in 2001 showed that for every Euro earmarked from the CDE budget, Euro 2.3 were secured from other external contributors.

The CDE envisages additional funding being mobilised in two principal forms:

- **resources generated on behalf of third parties;**

- **parallel funding of specific projects.**

Since 1997 the following additional resources have been mobilised by the CDE:

1997	2,843,000 euro
1998	2,670,000 euro
1999	2,316,000 euro
2000	2,471,000 euro
2001	2,469,000 euro

CDE Expenditures 1998–2002

	1998	1999	2000	2001	2002
Operational Budget	8,400,000	8,400,000	9,680,000	10,758,000	9,050,000
Commitments	8,999,000	8,523,000	10,191,000	10,379,000	9,032,000
Payments	7,863,000	9,352,000	8,817,000	8,8946,000	n/a

The CDE is managing an increasing number of private sector focused programmes financed by the European Commission, under the supervision of AIDCO. This includes the PROINVEST scheme and a project to assist ACP enterprises in complying with EU health standards in the fisheries sector.

How Does the CDE Work?

The CDE works through five major units: one with a geographical focus; two with a sectoral focus; one dealing with financial resources and advisory services; and another dealing with control and operational follow-up.

Geographical Co-ordination

- West Africa
- East Africa
- Pacific
- Caribbean
- Central Africa
- Southern Africa

Sector Co-ordination 1

- fisheries, cut flowers, organic products, essential oils, etc.
- cereals, milk and dairy, animal and poultry feed, transport of plants, meat, etc.
- fruit and vegetables, processed fresh products for export, plant processing, organic products
- timber furniture, metals
- construction materials, ornamental stone, clay, quarrying, processing and mining

Sector Co-ordination 2

- tourism and related activities, transport
- private infrastructure management
- trade, services and IT
- environment, ecology, quality
- health
- textiles, leather and skins
- tanning, leather products, etc.
- metal and machinery
- chemicals, cosmetics, fertilisers, pharmaceutical products, plastic, glass, packaging and printing

The **Financial Resources and Advisory Unit** deals with:

- European institutions (bilateral and multilateral);
- relationships with financial institutions (bilateral and multilateral);
- relationships with European programmes.

These four major divisions are supported by an **Administrative Division**.

The CDE is increasingly seeking to assist small and medium-sized enterprises through a programme approach which is sector based, multi-annual and increasingly regional in focus. The aim of this approach is to maximise the scope for synergy in one or more sectors in a country or region, so that optimal use can be made of CDE human and budgetary resources. It is hoped that by providing assistance to several enterprises in the same sector, the influence of CDE interventions will spread throughout the sector. Through this approach the CDE is seeking to work within a well-organised framework into which it can fit its facilities for support to ACP enterprises, intermediary organisations and consultants. The CDE is aiming to support the preparation of development projects that are more comprehensive, better structured, more fully integrated and coherent, and which bring benefits to the sector as a whole.

However, the CDE also maintains its assistance at the level of individual enterprises. Here again the CDE is seeking to deploy available instruments in a more integrated and coherent manner by extending assistance to individual enterprises in the context of the challenges facing the sector as a whole. It is hoped that this will lay a firmer basis for broadening interventions at the enterprise level into sector-wide programmes.

It should be borne in mind that while the CDE extends grants to improve service provision to ACP enterprises and to facilitate contacts between ACP and EU enterprises, it does not fund investments as such. Its role in this context is limited to helping companies to identify possible sources of investment funding, where appropriate.

More specifically, the CDE now focuses on three major areas of work:

- direct assistance;
- studies and information;
- the organisation of one-on-one and group meetings.

In the sphere of direct assistance the CDE supports the organisation of projects in the start-up and development phases and searches for financial and technical partners, especially in the EU. It offers two facilities for this purpose: the CDE **development facility** and the CDE **enterprise assistance facility**.

The **development facility** supports the creation, expansion or development of enterprises through the following phases:

- project definition;
- pre-feasibility, feasibility and market studies;
- searches for technologies and partners;

- financial engineering;

- assistance with legal packaging and setting up a project;

- quality and environmental studies.

The CDE **assistance facility** aims to support the long-term viability of enterprises through:

- start-up and technical assistance;

- training of personnel;

- diagnoses and audits (technical, financial and management);

- assistance with management and marketing;

- assistance with restructuring;

- support for integrating enterprises into national and regional networks and trade organisations;

- assistance with meeting requirements for quality and environmental protection labels and standards.

In the sphere of **studies and information** the CDE supports the provision of advice and the implementation of studies by experts in the fields required by the enterprise. The CDE seeks to maximise the impact of this practical work by compiling technical information and documentation which is then published in the form of practical guides and an electronic newsletter.

In the sphere of the **organisation of one-to-one or group meetings** the CDE organises at national and regional levels, technical or sectoral meetings or seminars aimed at bringing together ACP and EU entrepreneurs. The CDE can also support trade fairs, missions, trade gatherings and promotional events.

In supporting these activities the CDE is able to provide assistance covering:

- a maximum of two-thirds of the total cost of any operation for which support is requested;

- up to Euro 100,000 a year per enterprise;

- a cumulative total for successive operations of up to 20 per cent of assets or annual turnover.

In addition to these three major focal areas of activity, the CDE seeks to assist the development of ACP intermediary organisations involved in private sector development. This assistance is determined on a case by case basis but mainly takes the form of:

- assistance with their own management;

- introduction to other organisations in the same sector in European or ACP countries with which they might conclude partnership agreements;

- technical assistance in support of their services to member enterprises (identification of market outlets, partners, sources of finance or information, etc.).

In extending this assistance, priority is given to:

- the number of member enterprises the intermediary organisation services;

- an organisation's statutes, objectives and programmes;

- its own financial resources;

- the services it provides.

CDE assistance is always provided in parallel with the mobilisation of the organisation's own resources.

The CDE also provides assistance in developing the capacity of local consultants to provide business support services. This can involve specialised training of consultants in the appraisal of ACP enterprises projects, the preparation of presentations to potential backers and the technical training of consultants. The CDE has also supported the establishment and operation of networks of consultants in the Pacific, Caribbean and Africa. The CDE's contributions in this area of its activities are limited to two-thirds of the total cost of the operation and Euro 50,000 per annum.

The CDE maintains a network of contacts throughout the ACP and the EU. The network system through which the CDE now works in the ACP has a number of different levels, with different levels of responsibilities being devolved to different types of actors in the network.

The first level is the regional field office. The principal function of the regional field office is to strengthen the operational network of the CDE in the field by making CDE services more readily available to ACP enterprises. To date only one regional office has been set up – in the Caribbean (see Annex 9). The second level of network actors is the **decentralised management unit**. These consist of CDE network members which, on the basis of their abilities in the field of service provision to private sector operators, have been given an extended mandate in the deployment of CDE support instruments. This may or may not involve delegation of financial management responsibilities, depending on the nature and capacity of the local agency taking on the role of a decentralised management unit. While some 13 decentralised management units have been set up to date (see Annex 10), a total of 30 network members have been selected to become decentralised management units. The third level of actors on the CDE network is the basic antennae (see Annex 11), whose job is to inform local enterprises of CDE activities and procedures. Many of these institutions have long-standing relations with the CDE, although the extent to which they actively promote CDE activities varies considerably.

Trends in CDE Resource Deployment

	1997	1998	1999	2000	2001
Direct Assistance (%)	46.6	46.2	56.3	51.5	51.5
Planning Meetings (%)	19.4	23.5	22.8	21.9	24.8
Studies (%)	34.0	30.3	30.9	26.6	23.7

The network of contacts maintained in the EU (see Annex 12) is mainly concerned with assisting ACP operators to gain access to appropriate sources of finance.

The CDE's networking is thus seen as making a contribution in two key areas:

- **technical:** through identifying consultants, partners, markets, projects, gathering economic, technical and commercial information, validating information and projects;

- **financial:** by meeting the needs of ACP businesses for appropriate finance.

The CDE has also seconded experts to ACP countries to work on specific enterprise development initiatives, although this is commonly financed from other sources (the NIP or contributions from institutions in EU member states). One example of this is the Zambian Private Sector Development Programme.

What are the Main Focal Sectors for CDE Support?

In 2002 CDE assistance was heavily concentrated in **agro-industry** (42 per cent) and **construction, timber and metal** (25.5 per cent). The **textile sector** and **leather working** (10.6 per cent) are, however, areas of growing involvement for the CDE. In addition, specific sectoral programmes have been developed in the fisheries sector under a European Commission financed programme, linked to ensuring access to overseas markets in the context of stricter hygiene and health standards in the fisheries sector.

What is the Geographical Breakdown of CDE Support?

The three major regions receiving CDE assistance are **West Africa** (33.4 per cent), **Southern Africa** (17.5 per cent) and **East Africa** (17.7 per cent). The **Caribbean**'s share at 16.2 per cent of CDE assistance is relatively high given the population distribution of the ACP. In 2002 **Central Africa** received 9.8 per cent of CDE funding and the **Pacific** 5.4 per cent

Geographical levels of support, however, can vary greatly from year to year depending on the development of the local investment climate and the different cycles of programme development within the CDE's new programme approach.

This latter dimension is illustrated by the fact that while by the end of 2002 the CDE had a major timber programme under way in Central Africa, a similar programme in the Pacific was still under development.

The Geographical Distribution of CDE Operations

	1997	1998	1999	2000	2001	2002
Southern Africa (%)	20.7	21.1	23.1	23.6	22.6	17.5
Central Africa (%)	10.0	9.2	7.8	8.5	16.8	9.8
East Africa (%)	21.2	21.8	22.3	22.7	21.6	17.7
West Africa (%)	24.9	24.6	22.4	24.7	20.7	33.4
Caribbean (%)	12.8	11.6	11.8	13.9	12.6	16.2
Pacific (%)	10.4	11.7	12.6	6.6	5.7	5.4

What Current Programmes Does the CDE Have under Implementation?

Given that the CDE is seeking to move away from isolated interventions in response to the needs of individual enterprises towards a programme approach which seeks to combine various elements of CDE support within a well-organised and co-ordinated programme of mutually supporting activities, the CDE has a growing number of programme-based interventions and a consequently smaller number of overall interventions.

Currently the following CDE programmes are underway:

- timber certification and woodworking in Central Africa;
- timber certification and woodworking in the Pacific;
- timber certification and woodworking in the Caribbean;
- cotton and textile industry in West Africa;
- textiles programme in Southern Africa;
- livestock in West Africa;
- livestock in East Africa;

- leather programme for East and Southern Africa;
- EU health standards in Mozambican fisheries;
- EU health standards in Cape Verdean fisheries;
- marine resources in the Pacific region;
- medicines derived from tropical medicinal plants in ACP countries;
- Caribbean herbal products development;
- mining and quarrying technology and productivity in Southern Africa;
- productivity of the building materials sector in West Africa;
- productivity and environment of the ceramics and aggregates sector in the Caribbean;
- treatment of industrial toxic waste in the Seychelles and Mauritius;
- strengthening the organic products sector in the Pacific and improvement of its competitiveness on export markets;
- HACCP and quality control in the fruit and vegetable sector in the Caribbean;
- development and standardisation of West Africa's stock of hotels;
- hotel industry, eco-tourism and local communities in the Caribbean;
- hotel industry, eco-tourism and local communities in Southern Africa;
- hotel industry, eco-tourism and local communities in the Pacific;
- hotel industry, eco-tourism and local communities in East Africa;
- processing and regional trade among countries of the Indian Ocean Community.

In addition to these sector programmes within particular regions, the CDE maintains an *'integrated sole proprietorship support programme'*. This is to enable the CDE to continue to provide direct support to individual enterprises.

What Types of Support are Provided through CDE Programmes?

The forms of support that the CDE is now trying to bring together in a targeted and co-ordinated way under its evolving programme approach include the following elements:

- support for partnership meetings;

- support for regional trade associations;

- research into the competitiveness of the sector;

- introduction of technical improvements in the product process;

- enhancing product quality;

- a needs survey;

- pre-project surveys;

- assistance with project identification;

- support to project start-up and development;

- direct assistance to enterprises, including staff training;

- upgrading and transmission of know-how to intermediate structures;

- support to good environmental practice;

- assistance in securing investment finance.

What Level of Funding Does the CDE Provide?

Fifty per cent of the operations supported by the CDE apply to schemes involving less than Euro 5,000. These types of support cover participation in trade fairs, business and technical meetings.

The remaining CDE support is provided to larger schemes, although the average level of funding is only around Euro 20,000. Often ACP enterprises benefit from more than one CDE supported intervention. In addition, the CDE can play an important role in facilitating access to other sources of financial assistance.

In 2001, in the 783 enterprises supported by the CDE, using a total operational budget of Euro 10.4 million, new investments totalling Euro 2,112 million were made. While this level of investment mobilisation cannot be wholly attributed to CDE funding, it does illustrate the complementarity between CDE interventions and the support mobilised from other sources.

In 2002 the number of applications recorded fell to 2,161 (1,574 in 2001). This was largely due to the application of appraisal procedures through the decentralised management units, which resulted in a stricter screening of projects than in the past. It also reflected a conscious effort to refocus CDE support on a more programme-based approach.

In 2002 the number of enterprises assisted rose to 858. This was a by-product of the large number of meetings assisted by the CDE (up 14 per cent on 2001) which provided opportunities for more initial contacts. In 2002 the average unit value of a CDE contribution was lower than in previous years. This was because more operations were assisted from a fixed budget. However, the overall level of investment supported did not fall, since the lower CDE contribution was in many cases accompanied by a larger financial contribution from the enterprises being assisted.

In 2002 the average unit value of CDE contributions was Euro 8,000.

● How Should Applications for Support from the CDE be Made?

There are four routes in applying for support from the CDE:

- through the regional field office (see Annex 9);

- through a decentralised management unit (see Annex 10);

- through one of the CDE network partners in the ACP (see Annex 11) or one of the CDE's network partners in the EU (see Annex 12);

- through any bilateral, multilateral or local financial institution.

However, many successful initial contacts with the CDE are initiated on the fringes of sector or thematic meetings, since these requests correspond to the areas where the CDE is seeking to develop support programmes.

The first step in the application process is the compilation of a targeted assistance request detailing the assistance required from the CDE in accessing specific business services. The CDE is currently revising its standard application form and in due course will post a revised request form on its website. In the interim, private sector enterprises are advised to contact the decentralised management units (in the case of the Caribbean the regional field office) or one of the CDE network partners in ACP countries, who are empowered to accept or reject requests. The decentralised management units and network partners can also assist applicants in reformulating requests where the assistance request has not been fully developed. Where requests are accepted, they are forwarded to CDE headquarters for appraisal and final decision making.

2.7 The Programme Review Process

This section explains the process by which the utilisation of aid is reviewed. The review process has been substantially strengthened under the Cotonou Agreement. The section looks at:

- the aims of the strengthened and extended review process;

- how the review process will work both at the national and regional level;

- the different elements of the review process;

- the intended outcomes of the review process.

What is the Aim of the Review Process Set Out in the Cotonou Agreement?

The Agreement establishes a far more comprehensive review process for ACP-EU co-operation than under the previous Lomé Convention. It requires the National Authorising Officer in each ACP country and the EU Delegate to each ACP country to:

- *annually undertake an operational review of the indicative programme;*

  Annex IV, Chapter 1, Article 5.1

- *undertake a mid-term and end-of-term review of the Country Support Strategy and the indicative programme in the light of current needs and performance.*

Although in many respects the new review process builds on similar arrangements under earlier Lomé Conventions, a key new element is the rigour with which the whole review process is to be applied.

Clear performance indicators, with quantifiable objectives, are to be set out in the **Country Support Strategy** and the **National Indicative Programme**. The review process will then use these indicators and objectives as a yardstick against which to judge an ACP country's performance.

How will the Annual Review Process Work?

According to the Agreement the annual operational review process should cover:

Annex IV,
Chapter 1,
Article 5.4

- *the results achieved in the focal sector(s) measured against the identified targets and impact indicators and sectoral policy commitments;*

- *projects and programmes outside the focal sector(s)and/or in the framework of multi-annual programmes;*

- *the use of resources set aside for non-state actors;*

- *the effectiveness in implementation of current operations and the extent to which the timetable for commitments and payments has been respected;*

- *an extension of the programming perspective for the following years.*

The annual operational reviews will in turn be based on **regular monthly monitoring reports** and the ongoing reporting system established within the EU Delegations. This in turn will be based on **regular and ongoing dialogue with the office of the NAO**.[21]

It is hoped that this system of monthly reporting will allow any problems arising to be swiftly identified and appropriately addressed. The **annual operational review** should thus be the culmination of this ongoing monitoring and dialogue. In the Commission's view, the annual operational review should emerge naturally from the ongoing dialogue process and should impose no major substantive additional burden on ACP administrations.

The **annual joint Delegate/NAO reports** are to provide the basis for the annual assessment. The EU Delegation (in consultation with locally represented EU member states) will be expected to prepare a brief **position paper** on issues raised in the annual review. The **EDF Committee**, composed of representative of EU member states, will then have an **exchange of views** on the annual operational reviews. The results of the annual operational reviews of every ACP country programme will then be transmitted to the joint **ACP-EU Development Finance Committee**.[22]

This whole annual review should be completed within 60 days of the formal initiation of the in-field review phase. **The first trial annual operational review was scheduled to take place in mid 2001.** However, with the European Commission unable to legally spend 9th EDF resources until 1 April 2003, the annual operational review would have differed little from the Delegates' annual reports under the Lomé Convention. In reality, the first annual review of financial co-operation under the Cotonou Agreement will not be possible until mid-2004, by which time one full year of financial co-operation under the 9th EDF regulations will have been completed.

Significantly, in the light of these annual reviews, the National Authorising Officer and the EU Delegate can adapt and revise the Country Support Strategy and the indicative programme. ACP NAOs should take full advantage of this possibility to adjust the NIP in the face of any unforeseen problems. Modifying the CSS and the NIP in the light of unforeseen problems will allow performance targets to be established on a more realistic basis. This is important since the strategic mid-term review will involve decisions on the level of aid to be finally made available to each ACP country.

How will the Mid-term and End-of-Term Review Processes Work?

The **mid-term and end-of-term reviews** will build on and consolidate the annual reviews and will update and modify the programme if required. During this phase the Delegate's **position paper** will evaluate the effectiveness of the CSS and propose any necessary changes. This could also include proposals with regard to the amount of money to be made available to the ACP country concerned. This paper will in summary form:

- analyse the country's performance in meeting set targets;
- outline any substantive changes to be proposed to the CSS;
- contain a proposal for the confirmation or reallocation of resources.

The European Commission's HQ Policy Group, will discuss the mid-term/end-of-term draft position paper and confirm or modify its findings. Where major changes are proposed, the **Quality Support Group** will also consider the paper. This consolidated EU position will then be the basis for the EU Delegate's negotiations/discussions with the NAO and non-state actors in the ACP country concerned.

Formal conclusions initialled by both sides will then be submitted to the EDF Committee for their consideration and approval before a formal modification of the programme can take place. It is envisaged that these strategic reviews would be completed within 90 days.[23]

What will be the Outcome of the Review Process?

Under the 'rolling programming' concept this performance assessment is to be used to inform decisions on resource allocations. It will affect both the utilisation and **volume** of resources allocated to individual ACP country pro-grammes. If the aid utilisation performance falls short of the scheduled levels, or if the objectives jointly agreed in the Country Support Strategy are not being met, then **the volume of aid made available could be reduced and/or its utilisation changed**. Equally, those ACP countries that achieve their performance targets could benefit from additional aid allocations.[24]

This more rigorous review process, which links **how effectively aid is being used to the future availability of aid**, adds a new dimension to what was formerly seen as a routine reporting task.

One important implication of the more rigorous review process is that ACP governments will need to pay careful attention to the **objectives** set down in the **Country Support Strategy** and the **performance indicators** set out in the **National Indicative Programme**. If highly ambitious objectives and performance indicators are agreed, then ACP governments could find them-selves **losing part or all of the 'B' component of their country allocation**.

This raises the question of the basis for performance indicators. Will perform-ance targets be set with reference to the past experience of ACP-EU co-opera-tion, where it has taken up to 13 years to fully use aid under each five-year allocation? Or will performance targets be set with reference to the European Commission's new aspirations for more rapid deployment of available aid funds? Or will performance targets be set with reference to progress towards internationally agreed goals, such as those relating to access to education? Or will performance criteria be developed which take into account the specific circumstances of individual ACP countries and regions? To date it is still unclear what basis will be used for establishing performance indicators.

There would appear to be a need to ensure that performance targets are **real-istic in the light of the particular circumstances facing individual ACP countries** and the probability that unforeseen events may occur to undermine the achievement of jointly agreed objectives.

To summarise, the mid-term and end-of-term review process will lead to:

- a modification of the strategy and an internal redeployment of resources;

or

- a confirmation of the existing strategy and allocation;

This will mean:

- a downward revision of the initial resource allocation;

or

- an upward revision of the initial resource allocation.

It should be noted that the European Commission will take the resource alloca-tion decision after consultation with EU member states and the EDF Committee, but that **resource allocation decisions will not be discussed with the recipient ACP country in advance**.

How will the Regional Review Process Work?

Unlike under the Country Support Strategy, no annual reviews will be conducted on regional indicative programmes. However a mid-term and end-of-term review of the regional indicative programme will be undertaken with the aim of adapting the programme to *'evolving circumstances'* and in order to ensure that the programmes are being correctly implemented.

Annex IV,
Chapter 2,
Article 11

What will be the Outcome of the Regional Review Process?

As with the country review process, the regional mid-term and end-of-term reviews could lead to a revision of the resources allocated to the regional pro-gramme. However, unlike under the country programmes, no indicative 'B' allocations will be made to regional programmes under the 9th EDF.

What is the Annual Implementation Report?

According to the Cotonou Agreement, each year a joint assessment should be conducted of the implementation of co-operation programmes. This annual reporting on co-operation activities at the country level has been a long-standing feature of ACP-EU co-operation and was previously referred to as the 'Delegate's Annual Report'. Under the Agreement this annual reporting process is now a joint exercise carried out locally by the EU Delegate and the National Authorising Officer. It should provide an annual assessment of:

- the results achieved in the focal sector(s) measured against the identified targets, impact indicators and sectoral policy commitments;

Annex IV,
Chapter 1,
Article 5

- projects and programmes outside the focal sector(s) and/or in the frame-work of multi-annual programmes;

- the use of resources set aside for non-state actors;

- the effectiveness of implementation of current operations;

- the fulfilment of the planned timetable for commitments and payments;

- the perspective for future activities.

This joint assessment constitutes the Annual Implementation Report. It normally includes a summary review of each and every co-operation activity being implemented with the benefit of EU funding, including operations financed from the EU annual budget.

Once the annual implementation report has been compiled, it has to be submitted within 30 days to the Development Finance Co-operation Committee.[25] Depending on the results of the review, the Committee recommends modifications to the aid programme under implementation. The annual implementation report effectively provides the basis for the mid-term and end-of-term reviews.

2.8 Non-state Actors and the Cotonou Agreement

This section looks at:

- the definition of a non-state actor under the Cotonou Agreement;

- the wider role non-state actors are expected to play;

- the specific role non-state actors could be called upon to play within the ACP-EU co-operation process;

- the role the EC Delegate has in promoting non-state actor engagement with the ACP-EU co-operation process;

- the specific role non-state actors are seen to have in the preparation of the Country Support Strategy and the National Indicative Programme;

- the scope for non-state actor involvement in the implementation of co-operation activities;

- the possible scope for non-state actor involvement in the programme review process;

- the experience to date of non-state actor engagement with the programming process under the Agreement.

What is a Non-state Actor?

Under Article 6 of the Cotonou Agreement non-state actors are defined as:

- the private sector;

- economic and social partners, including trade union organisations;

- civil society in all its forms according to national characteristics.

Part 1, Title I, Chapter 2, Article 6

From a European Commission perspective, civil society organisations range from self-help groups, community organisations and registered charities through church organisations and farmers associations to independent research and academic institutions. The actual eligibility of individual non-state actor bodies to participate in ACP-EU co-operation activities will, however, depend on the extent to which they are perceived to:

Part 1, Title I,
Chapter 2,
Article 6.2

... address the needs of the population, on their specific competencies and whether they are organised and managed democratically and transparently.

While the definition of non-state actors allows for a wide range of organisations to engage in ACP-EU co-operation activities, it also allows for the **selective involvement of non-state actors**, based on the added value they bring to the development co-operation process.

What Wider Role are Non-state Actors Seen to Play?

The provisions of the Cotonou Agreement on the role of non-state actors should be seen against the background of the European Commission's conception of the role of non-state players in the wider development co-operation process. The European Commission no longer sees non-state actors simply as low-cost delivery systems. The Commission's outlook is now much broader with the emphasis being on bringing non-state actors into the political dialogue process and ensuring their participation in defining and evaluating development strategies and programmes. Including non-state actors in the ACP-EU co-operation process has been a main political priority during the Lomé renegotiations.

This emphasis on the involvement of non-state actors should not be seen as 'anti-state'. It is rather an attempt to mobilise all available capacities and resources in the fight against poverty, within the framework of a new and innovative state/non-state actor partnership.

The new approach is seen as offering an alternative to top-down approaches which offered little scope for local variations. It offers scope for improving sectoral policy formulation and programme implementation and is crucial to achieving the ambitious objectives of ACP-EU co-operation.

What Does the Cotonou Agreement Say about the Involvement of Non-state Actors in ACP-EU Co-operation Activities?

Under the Cotonou Agreement the important contribution that non-state actors can make to the development process is recognised. In this context it is agreed that, where appropriate, non-state actors shall:

- be informed and involved in consultation on co-operation policies and strategies, on priorities for co-operation especially in areas that concern or directly affect them, and on the political dialogue;

- be provided with financial resources, under the conditions laid down in this Agreement in order to support local development processes;

- be involved in the implementation of co-operation project and programmes in areas that concern them or where these actors have a comparative advantage;

- be provided with capacity-building support in critical areas in order to reinforce the capabilities of these actors, particularly as regards organisation and representation, and the establishment of consultation mechanisms including channels of communication and dialogue, and to promote strategic alliances.

Part 1, Title I,
Chapter 2,
Article 4

What Role Does the EC Delegate Have in Promoting Non-state Actor Involvement in ACP-EU Co-operation?

The EC Delegate to each ACP country will play a two-fold role in promoting the involvement of non-state actors: as a **critical observer** and as a **facilitator**.[26] As a critical observer, it will be the EC Delegate's responsibility to ensure that non-state actor involvement is representative and does not simply involve a 'rubber stamping' of government programmes and policies by government sponsored non-governmental bodies. In a context where deregulation and privatisation have led to the creation of a plethora of non-governmental organisations, a significant number of which in some ACP countries are state sponsored, this is likely to be a far from straightforward task. It will require EC Delegates to have a fairly **detailed local knowledge** and for the EC Delegate to be willing to **act on this knowledge where 'rubber stamping' involvement is the dominant trend** in non-state actor participation in ACP-EU co-operation programmes.

It will also require independent non-state actors in ACP countries to organise themselves and articulate their views and concerns. In this regard, European non-governmental development organisation (ENGDOs) could play an important role in providing financial and logistical support to local non-state actors.

In their role as **observers**, EC Delegates are also expected to ensure that local non-state actors are familiar with the programming process and are effectively involved in all stages of the programming process.

As a **facilitator** it is envisaged that the EC Delegate will:

- support capacity building for non-state actor participation;

- establish arrangements for dialogue between non-state actors and governments in the programming process;

- ensure that non-state actors can hold dialogues among themselves in preparation for programming.

It is envisaged that each EC delegate, in facilitating dialogue between the ACP government and non-state actors, will take the following steps:

- designate a contact point in the EC Delegation to deal with non-state actors;

- initiate a discussion with government and non-state actor representatives on categories of non-state actors eligible for involvement in the programming dialogue and the implementation of co-operation programmes;

- provide support to non-state actors to facilitate their participation;

- extend direct support to certain non-state actors in implementing programmes within the national ACP-EU co-operation programme;

- co-operate closely with other agencies seeking to promote non-state actor participation.

Given the human resource constraints on EC Delegations in effectively managing existing co-operation activities, and the far more intensive nature of the dialogue process which the EU's new approach to programming will entail, it is an open question as to whether EC Delegations will have the capacity to play the envisaged role of **critical observer** and **facilitator** effectively.

It is maintained that the rolling out of the de-concentration process, with increased powers and responsibilities being devolved to EC Delegations, will ease these human resource constraints and enhance the capacity of the European Commission Delegations to support participatory approaches to development co-operation. However, it remains to be seen how this process will work out in practice, and in particular whether the increased powers and responsibilities of EC Delegations will be matched by commensurate increases in properly trained staff.

What Role Do Non-state Actors Have in the Preparation of the Country Support Strategy?

According to the Cotonou Agreement the drawing up of the Country Support Strategy should involve:

... consultations with a wide range of actors in the development process.

Annex IV,
Chapter 1,
Article 2

The EU's initial timetable for the completion of the programming process, was extremely tight, extending over only a six-month period.[27] Given the limited scope of past non-state actor involvement in the programming process and the limited local knowledge in ACP countries on the procedures to be followed with regard to the compilation of the Country Support Strategy, the allocation of a six-week period for consultations at the very beginning of the process provided little scope for meaningful state/non-state actor dialogue.

The European Commission nevertheless tried to encourage a wide range of civil society bodies to contribute in an organised and constructive manner to the development of the Country Support Strategy.

The experience in individual ACP countries varied greatly. In some countries no consultation took place; in others consultations only took place at a late stage in preparing the Country Strategy Paper. In some countries a close correlation between government and non-state actors' views on issues in the Country Strategy Paper was identified, while in other countries non-state actors lacked the capacity to coherently put forward views on the issues to be addressed.[28]

According to the February 2002 Commission review of the involvement of non-state actors in the programming process, this created a situation where:

- in 42 of the 50 Country Strategy Papers reviewed, information activities or consultations with non-state actors had taken place;
- in 33 of these countries specific information activities were organised;
- in 36 countries non-state actors were involved in consultations at an early stage;
- in 25 countries the Country Strategy Paper was modified following the consultations with non-state actors.[29]

By March 2003 a new Commission review showed information activities or consultations with non-state actors in relation to 59 of 63 Country Strategy Papers then completed, with non-state actors being involved in consultations at an early stage in 46 of these countries and with 36 Country Strategy Papers being modified following these consultations.[30]

In some of these countries the programming process even led to the creation of new functional bodies involving state and non-state actors.

By March 2003, in 50 out of the 63 Country Strategy Papers reviewed, the following broad categories of non-state actors were involved in the information/consultation process:

- NGO and community-based organisations;
- labour organisations;
- chambers of commerce, private sector associations and business organisations;
- associations of churches and confessional movements;
- universities;
- media;
- representatives of parliamentary groups.

In Zimbabwe, where a specific Non State Actor Forum (ZNSAF) has been created for the implementation of a decentralised co-operation programme, a much more structured policy dialogue with government around programming issues was possible, as the ZNSAF sought to co-ordinate non-state actor inputs into the programming dialogue. Despite the high level of political confrontation in Zimbabwe, this experience of dialogue around aid programming and aid management has been seen as broadly positive. The experience in Uganda was also seen to be a positive one.

Overall, however, the February 2002 Commission review of the involvement of non-state actors in the programming process found that while there had been some form of consultation:

... few of these processes had an impact on the resulting document.[31]

What is more it was acknowledged that this was probably indicative of the fact that:

... consultation had been more formal than concrete.[32]

By March 2003 the Commission review maintained that in just over half (57 per cent) of the countries reviewed non-state actors had had an impact on the final version of the Country Strategy Paper.

In a number of Country Strategy Papers, while the need to work with non-state actors is identified, only vague references are made to the level of funding to be made available, with no specific funding arrangements being specified. The European Commission considers that it would be helpful in most ACP countries to reserve an amount to be made available to non-state actors. By March 2003 the European Commission was reporting that in more than half of all Country Support Strategies then concluded (63) such amounts had been reserved for non-state actors.[33]

In supporting non-state actors, legal problems have been identified which make it very difficult for the European Union to make EDF funds available to them without the prior approval of the National Authorising Officer (see 'How Can the Amount Reserved for Non-state Actors Under the EDF Be Made Available?').

Against this background the Commission services have noted that greater clarity is required on the possible modalities. The European Commission is currently preparing guidelines for European Commission Delegations on how the funding of non-state actors should be managed where specific amounts have been reserved for non-state actors in the NIP.

What Role Do Non-state Actors Have in the Preparation of the NIP?

Since the programming process determines how **all** future EU aid to each ACP country is to be used and **the channels through which such aid is to be deployed**, if non-state actors are to become effectively engaged in ACP-EU co-operation activities then scope for their participation needs to be allowed under the NIP. This requires non-state actors to establish mechanisms for effective dialogue with the **National Authorising Officer**, the principal contact point for all dealings with the EU related to the implementation of co-operation activities. Normally the NAO is a senior government official in the Ministry of Finance or similar government department.

Annex IV,
Chapter 6,
Article 35

For non-state actors, getting involved in the NIP process is not easy. The NAO already has to co-ordinate the inputs of different government departments, which is often a difficult task as different Ministries seek access to the available funding. Co-ordinating the inputs from a wide range of non-state actors adds considerably to the NAO's work load.

Against this background it is necessary for non-state actors to establish effective mechanisms for co-ordination of their inputs so as to minimise the additional workload placed on the NAO. If such mechanisms can be established, this facilitates the dialogue with the NAO.

To date, provision has been made for an amount reserved for non-state actor activities or capacity building for non-state actors in no less than 39 Country Strategy Papers. Under these 39 country programmes (the total value of which is more than Euro 3,500 million), Euro 170 million has been earmarked for the financing of activities involving non-state actors. This represents approximately 5 per cent of the 'A' envelope in the countries concerned.

What are the Financial Possibilities for Non-state Actor Involvement in ACP-EU Co-operation Programmes?

The European Commission initially proposed that up to 15 per cent of the 'A' allocation to each ACP country should be deployed through non-state actors.[34] However, effectively bringing in non-state actors into ongoing processes of ACP-EU co-operation is proving a difficult task. In the light of this, the Commission is now suggesting that a specified amount for co-operation with non-state actors should be indicated in the National Indicative Programme, but with no specific percentage being recommended.

The basis for non-state actor involvement in ACP-EU co-operation activities varies greatly. It can take the form of a broad decentralised co-operation programme, which is managed by non-state actor bodies within a commonly agreed framework (agreed by the EU, ACP government and non-state actors concerned through a multi-annual programme). Or it can take the form of non-state actor involvement in wider sectoral programmes (e.g. national strategies to combat HIV/AIDS). It can take the form of discreet co-operation programmes managed by non-state actors (e.g. a trade development programme managed by the private sector). It can even be a combination of the foregoing.

It should be noted that even where EDF funds are to be reserved for non-state actors, the process of legally committing the funds must comply with EDF rules. Current EDF rules require all projects and programmes funded under the NIP to be 'signed off' by the National Authorising Officer of the country concerned. The signature of the NAO is a legal requirement for all programmes falling under the NIP, including those involving non-state actors. No funding can legally be provided to non-state actors under country allocations without the signature of the NAO.

At this stage considerable emphasis is being placed on capacity building among non-state actors to facilitate their involvement in both the dialogue process and implementation of co-operation programmes.

How Can the Amount Reserved for Non-state Actors under the EDF Be Made Available?

There are three main ways of providing funding to non-state actors:

- an amount reserved for non-state actors under the NIP;
- participation in the implementation of focal and/or non-focal sector programmes;

- support via thematic EU budget lines which are available outside the Cotonou Agreement and which do not fall under EDF rules.[35]

However, under the Agreement the Commission faces a problem in opening 'direct access funding' to non-state actors. Legally, under the terms of the Agreement **no such 'direct access funding' expenditures may be made without first securing the approval of the concerned National Authorising Officer or Regional Authorising Officer.**[36] Under the terms of the Agreement the financing of activities from the EDF through non-state actors is:

> *... subject to the agreement of the ACP State or ACP States concerned.*

Part 4, Title I, Chapter 1, Article 58.2

This means that EDF funds can only be made directly available to non-state actors with the prior agreement of the NAO. This prior agreement could take different forms but it is essential that it provides a general agreement for **specified funds to be used to finance the activities of specified non-state actors**. Such consent and any conditions attached to it should be clearly expressed.

It should be noted that the inclusion of an envelope for support to civil society in the NIP is not sufficient to allow such expenditures to be made. There must be a clear identification by the concerned ACP authorities of the non-state actors eligible to receive funding. In contrast, even if no provision has been made for the financing of non-state actors under the NIP, the NAO is free at any time to give subsequent agreement to such funding. However, each funding activity would then require specific approval from the NAO concerned.

One way of ensuring that the amount reserved for non-state actors is efficiently made available is through the establishment of multi-annual programmes, with the consent of the National Authorising Officer or Regional Authorising Officer (depending on the source of the funding – NIP or RIP).

A second option is for the NAO to sub-delegate certain financial responsibilities to the EU Delegation to manage relations with non-state actors within a commonly agreed framework.

However, without prior approval from the NAO or, in the case of suspension of co-operation activities, the Chief Authorising Officer, the EU Delegate cannot enter into any contracts with non-state actors using EDF funding.

It is increasingly recognised that most solutions for making money available to non-state actors will require the establishment of a Programme Management Unit (PMU), with powers delegated to it by the NAO or ROA. The PMU would then be responsible for implementing the programme within a commonly agreed framework.

The Commission believes that EC delegations will need to be allowed flexibility to establish arrangements for NSA access to EDF funding which are consistent with local realities. In some cases, for example, it could be appropriate to contract out programme management to an existing local representative NGO platform.

Doing so, however, would mean that the EU could not pursue the normal tendering arrangements and would have to gain a special dispensation for contracting in the locally established representative NGO platform.

What Role Can Non-state Actors Play in the Implementation of Co-operation Activities?

In the European Commission's view, non-state actors should have a role in both the **design** and **implementation** of specific development co-operation activities. However, with the emphasis on concentrating EDF resources on focal sectors, it is envisaged that only a limited range of non-state actors will actually be involved in the implementation of co-operation activities. The actual non-state actors involved will depend on the relative expertise which specific non-state actors have in the focal sectors of ACP-EU co-operation, set out in the Country Support Strategy and the National Indicative Programme.

This, it is felt, will make it easier administratively to manage the whole process of non-state actor involvement. This means that while the EU will encourage a wide range of non-state actors to become involved in the ACP-EU co-operation process, only **a limited range of non-state bodies will actually be involved in concrete financial and technical co-operation activities**.

According to the Commission's February 2002 review, three main strategies for involving non-state actors in future co-operation activities can be identified:

- mainstreaming participation at all levels;
- an increased role in the focal sector at both policy and programme level;
- an increased role in non-focal sectors.[37]

According to the February 2002 Commission review, in 28 of the 50 Country Strategy Papers reviewed non-state actors were seen to have a role in both the focal and non-focal sector. In seven countries non-state actors are restricted to a role in the focal sector, while in five countries non-state actor involvement is restricted to the non-focal sector.[38]

The March 2003 Commission review, however, revealed that maintained non-state actors had a role in both the focal and non-focal sectors in 38 of the 63 Country Strategy Papers reviewed, with non-state actors restricted to a role in the focal sector in 14 countries and restricted to a role in the non-focal sector in six countries.[39]

Non-state actor engagement in focal sectors varies from participation in transport sector programme identification and design, through increased direct private sector participation in programmes, to the involvement of farmers' organisations in rural development activities and health sector organisations in social sector programmes. In terms of non-focal sector activities, considerable emphasis is placed on capacity building of non-state actors and direct assistance to non-state actor programmes aimed at poverty eradication.

What Role Do Non-state Actors Have in the Review Process?

Formally no specific provisions are made for non-state actor participation in the review process, although it is implicit in the Commission's new 'rolling programming' approach. However, given the recognition under the Cotonou Agreement of the need to involve non-state actors *'where appropriate'*, it would appear appropriate that mechanisms should be found for involving non-state actors in the review process, since efforts have already been made to involve them in consultations on the priorities to be adopted under the Country Support Strategy.

According to the Commission's February 2002 review of the involvement of non-state actors in the programming process:

> *Only 60 per cent of the documents mention arrangements for involving NSAs in ongoing monitoring and review processes, although some involvement is clearly specified in the Cotonou rolling programming provisions.*[40]

However, by March 2003 the Commission maintained this had risen to 68 per cent.[41]

As of February 2002, 31 Country Strategy Papers mentioned the need for follow- up. According to the Commission, by March 2003 this had risen to 43. This included references to:

- the creation of mechanisms to ensure the involvement of non-state actors in the formulation and implementation of sectoral policies (including, in the case of Zimbabwe, the idea of setting up a monitoring and evaluation plan in the health sector);

- the creation of mechanisms to ensure non-state actor participation in the rolling programming and review process;

- the establishment of specific indicators for sectoral policy implementation.[42]

One possible avenue for ensuring non-state actor participation in the review process would be to submit annual operational reviews to national ACP Parliaments through relevant Parliamentary Committee structures. The annual operational review could then be the subject of open discussion, with both state and non-state actors being invited to submit their views to the relevant Parliamentary Committee on the progress of implementation. This would not only encourage greater non-state actor engagement with the actual development co-operation process, but would also help develop more effective Parliamentary oversight of ACP-EU co-operation activities.

What Eligibility Criteria Exist to Guide Non-state Actor Participation in ACP-EU Co-operation Programmes?

Efforts are underway to establish an ACP-EU consensus on the eligibility criteria to be applied to non-state actor involvement in the Cotonou co-operation process. An ACP paper on 'Eligibility Criteria for Non-State Actors: Access To Funding Under the EDF' was formally adopted by the ACP-EU Council of Ministers on 16 May 2003.

The key features of this document cover the following areas:

- the extent to which non-state actor organisations should promote poverty reduction and sustainable development;

- the extent to which non-state actors should have relevant experience and proof of capacity in the area of proposed activity;

- the extent to which non-state actors should be non-profit making and have a clear and accountable organisational structure;

- the extent to which non-state actor organisations should be local in character through the predominant participation of ACP citizens;

- the extent to which non-state actors should be representative;

- the extent to which non-state actor organisations and management arrangements should be democratic and transparent;

- a requirement that non-state actors should act within existing ACP state law;

- the need to promote the participation of grassroots organisations;

- the financial situation of the organisation;
- the degree of independence from the state.[43]

Criteria for the exclusion of non-state actors from EDF funding were also set down in this paper and focused mainly on bankruptcy, misrepresentation in previous calls for tender or being in serious breach of contract. The only non-financial stipulation prohibiting the participation of non-state actors in EDF funding was if they were a political party.

However, it is widely recognised that in practice eligibility criteria will need to be drawn up by mutual agreement between the parties concerned (the ACP government, the EC delegate and local non-state actors). In 20 ACP countries eligibility criteria for non-state actor funding under the NIP have already been discussed with the NAO (Gambia, Gabon, Kiribati, Jamaica, St Lucia, Chad, Vanuatu, Zimbabwe, Burkina Faso, Guyana, São Tomé & Príncipe, Botswana, Ethiopia, Tanzania, Swaziland, Comores, Guinea Bissau, Angola, Seychelles and Sudan), while in two other countries studies are underway aimed at defining eligibility criteria for non-state actor access to EDF funding (Namibia and Uganda).[44]

What Has Been the Experience of Non-state Actor Participation under the Cotonou Agreement So Far?[45]

The participation of non-state actors in the programming process has varied greatly from ACP country to ACP country. In some countries a fairly extensive dialogue and involvement of non-state actors has taken place; in others, the consultation process has been only poorly defined. Even in some of these cases, however, provision has been made in the National Indicative Programme for the involvement of non-state actors. In still other countries, no effective consultations have taken place with non-state actors and there is no indication that there is any desire to see a role for non-state actors in the ACP-EU co-operation process.

In 42 of the 50 Country Strategy Papers prepared by the end of January 2002, there was some level of consultation with non-state actors. In 25 of the 50 Country Strategy Papers reviewed, modifications were made following consultations with non-state actors. By March 2003 the European Commission maintained that in 59 of 63 Country Strategy Papers there had been some level of consultation with non-state actors and that in 36 cases modifications were made to the Country Strategy Paper following these consultations. In some countries the EU response strategy has been geared explicitly towards enhancing non-state actor participation in all sectors of co-operation. In other countries it has restricted itself to promoting non-state actor engagement in focal sector activities, while in still other countries non-state actor involvement is only being promoted in non-focal sectors, as a means of targeting poor groups or promoting good governance and conflict prevention.

Factors limiting non-state actor involvement identified to date include:

- the reluctance of national authorities to bring non-state actors more fully into the co-operation process;

- the difficult in identifying eligible interlocateurs among non-state actor formations;

- the lack of time and staff capacity to set up appropriate consultative mechanisms;

- limited capacity among non-state actor formations to engage in a coherent manner on policy and programming issues.

In reviewing the experience to date the Commission has developed a three-fold typology of ACP countries:[46]

Type I: an ACP country with a culture of participation, an organised civil society and a strong tradition of dialogue;

Type II: an ACP country with some tradition of dialogue and participation, but where much remains to be done in mainstreaming participation;

Type III: an ACP country where there is limited political space for participation or a very weakly organised civil society.

Somewhat surprisingly, the practical experience of non-state actor engagement with the preparation of the Country Support Strategy and the NIP process has shown little correlation with this typology. Some countries with a strong culture of participation, a well-organised civil society and a strong tradition of dialogue have seen little non-state actor engagement with the ACP-EU co-operation process. Other countries with a limited tradition of dialogue and ACP participation have seen a strong effort to engage non-state actors in the process.

Experience suggests that given the difficulties faced in effectively bringing non-state actors into the ACP-EU co-operation process, non-state actor organisations in ACP countries are making a hard-headed assessment of the benefits and costs associated with seeking to engage with the process. Only where there are real benefits to be gained from increasing the role of non-state actors in setting national priorities, designing specific programmes or implementing specific co-operation activities, are non-state actors investing their limited capacities in becoming involved.

Preliminary Questions to be Addressed by Non-state Actors

What local non-state actors are interested in becoming more involved in the planning and implementation of EU financed co-operation programmes and with what objectives in mind?

- Do local non-state actors have the organisational capacity to prepare a dialogue with government on the priorities and types of assistance most appropriately sought from the EU?

- Do local non-state actors have the information base from which to prepare a dialogue with government on the priorities and types of assistance most appropriately sought from the EU?

- Is the ACP government willing to support this process of widening involvement in the programming process?

- Can local non-state actors organise themselves quickly enough to be able to participate?

- Do local non-state actors have the resources and capacity to work jointly together in any dialogue with government?

- What, concretely, will non-state actors gain from their engagement with the ACP-EU dialogue process either in financial terms or in terms of the promotion of their specific sectoral or thematic policy agenda?

What is Decentralised Co-operation?

Decentralised co-operation emerged under Lomé IV as a vehicle for reaching beyond the state to non-state actors and promoting their greater involvement in the ACP-EU co-operation process. Under the Lomé Convention decentralised co-operation programmes were launched in Benin, Ghana, Uganda, Dominican Republic, Haiti, Zimbabwe, Senegal, Guinea Conakry and Madagascar. This more sophisticated approach reached beyond the micro-project approach previously adopted to bring in a more diverse range of non-state actors, and it was seen as much more than just a way of financing grassroots projects.

Decentralised co-operation was seen as a distinct approach to development co-operation. The European Commission sees this approach as being based on five central ideas:

- the active participation of a wide range of actors;

- the promotion of greater co-ordination and complementarity between various actors through dialogue;

- the delegation of administrative and financial responsibilities to the hierarchy closest to the actors concerned;

- the adoption of a process approach, with a view to ensuring genuine local participation;

- promoting capacity and institutional development to enable action and control at the local level.[47]

In practice the European Commission sees its decentralised co-operation programmes developing along two main lines:

- as support for the process of decentralisation, aimed at the establishment of legitimate and effective systems of local government;

- as support for local development initiatives and processes, making it possible to ensure consistency between previously isolated activities.

In the Commission's view it will take a considerable amount of time for this decentralised co-operation concept to take root. This is because the Commission's decentralised co-operation concept will require a rethinking of the approach adopted over the past 25 years, which in large part focused development co-operation on the state.[48] The European Commission takes the view that new experiences will have to be developed, with lessons being learned along the way and, where appropriate, existing institutional arrangements for co-operation being modified.

It is acknowledged that this will require a redefinition of the role of the state in the co-operation process, with greater emphasis being placed on the 'facilitation' role which the state can play. However, it is acknowledged that this will require the development of new capacities both within government and within the broader non-governmental sector.

2.9 The Private Sector and the Cotonou Agreement

This section reviews:

- what the Cotonou Agreement says about the involvement of the private sector in the ACP-EU co-operation process;

- the role of the private sector in the preparation of the Country Support Strategy and the National Indicative Programme;

- the various co-operation instruments potentially of interest to the private sector;

- the procedures for accessing funds from the Investment Facility;

- the procedures for securing support under CDE programmes;

- the procedures for securing assistance under CTA programmes;

- the role the private sector can play in the implementation of co-operation activities;

- the tendering preferences extended to ACP private sector operators under the Cotonou Agreement.

What Does the Cotonou Agreement Say about Supporting Private Sector Development in ACP Countries?

The provisions of the Agreement dealing with the involvement of the private sector in ACP-EU co-operation can be divided into two distinct components:

a) the provisions which deal with the involvement of non-state actors, including the private sector;

b) the provisions which refer specifically to support for the development of the private sector in ACP countries.

As part of the broader community of non-state actors, the private sector is expected to participate in the ACP-EU co-operation process at all appropriate levels. In particular, the private sector should be:

- informed and involved in consultations on co-operation policies, strategies and priorities in areas that affect the private sector;

- involved in implementing co-operation activities in areas of direct concern to the private sector;

- involved, where appropriate, in the review process.

Private sector organisations, however, enjoy a wider range of possibilities for obtaining financial assistance under the Cotonou Agreement than other non-state actors as a result of the specific provisions on the promotion of investment and private sector development.

These provisions are contained in Part 3 of the Agreement, 'Co-operation Strategies', Chapter 2. The main article dealing with investment and private sector development is Article 21, although in this section references are also made to private sector development in Articles 19, 20, 22, 23 and 24.

Article 21 states:

Part 3, Title I, Chapter 2, Article 21.1

... co-operation shall support the necessary economic and institutional reforms and policies at national and/or regional level, aiming at creating a favourable environment for private investment, and the development of a dynamic, viable and competitive private sector.

Specifically it should support:

a) *the promotion of public-private sector dialogue and co-operation;*

b) *the development of entrepreneurial skills and business culture;*

c) *privatisation and enterprise reform; and*

d) *development and modernisation of mediation and arbitration systems.*

In addition, Article 21.2 highlights the need to improve:

Article 21.2

... the quality, availability and accessibility of financial and non-financial services to private enterprises.

This is to be done by:

- supporting the development of a modern financial sector;

- developing and strengthening business institutions and intermediary organisations;

- supporting the transfer of technologies and know-how on all aspects of business development.

Further specific commitments are made on supporting the development of financial institutions and business services, including with reference to trade development. Specific reference is also made to the need to support micro-enterprise development through improving access to both financial and non-financial services.

Looking beyond Article 21, Article 22 deals with macroeconomic and structural reform and places considerable emphasis on getting the policy framework for private sector development right. More broadly, these provisions of the Agreement commit the EU to supporting all aspects of private sector development in all sectors. Thus the Agreement has seen the broadening out of the mandate of the Centre for the Development of Industry (CDI) and its transformation into the Centre for the Development of Enterprise.

Part 3, Title I, Chapter 2, Article 22

Against this background other provisions of the Agreement which are of interest to the private sector include:

- the provisions dealing with the CDE;

- the provisions dealing with the Investment Facility;

- the provisions dealing with the CTA;

- the provisions dealing with the tendering procedures, in particular those dealing with the tendering preferences extended to ACP suppliers and contractors.

What Role Does the Private Sector Have in the Preparation of the Country Support Strategy?

According to the Agreement, the drawing up of the Country Support Strategy should involve *'consultations with a wide range of actors in the development process'*, including the private sector.

Annex IV, Chapter 1, Article 2

The February 2002 Commission review of the involvement of non-state actors in the programming process found that chambers of commerce, private sector associations and other business organisations, together with other non-state actors, had participated in the various information and consultation processes which took place around the Country Strategy Papers. However, the review concluded overall that while there had been some form of consultation:

> *... few of these processes had an impact on the resulting document.*[49]

While the review suggested that this was probably indicative of the fact that *'consultation had been more formal than concrete'*,[50] it acknowledged that in some ACP countries (e.g. Mauritius) dialogue between government and the private sector was well developed with regular consultations on pertinent issues.

To What Extent is the Private Sector to Be Involved in National Indicative Programmes in ACP Countries?

An April 2002 review of ACP-EU co-operation based on 23 Country Support Strategies[51] posted on the web by the Commission found that:

- in some countries (e.g. Jamaica) private sector development was a focal sector for aid deployment;

- in some countries (e.g. Zambia) the private sector was the leading sector when it came to non-state actor involvement in ACP-EU co-operation;

- in some countries (e.g. Cape Verde) public-private sector partnerships were being envisaged for the implementation of major focal sector co-operation activities;

- in some countries (e.g. Suriname) support for privatisation was seen as an important non-focal sector area of activity.

The private sector is also likely to be heavily involved in programmes of macroeconomic support extended under the NIP through the vehicle of sectoral or general import programme aid.

What Instruments of Co-operation are of Most Interest to the Private Sector?

The following instruments of support are of greatest interest to the private sector in ACP countries:

- the Investment Facility;

- the National Indicative Programme;

- the Regional Indicative Programme;

- the Centre for the Development of Enterprise;

- the Technical Centre for Agricultural and Rural Co-operation.

The importance of these various instruments varies from region to region throughout the ACP depending on:

- the choices made under the NIP with regard to the focal and non-focal sectors;

- the choices made under the RIP with regard to the focal and non-focal sectors;

- the relevance of particular CDE sectoral programmes to the economy of the ACP country concerned;

- the existing level of CDE activities underway in the country or region concerned and the effectiveness of the local antennae;

- the relevance of particular CTA programmes to the economy of the ACP country concerned;

- the existing level of CTA activities underway in the country or region concerned;

- the stage of development of the local private sector and the wider environment created for private sector development (this will affect the ability of enterprises to obtain loans from the Investment Facility);

- the types of assistance being provided under the various NIPs and RIPs.

In addition, given the importance of the market potentially created by EU financed aid programmes in certain ACP countries and regions facing currency convertibility problems, a major area of potential interest to ACP private sector operators is the **tendering preferences extended under the Agreement**. Targeting this aid-financed market can provide an important stimulus to local economic activity in certain ACP countries and regions.

The choices made under the NIP/RIP over the **sectors** to be supported and the **types of assistance** to be provided will have important implications for the extent to which the local private sector benefits from NIP interventions. For example, direct budget support is unlikely to benefit the private sector directly (though it may create local demand for goods and services provided by the private sector), whereas sector or general import programme support is likely primarily to benefit the private sector by improving the supply of raw materials and intermediate goods. In addition, credit lines, credit guarantees and the promotion of equity participation in enterprises will directly benefit the private sector.

This is not to suggest that other types of assistance do not benefit the private sector. A transport sector programme, by easing input and marketing problems, may provide a major indirect stimulus to private sector development, while general education and health sector programmes may, in the long term, bring huge benefits to the private sector in terms of increased labour productivity.

The private sector can thus benefit directly and indirectly in a multiplicity of ways from the choices made under the NIP/RIP, with regard to the **sectors for aid deployment, the type of programmes to be implemented** and **the types of assistance to be sought**.

How Can ACP Private Sector Operators Access Funds from the Investment Facility?

Procedures for accessing Investment Facility funding vary depending on the size of the funding requested. Normally the EIB does not provide loans directly to enterprises below Euro 1.5 million. Given that the EIB normally provides loans equivalent to between 25 per cent and 30 per cent of the project cost, this implies an average project size of around Euro 4.5 million. Given the size of most ACP economies and the scale of small and medium-sized enterprises in the ACP, this is a relatively high minimum size for the provision of direct loans.

Funds to small and medium-scale enterprises in ACP countries are largely made available though global loans administered through intermediate financial institutions or through 'Apex' facilities that allow a range of local financial institutions to make use of different forms of credit for on-lending. An intermediate financial institution is a commercial bank or a development finance institution locally established in the ACP country. The EIB then makes available what is known as a 'global loan', which is then broken down into smaller amounts by the local financial institution and on-lent to their own clients, using their own credit judgement but acting within the criteria agreed by the EIB when drawing up the global loan agreement.

Currently the EIB provides financing for small and medium-sized enterprises in 33 countries (see Annex 7).

The first stage in securing funds for larger projects directly from the Investment Facility is the submission of a **funding request** to the EIB. Initial contacts with the EIB over a project can be quite informal, taking place by phone or fax. A funding request should include **a description of the project** (nature, purpose, cost, working capital requirement, financial plan, timetable, expected return) and **information on the financial status of the promoter** (recent annual reports and financial statements).

More specifically it should include:

- **General and legal information about the enterprise, its principal partners or promoters;**
- **Technical data on the project;**

- Economic data on the project;

- Financial data on the project.

Private sector operators seeking EIB funding must first secure the formal support of their government before submitting a loan request to the EIB. This rarely poses a problem.

Once a funding request has been submitted, it is subjected to a rigorous appraisal of its **economic, financial, technical and environmental viability**.

The key factors in accessing funding directly from the EIB are:

- the economic, financial, technical and environmental viability of the investment project;

- the quality of the funding request;

- the relationship built up with the individual EIB loan officer responsible for loans to the country from which the funding request originates.

In the EIB management system considerable powers of decision making are devolved down to the individual loan officers. The relationship established with the loan officer can help resolve any problems arising from the inadequacy of data supplied in the funding request or within the project appraisal process. Establishing a good working relationship with the individual loan officer will also assist the private sector operator in understanding more precisely the timeframes within which individual decisions will be taken and the scope for tailoring the terms and conditions of the loan to the specific needs of the investment project (including, where appropriate, the extent and utilisation of the interest rate subsidy).

How Can ACP Private Sector Operators Access CDE Funds?

The CDE is increasingly seeking to work through a programme approach. The first starting point, therefore, for a private sector operator seeking CDE assistance should be to identify whether the CDE already has a relevant sector programme in place in their region, or whether such a programme is under preparation.

This can best be done in one of three ways: making contact with the regional field office or the local decentralised management unit (see Annexes 9 and 10); making contact with the local CDE network member (see Annex 11) or by direct contact with CDE on the fringes of sectoral partnership meetings.

Should the activities of the enterprise seeking support not fall within an existing or planned CDE programme, possibilities for assistance still exist under the CDE's **Integrated Sole Proprietorship Support Programme**, which enables the CDE to provide direct support to individual enterprises.

Enquires about possible CDE support should first be directed to one of the local contact points, decentralised management units or, in the case of the Caribbean, the regional field office. These bodies can provide assistance in preparing suitable applications for CDE support.

Sectorally Defined and Geographically Focused CDE Programmes

Timber Sector
- Timber certification and woodworking in Central Africa
- Timber certification and woodworking in the Pacific
- Timber certification and woodworking in the Caribbean

Cotton and Textiles
- Cotton and textile industry in West Africa
- Textiles programme in Southern Africa

Livestock Sector Related
- Livestock in West Africa
- Livestock in East Africa
- Leather programme for East and Southern Africa

Fisheries Sector Related
- EU health standards in Mozambican fisheries
- EU health standards in Cape Verdean fisheries
- Marine resources in the Pacific region

Pharmaceutical Sector
- Medicines derived from tropical medicinal plants in ACP countries
- Caribbean herbal products development

Mineral Sector
- Mining and quarrying technology and productivity in Southern Africa
- Productivity of the building materials sector in West Africa
- Productivity and environment of the ceramics and aggregates sector in the Caribbean.

Sectorally Defined and Geographically Focused CDE Programmes (continued)

Environmental

- Treatment of industrial toxic waste in the Seychelles and Mauritius

Fruit and Vegetables

- Strengthening of the organic products sector in the Pacific and improvement of its competitiveness on export markets
- HACCP and quality control in the fruit and vegetable sector in the Caribbean

Tourism Sector

- Development and standardisation of West Africa's stock of hotels
- Hotel industry, eco-tourism and local communities in the Caribbean
- Hotel industry, eco-tourism and local communities in Southern Africa
- Hotel industry, eco-tourism and local communities in the Pacific
- Hotel industry, eco-tourism and local communities in East Africa

Regional

- Processing and regional trade among countries of the Indian Ocean Community

It should be borne in mind that 50 per cent of operations supported by the CDE apply to schemes involving less than Euro 5,000, although support is also extended to larger studies of an average size of Euro 20,000. While this appears a relatively low level of funding, it should be borne in mind that ACP enterprises can benefit from more than one CDE-supported intervention and that the CDE can play an important role in facilitating access to other sources of financial assistance.

In planning to approach the CDE, private sector operators in ACP countries should be aware of the types of assistance which the CDE makes available, namely:

- support for partnership meetings linking up ACP and EU operators in the same sector;

- support for regional trade associations;

- support for research into the competitiveness of the sector;

- support for the introduction of technical improvements in the product process;

- support for enhancing product quality;

- support for a needs survey;

- pre-project surveys;

- assistance with project identification;

- support for project start-up and development;

- direct assistance to enterprises, including staff training;

- upgrading and transmission of know-how to intermediate structures;

- support for good environmental practice;

- assistance in securing investment finance.

How Can the Private Sector Benefit from CTA Programmes?

The CTA is primarily concerned with improving access for concerned ACP stakeholders (including the private sector) to information on agricultural and rural development and with strengthening the capacity of ACP stakeholders to manage information and communication on agricultural and rural development issues.

The CTA's work is channelled through three main programmes:

- Information Products and Services Programme;

- Communication Channels and Services Programme;

- Information and Communication Management Skills and Systems Programme.

In approaching the CTA, private sector operators will need to assess the extent to which individual programmes currently under design and implementation by the CTA can contribute to assisting them in developing their information and communication activities in the sphere of agricultural and rural development.

Probably the CTA programmes of greatest interest to private sector operators are the market information systems programmes, the trade policy related programmes and the sectorally focused programmes (for example, sectoral meetings on herbs and medicinal plants or fisheries hygiene issues). In the implementation of these sectorally focused programmes, the CTA is increasingly co-operating with the CDE. The Agritrade Project is particularly relevant with regard to assessing the market implications of trade policy developments, providing background and monthly updates on key sectors (e.g. sugar, beef, rice and bananas) and around key themes (e.g. the trade implications of CAP reform, EU-ACP economic partnership agreement negotiations, developments in the sphere of food safety and EU positions in the WTO negotiations on agriculture). This website seeks to look at the market implications of policy developments in ACP-EU agricultural trade.

Other technical publications and information dissemination activity programmes of the CTA could also be of considerable interest to various agricultural related private sector producer associations throughout the ACP.

Once private sector operators have identified the CTA programmes of greatest relevance to their concerns, contact should be made either through the office of the Director of the CTA or via the relevant department head.

What Role Can the Private Sector Play in the Implementation of Co-operation Activities?

The role of private sector organisations in the implementation of co-operation activities can be divided into a number of distinct components. As part of the general non-state actor community, the private sector can benefit from the direct allocation of funds to implement specific projects under the NIP, RIP or Investment Facility.

At the level of the NIP, the European Commission initially proposed that up to 15 per cent of the 'A' allocation should be deployed through non-state actors. However, bringing non-state actors into co-operation programmes has not proved easy. In the light of this, the Commission is now only suggesting that an amount be specified in the NIP for the financing of programmes involving non-state actors.

In some countries (for example Jamaica), programmes under design solely dedicated to private sector development account for 22 per cent of NIP funds. In other countries (for example Zimbabwe), specific private sector managed components of broader trade development programmes have been established, and in others public-private sector partnerships are being developed to implement specific sectoral programmes (for example water and sanitation programmes in Cape Verde).

Looking beyond the establishment of programmes of direct support to private sector development and public-private sector partnerships in the implementation of specific sectoral programmes, the other major role which ACP private sector operators play in ACP-EU co-operation activities is through their role in contracting and sub-contracting for the implementation of specific co-operation activities. The key provisions of the Cotonou Agreement influencing this element of private sector participation in ACP-EU co-operation activities are those dealing with the tendering process.

What Tendering Preferences Do ACP Private Sector Operators Enjoy under the Cotonou Agreement?

Under the tendering rules set out in the ACP, private sector operators can tender for all goods and service contracts put out to tender under the European Development Fund. Under Article 26 of Annex IV on 'Implementation and Management Procedures' of the Cotonou Agreement, ACP operators are even extended certain preferences within the tendering process. Article 26 is designed to encourage *'the widest participation'* of ACP private sector operators in the implementation of contracts financed under the EDF. With this objective in mind, the following tendering preferences are extended to ACP private sector operators (in fact all natural and legal persons of ACP states):

Works Contracts

Annex IV, Article 26

Where at least one-quarter of the capital stock and management staff originates from one or more ACP states, for works contracts of less than Euro 5,000,000, ACP tenders are accorded a *'10 per cent price preference where tenders of an equivalent economic, technical and administrative quality are compared'*.

Supply Contracts

For all supply contracts where tenders in ACP states offer supplies of ACP origin for at least 50 per cent of the contract value, they are accorded a *'15 per cent price preference where tenders of an equivalent economic, technical and administrative quality are compared'*.

Service Contracts

Where competence is the same, preference is given to:

a) experts, institutions and consultancy companies or firms from ACP states where tenders of an equivalent economic, technical and administrative quality are compared;

b) offers submitted by an ACP firm in a consortium with European partners;

c) offers presented by European tenders with ACP sub-contractors or experts.

These preferences also apply to sub-contracting.

2.10 Project Submission

This section looks at:

- what a financing proposal is and what information should be included in it;
- the process by which a financing proposal becomes a financing decision, paying particular attention to the role of internal European Commission structures;
- what is included in the financing agreement;
- the scope and procedures for the establishment of multi-annual programmes.

What is a Financing Proposal?

A **financing proposal** is the final stage of the project preparation process. It follows on from the project identification, presentation and appraisal processes. The financing proposal summarises the previous stages and is drawn up by a European Commission official in close consultation with the government of the ACP country presenting the proposal. It is on the basis of the financing proposal that a decision is taken on whether to finance that particular activity. The financing proposal is subject to appraisal by both European Commission decision-making structures **(Quality Support Group)**, and the European Union decision-making body **(European Development Fund Committee (EDF) Committee)**.

What Information Should Be Included in a Financing Proposal?

The financing proposal should be a maximum of 12 pages long and should consist of three major sections dealing with:

- the **relevance** of the project;

- the **feasibility** of the project;
- the **sustainability** of the project.

The financing proposal should be submitted in the following format:

A. RELEVANCE

1 Consistency with global objectives

1.1 EC aid policy objectives and priorities

1.2 Objectives of NIP/RIP (focal/non-focal sector)

1.3 Link with annual country review

2 Sectoral analysis

2.1 Features of this sector

2.2 Status of national/regional policy

3 Problem analysis

3.1 Target groups, beneficiaries, stakeholders

3.2 Specific problems

4 Origins and preparation of the project

B. FEASIBILITY

5 Project description

5.1 Overall objectives

5.2 Project purpose

5.3 Results

5.4 Activities

5.5 Indicators

6 Project analysis

6.1 Lessons from past experience

6.2 Linkage with other operations

6.3 Results of economic and cross-sectoral appraisals

6.4 Risks and assumptions relating to implementation

7 Project implementation

7.1 Physical and non-physical means

7.2   Organisational and implementation procedures

7.3   Appropriate technology

7.4   Timetable, cost and financing plan

7.5   Special conditions and accompanying measures to be taken by the government

7.6   Monitoring arrangements and follow-up

7.7   Reviews/evaluations/audits: procedures and reports

C. SUSTAINABILITY

8   Measures ensuring sustainability

8.1   Ownership by beneficiaries

8.2   Cross-sectoral sustainability

8.3   National policy measures

8.4   Institutional and management capacity

8.5   Complementarity and sectoral co-ordination between donors

8.6   Economic and financial sustainability [52]

What is Involved in Turning a Financing Proposal into a Financing Decision?

The first stage in moving from a financing proposal to a **financing decision** is consideration of the financing proposal by the **Quality Support Group** (QSG). This has two stages: consideration of an initial project **identification sheet** and **full consideration of the financing proposal**. The identification sheet has to be adopted by the **Quality Support Group** before consideration can be given to the full financing proposal.

Financing proposals submitted to the Quality Support Group must be accompanied by a one-page summary and appropriate annexes, including a logical framework matrix. They should also be accompanied by:

- the request from the National Authorising Officer (or RAP);

- the finalised project identification sheet;

- a copy of the minutes of the QSG meeting at which the project was initially discussed;

- the draft Commission Decision signed by the relevant director;

- the technical and administrative provisions (DTA) drawn up in consultation with the appropriate services;

- a 500-word press release on the project;

- a *note verbale* informing the ACP government concerned of the adoption of the project.[53]

Prior to submission the endorsements (visas) of the concerned departments of the Commission services must be obtained and must accompany the submission of the financing proposal.

The Quality Support Group may suggest amendments to financing proposals to improve the quality of project preparation or it may reject the proposals. If amendments are suggested, these should be incorporated into the financing proposal prior to submission to the EDF Committee.

Once the proposal has been approved by the Quality Support Group, the financing proposal can be submitted to the EDF Committee.

The EDF Committee consists of representatives of the governments of EU member states and is chaired by a representative of the European Commission (which also provides the Secretariat to the Committee). The EDF Committee must give an opinion on:

- financing proposals for projects or programmes with a value greater than Eur 8 million or representing more than 25 per cent of an indicative programme.[54]

- financing proposals from the Commission itself linked to the administration and implementation of the EDF (proposals for reinforcing the Commission's administrative capacity, studies, assessments, audits, consulting services, and monitoring and evaluation).

Financing proposals costing more than Euro 15 million or representing over 25 per cent of the indicative programme are approved by an oral procedure, while financing proposals costing between Euro 8 million and Euro 15 million are approved by a written procedure.

For programmes less than or equal to Euro 8 million or less than 25 per cent of the national indicative programme (or RIP), the Commission may approve projects without first obtaining the opinion of the EDF Committee. However, any member state's representative to the EDF Committee may request discussion of any of these projects at the EDF Committee.

Once the financing proposal has been approved under these procedures, a financing agreement is drawn up and signed by the Commission and the government concerned. According to the Cotonou Agreement this process should be completed:

> *... within 120 days from the date of communication of the financial proposal.*

Annex IV,
Article 16.4

If a financing proposal is not approved, the ACP government(s) concerned have to be immediately informed. Within 60 days they can then request either:

a) *that the matter be referred to the ACP-EC Development Finance Committee; or*

Article 16.5

b) *that they be given a hearing by the Community's decision-making body.*

If either of these options is pursued, the supplementary information then made available has to be taken into account in the final decision.

What is a Financing Agreement?

All funds committed through an NIP/RIP are subject to a **financing agreement** drawn up between the European Commission and the ACP government concerned. The financing agreement sets out in detail:

Annex IV,
Chapter 3,
Article 1

- the financial commitment made under the project;

- the terms and conditions on which the finance is made available;

- the arrangements for making the financial transfer;

- the general and specific commitments made relating to the project;

- the timetable for the technical implementation of the project;

- provisions for cost increases and contingencies.

The financing agreement should be drawn up within 60 days of the financing decision having been made. Once the financing agreement is signed, disbursements of funds may be made in line with the financing plan laid down in the agreement.

While as a rule no disbursements may be made without a financing agreement having been concluded, provision is made for retroactive financing. This is especially the case with regard to projects which follow on from each other. The aim of the retroactive financing provisions is to avoid any gaps in project implementation and unnecessary delays.

Providing the Commission agrees, between the project appraisal and the financing decision stage ACP governments may pre-finance activities linked

Annex IV,
Chapter 3,
Article 19

to the start-up of the project, particularly where seasonal factors come into play or there are long delivery times. ACP governments may also issue invitations to tender with appropriate suspension clauses. However, these provisions on retroactive financing in no way prejudice the final decision of EU bodies.

What is a Multi-Annual Programme?

Under the Cotonou Agreement provision is made for the financing of multi-annual programmes. These multi-annual programmes can cover the following activities:

Article 16.7

- training;
- decentralised co-operation;
- microprojects;
- trade promotion;
- trade development.

The aim of multi-annual programmes is to allow for the financing of sets of activities in a given sector, which individually are limited in their scope.

Financing proposals for multi-annual programmes do not need to set out in detail all the activities to be pursued; they merely have to set out the broad outlines of the types of activities envisaged and the overall financial framework proposed for the financing of these sets of activities over a multi-annual period.

How are Multi-Annual Programmes Approved?

Article 16.8

Financing decisions on multi-annual programmes are taken in response to a request from the NAO on the basis of a letter from the Chief Authorising Officer notifying the NAO of the decision to finance the multi-annual programme. This letter constitutes the financing agreement. Decisions on individual activities to be financed under the multi-annual programme are then taken in the light of the framework established under the proposal for the multi-annual programme by the NAO or the agent to whom authority has been delegated (e.g. the agent of decentralised co-operation or a specifically constituted Programme Management Unit).

The NAO and the EC delegate, however, remain responsible for monitoring the implementation of the multi-annual programme and ensuring the proper utilisation of the finance made available in the light of the objectives of the programme. Each year a report on the implementation of the multi-annual programme must be made, with satisfactory reporting and accounting for the utilisation of funds paid out in the past year being essential to the release of subsequent tranches of funding.

Annex IV,
Chapter 3,
Article 16.9

2.11 Administrative Structures

This section reviews the administrative structures involved in the planning, commitment and monitoring of ACP-EU development co-operation activities. It deals primarily with the actors referred to in the Cotonou Agreement and two internal EU structures involved in overseeing programme development and reviewing programme implementation.

However, it does not deal with the internal European structures dealing with day-to-day aid management, since these arrangements are determined internally by the EU and are not governed by the provisions of the Cotonou Agreement.

The section reviews the roles of:

- the National Authorising Officer;
- the EC delegate;
- the Chief Authorising Officer;
- the Quality Support Group;
- the EDF Committee;
- the ACP-EU Development Finance Co-operation Committee.

What is a National Authorising Officer?

The **National Authorising Officer** is an official appointed by the ACP government in each country where the EU has co-operation programmes under the Cotonou Agreement. The NAO is the principal point of contact for the European Commission in all its dealings around the programming and management of co-operation activities under the Agreement. As such it is the NAO who plays the major co-ordinating role in putting together the Country Support Strategy and the National Indicative Programme.

Legally, no expenditures can be made under the EDF country programmes without the approval of the National Authorising Officer. The only exception to this is where the functioning of the ACP state has broken down to such an extent that the ACP authorities cannot carry out the basic functions of a modern state. Under these circumstances, where co-operation programmes have been suspended under Article 96 of the Agreement, the **Chief Authorising Officer** may take over the functions of the National Authorising Officer.

According to the provisions of the Agreement, acting in close co-operation with the Head of the EC Delegation (the Delegate), the National Authorising Officer is responsible for:

Annex IV,
Chapter 6,
Article 35

- the preparation, submission and appraisal of projects and programmes;
- issuing invitations for local tenders;
- receiving both local and international tenders;
- presiding over the examination of tenders;
- evaluating tenders;
- establishing the results of examination of tenders;
- signing contracts and approving expenditures;
- adapting projects under implementation (within limits) in order to ensure the proper execution of activities in line with the programme's objectives.

Who is the EC Delegate?

The European Commission is represented in each ACP country by a local office, which is referred to as a **delegation**.[55] Each local office is headed by a **delegate**. As the name suggests, the head of the local EC office in each ACP countries has certain powers delegated to him/her.

Under the Agreement the EC Delegate is mandated to provide a range of support for the technical preparation of co-operation activities (preparing projects and programmes, appraising dossiers, preparing financing proposals and supervising various aspects of tendering), with an emphasis on simplifying project and programme appraisal and implementation procedures. The EC Delegate is also responsible for ensuring that projects and programmes are properly implemented and for evaluating co-operation activities.

Overall, the Delegate provides the principal route for all communications between the EU and individual ACP governments on matters of ACP-EU co-operation. As such the Delegate has a major role to play in the dialogue with the ACP government on both the Country Support Strategy, and the National Indicative Programme.

The Delegate is required to work in close co-operation with the National Authorising Officer in carrying out the following specific responsibilities:

Annex IV,
Chapter 6,
Article 36.2

- to assist on request in the *'preparation of projects and programmes and in negotiating technical assistance contracts'*;

- to *'participate in appraising projects and programmes, preparing tender dossiers and seeking ways to simplify project and programme appraisal and implementation procedures'*;

- preparing financing proposals;

- approving local open invitations to tender;

- the opening and examination of tenders.

The EC Delegate is required to ensure that the lowest cost tenders complying with the specification are accepted and that the tender does not exceed the sum earmarked for the contract. The EC Delegate is also required to ensure that the project and programmes financed from the EDF are properly executed from both a technical and financial point of view.

The EC Delegate is also nominally required to keep the ACP government to which they are accredited fully informed of developments affecting the management of co-operation activities and of any wider developments in EU activities which might directly concern co-operation between the EU and the ACP state concerned.

While according to the provisions of the Cotonou Agreement the Country Support Strategy should be prepared by the ACP state, in many ACP countries the EC Delegate has come to play a major role in preparing the Country Support Strategy. The European Commission guidelines for programming indicate that the *'primary priority of a Delegation'* should be *'designing, implementing and quality controlling the Country Support Strategy'*.[56]

The EC Delegate also has a major role in conducting the annual operational reviews and the mid-term and end-of-term reviews. Indeed, the EC Delegate is meant to be involved in ongoing monitoring of all EU co-operation activities in the country to which he/she is accredited.

The European Commission guidelines also give the EC Delegate specific functions with reference to promoting the involvement of non-state actors in ACP-EU co-operation activities. The EC Delegate is expected to assume a dual role in promoting the involvement of non-state actors as a **critical observer** and as a **facilitator**.[57]

As a critical observer, it is the EC Delegate's responsibility to ensure that non-state actor involvement is representative and does not simply involve a 'rubber stamping' of government programmes and policies by government sponsored non-governmental bodies. In their role as observers, EC Delegates are also expected to ensure that local non-state actors are familiar with the programming process and are effectively involved in all stages of the programming process.

As a facilitator, it is envisaged that the EC Delegate will:

- support capacity building for non-state actor participation;
- establish arrangements for dialogue between non-state actors and governments in the programming process;
- ensure that non-state actors can dialogue among themselves in preparation for programming.

It is envisaged that each EC Delegate, in facilitating dialogue between the ACP government and non-state actors, will take the following steps:

- designate a contact point in the EC Delegation to deal with non-state actors;
- initiate a discussion with government and non-state actors' representatives on categories of non-state actors eligible for involvement in the programming dialogue and the implementation of co-operation programmes;
- provide support to non-state actors to facilitate their participation;
- extend direct support to certain non-state actors in implementing programmes within the national ACP-EU co-operation programme;
- co-operate closely with other agencies seeking to promote non-state actor participation.

In situations where ACP governments cannot carry out the basic functions of a modern state, and where co-operation has been suspended under Article 96 and the Chief Authorising Officer has assumed the functions of the NAO, delegates may be called on to carry out certain of the functions assumed by the Chief Authorising Officer.

Who is the Chief Authorising Officer?

The Chief Authorising Officer is appointed by the Commission and is responsible for managing the resources of the EDF. The Chief Authorising Officer is responsible for the commitment clearance, authorisation and accounting of expenditures under the European Development Fund.

According to the Cotonou Agreement the Chief Authorising Officer shall:

> *(a) commit, clear and authorise expenditure and keep account of commitments and authorisations;*

Annex IV,
Chapter 6,
Article 34.2

(b) *ensure that financing decisions are carried out;*

(c) *make commitment decisions and financial arrangements that prove necessary to ensure proper execution of approved operations from the economic and technical viewpoints;*

(d) *... prepare the tender dossier before the invitations to tender are issued for (i) open international tender, and (ii) restricted international invitation to tender with pre-qualification;*

(e) *approve the proposals for the placing of contracts ...;*

(f) *ensure publication in reasonable time of international invitations to tender.*

The Chief Authorising Officer has overall legal responsibility for the management of EDF resources.

Where an ACP state can no longer carry out the functions of a modern state, the Chief Authorising Officer may assume the functions of the National Authorising Officer of the ACP state concerned.

The functions of the Chief Authorising Officer have often been taken on by the European Commissioner Responsible for Development Co-operation.

What is the Quality Support Group?

The **Quality Support Group** is an internal body established by the European Commission with the explicit aim of improving the quality of EU external assistance.

The development of the Quality Support Group concept needs to be seen against the background of the general reform of EU external assistance programmes. This process of reform aims to make all aspects of EU aid deployment more results orientated, with the establishment of clear indicators that will allow subsequent assessment of the effectiveness of the implementation of aid operations. Since the establishment of the Quality Support Group structures is rooted in efforts to reform the management of *all* EU external assistance, it is not rooted in any provisions of the Cotonou Agreement.

The aim of the various Quality Support Group structures is to contribute to the improvement in the quality of **strategic planning**, **programming** and **implementation of EU aid programmes**, with the ultimate aim of improving the impact of EU aid on the beneficiary country and target group. It aims to assess the **relevance**, **feasibility** and **sustainability** of all measures proposed.

The Quality Support Group concept is to be introduced progressively over

2002, with the aim of it being fully operational by 2003. The European Commission emphasises how the Quality Support Group should:

> ... not be seen as an extra layer of bureaucratic control.[58]

The Quality Support Group operates on three levels:

- Inter-service Quality Support Group (I-QSG) (see Annex 13);
- Office Quality Support Group (O-QSG) (see Annex 14);
- Directorate Quality Support Group (D-QSG) (see Annex 15).

The opinion of one of the structures of the Quality Support Group on the Proposal for Identification is a necessary precondition for the actual commitment of funds for any operation, including funds for initial identification and feasibility studies.

In the Commission's view, this whole process of assessment by the Quality Support Group, including approval by the Geographical Director, should not take more than one month.[59]

What Information Should a Proposal for Identification Contain?

A **proposal for identification** has to be prepared for all operations over Euro 2 million. Ultimately, each proposal for identification should be compiled by the EC Delegation. However, during the phasing-in stage the operational unit concerned in AIDCO will take the responsibility for producing each proposal for identification. A proposal for identification should include information allowing an understanding of:

- *how the identification and appraisal of the proposed operation is being prepared, in terms of timing, of its main activities and of resources required;*

- *what are the key policy and operational elements that are going to be the subject of the detailed feasibility analysis in order for a complete measure to be presented after the successful completion of the identification and appraisal stage;*

- *the detailed specific information on the proposed operations (e.g. the exact cost of the road section, duration of construction, ECOFIN analysis of the road) will be provided at the end of the phase, in the form of a more complete measure.[60]*

Each Proposal for Identification should in summary form (12 or so lines) cover 11 main areas:

- the measure's name and title;
- the authority submitting the proposal;
- funding sources to be mobilised for the programme;
- estimated costs and contributions involved;
- summary of statistical information (recorded according to the OECD Development Assistance Committee standard);
- any link with previous actions;
- the units and official in the Commission services involved;
- the funding needed for the identification and appraisal phase;
- the data required for monitoring the identification and appraisal phase;
- background to the institutional and economic context within which the appraisal is being undertaken;
- the Quality Support Group Review.

The most detailed section of the proposal for identification is Section 10 which includes a review of:

- the coherence of the project with the wider aid programme's objectives;
- background information on the sector of intervention;
- problems to be addressed;
- objectives and expected results;
- intended beneficiaries.

Section 11, the Quality Support Review, is completed at the end of the process of compilation of the proposal for identification.

What is the European Development Fund Committee?

The European Development Fund Committee is the main decision-making body involved in the supervision of ACP-EU co-operation under the Cotonou Agreement. The EDF Committee consists of representatives of EU member states' governments and is chaired by the Commission. Under earlier Lomé Conventions the approval of the EDF Committee was required for all major projects and programmes funded under the EDF. Under the Cotonou Agreement, however, its role has been redefined to give it more of a supervisory role at the policy level and less of a role in the approval of individual projects and programmes. According to the Internal Agreement the tasks of the EDF Committee cover three levels:

- *programming of Community aid and programming reviews in particular focusing on country and regional strategies, including identification of projects and programmes;*

- *participation in the decision-making process related to financing from the European Development Fund; and*

- *monitoring the implementation of Community aid, including sectoral aspects, cross-cutting issues and the functioning of field level co-ordination.*[61]

With regard to programming, the EDF Committee is required to give its opinion on the Country Support Strategy and the draft National Indicative Programme and needs to be informed of the finalised Country Support Strategy and NIP. The EDF Committee also gives its opinion on resource allocations made to national and regional programmes. The EDF Committee is further required to discuss the annual implementation reviews and give an opinion on the mid-term and end-of-term reviews.

The European Commission is required to **'take measures'** in the light of the opinions expressed by the EDF Committee. If an unfavourable opinion is delivered, the Commission either has to withdraw the proposal or refer it to the EU Council.

Under the Agreement increased emphasis has been placed on the role of the EDF Committee in promoting:

... consistency and complementarity between Community aid and aid from the member states.[62]

The EDF Committee now has a more limited role in approving individual projects and programmes. Under the Internal Agreement, without reference to the EDF Committee, the Commission is allowed to approve projects and programmes:

... with a value of less than or equal to Eur 8 million and representing less than 25 per cent of the indicative programme.[63]

Different procedures apply in terms of the information which needs to be made available to the EDF Committee depending on the size of the programme. For activities with a value of Euro 2–8 million the Commission is required to provide *ex ante* information on:

- the relevance of the project to the development of the country concerned and the achievement of the objectives set out in the Country Support Strategy;

- the expected impact of the programme, its feasibility and sustainability;

- the timetable for implementation along with key indicators for assessing achievement of expected results and objectives.

This information should be made available at least two weeks before the Commission plans to take a decision.

For activities between Euro 0.5 million and Euro 2.0 million similar information has to be provided at least two weeks before any decision is taken but in a more succinct form.

For activities costing less than Euro 500,000 the Commission only has to inform the EDF Committee after the decision has been taken.

Each EU member state may demand that those projects and programmes approved directly by the Commission under the above procedure are discussed in the EDF Committee. However, the aim is that this should be the exception rather than the rule.

For activities over Euro 8 million or representing more than 25 per cent of an NIP, the EDF Committee must give an opinion. Without a favourable opinion from the EDF Committee the project or programme cannot go ahead. Financing proposals greater than Euro 15 million are discussed in actual meetings of the EDF Committee, while for financing proposals between Euro 8 million and Euro 15 million a written procedure for canvassing the opinion of EDF Committee members is followed.

The EDF Committee should make final decisions on financing proposals within 60 days of their submission.

In terms of monitoring the implementation of ACP-EU co-operation, the EDF Committee is required to discuss:

- general development issues which affect the implementation of the EDF;

- sectoral strategies developed by the Commission in consultation with member states' experts, where this is needed to ensure coherence;

- results of evaluations;

- the mid-term appraisal of projects and programmes.

The EDF Committee takes decisions on the basis of a qualified majority of 145 votes, with at least eight member states in favour of the decision. A system of weighted voting is used based on the contribution of member states to the financing of the EDF. The following weight is given to the votes of different EU member states:

Member State	Votes
Belgium	9
Denmark	5
Germany	50
Greece	4
Spain	13
France	52
Ireland	2
Italy	27
Luxembourg	1
Netherlands	12
Austria	6
Portugal	3
Finland	4
Sweden	6
United Kingdom	27
Total	**220**

What is the ACP-EC Development Finance Co-operation Committee?

The ACP-EU Development Finance Co-operation Committee consists of equal numbers of ACP and EU ministerial representatives. However, the Ministers can delegate their responsibilities to authorised representatives. The ACP-EU Development Finance Co-operation Committee is responsible for:

- examining overall progress in achieving the objectives and principles of co-operation activities;

  Part 4, Title IV, Article 83.2

- establishing guidelines for the timely and effective implementation of co-operation activities;

- examining problems as they arise and suggesting appropriate responses;

- reviewing the various annexes to the Agreement to see that they remain relevant and, where necessary, recommending appropriate amendments;

- examining the effectiveness of measures to enhance private sector development, particularly through the operation of the Investment Facility.

The ACP-EU Development Finance Co-operation Committee should meet every quarter, with Ministerial level consultations at least once a year.

The Committee can also take initiatives to convene expert meetings to address particular problems that may hinder the efficient implementation of co-operation activities.

2.11 Implementation of Co-operation Activities

This section provides a brief overview of the implementation of co-operation activities, looking in general at how co-operation programmes are managed and at the tendering process through which contracts for the implementation of specific co-operation activities are placed.

How are Co-operation Programmes Implemented?

The actual implementation of development co-operation activities lies with those agencies specified in the individual **Financing Agreement**. This may be a government department, a private sector body, a non-state actor body or a specially established programme management unit. These activities are then implemented in line with the timetables set down in the individual Financing Agreement.

In the past, responsibility for project and programme implementation lay largely with the relevant ACP line Ministry responsible for the sector in which the activities were being implemented (e.g. a road project would be implemented by the Roads Department of the Ministry of Transport). Day-to-day supervision of programme implementation then lay with the contracting parties who won the tender to implement the programme. Increasingly, however, with the EU favouring the financing of larger and larger programmes, specifically established **Programme Management Units** are being created with responsibility for overseeing programme implementation.

This can have important implications for capacity building in government service in ACP countries, with scarce trained staff being siphoned off into specially constituted Programme Management Units whose terms and conditions of remuneration are often better than those available in the public service.

What is the Tendering Process?

The tendering process is the system of rules under which it is determined who will actually implement the contracts placed in order to carry out the activities envisaged under the project or programme. All tenders placed under the EDF are open on equal terms to:

- *natural persons, companies or firms or public or semi-public agencies of the ACP States and the Member States;*

  Annex IV, Chapter 4, Article 20

- *co-operative societies and other legal persons governed by public or private law, of the Member States and/or the ACP States; and*

- *joint ventures or groupings of companies or firms of ACP States and/or of a Member States.*

A commitment is made under the Cotonou Agreement ensuring:

... the widest possible participation on equal terms in invitations to tender for works, supplies and services contracts.[173]

Article 21

Where major cost considerations arise, provision is made for the purchase of goods and services from non-ACP developing country suppliers (so-called 'derogation'). Five major factors are taken into account in considering derogation requests:

- geographical location;

- competitiveness;

- the need to avoid excess cost increases;

- transport problems or delivery delays;

- local technology needs.

Tenders can also be accepted from other third country suppliers where there is an emergency or where the third country is also supporting regional schemes or where the third country is co-financing the project.

What Tendering Procedures Apply?

Disbursements under the financing agreement must comply with the tendering rules established under the Cotonou Agreement.

Tenders may be awarded through the following procedures:

- **Open International Invitation to Tender** for **'works contracts'** over Euro 5 million and supply contracts over Euro 0.15 million;

  Article 23

- **Open Local Invitation to Tender** for **'works contracts'** under Euro 5 million and **'supply contracts'** under Euro 0.15 million;

- **Restricted Invitations to Tender** for **'service contracts'** under Euro 0.2 million;

- **Direct Agreement Contracts** for **'works contracts'** under Euro 0.3 million, **'supply contracts'** under Euro 0.03 million and **'service contracts'** under Euro 0.2 million;

- **Direct labour arrangements** implemented through public or semi-public agencies;

- **Framework Contracts** for implementation of multi-annual framework programmes.

While the ACP government carries responsibility for awarding the contracts on the basis of criteria laid down in the Cotonou Agreement, where restricted invitations to tender are issued, the short list is drawn up in consultation with the EC Delegate.

Notes

1   Communication from the Commission to the European Parliament, the Council and the Court of Auditors, 'Financial Analysis of the 6th, 7th and 8th European Development Funds – 2000', Brussels, 22.8.2001 COM(2001) 479 final, p. 3.
2   Total grant financing made available under that EDF for co-operation with ACP countries.
3   The amount of money for which financing agreements have been signed.
4   The amount of money for which contracts with implementing agents have been signed.
5   The amount of money which the European Commission has actually paid out.
6   See the section of the *User's Guide* 'Project Submission: What is a Multi-Annual Programme?' for more details on multi-annual programmes.
7   See 'Sectoral Breakdown of 9th EDF Resources Programmed in Draft CSPs for ACP Countries', 14.05.2002, DEV/A/1.
8   Ibid.
9   See 'ACP 9th EDF Programming Guidelines', B. Underlying Principles, DG Development, 12.05.00.
10   Ibid., Note No. 9, p. 7.
11   Ibid., p. 3.
12   Ibid., p. 9.
13   Ibid., pp. 11, 13, 15.
14   See 'Financing in the ACP', European Investment Bank.
15   Ibid., p. 8.
16   Ibid., p.7.
17   See 'Applying for EIB Funding', European Investment Bank.
18   For details of the composition and operation of the Investment Facility Committee, see the Internal Agreement, Chapter V, Articles 29–30.
19   Strategic Plan and Framework for Action 2001–2005, Wageningen, The Netherlands, October 2001, p. 31.
20   Ibid.
21   ACP 9th EDF Programming Guidelines, Section 11.1, 'Rolling Programming and the Review Mechanism', DG development, 12 May 2000.
22   Ibid.
23   For more details on all these aspects see annex, 'ACP 9th EDF Programming Guidelines', DG Development, 12 May 2000.
24   With a growing tendency to use unallocated reserves in support of global thematic programmes (e.g. the Global Fund for AIDS, TB and Malaria, the HIPC Initiative and the new EU Water Fund), it is far from clear what additional resources will in fact be available for allocation to ACP countries which meet their performance targets.
25   For details of the composition and operation of the ACP-EU Development Finance Co-operation Committee see the section of the *User's Guide* on Administrative Structures, 'What is the ACP-EU Development Finance Committee?'.
26   Details on the role the EU Delegate is expected to play vis à vis the promotion of non-state actor involvement in the ACP-EU co-operation process can be found in 'ACP 9th EDF Programming Guidelines', Section 9.4., DG Development, 12 May 2000.
27   This timetable was set out in 'ACP 9th EDF Programming Guidelines', Section

4.2, DG Development, 12 May 2000.

28   Information on the experience of non-state actor engagement in the Country Support Strategy process is drawn from 'Implementation of the Cotonou Agreement, Involvement of Non-State Actors in the Programming Process: A Preliminary Assessment', Development Policy, Coherence and Forward Studies, DG Development, 6 February 2002.

29   'Implementation of the Cotonou Agreement: Involvement of Non-State Actors in the Programming Process: A Preliminary Assessment', p. 15, DG Development, European Commission, 6 February 2002.

30   This is based on comments by Commission staff on the initial draft of the *User's Guide*. There are a number of logical inconsistencies in the figures cited in the February 2002 Commission paper and the information cited by Commission staff from the March 2003 paper. These can perhaps be accounted for by some degree of non-state actor involvement after the Country Support Strategies had been drawn up between February 2002 and March 2003. Given these inconsistencies, the decision has been taken to cite both the Commission review from February 2002 and the Commission staff's observations based on the March 2003 internal Commission review.

31   'Implementation of the Cotonou Agreement: Involvement of Non-State Actors in the Programming Process: A Preliminary Assessment', p. 15, DG Development, European Commission, 6 February 2002.

32   Ibid.

33   This is based on comments by Commission staff on the initial draft of the *User's Guide*.

34   See 'ACP 9th EDF Programming Guidelines', Section 9.4, DG Development, 12.5.2000.

35   See 'Implementation of the Cotonou Agreement: Involvement of Non-State Actors in the Programming Process: A Preliminary Assessment', pp. 11–12, DG Development, European Commission , 6 February 2002.

36   This issue is explored in the following notes: 'Use of 9EDF by Civil Society Actors', Legal Service, European Commission 18 April 2002; 'Direct Access Fund for Civil Society Under the 9th EDF', Development Policy, Coherence and Forward Studies, 14 December 2001; Explanatory note: Involvement of Civil Society under the Cotonou Agreement, 14 March 2002.

37   'Implementation of the Cotonou Agreement: Involvement of Non-State Actors in the Programming Process: A Preliminary Assessment', p. 10, DG Development, European Commission, 6 February 2002.

38   Ibid., p. 9.

39   This is based on comments by Commission staff on the initial draft of the *User's Guide*.

40   'Implementation of the Cotonou Agreement: Involvement of Non-State Actors in the Programming Process: A Preliminary Assessment', p. 15, DG Development, European Commission, 6 May 2002.

41   This is based on comments by Commission staff on the initial draft of the *User's Guide*.

42   'Implementation of the Cotonou Agreement: Involvement of Non-State Actors in the Programming Process: A Preliminary Assessment', p. 14, DG Development, European Commission, 6 February 2002.

43   Extracted from 'Eligibility Criteria for Non-State Actors: Access to Funding

Under the EDF', ACP, Brussels, 25 February 2003.

44   'Implementation of the Cotonou Agreement: Involvement of Non-State Actors in the Programming Process: A Preliminary Assessment', p. 13, DG Development, European Commission, 6 February 2002, supplemented by information communicated by the responsible Commission official.

45   This section draws on the analysis contained in 'Implementation of the Cotonou Agreement: Involvement of Non-State Actors in the Programming Process: A Preliminary Assessment', DG Development, European Commission, 6 February 2002.

46   Ibid., p. 4.

47   See 'Support for Decentralised Co-operation: Operational Guide to Decentralised Co-operation', DG Development, Brussels, January 2000.

48   'The Role of Non-Governmental Actors in the New ACP-EU Partnership Agreement', p. 4, DG Development, 26 April 2000.

49   'Implementation of the Cotonou Agreement: Involvement of Non-State Actors in the Programming Process: A Preliminary Assessment', p. 15, DG Development, European Commission, 6 February 2002.

50   Ibid.

51   'Table Summarising Some Aspects of the Country Support Strategies', APRODEV, 9 April 2002.

52   For a summary see 'Revision to Format of Financing Proposals', DG Development, European Commission, Brussels, March 2000; for a more comprehensive review of what should be included see 'Guidelines for the presentation of financing proposals to the European Development Fund Committee', DG Development, European Commission, Brussels, March 2000.

53   Ibid., p. 6.

54   'Internal Agreement between representatives of the government of member states on the financing and administration of Community aid under the Financial protocol of the Partnership Agreement between the ACP states and the European Community signed in Cotonou (Benin) on 23 June 2000 and the allocation of financial assistance for the Overseas Countries and Territories to which part four of the European Community treaty applies', Article 24.1 (hereafter referred to as the 'Internal Agreement').

55   For small ACP countries, one EU Delegate may be accredited to more than one country.

56   ACP 9th EDF Programming Guidelines, Section 4, The Programming Process, 12 May 2000, DG Development.

57   Ibid., Section 9.4, The Programming Process.

58   Interservice Quality Support Group: Launching the Work of the Group, 30 November 2000.

59   For details on the various Quality Support Group structures see 'Draft Guidelines, Quality Support Group in the Office', Brussels, 11 April 2002 AIDCO/HCS/JB D(2002), EuropeAid Co-operation Office.

60   'Guidelines for Submitting A Proposal for Identification and Appraisal,' Europe Aid Co-operation Office, European Commission, 19 March 2002.

61   Internal Agreement, Article 22.2.

62   Ibid., Article 23.2.

63   Ibid., Article 24.3.

Part 3

Trade Arrangements under the Cotonou Agreement

3.1 Overview

This section reviews the provisions of the Cotonou Agreement dealing with ACP-EU trade. It outlines in broad terms:

- what the trade provisions of the Cotonou Agreement cover;
- the main objectives and principles of the Cotonou trade provisions;
- where the various detailed provisions of the current Cotonou trade arrangements can be found;
- the institutional arrangements for ACP-EU consultations on trade matters.

What Do the Cotonou Trade Provisions Cover?

The trade provisions of the Cotonou Agreement are dealt with under Part 3, Title II, Articles 34–54, under the heading 'Economic and Trade Co-operation' and in a series of detailed annexes and Protocols. These provisions cover:

Part 3,
Title II
Articles 34–54

- the objectives and principles underpinning ACP-EU economic and trade co-operation;
- the general trade arrangements to be applied during what is referred to as the 'preparatory period' (2000–2008);
- the commodity protocols;
- the modalities and procedures for the negotiation of longer-term frameworks for ACP-EU trade relations;
- institutional arrangements for joint consultations on trade issues;
- commitments on co-operation in international fora;
- trade in services and trade-related areas.

What are the Main Objectives and Principles of the Cotonou Trade Provisions?

The primary aim of economic and trade co-operation under the Cotonou Agreement is:

Part 3, Title II,
Chapter 1,
Article 34.3

... fostering the smooth and gradual integration of the ACP States into the world economy.

The ultimate objective of ACP-EU economic and trade co-operation is seen as being:

Article 34.2

... to enable the ACP States to play a full part in international trade.

Some ACP states emphasise how ACP-EU trade co-operation needs to be seen in the context of the wider objectives of the Cotonou Agreement, namely the commitment to reducing, and eventually eliminating, poverty and to promoting sustainable development. However, this is left implicit in the 'Economic and Trade Co-operation' provisions.

Emphasis is placed on promoting ACP states' active participation in multilateral trade negotiations and assisting ACP states in managing the challenges of globalisation and facilitating their transition to a liberalised global economy.

Against this background the aims of ACP-EU economic and trade co-operation are stated as being to:

Article 34.1

- enhance the production, supply and trading capacities of ACP states;
- produce a new trade dynamic;
- strengthen ACP trade and investment policies;
- improve the capacity of ACP states to handle trade-related issues.

This, it is maintained, should:

Article 34.4

... be implemented in full conformity with the provisions of the WTO, including special and differential treatment, taking account of the Parties' mutual interests and their respective levels of development.

Article 35.1

The Cotonou Agreement commits the ACP and the EU to a *'strengthened and strategic partnership'* which will adopt a comprehensive approach and build on the achievements of previous ACP-EU co-operation agreements. It further commits ACP and EU countries to:

... using all means available to achieve the objectives set out by addressing supply and demand side constraints.

It emphasises the importance of trade development measures in establishing national development strategies. Significantly, the Agreement emphasises how:

> *... economic and trade co-operation shall build on regional integration initiatives of ACP states.*

Part 3, Title II,
Chapter 1,
Article 35.2

The general provisions on objectives and principles commit ACP-EU economic and trade co-operation to taking:

> *... account of the different needs and levels of development of the ACP countries and regions.*[8]

Article 35.3

and reaffirm the attachment of all parties to:

> *... ensuring special and differential treatment for all ACP countries and to maintaining special treatment for ACP LDCs and to taking due account of the vulnerability of small, landlocked and island countries.*

Where Can the Details of the Trade Provisions Applied during the Transitional Period be Found?

The detailed provisions dealing with ACP market access during the 'preparatory period' are set out in Part 3, Title II, Article 36 and Annex V of the Cotonou Agreement. Annex V includes five Protocols and various annexes.

Issues Dealt with by Annexes and Protocols on Trade Provisions during the Transitional Period

The details of the trade regime to be applied during the preparatory period (2000–2008)	Annex V
The definition of the concept of originating products	Annex V, Protocol 1
The processing required on non-originating materials in order for manufactured products to obtain originating status and hence qualify for duty free access	Annex II, Protocol 1 attached to Annex V
Movement certificates and associated administrative arrangements	Protocol 1, Title IV, Articles 14–21, Annexes IV, V, VIA, VIB, VII to Protocol 1 attached to Annex V
Derogation applications	Annex VIII to Protocol 1, attached to Annex V
The specific processing requirements for textile products to be granted originating status	Annex IX to Protocol 1, attached to Annex V
Textile products excluded from cumulation provisions in Article 6(3)	Annex X to Protocol 1, attached to Annex V
The cumulation provisions to be applied under Article 6(3) to South African originating materials after 3 and 6 years of application of the South Africa-EU Trade and Development Co-operation Agreement	Annexes XI and XII to Protocol 1, attached to Annex V
The products not covered by the cumulation provisions	Annex XIII to Protocol 1, attached to Annex V
Fisheries products temporarily excluded from the cumulation provisions	Annex XIV to Protocol 1, attached to Annex V

Issues Dealt with by Annexes and Protocols on Trade Provisions during the Transitional Period (continued)

A joint declaration on cumulation	Annex XV to Protocol 1, attached to annex V
The Sugar Protocol	Protocol 3
The Beef and Veal Protocol	Protocol 4
The Second Banana Protocol	Protocol 5
Declaration XXII, Joint Declaration concerning agricultural products	Article 1(2)(a) of Annex V
Declaration XXIV, Joint Declaration on Rice	

What Institutional Arrangements are Provided for ACP-EU Trade Co-operation?

In order to intensify ACP-EU trade co-operation and to address problems arising in the implementation of the Agreement provision is made for the establishment of a **Joint Ministerial Trade Committee**. This Joint Ministerial Trade Committee is scheduled to meet once a year with a particular focus on:

- multilateral trade negotiations;

- the impact of liberalisation on ACP-EU trade;

- the impact of liberalisation on the development of ACP economies;

- how best to preserve the benefits of the existing ACP-EU trade arrangement.

Part 3, Title II, Chapter 1, Article 38

This is supplemented on the ACP side by the establishment of an **ACP Trade Ministers Committee**, which meets more frequently. Currently the deliberations of the ACP Ministerial Trade Committee have largely been focused on preparations for the ACP-EU negotiations on the future trade arrangement to succeed the existing non-reciprocal trade arrangement.

3.2 Current Market Access Arrangements

This section reviews:

- the current market access arrangements and the qualifications to duty free access currently applied;

- the specific trade arrangements applied to agricultural products as a result of the Common Agricultural Policy;

- the rules of origin applied under the Cotonou Agreement which must be adhered to if a good exported from an ACP country is to benefit from the preferential access granted under the Cotonou Agreement;

- the administrative arrangements to be followed to secure the benefits of the trade preferences extended under the Cotonou Agreement;

- the safeguard provisions;

- the commitments entered into through the Cotonou Agreement in the area of trade in services;

- the commitments entered into with regard to trade-related areas.

What Do the Current Market Access Provisions Allow?

The trade arrangements established for the period 2000–2008 should be seen against the background of the commitment made to concluding:

Part 3, Title II, Chapter 2, Article 36.1

... new World Trade Organisation (WTO) compatible trading arrangements.[1]

Since it is recognised that new WTO compatible trading arrangements will need to be introduced gradually, it was agreed that during the preparatory period:

> *... the non-reciprocal trade preferences applied under the Fourth ACP-EC Convention shall be maintained.*

Part 3, Title II, Chapter 1, Article 36.3

This means that until 1 January 2008 ACP exporters will continue to enjoy duty free access for more or less all exports to the EU market which 'originate' in ACP countries.

There are, however, three qualifications to the duty free access granted ACP exports under the Agreement:

- restrictions placed on duty free access as a result of the Common Agricultural Policy;

- rules of origin;

- the safeguard provisions.

How is the Trade in Agricultural Products Dealt with under the Cotonou Agreement?

With regard to those agricultural and processed agricultural products which fall under the EU's Common Agricultural Policy or which potentially compete with goods falling under the CAP, the principle of duty free access is qualified by the imposition of quotas on the duty free access granted and, in some instances, the application of a part of the special duty.

The specific quota restricted access permitted for agricultural products under the Agreement is set out in:

- the Beef Protocol;

- the Sugar Protocol;

- Declaration XXII, the Joint Declaration concerning agricultural products referred to in Article 1(2) (a) of Annex V.

However, no specific commitments were made under the Agreement on access for ACP banana exports.

While reaffirming the importance attached to the commodity protocols, the Agreement also acknowledged the need to review them:

> *... as regards their compatibility with WTO rules.*

Article 36.4

It was maintained, however, that this review would be undertaken:

> *... with a view to safeguarding the benefits derived therefrom, bearing in mind the special legal status of the Sugar Protocol.*

However, it should be noted that the Agreement also renewed the provisions with regard to **safeguard measures**, which allow the EU to re-introduce import controls where ACP exports threaten to disrupt the EU market.

Can the Treatment Accorded to Agricultural Products Be Modified?

Provision is made under the Cotonou Agreement for modification of the treatment accorded to ACP agricultural products. The procedures to be followed for the addition of new products to the list of products subject to special arrangements under Declaration XXII are set out in Annex V, Chapter 1, Article 1(b), (c) of the Agreement.

These provisions state:

Annex V,
Article 1(b)(c)

... if during the application of this Annex, the ACP State request that new lines of agricultural production or agricultural products which are not the subject of specific arrangements when this annex enters into force should benefit from such arrangements, the Community shall examine these requests in consultation with the ACP States.

Notwithstanding the above the Community shall in the context of the special relations and special nature of ACP-EC co-operation, examine on
a case-by-case basis the requests from the ACP States for preferential access for their agricultural products to the Community market and shall notify its decision on those reasoned requests if possible within four months, and in any case not more than six months after the date of their submission.

Concessions granted in this regard should take account of:

Article 1(c)

... the possibilities offered by the off season market.

The concessions granted under Declaration XXII, the Joint Declaration concerning agricultural products referred to in Article 1(2) (a) of Annex V, can be modified if under the Common Agricultural Policy the treatment accorded the product concerned is changed. In such cases the provisions of the Agreement commit the EU to ensuring:

Article 1(d)

... that products originating in the ACP States continue to enjoy an advantage comparable to that previously enjoyed in relation to products originating in third countries benefiting from the most favoured nation clause.

What Market Access Does the Beef Protocol Allow?

The provisions allowing preferential access for traditional suppliers of beef to the EU were rolled over under the Cotonou Agreement, allowing the export of the following tonnage of chilled or frozen de-boned beef and veal:

	Tonnes
Botswana	18,916
Namibia	13,000
Zimbabwe	9,100
Madagascar	7,579
Swaziland	3,362
Kenya	142

Protocol 4 on beef and veal, Article 2

Exports within this quota do not have to pay the ad valorem duty applied to beef imports but must pay 8 per cent of the special duty applied to beef imports (that is to say, ACP beef exported under the quota enjoys a 92 per cent reduction in the special duty).

Provision is also made under the Beef Protocol for rolling over unutilised quotas to the following year and re-allocating quotas between countries.

In Declaration XXVI the EU committed itself to:

Declaration XXVI, Joint Declaration on beef and veal

- establishing appropriate rules and procedures for the application of the Beef Protocol;

- facilitating year-round marketing and assisting in addressing supply side constraints.

The EU also agreed to consider requests from least developed ACP countries to export beef and veal under preferential conditions. The new agreement thus secures the current levels of access to the EU market granted to Beef Protocol beneficiaries until 1 January 2008.

CAP Reform vs. Beef Protocol

Under the impetus of CAP reform the value of preferential access for beef and veal has been declining. According to EU Agricultural Commissioner Franz Fischler, two-thirds of the decline in the average price of beef in the EU since 2000 has been the result of the process of CAP reform, with one-third of the price decline being a consequence of the BSE and foot and mouth disease crises.

In April 2002 Swaziland Meat Industries reported that the UK price of chilled steak cuts had fallen from £4.05 per kg in the 1995/96 season (the season before the major BSE crisis in the UK) to £2.91 per kg in the 2002 season (a 28 per cent decline), while the price of forequarter frozen cuts fell from £2.10 per kg to 1.40 per kg (a 30 per cent decline). Similar price falls are reported for Namibian and Botswanan beef exports. Clearly the process of CAP reform is reducing the value of traditional beef sector trade preferences extended to ACP countries.

This has led ACP beef suppliers to call for the introduction of *'compensatory trade measures'* in order to **maintain the value of the trade preferences granted to ACP countries in the beef sector**. Specifically, Southern African beef exporters have called for:

- the abolition of the remaining 8 per cent special duty (formerly the agricultural levy) applied to beef imports from ACP countries, which currently costs ACP beef exporters around 15 pence per kg of exported beef;

- a broadening of the beef product range which can be exported within the scope of the Beef Protocol, allowing the export of higher value products and reducing dependence on declining commodity markets;

- reform of the licensing arrangements to allow greater flexibility to respond to market signals, and other administrative changes to facilitate the marketing of beef *'without undue restrictions'*.

What Market Access Does the Sugar Protocol Allow?

Annex V,
Protocol 3
on ACP sugar

The EU reaffirmed its commitment under the Sugar Protocol to importing an agreed volume of ACP **sugar** at guaranteed prices for an indefinite period. In the Cotonou Agreement the provisions dealing with access for ACP sugar exports are dealt with under Protocol 3 and various declarations and annexes containing letters on the application and extension of sugar sector preferences to ACP countries. Taken together, these provisions extend the following duty free quotas to ACP sugar exports:

ACP Sugar Quotas (Tonnes White Sugar)[1]

St Kitts and Nevis	14,800	Guyana	157,700
Belize	39,400	Swaziland	116,400
Barbados	49,300	Fiji	163,600
Trinidad and Tobago	69,000	Mauritius	487,200
Malawi	20,000	Jamaica	118,300
Tanzania	10,000	Madagascar	10,000
Zimbabwe	25,000	Congo	10,000
Kenya	5,000	Uganda	5,000
Suriname	4,000	Ivory Coast	2,000
Zambia	0		

Annex V,
Protocol 3,
Article 3

The Sugar Protocol has brought considerable benefits to ACP countries, given the high prices prevailing on the EU market. A study of the EU sugar regime by the Netherlands Economic Institute[2] estimated that in 1997/98 the total **income transfer**[3] to ACP countries under the EU preferential sugar arrangements totalled 501.83 MECU. With world market prices declining by more than half between 1997/98 and 1999/2000, the income transfer to ACP countries would have exceeded 1,000 MECU by 1999/2000.

While the Cotonou Agreement preserves the preferential access traditionally extended to ACP sugar suppliers under the Sugar Protocol, the value of these preferences have been declining as the Euro has lost value against the US dollar.[4] This has been a particular point of concern for Caribbean sugar suppliers whose imports largely come from the United States.[5] The value of the sugar preferences extended to ACP countries under the Sugar Protocol is also likely to be undermined as the EU seeks to extend to the sugar sector the process of reform already underway in all other major agricultural sectors. This reform process involves **a shift from price support to direct aid to farmers**. In other sectors this has led to substantial reductions in the intervention price.

In October 2000 the European Commission estimated that if reform of the sugar sector were to be pursued involving a 25 per cent reduction in the EU sugar price, this would result in annual income losses to ACP sugar exporters of around US$250 million.[6] While sugar sector reform has been consistently deferred since 1992, it now appears inevitable that reform involving some level of production and quota cuts will be introduced in the sugar sector by

2006. As a consequence, in the coming years the high returns enjoyed on ACP sugar exports to the EU market are likely to decline significantly.[7] This could make the position of a number of ACP sugar suppliers, particularly in the Caribbean, extremely difficult.

In addition to the Sugar Protocol, ACP suppliers also enjoy preferential access to the EU sugar market through the **special preferential sugar (SPS) arrangement**. The key to the special preferential sugar arrangement is the concept of *'maximum supply needs'*. These are established with reference to the needs of seven sugar cane refineries (two each in the UK, France and Portugal, and one in Finland and are currently set at 1,779,000 tonnes of white sugar equivalent. Any imports above these requirements have to pay the full duty and receive no processing aid.

The 'maximum supply needs' were formerly met through:

- an ACP Sugar Protocol quota of 1,294,700 tonnes;
- an Indian quota of 10,000 tonnes;
- the Finnish MFN quota of 85,463 tonnes;
- the exportable production of the French Overseas Territories;
- the Special Preferential Sugar arrangement for ACP countries and India.

With the production of the French Overseas Territories varying, the amount of special preferential sugar imports allowed from the ACP and India is effectively a residual amount.

This residual access under the SPS arrangement is now being reduced through the implementation of the sugar preferences extended to least developed countries under the EU's Everything But Arms (EBA) initiative. As the quota granted to least developed country sugar exports is expanded up to 2009, so the amount of sugar allowed access to the EU market under the SPS arrangement will decline.

EBA Transitional Quotas

Year	Tariff Quota (tonnes)
2001–2002	74,185
2002–2003	85,313
2003–2004	98,110
2004–2005	112,827
2005–2006	129,751
2006–2007	149,213
2000–2008	171,595
2008–2009	197,335

After the transitional period LDC sugar exporters will enjoy unrestricted duty free access to the EU market for 'originating' sugar. This will effectively do away with SPS access for ACP sugar exports. However, the SPS arrangement is not part of the Cotonou Agreement.

What Market Access Does the Banana Protocol Allow?

In the light of the 1999 WTO rulings on **bananas**, the Cotonou Agreement made only limited commitments to protecting the interests of ACP banana producers. It specifically committed the EU only to:

> *... examine where necessary the measures aimed at ensuring the continued viability of their banana export industries and the continuing outlet for their bananas in the Community market.*

Annex V, Protocol 5, Second Banana Protocol, Article 1

The measures to be implemented to ensure the continued viability of ACP banana exports, however, were not elaborated in the Agreement, beyond the commitment to:

> *... pursuing through all the means available ... measures designed to enable ACP states ... to become more competitive.*

Article 2

Thus the Agreement did not secure the future of the ACP Banana regime. Subsequent developments in the EU-US banana dispute have, however, seen the basis laid for the phasing out of country-specific ACP banana preferences.

The final agreement in the transatlantic banana dispute reached in April 2001 established a bound duty on banana imports of Euro 630 per tonne (down from Euro 850 per tonne at the conclusion of the Uruguay Round). However, virtually all imports take place under preferential tariff quota arrangements, with few imports paying the full duty.

On 2 May 2001 the European Commission announced new tariff quota arrangements designed to bring the dispute in the WTO to an end. The agreement reached was a two-phased arrangement involving a transitional tariff quota arrangement to run from July 2001 to 2006 and the establishment of a flat tariff system after 2006.

After much debate it was agreed that the licensing system should be managed on the basis of *'historical references'*. According to the Commission the first step in implementing this new arrangement involved:

- the establishment of a new definition of traditional operators (based on primary importers, that is, the importers who own or buy bananas in the country of origin and ship them to the EU);

- Eighty-three per cent of the quantities being managed on the basis of 'historical reference';

- Seventeen per cent of the quantities being managed through a 'simultaneous examination' system (this involves operators asking for certain quantities and licences being allocated on a pro rata basis determined by the total amount of licences available).

The new arrangement established three tariff quotas:

Quota A: 2,200,000 tonnes (Euro 75 duty, ACP 0);

Quota B: 353,000 tonnes (Euro 75 duty, ACP 0) increased to 453,000 tonnes (from January 2002);

Quota C: 850,000 tonnes (from January 2002 750,000 exclusively for ACP).

Significantly, the former country allocations of import licences formally ceased to have effect from 1 July 2001.

Formerly, under the Lomé Convention the European Commission was committed to granting traditional ACP suppliers a quota that matched the best ever export volumes achieved in any year up to 1991. However, during the transition period to 2006 bananas will be imported into the EU through licences issued to companies on the basis of past trade. These licences will no longer be tied to purchases from a specific country and may be used to import bananas from any of the countries covered by the licence.

Theoretically, this could allow a Windward Island company holding a valid licence to import Ivory Coast bananas. With current patterns of ownership, production and licence allocation this is unlikely to happen. However, should new patterns of ownership of the companies concerned emerge, or should new production be developed in non-traditional suppliers by companies currently holding licences, then this situation could change.

Thus, this does not mean that the more efficient ACP banana producers cannot increase their exports to the EU. In the mid-1990s Cameroon, Ivory Coast and Belize expanded their exports beyond their traditional ceilings to take up temporary shortfalls in the supplies from traditional ACP suppliers. The change in method of licensing will now ensure that all existing quotas are fully filled, regardless of the production conditions in any particular country.

The second step in the implementation of this new arrangement involved the re-allocation of 100,000 tonnes from the 'C' quota to the 'B' quota as of 1 January 2002. This has resulted in an increase in the 'B' quota to 453,000 tonnes and a decrease in the 'C' quota (now exclusively available to the ACP) to 750,000 tonnes. This effectively expands access for non-ACP suppliers, but will allow the maintenance of ACP access above the actual average level of imports in recent years.[8]

What Market Access Does the Declaration on Rice Make Provision For?

Under Declaration XXII, the 'Joint Declaration Concerning Agricultural Products Referred to in Article 1(2) (a) of Annex V', the market access arrangements for ACP rice exports are set out. This establishes two ACP rice quotas:

Declaration XXII, referred to in Article 1(2)(a) of Annex V

- a quota of 125,000 tonnes for direct husked rice exports to the EU;

- a quota of 20,000 tonnes for direct broken rice exports to the EU.

On these quotas a 65 per cent reduction in the duty charged is granted. ACP rice exported under these quotas pays only 35 per cent of the standard import duty minus Euro 4.35 per tonne for husked rice and minus Euro 3.62 per tonne for broken rice. The actual duty applied varies on a fortnightly basis depending on the level of the reference price used. The principal ACP rice exporters are Guyana (±70 per cent) and Suriname, with small volumes of rice from Madagascar also being exported to EU territories.

Looking beyond the Cotonou Agreement, exports of rice from Guyana to the EU were strongly affected by the adoption in 1996 of EU safeguard measures against rice being exported to the EU market via EU overseas countries and territories (OCTs), including Aruba, Bonaire, Curaçao, St Maarten, and the Turks and Caicos Islands). Before this date Guyana had exported up to 250,000 tonnes of rice to the EU market, with 90 per cent of it going via the OCTs, where it underwent a certain level of processing before being shipped duty free to the EU market. However, under pressure from Southern European rice producers, a 35,000 tonne quota on ACP rice exported via OCTs was introduced in 1997.

The effect of this measure on the Guyanese rice industry was dramatic, coinciding as it did with declining EU rice prices resulting in part from a partial shift from price support to direct aid in the rice sector.[9] This situation was further compounded by unusually bad weather conditions in Guyana.

The system of quotas is administered through import licences. Licences for the import of rice under the 125,000 tonne husked rice quota are issued three times a year – in January, May and September. Licences for the import of the 20,000 tonnes of broken rice are issued in January and May. Licences for the import of 35,000 tonnes of husked rice equivalent via OCTs are allocated in January. Importers are required to pay a deposit on the licences issued equivalent to Euro 120 per tonne. No single importer can import less than 100 tonnes or more than 2,080 tonnes.[10]

While no agreement could be reached on a further round of EU rice sector reform in 2000, the European Commission in its July 2002 Mid-term Review of the CAP proposed an immediate rice price reduction of 50 per cent[11] with the aim of bringing the EU rice market back into balance. While no agreement has yet been reached on this measure, such a price reduction would profoundly affect the benefits derived by ACP rice exporters from the preferences currently extended under the Cotonou Agreement. European Commission financed studies suggest an immediate reduction in EU rice prices of 34 per cent in 2004 and a 41 per cent reduction by 2009.[12]

There is also considerable concern among ACP rice suppliers over the effects of the progressive extension of duty free access to least developed country rice exporters under the EU's EBA initiative.

Declaration XXIV 'Joint Declaration on Rice'

Against this background, the Cotonou Agreement contains a commitment on support to ACP **rice** exports. In Declaration XXIV on rice, the EU commits itself to financing an integrated sector-specific programme for the development of ACP rice exports. This programme will include:

- improvement of conditions of production and enhancement of quality through assistance in the areas or research, handling, harvesting, transport and storage;

- enhancing the competitiveness of existing rice exporters;

- assisting ACP rice exporters in meeting environmental and waste management standards, and other international and EU norms;

- assistance with marketing and trade promotion;

- assistance in developing value added products.

There have, however, been complaints over the delays experienced in putting in place various rice sector programmes.[13]

The EU's decision to invoke safeguard measures with regard to rice exports via the OCTs, the consequences of internal EU processes of agricultural reform and the implementation of trade preferences in favour of least developed countries in the rice sector illustrate clearly how the value of ACP trade preferences extended under the Cotonou Agreements is intimately connected with wider agricultural and trade policy developments.

What Provisions Have Been Made for Support for ACP Rum Exporters?

Under the Lomé Convention duty free access was granted to ACP exporters for certain specified volumes of rum. However, with the elimination of EU duties on rum imports from the US, the value of the duty free access granted to ACP rum exporters has been effectively removed.

Against this background and recognising:

> ... *the importance of the rum sector for the economic and social development of several ACP countries and regions ...*

Declaration XXV, Joint Declaration on Rum

the EU has committed itself under the Cotonou Agreement to supporting a programme of measures designed to enhance the competitiveness of ACP rum exports. These measures include:

- a commitment to unrestricted duty free access for ACP rum, arak and tafia exports;

- a commitment to ensuring that ACP rum exporters are not disadvantaged or discriminated against compared to third country rum producers;

- a commitment to financing an *'integrated sector-specific programme for the development of ACP exporters of rum'*. Such a programme could include the following measures:

  - *enhancing the competitiveness of existing exporters of rum*

  - *assistance with the creation of rum marques or brands by ACP region or country*

  - *enabling marketing campaigns to be designed and implemented*

  - *assisting ACP rum producers to meet environmental and waste management standards and other norms in the international markets including the EC market*

  - *assisting the ACP rum industry to move out of bulk commodity production into higher value branded rum products.*

This programme is to be financed from unallocated EDF resources by agreement with concerned national and regional authorities. The programme is now being implemented in close collaboration with representative private sector bodies from the West Indian rum sector. The EU also commits itself to consulting ACP states on any measures it plans to take affecting the rum sector.

How are Other Agricultural Products Treated under the Cotonou Agreement?

The preferential treatment extended to a range of other ACP agricultural products is set out in Declaration XXII, the **'Joint Declaration Concerning Agricultural Products Referred to in Article 1(2) (a) of Annex V'**. The products covered include certain categories of the ones listed in the table below:

Agricultural Products in Declaration XXII

- Live animals (01)
- Meat and edible meat offal (02)
- Fish, crustaceans, molluscs and other acquatic invertebrates (03)
- Dairy products (0401–0406)
- Bird eggs (0407–0408)
- Natural honey (0409)
- Turtle eggs and others not specified (0410)
- Other animal products (05)
- Live trees and plants (06)
- Potatoes (0701)
- Tomatoes (0702)
- Onions, shallots, garlic, leeks etc – fresh and chilled (0703)
- Cabbages, cauliflowers or similar vegetables (0704)
- Lettuces – fresh and chilled (0705)
- Carrots, turnips, beetroot and similar edible roots (0706)
- Cucumber and gherkins – fresh and chilled (0707)
- Leguminous vegetables (0708)
- Other vegetables – fresh and chilled (0709)
- Vegetables uncooked or cooked by steaming or boiling (0710)
- Vegetables provisionally preserved (0711)
- Dried vegetables (0712)
- Dried leguminous vegetables (0713)
- Manioc, arrowroot and similar roots and tubers (0714)
- Coconuts, brazil and cashew nuts (0801)
- Other nuts (0802)
- Dates, figs, pineapples, avocados, guavas and mangoes (0804)
- Citrus fruit – fresh or dried (0805)
- Grapes (0806)
- Melons (0807)
- Apples, pears, quinces – fresh (0808)
- Apricots, cherries, peaches, nectarines, plums (0809)
- Strawberries, raspberries, blackberries, currants, gooseberries (0810)
- Fruit and nuts falling under 0811
- Fruit and nuts provisionally preserved (0812)
- Apricots, prunes and other dried fruit falling under 0813
- Peel of citrus and other fruit – fresh frozen or dried (0814)
- Coffee, tea and spices (09)
- Cereals (1001–1005)
- Rice (1006)
- Sorghum (1007)
- Buckwheat (1008)
- Wheat or meslin flour (1101)
- Cereal flour – excluding wheat and meslin (1102)
- Cereal, groat, meal and pellets (1103)

Agricultural Products in Declaration XXII (continued)

- Cereal grains otherwise worked (1104)
- Flour, meal flakes (1105)
- Flour of leguminous vegetables in headings 0713, 0714 and 8 (1106)
- Oil seeds (1208–1211)
- Locust beans and other products falling under 1212
- Swedes, fodder roots and other product falling under 1214
- Lacs, gums resins and other vegetable sap (13)
- Lard and pig and poultry fat rendered (1501)
- Fats of bovine animals falling under 1502–1508
- Palm oil (1511)
- Sunflower seed and cotton seed and other oils falling under 1512–1516
- Margarine (1517)
- Other animal and vegetable fats falling under 1518
- Glycerine (1520)
- Vegetable and bees wax (1521)
- Sausages (1601)
- Prepared and preserved meats (1602)
- Meat and fish extracts and juices (1603)
- Prepared or preserved fish (1604–1605)
- Sugars and sugar confectionery (17)
- Molasses (1703)
- Sugar confectionery not containing cocoa (1704)
- Cocoa and cocoa preparations falling under 1801–1805
- Chocolate and other food preparations containing cocoa falling under 1806
- Preparations of cereals, flour, starch and milk pastries (1901)
- Pasta (1902)
- Tapioca (1903)
- Food preparations falling under 1804
- Breads, biscuits, cakes, etc. falling under 1905
- Preparations of vegetables, fruit and nuts and other products falling under 2001
- Prepared and preserved tomatoes (2002)
- Mushrooms, etc. falling under 2003
- Other preserved vegetables falling under 2004
- Other prepared and preserved vegetables falling under 2005
- Fruit and nuts falling under 2006
- Jams, jellies, etc. falling under 2007
- Fruits and nuts and other products falling under 2008
- Fruit juices falling under 2009
- Miscellaneous edible products falling under 21
- Beverages and spirits falling under 22
- Residues and waste for animal fodder falling under 23
- Tobacco (24)

Agricultural Products in Declaration XXII (continued)

- Organic chemicals (29)
- Essential oils falling under 33
- Casein, casseinate products falling under 3501
- Whey proteins falling under 3502
- Gelatine falling under 3503
- Pephones and other derivatives falling under 3504
- Dextrons and other modified starches falling under 3505
- Miscellaneous chemical products falling under 38
- Silk (50)
- Cotton (52)

In the agricultural sector two types of import duty may be applied by the EU: **ad valorem duties** and **special duties**. While products may enjoy a 100 per cent reduction in the ad valorem duty, they may still be subjected to variable special duties.

Against this background, certain of these products may enjoy:

- full duty free access (full exception from ad valorem duties and special duties);

- quota restricted ad valorem duty free and special duty free access;

- quota restricted ad valorem duty free access and a partial reduction in the special duty;

- quota restricted reductions in the ad valorem and special duties;

- seasonal quota restricted ad valorem and special duty free access;

Declaration XXII,
Joint Declaration
on Agricultural
Products

- seasonal quota restricted ad valorem and special duty reductions (see Annex 16) which reproduces the tariff preferences granted to the agricultural products listed under 'Declaration XXII').

If agricultural products are not explicitly referred to in the list contained in Declaration XXII then no preferential access is extended.

Many of the products enjoying preferential access under the terms of Declaration XXII still need to comply with EU sanitary and phytosanitary standards, which can effectively prevent the export of certain products. The detailed issue of how SPS standards are applied to imports from ACP countries is not dealt with in the Cotonou Agreement but is subject to internal EU regulations.

While duty free access is granted for fisheries products, detailed rules of origin over what constitutes an ACP 'originating' fisheries product are laid down in the Agreement and this can limit the duty free access granted to fish caught in the Exclusive Economic Zones of ACP countries (see Annex 17).

What are Rules of Origin?

Rules of origin define what goods can and cannot be given duty free access to the EU market under any preferential trade arrangement. The aim of rules of origin is to prevent third countries that do not enjoy preferential access from simply routing products to the EU market through preferred trading partners. Rules of origin generally specify what proportion of the final product must have been produced in the country (or, in the case of the ACP, countries) to which the trade preferences have been extended. These local content requirements vary from sector to sector and from product to product, particularly for those products considered sensitive by the EU.

An important aspect of rules of origin is the administrative requirements they impose on exporters. If the paperwork dealing with rules of origin questions accompanying a consignment of exports to the EU is not entirely in order, this can result in the consignment being held up or being subjected to the standard MFN import duties.

What Rules of Origin Apply under the Cotonou Agreement?

The specific definition of what constitutes an originating product under the Cotonou Agreement can be found in **Annex V, Protocol 1** of the Agreement.

Annex V, Protocol 1

A product is considered 'originating' if it is **'wholly' obtained in an ACP country** or it has **undergone one of the various stages of processing** which grants the status of originating product on 'non-wholly obtained products'. 'Wholly obtained products' are defined as:

(a) mineral products extracted from their soil or from the sea bed;

(b) vegetable products harvested there;

(c) live animals born and raised there;

(d) products from live animals raised there;

(e) products obtained by hunting or fishing conducted there;

(f) products of sea fishing and other products taken from the sea outside the territorial waters by their vessels;[14]

(g) products made aboard their factory ships exclusively from originating fish products;

(h) used articles collected there fit only for the recovery of raw materials, including used tyres only for retreading or for use as waste;

(i) waste and scrap resulting from manufacturing operations conducted there;

(j) products extracted from marine soil or subsoil outside their territorial waters provided that they have sole rights to work that soil or subsoil;

(k) goods produced there exclusively from the products set down as wholly originating.

Annex V, Protocol 1, Title II, Article 4

The detailed rules on processing which must take place in an ACP country in order for materials that are not wholly obtained there to gain originating status are set out in **Annex II to Protocol 1**, attached to Annex V of the Agreement (see Annex 18). 'Non-originating materials' can be used in a manufacturing process without losing 'originating' status if:

(a) their total value does not exceed 15 per cent of the ex works price of the product;

(b) any of the percentages given in the list for the maximum value of non-originating materials are not exceeded.

Operations considered insufficient to qualify non-originating materials for originating status include:

Article 5

- simple preservation processes linked to transport or storage;
- simple sifting, screening, cleaning, sorting, matching, painting or cutting up processes;
- simple changes in packaging;
- simple labelling exercises;
- simple mixing operations;
- simple assembly operations;
- slaughtering of animals;
- simple combinations of the above.

Article 6

Under both the Cotonou Agreement and the earlier Lomé Convention it was agreed that any good produced in one ACP country could be counted as if it were produced in any ACP country in terms of its 'originating' status. This is known as **'cumulation'** and is designed to encourage trade and economic co-operation between ACP countries which have different resource endowments.

What Do the Regional Cumulation Provisions Allow?

Since 1995 ACP countries have been allowed to make more extensive use of products originating in neighbouring non-ACP developing countries (where ACP and non-ACP countries form part of a 'coherent geographical entity'), without losing the 'originating' status which allows the product to benefit from duty free access under the ACP-EU agreement. This is known as **regional cumulation**. This provision was extended and elaborated in more detail under the Cotonou Agreement. Under the Agreement the expression 'neighbouring developing country belonging to a coherent geographical entity' was defined as including:

- **Africa:**   Algeria, Egypt, Libya, Morocco, Tunisia

- **Caribbean:**   Colombia, Costa Rica, Cuba, El Salvador, Guatemala, Honduras, Nicaragua, Panama, Venezuela

- **Pacific:**   Nauru

The provisions dealing with regional cumulation can be found in various annexes to Protocol 1 to Annex V. These various annexes specify both where regional cumulation rules can apply and the instances where regional cumulation is not allowed.

Annex IX to Protocol 1	provides a list of the processing or working which must be carried out in ACP countries in the sphere of textiles and textile articles for a product originating in a neighbouring non-ACP country to be granted 'originating' status (see Annex 19).
Annex X to Protocol 1	sets out the textile products excluded from the regional cumulation procedures (see Annex 20).
Annexes XI, XII, XIII	deal with the specific regional cumulation and arrangements for XIV to Protocol 1 South Africa, which is a member of the ACP Group.

Detailed administrative procedures for the invocation of regional cumulation arrangements exist. These are set out in Annex I, Protocol 1, Article 20 and closely follow the suppliers' declarations required in support of an EUR 1 certificate. Decisions on the application of the rules on regional cumulation are made by the ACP-EU Customs Co-operation Committee.

What Specific Rules of Origin are Applied to Cumulation Involving South Africa

The basic provisions on regional cumulation with South Africa are set out in Annex I to Protocol 1, Title II, Article 6.3–6.10. Article 6.3 states:

Annex I to
Protocol 1,
Title II,
Article 6.3

... materials originating in South Africa shall be considered as originating in the ACP states when incorporated into a product obtained there.

This will only continue to be the case when:

... the value added there exceeds the value of the materials used originating in South Africa.

However, these provisions only apply to the products listed in Annexes XI and XII under the conditions stipulated.

Annex XI to
Protocol 1,

Annex XI to Protocol 1 sets out the products for which cumulation is allowed with South Africa after three years of implementation of the EU-South Africa Trade, Development and Co-operation Agreement (see Annex 21). Annex XII to Protocol 1 sets out the products for which cumulation is allowed with South Africa after six years of implementation of the EU-South Africa Trade, Development and Co-operation Agreement (see Annex 22). These provisions are linked to the timetable for the implementation of the EU-South Africa Trade, Development and Co-operation Agreement.

Annex XIII to
Protocol 1,

Annex XIII to Protocol 1 sets out the products for which cumulation with South Africa is not allowed. This includes a wide range of products from motor vehicles and parts through a wide variety of agricultural and processed agricultural products to certain processed mineral products (see Annex 23).

Annex XIV to
Protocol 1,

Annex XIV to Protocol 1 sets out the fisheries products to which cumulation provisions with South Africa do not apply at the moment. Nominally these fisheries products will only be included in the cumulation provisions where the tariffs on these products have been eliminated within the framework of the EU-South Africa Trade Development and Co-operation Agreement. However, these provisions on fisheries products are linked to the development of EU-South Africa fisheries sector relations, specifically the progress made in the conclusion of an EU-South Africa fisheries access agreement (see Annex 24).

To invoke these regional cumulation provisions ACP states must request the export of products under these provisions. The ACP-EU Committee of Ambassadors then decides on the request on the basis of a report drawn up by the ACP-EU Customs Co-operation Committee.

Special provision is made for the fellow members of the Southern African

Customs Union – Botswana, Lesotho, Namibia and Swaziland. Article 6.9 states:

> *Without prejudice to paragraphs 5 and 7, working and processing carried out in South Africa shall be considered as having been carried out in another member state of the South African Customs Union (SACU) when the materials undergo subsequent working or processing in that other member state of SACU.*

Annex V,
Protocol 1,
Title II,
Article 6.9

The 'without prejudice provisions' mean that this only applies to the products listed in Annex XI and Annex XII after three and six years respectively.

What Do the Derogation Provisions Allow?

The derogation provisions of the rules of origin allow exceptions to the general rules of origin. This allows non-originating products to be used to a greater degree than the normal rules of origin would allow, without losing the benefits of the trade preferences extended under the Cotonou Agreement.

Derogations from the rules of origin have to be specifically requested through the ACP group. All derogation requests are subject to assessment and approval by the ACP-EU Customs Co-operation Committee. Derogation requests may be granted where:

> *... the development of existing industries or the creation of new industries justifies them.*

Title V
Article 38.1

Once granted, each derogation request is generally valid for five years and may be renewed, provided that three months before the end of the derogation period proof is provided that the producer is still unable to meet the normal rules of origin requirements.

How is a Derogation Obtained?

A derogation is obtained by submitting a justified request to the ACP-EU Customs Co-operation Committee (see Annex 25). The request should include information on:

- a description of the finished product;

Article 38.2

- the nature and quantity of the materials originating in a third country;

- the nature and quantity of materials originating in ACP states, the Community or the OCT which have been processed there;

- manufacturing processes;

- value added;

- number of employees in the enterprise concerned;

- anticipated volume of exports to the Community;

- other possible sources of supply for raw materials;

- reasons for the duration requested in the light of efforts made to find new sources of supply;

- other pertinent observations.

The Cotonou Agreement stipulates that once a request has been formally submitted in the right format, the Customs Co-operation Committee should:

Annex V,
Protocol 1,
Title V,
Article 38.1

... respond positively to all the ACP requests which are duly justified in conformity with this Article and which cannot cause serious injury to an established Community industry.

In examining a derogation request the Customs Co-operation Committee should take into account:

Article 38.3

- *the level of development or the geographical situation of the ACP State or States concerned;*

- *cases where the application of the existing rules of origin would significantly affect the ability of an existing industry in an ACP State to continue its exports to the Community, with particular reference to cases where this could lead to cessation of its activities;*

- *specific cases where it can be clearly demonstrated that significant investment in an industry could be deterred by the rules of origin and where a derogation favouring the realisation of the investment programme would enable these rules to be satisfied by stages.*

Article 38.5

In the case of least developed countries the Customs Co-operation Committee should also take into account the socio-economic impact of the decisions, particularly on employment and the length of time requested.

According to the provisions of the Agreement derogations should be granted where:

Article 38.7

the value added to the non-originating products used in the ACP State or States concerned is at least 45% of the value of the finished product, provided that the derogation is not such as to cause serious injury to an economic sector of the Community or of one or more Member States.

Specific provision is made for derogations related to canned tuna and tuna loins. These provisions stipulate that derogations will only be granted within an annual quota of 8,000 tonnes of canned tuna and 2,000 tonnes of tuna loins. However, within these quotas derogations will be granted automatically.

Annex V, Protocol 1, Title V, Article 38.8

A decision on a derogation request needs to be made by the Customs Co-operation Committee not later than 75 working days after the request is received by the EC co-Chairman of the Customs Co-operation Committee. If an ACP state is not informed of the decision within this timeframe the request is deemed to be accepted.[54]

Article 38.9

What Specific Rules of Origin are Applied to ACP Fisheries Products?

For fisheries products to qualify as originating from an ACP state and hence qualify for duty free access to the EU market, fish products must be caught by *'their vessels'*. The term 'their vessels' is held to apply to:

Title II, Article 3.1(f)

- vessels registered or recorded in an EC member state, in an ACP state or in an OCT;

- vessels which sail under the flag of an EC member state, an ACP state or an OCT;

- vessels which are

  - owned at least 50 per cent by EC, ACP or OCT nationals or a company with its head offices in an EC, ACP or OCT country and the Chairman and the majority of the Board members of which are EC, ACP or OCT nationals;

    Article 3.2

  - at least 50 per cent crewed by EC, ACP or OCT nationals.

Vessels which are chartered or leased by ACP states may also be granted the status 'their vessel' where:

- the EU was offered a fisheries agreement but did not accept it;

  Article 3.3

- at least 50 per cent of the crew are ACP, EU or OCT nationals;

- the charter or lease contract has been accepted by the Customs Co-operation Committee as providing adequate opportunities for developing an ACP state's own fishing capacity.

If fish are not caught on vessels deemed to be 'their vessels' then they are not eligible for the trade preferences extended to fisheries products under the terms of the Agreement.

Declaration XXXIX, 'ACP Declaration relating to Protocol 1 of Annex V on the origin of fishery products'

These rules of origin for fisheries products have been a source of contention in ACP-EU fisheries relations. This is reflected in the ACP Declaration on the rules of origin for fisheries products attached to the Cotonou Agreement, which calls for all catches effected in the exclusive economic zones of ACP states and obligatorily landed in ACP ports for processing to be granted originating status.

What Administrative Steps Should Be Followed to Ensure That Goods are Allowed Preferential Access to the EU Market under the Terms of the Cotonou Agreement?

All shipments from ACP countries need to be accompanied by either:

- a movement certificate (EUR 1) (see Annex 26); or

- a declaration by the exporter (referred to as an 'invoice declaration') (see Annex 27).

Annex II to Protocol 1

These documents declare that the goods being exported to the EU meet the requirements necessary for them to qualify for the trade preferences extended under the Cotonou Agreement (e.g. they are produced from wholly 'originating' materials or that non-originating raw materials have undergone sufficient processing in an ACP state to qualify for originating status under the terms set out in Annex II to Protocol 1 attached to Annex V).

The **invoice declaration** applies to small value consignments of products that originate in ACP states (below Euro 6,000). An 'invoice declaration' has to be made out by the exporter and follow a specimen text, which can be found annexed to this *User's Guide* (Annex 27). The 'invoice declaration' must bear the original signature of the exporter. For small consignments which are shipped regularly, authorisation may be given by the ACP authorities to 'approved exporters' to make out the 'invoice declaration', subject to monitoring by the customs authorities of the ACP state concerned. The EUR 1 document is used for larger consignments. In both instances the ACP states' customs authorities remain ultimately responsible for ensuring compliance with the rules of origin set out under the Agreement and for ensuring that all 'movement certificates' and 'invoice declarations' are authentic.

Both the **EUR 1** and the 'invoice declaration' include a commitment on the part of the exporter to submit, where necessary, supporting documentation should the appropriate authorities request it. This supporting documentation includes suppliers' declarations that inputs meet the criteria required for originating status or suppliers' declarations that the inputs do not qualify for originating status.

This documentation must be accompanied by an 'Information Certificate' (see Annex 28), which *de facto* constitutes an endorsement by the customs department of the ACP government concerned that the declaration certificates are accurate. The information certificate is intended to facilitate the issuing of the EUR 1 movement certificate.

All these certification documents must be laid out in a specified format and be printed on a specified type of paper by an approved printer.

What is a EUR 1 Movement Certificate?

The EUR 1 movement certificate is the main administrative form which must accompany major consignments of ACP exports to the EU wishing to benefit from the trade preferences extended under the Cotonou Agreement. The EUR 1 takes a specific format and must be printed by an approved printer, with the name and address of the printer or a recognised printer's mark appearing on the document. Each certificate must bear a serial number, which allows it to be individually identified.

A movement certificate must include:

- the name and address of the exporter;
- where different, the name of the consignee;
- the date of issue;
- a description of the goods, the number and type of packing;
- the mass of the product;
- a declaration by the exporter that the goods meet the conditions required for the issue of a certificate;
- an endorsement by the customs service of the exporting country;
- a verification certification.

It may also include transport details and invoices.

A EUR 1 movement certificate is obtained by applying to the customs department of the ACP state of origin on a specified application form (see Annex 29). Both the application for a EUR 1 movement certificate and the information certificate must be filled in by the exporter or the exporter's authorised representative. The EUR 1 movement certificate has to be carefully filled in. No erasures or crossing out is allowed and no gaps should be left in the form. This is particularly the case for the section dealing with the description of the goods, where once all details have been given, a horizontal line must be drawn through the remaining empty space.

What is the Safeguard Clause?

Annex V,
Articles 8–11

Annex V,
Protocol 2

The basic safeguard clause is set out in Article 8 of Annex V of the Cotonou Agreement and is elaborated in the succeeding articles (Articles 9, 10 and 11) and Protocol 2 to Annex V. The safeguard clause allows the EU to take appropriate measures against ACP exports where imports into the EU:

Annex V,
Article 8.1

- cause or threaten to cause serious injury to EU producers of the same or directly competing products;

- threaten serious disturbances in any sector of the economy;

- threaten to create difficulties which could bring about serious deterioration in the economic situation of a region of the EU.

Article 8.3

Article 8.4

These safeguard measures, however, should be restricted to those measures which least disturb ACP exports. In invoking the safeguard clause, particular attention should be paid to the interests of the least developed, landlocked and island ACP states.

Article 9.1

The provisions of Article 9 call for *'prior consultations'* before the invocation of the safeguard clause, with ACP states having a right to detailed information from the EU demonstrating the extent to which imports from an ACP state have caused the problems giving rise to the invocation of the safeguard clause.

These consultations should give rise to jointly agreed measures. However, the EU retains the right to take immediate decisions where this is deemed necessary.

Article 9 also makes provision for regular consultations and statistical surveillance in areas where the safeguard clause has been invoked. The detailed provisions for the invocation of the safeguard clause are set out in Protocol 2 to Annex V. This protocol makes provision for advanced consultations, the aim of which is:

Article 3

... to limit, in the case of sensitive products, the risks of sudden or unforeseen recourse to safeguard measures.

These provisions are intended to allow a close monitoring of trends in sensitive sectors in order to:

... detect problems which could arise.

The provisions of Protocol 2 effectively allow the EU to encourage voluntary restraint in sensitive areas, thereby reducing the actual use of formal safeguard measures.

What Commitments on Trade in Services are Entered into through the Cotonou Agreement?

The provisions on trade in services are dealt with in Part 3, Title II, Chapter 4, Articles 41–43. The general provisions reaffirm the commitments entered into under the General Agreement on Trade in Services (GATS). The provisions of the Agreement furthermore commit the EU and the ACP to liberalising services in accordance with the provisions of the GATS *'under the economic partnership agreements'*.

Part 3, Title II, Chapter 4, Article 41.4

The Agreement also commits the EU to assist ACP countries in developing their service sectors, particularly in the fields of:

- tourism;
- financial services;
- telecommunications;
- culture;
- construction and related engineering services.

With regard to maritime services, the provisions of the Agreement commit the EU and ACP to extend national treatment to shipping operators:

> *... with respect to access to ports, the use of infrastructure and auxiliary maritime services of those ports, as well as related fees and charges, customs facilities and assignment of berths and facilities for loading and unloading.*

Article 42.3

These provisions furthermore commit the EU to supporting:

> *... ACP States' efforts to develop and promote cost-effective and efficient maritime transport services in the ACP States with a view to increasing the participation of ACP operators in international shipping services.*

Article 42.4

Article 43 of the Agreement recognises the important role which information and communication technology can play in:

> *... the successful integration of ACP countries into the world economy.*

Article 43.1

It reaffirms the commitments made under multilateral agreements, particularly the Protocol on Basic Telecommunications attached to the GATS. It commits the EU to take measures that will:

> *... enable inhabitants of ACP countries easy access to information and communication technologies through, among other, the following measures:*

Part 3, Title II,
Chapter 4,
Article 43.4

- *the development and encouragement of the use of affordable renewable energy resources;*

- *the development and deployment of more extensive low-cost wireless networks.*

There is also a commitment to co-operation in ensuring:

Article 43.5

... greater complementarity and harmonisation of communication systems, at national, regional and international level and their adaptation of new technologies.

Overall, these commitments made on **services** are seen by the European Commission as providing the basis for negotiations leading to a comprehensive liberalisation of trade in services under any successor trade agreement.

What Commitments in Trade-related Areas are Entered into through the Cotonou Agreement?

The Agreement contains provisions on a range of trade-related areas, with the EU committing itself to assisting ACP countries in strengthening their regulatory frameworks with regard to:

- competition policy;

- intellectual property rights;

- standardisation and certification;

- sanitary and phytosanitary standards;

- trade and environmental issues;

- labour standards;

- consumer policy.

The provisions on **competition policy** embody a recognition of the importance of competition policy and a commitment to implementing national and regional rules and policies to control and prohibit:

Chapter 5,
Article 45.2

... agreements between undertakings, decisions by associations of undertakings and concerted practices between undertakings which have as their object or effect the prevention, restriction or distortion of competition ...

and prevent abuse of a dominant market position. A commitment is also made to co-operate in formulating competition policies and drafting competition legislation.

The provisions on **intellectual property rights** embody a recognition of the importance of affording protection to intellectual property and

> *... other rights covered by TRIPS including protection of geographical indications.*

Chapter 5, Article 46.1

The importance of adhering to the WTO TRIPS agreement and the Convention on Biological Diversity and acceding to all relevant international conventions is emphasised.

A commitment to considering the conclusion of agreements on the protection of trademarks and geographical indications is included in the Agreement's provisions on intellectual property rights. A commitment to strengthening co-operation in intellectual property rights is also included.

Article 46

The provisions on **standards and certification** embody commitments on closer co-operation aimed at establishing *'compatible systems'*. A provision is also made on consideration to be given to negotiating mutual recognition agreements.

Article 47

The provisions on **sanitary and phytosanitary measures** recognises the right to protect human, animal and plant health through such measures so long as the measures taken are not discriminatory and are not a form of disguised trade restriction. The commitments made under the WTO SPS agreement are reaffirmed and a commitment is made to achieve stronger co-ordination and consultation.

Article 48

The provisions on **trade and environment** reaffirm the commitment to promoting the development of international trade in ways that are sustainable and in accordance with international conventions. The provisions recognise, however, that the ACP may have special requirements which need to be taken into account in designing and implementing measures. A commitment to strengthening co-operation is also included in these provisions.

Article 49

The provisions on **trade and labour standards** reaffirm the commitment to internationally recognised core labour standards. A commitment to enhanced co-operation is also contained in these provisions.

Article 50

The provisions on **consumer policy and protection of consumer health** commit the EU and the ACP to closer co-operation in a multiplicity of areas specified in the text.

Article 51

Overall, these commitments are now being interpreted by the European Commission as providing the basis for negotiation of a comprehensive set of agreements on trade-related areas, including the liberalisation of public procurement, which is not mentioned in the Agreement.

3.3 Future ACP-EU Trade Arrangements

This section looks at the commitments entered into in the text of the Cotonou Agreement with regard to the establishment of ACP-EU trade arrangements beyond 2008. This section examines:

- the different views on the experience of ACP-EU trade relations to date;

- what the Agreement says on future ACP-EU trade relations;

- the commitments entered into with regard to Economic Partnership Agreements (EPAs);

- the commitments made on alternative trade arrangements;

- the treatment to be accorded to least developed countries;

- the commitments made with regard to matching the requirements of EPAs to the level of development of individual ACP countries;

- the nature of the relationship between WTO rules and the negotiation of future ACP-EU trade arrangements.

What Has Been the Experience of Non-Reciprocal ACP Trade Preferences?

There is considerable disagreement over the experience of ACP-EU trade relations over the past 27 years. The European Commission believes that the past system of non-reciprocal trade preferences extended to ACP countries has manifestly failed to deliver economic and social development. It points out how between 1976 and 1992 the ACP's share of imports into the EU fell from 6.7 to 3.7 per cent. While **ACP** exports to the EU grew on average at **2 per cent per annum** over the period, exports from **Mediterranean and Latin American** countries grew at an average of **6 per cent per annum**, while exports from **Asian** developing countries grew at an average of **12 per cent**

per annum. As a result of these divergent export growth rates, by 1992 Asian countries had replaced the ACP as the main developing country exporters to the EU. With these trends having continued throughout the 1990s, this appears to provide a strong case for arguing that Lomé trade preferences failed to promote strong growth in ACP exports and that therefore a new approach is needed.

However, as two respected ACP Parliamentarians[15] have recently pointed out, this overall picture of ACP-EU trade performance gives a very distorted view of the performance of individual ACP economies in those areas where trade preferences have provided real margins of preference over other developing country suppliers. Disaggregating the trade data they point out that:

> *Some 26 ACP countries have enjoyed higher export growth to the EU than the average for Mediterranean and Latin American developing countries. Some 8 ACP countries have enjoyed higher export growth to the EU than the average for Asian developing countries.*[16]

Looking at the trade performance of the ACP in those products where significant margins of preference have been extended under the earlier Lomé Conventions, they point out that:

> *While ACP exports to the EU as a whole increased in volume terms between 1988 and 1997 by only **3.6%** compared to **76%** for non-ACP developing countries, in those products where the trade preferences provided margins of preference greater than 3%, the expansion in exports in volume terms was **61.9%** – an export performance **17 times better than the general export performance**.*[17]

Looking at the performance of Southern African ACP economies they point out that:

> *... whereas overall SADC exports to the EU in volume terms have declined by 5.4%, in those areas where margins of preference over GSP beneficiaries were greater than 3%, **SADC exports to the EU have increased by 83.6%**. This suggests that, despite the difficult circumstances faced by Southern Africa in the past decades, trade preferences have **helped certain sectors of SADC economies to buck the generally poor trend in overall export performance**. Indeed, in those areas where trade preferences are most significant, export growth to the EU has exceeded the average for non-ACP developing countries.*[18]

Overall, on this evidence the authors suggest that rather than ACP trade preferences having failed:

> *... trade preferences played an important role in slowing down the marginalisation of ACP economies within the world economy.*[19]

The authors go on to suggest that the Commission's analysis of the trade performance of ACP economies has singularly failed to take into account two important factors, namely that:

- *the Lomé trade preferences provided the ACP countries with either zero or very limited preference over their major competitors for the greater part (by value around 64%) of their exports;*

- *ACP exports are more heavily concentrated on poor-performing commodities than those of developing countries as a whole.*[20]

The authors suggest that the debate around the effectiveness of ACP trade preferences is far more complicated than the European Commission approach implies and call for these complexities to be:

> *... carefully considered and taken into account in the formulation of any future trade arrangements to succeed the current non-reciprocal Cotonou trade preferences.*[21]

What Does the Cotonou Agreement Say on Future ACP-EU Trade Relations?

Under the Cotonou Agreement it has been agreed that where appropriate during the period when the transitional trade arrangements are in place (up to 2008), negotiations will commence on the establishment of reciprocal preferential trade arrangements. Specifically it has been agreed that **Economic Partnership Agreements** will be negotiated with those:

Part 3, Title II,
Chapter 2,
Article 37.5

> *... ACP countries which consider themselves in a position to do so, at the level they consider appropriate and in accordance with the procedures agreed by the ACP Group, taking into account regional integration process within the ACP.*

Article 37.7

It has furthermore been agreed that:

> *... negotiations of the Economic Partnership Agreements shall aim notably at establishing the timetable for the progressive removal of barriers to trade between the parties, in accordance with the relevant WTO rules ...*

and that such agreements will lead to the conclusion of:

... new WTO compatible trading arrangements, removing progressively barriers to trade between them and enhancing co-operation in all areas relevant to trade.

Part 3, Title II, Chapter 2, Article 36.1

More specifically, the new agreement stipulates that:

Formal negotiations of the new trading arrangements shall start in September 2002 and the new trading arrangements shall enter into force by 1 January 2008, unless earlier dates are agreed between the Parties.

Article 37.1

However, it is also stipulated that:

... the period up to the start of the formal negotiations of the new trading arrangements shall be actively used to make initial preparations for these negotiations.

Article 37.2

and that furthermore:

... all the necessary measures shall be taken so as to ensure that the negotiations are successfully concluded within the preparatory period.

What Commitments Have Been Made on the Negotiation of Economic Partnership Agreements?

It has been agreed that **Economic Partnership Agreements** will be negotiated with those:

... ACP countries which consider themselves in a position to do so, at the level they consider appropriate and in accordance with the procedures agreed by the ACP Group, taking into account regional integration process within the ACP.

Article 37.5

In this context it was agreed that:

The Parties will regularly review the progress of the preparations and negotiations and, will in 2006 carry out a formal and comprehensive review of the arrangements planned for all countries.

Article 37.4

It is furthermore stipulated that this review is intended to:

... ensure that no further time is needed for preparations or negotiations.

In the text of the Agreement it is implicitly recognised that the introduction of reciprocal trade preferences with the EU will pose a major competitive challenge to producers in ACP countries. It is therefore proposed that:

Part 3, Title II,
Chapter 2,
Article 37.3

The preparatory period shall also be used for capacity-building in the public and private sectors of ACP countries, including measures to enhance competitiveness, for strengthening of regional organisations and for support to regional trade integration initiatives, where appropriate with assistance to budgetary adjustment and fiscal reform, as well as for infrastructure upgrading and development, and for investment promotion.

The proposal to use the preparatory period to assist budgetary adjustment and fiscal reform is a particularly significant commitment. In many ACP countries import duties (given the relative ease and cheapness of collection) constitute an important source of government revenue. With duties imposed on imports from the EU constituting a major part of total customs revenues, eliminating these duties (as opposed to reducing them) is likely to have profound implications for government revenues, requiring substantial fiscal reform. This lends particular significance to this provision of the Agreement.

What Commitments Have Been Made on Alternative Trade Arrangements?

Provision is made under the Cotonou Agreement for assessing in 2004 the situation of non-least developed countries that decide that they are not in a position to enter into Economic Partnership Agreements and for examining:

Article 37.6

... all alternative possibilities, in order to provide these countries with a new framework for trade which is equivalent to their existing situation and in conformity with WTO rules.

However, no provision is made in the EU negotiating directives for alternative trade arrangements which, under the terms of the Agreement, remain an option for individual ACP countries. There is concern that all ACP countries should be provided with a non-punitive[22] alternative to EPAs in developing their future trade relationship with the EU, so that ACP countries have a genuine choice in their options for future trade relations with the EU.

How are Least Developed Countries to be Treated in the Development of Future Trade Arrangements with the EU?

In the case of least developed countries, under the terms of the Cotonou Agreement, the EU committed itself to starting in 2000:

... a process which by the end of multilateral trade negotiations and at the latest 2005 will allow duty free access for essentially all products from all LDC.

Part 3, Title II, Chapter 2, Article 37.9

This, it is maintained, will build:

... on the level of the existing trade provisions of the fourth ACP-EC Convention and which will simplify and review the rules of origin, including cumulation provisions, that apply to their exports.

Article 37.9

This objective has been largely achieved with reference to the abolition of tariffs and measures having equivalent effect by the approval in 2001 of the European Commission's 'Everything But Arms' Initiative in favour of least developed countries. The EBA Initiative grants full duty free access for all originating LDC products except **arms**, **munitions** and, for a transitional period, **sugar**, **bananas** and **rice**, for which quota restricted duty free access will be allowed during a transitional period. However, with regard to rules of origin questions and, in particular, cumulation arrangements between non-LDC ACP countries and ACP LDCs wishing to export under the terms of the EBA, no progress has yet been made.

The treatment to be accorded to least developed countries in the development of future trade arrangements with the EU thus appears straightforward enough, recognising as it does the right which least developed countries have under the WTO agreement to 'special and differential treatment'.

However, the EU has subsequently made it clear that least developed countries which form part of regional groupings **will be expected to carry all the same obligations with regard to the implementation of economic partnership agreements as are negotiated regionally by the region as a whole**.

The Commission has recognised that this could entail extra adjustment costs for least developed countries and so has committed itself to providing additional aid from EDF funds to help with the adjustment costs which may arise. Given that all regional groupings in the ACP to varying degrees consist of a mixture of non-least developed and least developed countries with, in most regions, the least developed countries forming the majority, this elaboration of the EU's position carries important implications for least developed ACP countries, in terms of the future basis for their trade relations with the EU.

What Commitments Have Been Made on Matching EPAs to the Levels of Development of ACP Countries?

For those ACP countries who consider **Economic Partnership Agreements** appropriate, it is held that the process of negotiations:

Part 3, Title II,
Chapter 2,
Article 37.7

... shall take account of the level of development and the socio-economic impact of trade measures on ACP countries, and their capacity to adapt and adjust their economies to the liberalisation process.

Against this background it is held that the negotiations will therefore be:

... as flexible as possible in establishing the duration of a sufficient transitional period for the final product coverage, taking into account sensitive sectors, and the degree of asymmetry in terms of timetables for tariff dismantlement.

However, this flexibility is qualified by the stipulation that it must remain:

... in conformity with WTO rules then prevailing.

It is far from clear how the commitment to taking into account the different levels of development of ACP countries is to be translated into practice in a context where, in most ACP regions, least developed countries form the majority of the countries involved in regional integration initiatives. The European Commission's approach envisages allowing for a slower pace of implementation of tariff reduction commitments in the least developed countries. This, however, could simply give rise to increased smuggling and serve to undermine the domestic trade policy regime of least developed countries.

What is the Nature of the Relationship between WTO Rules and the Development of Future ACP-EU Trade Relations?

Part 3, Title II,
Chapter 1,
Article 34

The limited scope for accommodating the different levels of development of ACP countries within the same region is in large part attributable to the requirement to ensure compliance with WTO rules. While both the EU and the ACP are agreed on the need to ensure compliance with WTO rules, there are differences in interpreting what this means. Currently, the European Commission considers that this commitment means ensuring that any future ACP-EU trade agreement complies with the provisions of Article XXIV, the WTO provision dealing with the establishment of free trade areas. A number of ACP governments, however, would like to see a joint ACP-EU initiative to revise WTO rules to accommodate the specificities of reciprocal preferential trade arrangements between non-contiguous developed, developing and least developed economies. This is reflected in the ACP guidelines for negotiations that call for ACP-EU co-operation in the WTO to bring about a change in rules on regional trade arrangements.

Questions have been raised over whether the EU would be willing to pursue such a joint initiative in the WTO. Davies and Mbuende have pointed out how:

> *Following the Doha WTO Ministerial meeting, the European Commission expressed the view that the Ministerial resolution in Doha allowed negotiations to start on **'clear and quite strict rules defining the conditions to be met for free trade areas and regional agreements to be WTO compatible'**. If this is the case, then it is difficult to reconcile the Development Directorate's commitment to **'defending'** flexibility in ACP-EU Economic Partnership Agreement negotiations, with the Trade Directorate's efforts to ensure that **'clear and quite strict rules'** are drawn up on what is a WTO compatible free trade area arrangement. Indeed, the EU's commitment to **'clear and strict rules'** would appear to run counter to the need for **'flexibility'** in order to accommodate within Economic Partnership Agreement negotiations the very different economic and social constraints facing ACP countries.*[23]

Notes

1   The figures are drawn from Protocol 3 'on ACP Sugar' and the attached annexes to Protocol 3 including the exchange of letters.

2   'Evaluation of the common organisation of the market in the sugar sector', Netherlands Economic Institute, September 2000.

3   The income transfer is calculated by comparing earnings derived from exports of sugar to the EU market at preferential prices with what could be earned if this sugar had been sold on the world market. This simple calculation does not take into account, however, the price-depressing effects of the EU sugar regime on world sugar markets.

4   With the strengthening of the Euro against the US dollar this trend has now been reversed. It has, however, provided Caribbean sugar exporters with an indication of the likely impact of the first stages of sugar sector reform on their economies.

5   Between October 1999 and April 2002 the dollar price of Caribbean sugar exported under the Sugar Protocol fell from 24.24 US cents per lb f.o.b. to 19.67 cents per lb f.o.b.

6   Council Regulation on the Common Organisation of the Market in the Sugar Sector, Brussels, 4.10.2000 COM (2000) 604 final.

7   The impact of any price reductions could be offset to a certain degree by a recovery in the US dollar value of the Euro.

8   Information on the banana arrangements agreed since the signing of the Cotonou Agreement is drawn from the CTA agritrade website:
http://www.agricta.org/agritrade/news.htm

9   From 1995 the EU intervention price for rice was reduced by 15 per cent over a three-year period, with direct aid payments to increasing in tandem to fully compensate EU rice farmers for the reduction in the intervention price

10 Information on the rice arrangements is drawn from the CTA agritrade website http://www.agricta.org/agritrade

11 88 per cent of the reduction would be compensated for by increased levels of direct aid payments to EU rice farmers.

12 See 'FAPRI Analysis of the European Commission's Mid Term Review Proposals', the text of which can be found on
http://europa.eu.int/comm/agriculture/publi/reports/mtrimpact/rep3-en.pdf

13 See the resolution of the ACP-EU Joint Parliamentary Assembly from 21 March 2002 (ACP-EU/3379/02/fin) on 'Stagnation in the production sectors for bananas, rice and other products'.

14 See 'What Specific Rules of Origin Are Applied to ACP Fisheries Products?' for a definition of 'their vessels'.

15 Rob Davies and Kaire Mbuende, 'Beyond the Rhetoric of Economic Partnership Agreements', Cape Town, March 2002.

16 Ibid.

17 Ibid.

18 Ibid.

19 Ibid.

20 Ibid.

21 Ibid.

22 Currently non-least developed ACP countries who declined to conclude econ-
    omic partnership agreements with the EU would face a reversion to standard
    Generalised System of Preferences trade treatment. Under the EU GSP system
    this would result in a re-imposition of import duties on a range of products on
    which ACP non-least developed countries currently enjoy duty free access under
    the trade provisions of the Cotonou Agreement.
23 Davies and Mbuende, op. cit.

Part 4

Political Relations under the Cotonou Agreement

4.1 Political Relations under the Cotonou Agreement

The political dialogue section of the *User's Guide* looks at the political underpinnings of the ACP-EU partnership arrangement. It outlines:

- the main areas covered by ACP-EU political dialogue;

- the basic principles which underpin EU-ACP co-operation;

- the provisions and commitments entered into under the 'essential element' and 'fundamental element' clauses;

- the provisions made for dealing with corruption;

- the provisions for the institutionalisation and strengthening of political dialogue;

- the commitments made on peace building, conflict prevention and conflict resolution;

- the political dialogue aspects of the move over to performance-based aid allocations;

- the commitments made on migration;

- the commitments made on consultations on issues of coherence;

- the institutional arrangement for political consultation.

What are the Main Areas Covered by ACP-EU Political Dialogue?

The major areas covered by political dialogue between the EU and the ACP relate to:

- respect for the 'essential elements';

- respect for the fundamental element and anti corruption measures;

Part 1, Title II,
Article 8.2

- general consultations to *'facilitate the establishment of agreed priorities and shared agendas'*;

- consultations on issues to be discussed in international fora;

Article 8.4

- a political dialogue on *'specific political issues of mutual concern or of general significance for the attainment of the objectives of the agreement'*, including the arms trade, excessive military expenditures, drugs, organised crime, ethnic, religious and racial discrimination;

Article 8.5

- a dialogue on *'policies to promote peace and to prevent, manage and resolve violent conflicts'* – particular attention is paid to peace-building policies, conflict prevention and resolution;

- consultations on measures which the EU might take which *'affect the interests of the ACP states, as far as this agreement's objectives are concerned'*;

Article 13

- an in-depth dialogue on the issue of migration.

What are the Basic Political Principles Which Underpin ACP-EU Co-operation?

From an ACP perspective, the foundations of the ACP-EU political relationship were laid down in the 1974 George Town Agreement, which established the ACP group. This Agreement called for the establishment of a *'partnership between equals'*, based on mutual rights and obligations. However, the nature and content of the ACP-EU political relationship has evolved considerably since the signing of the first Lomé Convention under the impetus of wider global political changes. This has led to a progressive strengthening of the mutual commitments entered into under the political dimension of the ACP-EU relationship.

The fundamental principles that currently underpin ACP-EU co-operation are set out in Article 2 of the Cotonou Agreement. These fundamental principles involve the recognition of:

- the equality of the ACP and EU partners involved in the relationship;

- the importance of local ownership of development strategies;

Part 1, Title I,
Chapter 1,
Article 2

- the sovereign right of ACP states to determine their own development strategies *'with due regard for the essential elements'*, to which both the ACP and the EU commit themselves;

- the importance of the participation of different actors in the co-operation process and *'the mainstream of political, economic and social life'*;

- the pivotal role of dialogue in the co-operation process;

- the importance of fulfilling mutual obligations entered into within the framework of the dialogue.

What are the 'Essential Elements'?

The 'essential elements' which must be respected by all parties to the co-operation relationship are set out in Article 9 of the Agreement. These elements of the relationship are seen as being an essential and integral part of efforts to promote sustainable development. They include:

Part 1, Title II, Article 9

- respect for human rights and fundamental freedoms (including social rights);

- respect for *'universally recognised'* democratic principles;

Article 9.2

- the exercise of government powers *'founded on the rule of law'*, including *'effective and accessible means of legal redress'*, *'an independent legal system guaranteeing equality before the law'* and making the exercise of powers by the executive subject to the rule of law.

What is the 'Fundamental Element'?

The promotion of good governance in the form of *'the transparent and accountable management of human, natural, economic and financial resources for the purposes of equitable and sustainable development'*, is seen as a **'fundamental element'** of the development co-operation relationship.

Article 9.3

The use of the concept 'fundamental element' represented a compromise, given ACP concerns over the difficulties of arriving at universal criteria for the assessment of governance. There were concerns on the ACP side that any definitions of good governance would necessarily have to leave considerable scope for the exercise of discretionary powers and that this could result in rather arbitrary decisions. The ACP therefore resisted inclusion of good governance as an 'essential element'. A consensus was, however, reached on a definition of 'good governance' and its establishment as a 'fundamental element'.

What Commitments are Entered into through the Essential Element and Fundamental Element Clauses?

Where either an ACP or EU state fails to respect human rights, democratic principles and the rule of law, consultations should be initiated on the meas-

**Part 6,
Article 96.2**

ures necessary to *'remedy the situation'*. If such consultations are refused or no mutually acceptable remedies can be found then *'appropriate measures may be taken'*. These appropriate measures must be taken *'in accordance with international law'* and be *'proportional to the violation'*. Suspension of a country from the application of the Cotonou Agreement is seen as a *'measure of last resort'*.

In addition to commitments on respecting human rights, fundamental freedoms, democratic principles and the rule of law and good governance, the Agreement commits ACP and EU member states to actively supporting:

**Part 1,
Title II,
Article 9.4**

... the promotion of human rights, processes of democratisation, consolidation of the rule of law and good governance.

Support for these positive measures is seen as an important subject of political dialogue. Indeed, it is maintained that the need to actively promote respect for human rights, fundamental freedoms, democratic principles and the rule of law and good governance should be reflected in the design of development strategies and the deployment of EDF assistance.

What Procedures Need to be Followed to Invoke the 'Suspension Clause'?

Where countries fail to execute the provisions of the Cotonou Agreement dealing with essential elements, provision is made for suspending the application of the Agreement in that country. The provisions dealing with these instances are popularly referred to as the 'suspension clause' (and more formally the 'non-execution clause').

The provisions dealing with the suspension of the application of the provisions of the Agreement are set out in Article 96. Under these provisions, with the exception of especially urgent cases, if a country is felt to be failing to respect human rights, democratic principles and the rule of law then the government of the country concerned should be informed of the concerns and be provided with:

**Part 6,
Article 96**

... the relevant information required for a thorough examination of the situation with a view to seeking a solution acceptable to the Parties.

The aim in the first instance is to initiate consultations at an appropriate level in order to reach agreement on mutually acceptable measures to remedy the situation causing concern. These consultations should begin not later than 15 days after the initial invitation to consultations has been issued and should not last more than 60 days.

If the consultations fail to reach an acceptable solution or if consultations have been refused then *'appropriate measures may be taken'*. These appropriate measures should be in accordance with international law and be proportional to the violation which has caused them to be invoked. The measures should, however, generally be measures which least disrupt the application of the Cotonou Agreement. The measures taken should be revoked as soon as the reasons for taking them have disappeared.

In 'cases of special urgency' appropriate measures may be taken immediately, with consultations being initiated afterwards should the party concerned request such consultations. It should be noted that the suspension of the application of the Agreement in the case of individual countries failing to respect the 'essential element' provisions is seen as a *'measure of last resort'*.

Part 6,
Article 96.2

What Provisions are Made to Deal with Corruption?

The provisions dealing with corruption are set out in Article 97 of the Agreement. This article stipulates that where the EU is a 'significant partner' in economic and sectoral programmes of policy dialogue and serious cases of corruption arise, then consultations should take place. Such consultations should take place within 21 days of the issuing of an invitation to such consultations and should last no longer than 60 days.

Where consultations fail to result in an agreement on an acceptable solution to the problem (or where consultations are refused), 'appropriate measures' can be taken. Emphasis is placed on the authorities of the state where the corruption is taking place taking the measures necessary to remedy the situation immediately. The measures taken have to be proportional to the seriousness of the situation and should be measures which least disrupt the application of the Agreement. In cases of serious corruption, once again suspension of the application of the Agreement is a measure of last resort.

Article 97.3

How Has the Cotonou Agreement Sought to Institutionalise and Reinforce Political Dialogue?

The new Agreement contains a wide range of provisions that deal directly or indirectly with the stronger political dimensions of ACP-EU co-operation. The Agreement seeks to deepen and widen the scope of dialogue by including a range of new areas, establishing more flexible and diversified institutional arrangements for dialogue and by extending the dialogue to include non-state actors.

Nominally the Agreement provides for regular, comprehensive, balanced and deep political dialogue leading to commitments on both sides. The objective of this institutionalised and reinforced dialogue is to:

Part 1,
Title II,
Article 8.2

... exchange information, foster mutual understanding, and to facilitate the establishment of agreed priorities and shared agendas, in particular by recognising existing links between the different aspects of the relations between the Parties and the various areas of co-operation.

The reinforced political dialogue is also intended to facilitate consultations between the EU and the ACP on issues arising in international fora. This provision potentially opens up scope for closer ACP-EU co-operation on issues arising in the WTO.

The primary objective of this political dialogue process is seen as being to prevent situations arising in which one Party might deem it necessary to have recourse to the 'non-execution clause', which forms an integral part of the Cotonou Agreement and which allows co-operation programmes with individual ACP countries to be suspended where **'essential element'** provisions have been violated.

Other objectives for the reinforced dialogue are:

- to facilitate agreement on co-operation priorities with a view to promoting the development objectives of ACP-EU co-operation;

- to allow the partners to assess progress on human rights, democratic principles and the rule of law, the so-called 'essential elements' of the partnership;

- to help avoid recourse to measures of last resort such as the suspension of aid;

- to address new areas with a major impact on development such as peace, conflict prevention, regulation of the arms trade and migration.

The Agreement provides for more **flexible** forms of both formal and informal dialogue. Dialogue is now to be structured according to need and the issue under consideration. This reinforced ACP-EU dialogue takes place at a number of different levels. Geographically, it can be conducted at the national, regional or pan-ACP level. Hierarchically, it can be conducted at the level of government officials or at ministerial level. Increasingly, following the 2001 initiative of the Belgian Presidency of the EU Council of Ministers, political dialogue can also be pursued at the level of civil society. In theory, the ACP-EU political partnership now rests on much more solid political foundations.

However, while the EU emphasises the virtues of this more flexible approach, the ACP fears that it will allow the EU to progressively disengage from high-level political consultations, with ACP countries being represented at ministerial level, while the EU is represented by senior Commission officials with only limited direct involvement of responsible EU Ministers.

What Commitments Have Been Made on Peace Building, Conflict Prevention and Conflict Resolution?

The provisions on peace building, conflict prevention and resolution constitute an important new element of the ACP-EU political dialogue process. It commits the EU and ACP countries to an:

> *... active, comprehensive and integrated policy of peace-building and conflict prevention and resolution.*

Part 1,
Title II,
Article 11

In broad terms these provisions commit the EU and ACP governments to pursue policies to promote peace and to prevent, manage and resolve violent conflicts. It commits all parties to take full account of the objective of peace and democratic stability in the definition of priority areas of co-operation.

Significantly, work in this area is to be based on the principle of ownership. Particular emphasis is placed on building regional, sub-regional and national capacities, and on preventing violent conflicts at an early stage by addressing their root causes in a targeted manner, using whatever instruments are available and appropriate.

The Agreement commits all parties in situations of violent conflict to take all suitable action to prevent an intensification of violence, to limit its territorial spread and to facilitate a peaceful settlement of existing disputes. Under these provisions particular attention is to be paid to ensuring that financial resources for co-operation are used in accordance with the principles and objectives of the ACP-EU partnership, and to preventing a diversion of funds for belligerent purposes.

In addition, ACP-EU political dialogue is to focus on specific political issues of mutual concern or of general significance such as:

- the arms trade;
- excessive military expenditure;
- drugs and organised crime;
- ethnic, religious or racial discrimination.

How Does the Political Dialogue Process Relate to the Performance-based Aid Allocations?

Under previous Lomé Conventions clearly defined entitlements to EU aid were established at the beginning of each five-year aid deployment cycle. This money remained allocated to the ACP country concerned regardless of its aid utilisation performance. Under the Cotonou Agreement this fixed aid entitlement, linked to a five-year programming cycle, has been abandoned in favour of 'rolling programming', where additional aid allocations are made subject to aid utilisation performance and respect for 'essential elements'. This is seen by the EU as a more efficient way of using available aid resources, since it allows the EU and the beneficiary country to regularly review and adjust their co-operation programmes and the overall budget allocated, in the light of what is actually being achieved.

This in part reflects the heightened profile of the multi-faceted 'political dialogue' process. The EU has made it clear to the ACP that aid will be made available to those that are firmly committed to helping themselves. In political terms, this means the introduction of greater 'selectivity' in the allocation of aid. Allocations are now to be based not only on **need** (i.e. objective development indicators) but also on **merit** (i.e. qualitative performance indicators). The idea is to reward countries and regions with additional resources when they perform well in implementing the objectives of the Agreement. Negative incentives, in the form of decreased aid allocations or sanctions, will be used against those countries that do not perform well in implementing the objectives of the Agreement.

Through such a performance-based partnership, the EU wants to ensure a more flexible use of resources while improving overall aid effectiveness. This innovation was not entirely new under the Cotonou Agreement. Elements of a performance-based approach had been introduced under the revised Lomé IV Agreement and have become common practice among certain EU member states. Nevertheless, the ACP found the new approach controversial. It was felt that it eroded the partnership idea and that it would result in the imposition of new conditionalities, checklists of quantifiable performance indicators and unilateral sanctions.[1] Eventually, however, both parties acknowledged that the period of 'aid entitlements' could no longer be upheld and the positive aspects of the new approach were emphasised, namely that it would ensure a movement away from externally imposed conditionalities towards locally-owned aid performance monitoring, geared towards the effective promotion of commonly shared objectives.

To date it is unclear how these new features are working out in practice since the Cotonou Agreement only legally came into force on 1 April 2003.

What Commitments Have Been Made on Migration?

Under the provisions of the Cotonou Agreement dealing with migration the EU and the ACP have committed themselves to:

- an in-depth dialogue;

- respect for international obligations and laws;

- non-discrimination between each other's nationals legally employed in each other's territories;

- extending 'rights and obligations comparable to those of their citizens';   Part 1, Title I, Article 13.2

- respecting the *'rights and dignity of individuals'* when dealing with illegal immigrants;   Article 13.5

- measures aimed at *'reducing poverty, improving living and working conditions, creating employment and developing training'*, so as to contribute to the normalisation of migratory flows;   Part 1, Title I, Article 13.4

- developing *'co-operation programmes to facilitate the access of students from ACP states to education'*.

It was furthermore agreed that:

- *each Member State of the European Union shall accept the return of and readmission of any of its nationals who are illegally present on the territory of an ACP State, at the State's request and without further formalities;*   Article 13.5

- *each of the ACP States shall accept the return of and readmission of any of its national who are illegally present on the territory of a Member State of the European Union at that member State's request and without further formalities.*

Controversially, provision was made for *'bilateral agreements governing specific obligations for the readmission and return of their nationals'* which could *'if deemed necessary'* include *'arrangements for the readmission of third country nationals or stateless persons'*.

These bilateral agreements would establish the categories of persons covered by this provision and the arrangements for the readmission of third country citizens and stateless persons. Provision is also made for the extension of assistance in the implementation of these bilateral agreements.

There were fears in the ACP that these provisions could be used to compel ACP countries to accept the 're-admission' of third country citizens who just happened to have transited through their territories en route to the EU.

What Commitments Have Been Made on Consultations on Issues of Coherence?

Part 1, Title I,
Article 12

In the light of the EU's commitment to **coherence**, the provisions of the Lomé Convention dealing with consultations where the EU is adopting policies that impinge on ACP countries' development efforts have been reformulated under the Cotonou Agreement.

Under these provisions ACP states have the right to initiate consultations with the EU in areas where it is felt that a development in EU policy will have effects on the ACP country concerned. The ACP state may then request specific changes. These provisions and procedures for dialogue could potentially prove of considerable value to the ACP.

For example, the European Commission has estimated that any reform process involving a 25 per cent reduction in the EU sugar price would result in income losses for ACP sugar exporters of Euro 250 million per annum. In this context consultations on how sugar sector reform is to be managed could prove extremely valuable.

What Institutional Arrangements Exist for Political Consultations?

Part II,
Article 15

The ACP-EU Council of Ministers represents the highest level of joint decision making within the ACP-EU partnership. It consists of ACP and EU Ministers, plus the European Commission and should meet once a year. It is responsible for the conduct of the political dialogue and sets the policy guidelines for co-operation activities. It is also the body which resolves any disputes arising from the implementation of the provisions of the Cotonou Agreement.

Under the Agreement provision is made for Ministers to delegate their role to other representatives who shall exercise all the rights accorded a ministerial representative. As the number of dialogues in which the EU is engaged has multiplied, so the level of engagement of EU Ministers in these routine consultations with ACP governments has declined.

In addition to the joint meetings, ACP Ministers meet among themselves to discuss issues of common concern and to prepare positions ahead of joint meetings.

Part II,
Article 16

The joint ACP-EU Council of Ministers may delegate powers to the joint ACP-EU **Committee of Ambassadors**, which consists of each ACP state's Head of Mission to the EU and the Permanent Representatives of each EU member state to the European Union. Within its delegated powers the Committee of Ambassadors is responsible for monitoring the implementation of the provisions of the Agreement. In many respects the Committee of Ambassadors is the framework within which detailed questions about ACP-EU relations are thrashed out in preparation for deliberation by the ACP-EU joint Council of Ministers.

The ACP side of the Committee of Ambassadors meets more regularly than the joint Committee of Ambassadors and has a number of sub-committees. They prepare the work of the full committee, which in turn supervises the policy dimension of the routine work undertaken by the ACP Secretariat.

The third level of consultation within the ACP-EU co-operation process is the **ACP-EU Joint Parliamentary Assembly**. This consists of equal numbers of Parliamentary representatives from the EU and ACP states. The European parliamentary representatives are drawn from the European Parliament, while ACP representatives are drawn from each ACP member state's Parliament. Formally the role of the Joint Parliamentary Assembly is purely consultative and has the aim of:

Part II,
Article 17

- promoting democratic processes through dialogue and consultation;

- facilitating greater understanding between peoples and raising public awareness on development issues;

- discussing issues pertaining to development and the ACP-EU partnership;

- adopting resolutions and making recommendations to the Council of Ministers with a view to promoting the objectives of the Cotonou Agreement.

The Joint Parliamentary Assembly meets twice year, alternately in an ACP and an EU member state.

Under the Cotonou Agreement the rules on participation in the Joint Parliamentary Assembly have been tightened up. In the absence of parliamentary representatives from a particular ACP state, a representative of the ACP state concerned may participate 'subject to the prior approval of the Joint Parliamentary Assembly'. This modification is reflected in the rules of procedure of the Joint Parliamentary Assembly, with greater emphasis being placed on Parliamentary participation.

Under the Agreement a number of innovations to the institutional arrangements for consultations were introduced. Perhaps the most striking was the initiation of a joint **ACP-EU Trade Ministers meeting**, to discuss trade issues in ACP-EU co-operation more intensively. This supplements the work of the long-established joint Council of Ministers, which on the ACP side is drawn largely from Ministers of Finance (although not always, since this is the sovereign decision of each ACP government), and on the EU side from EU Development Co-operation Ministers. In many respects this innovation

Part III,
Title II
Article 38

reflects the increased prominence being given to trade issues under the Agreement.

In parallel with the greater emphasis in the Agreement on broadening participation in the development co-operation process to include a more substantive role for non-state actors, the provisions dealing with the work of the Council of Ministers commit it to conducting:

> *... an ongoing dialogue with the representatives of the social and economic partners and other actors of civil society in the ACP and the EU.*

To this end it is stipulated that consultations with civil society may be held alongside Council of Ministers meetings. This extends and builds on the provisions contained in Lomé IV, by committing to an ongoing dialogue and not simply consultations on practical modalities for the implementation of co-operation activities.

Note

1   ECDPM, 2001, Cotonou Infokit: Performance Based Partnership (21). Maastricht: ECDPM.

Annexes

Annex 1

Financial Protocol

1. For the purposes set out in this Agreement and for a period of five years commencing 1 March 2000, the overall amount of the Community's financial assistance to the ACP States shall be EUR 15 200 million.

2. The Community's financial assistance shall comprise an amount up to EUR 13 500 million from the 9th European Development Fund (EDF).

3. The 9th EDF shall be allocated between the instruments of cooperation as follows:

    (a) EUR 10 000 million in the form of grants shall be reserved for an envelope for support for long-term development. This envelope shall be used to finance national indicative programmes in accordance with Articles 1 to 5 of Annex IV 'Implementation and management procedures' to this Agreement. From the envelope for support for long-term development:

    (i) EUR 90 million shall be reserved for the financing of the budget of the Centre for the Development of Enterprise (CDE);

    (ii) EUR 70 million shall be reserved for the financing of the budget of the Centre for the Development of Agriculture (CTA); and

    (iii) an amount not exceeding EUR 4 million shall be reserved for the purposes referred to in Article 17 of this Agreement (Joint Parliamentary Assembly).

    (b) EUR 1 300 million in the form of grants shall be reserved for the financing of support for regional cooperation and integration of the ACP States in accordance with Articles 6 to 14 of Annex IV 'Implementation and management procedures' to this Agreement.

    (c) EUR 2 200 million shall be allocated to finance the Investment Facility according to the terms and conditions set out in Annex II 'Terms and conditions of financing' to this Agreement without prejudice to the financing of the interest rate subsidies provided for in Articles 2 and 4 of Annex II to this Agreement funded from the resources mentioned in paragraph 3(a) of this Annex.

4. An amount of up to Eur 1 700 million shall be provided from the European Investment Bank in the form of loans made from it sown resources. These resources shall be granted for the purposes set out in Annex II 'Terms and Conditions of financing' to this Agreement in accordance with the conditions provided for by its statutes and the relevant provisions of the terms and conditions for investment financing as laid down in the aforesaid mentioned Annex. The Bank may, from the resources it manages, contribute to the financing of regional projects and programmes.

5. Any balances remaining from previous EDFs on the date of entry into force of this Financial Protocol, as well as any amounts that shall be decommitted at a later date from ongoing

projects under these Funds, shall be transferred to the 9th EDF and shall be used in accordance with the conditions laid down in this Agreement. Any resources thus transferred to the 9th EDF that previously had been allocated to the indicative programme of an ACP Sate or region shall remain allocated to that State or region. The overall amount of this Financial Protocol, supplemented by the transferred balances from previous EDFs, will cover the period of 2000–2007.

6. The Bank shall administer the loans made from its own resources, as well as the operations financed under the Investment Facility. All other financial resources of this Agreement shall be administered by the Commission.

7. Before the expiry of this Financial Protocol, the Parties shall assess the degree of realisation of commitments and disbursements. This assessment shall constitute the basis for re-evaluating the overall amount of resources as well for evaluating the need for new resources to support financial cooperation under this Agreement.

8. In the event of the funds provided for in any of the instruments of the Agreement being exhausted before the expiry of this Financial Protocol, the joint ACP-EC Council of Ministers shall take the appropriate measures.

Annex 2

General Provisions[1]

The <*name of the region*[2]>, represented by <*name of the duly mandated regional organisa-tion(s) and/or the Government(s) of the ACP(s) country(ies) concerned*> and the European Commission hereby agree as follows:

(1) The <*name of the duly mandated regional organisation(s) and/or the Government(s) of the ACP(s) country(ies) concerned*>, (represented by <*name and title*>), and the European Commission, (represented by <*name and title*>,) hereinafter referred to as the Parties, held discussions in <*place*> from ...... to ...... with a view to determining the general orien-tation for co-operation for the period <*year of signature*>–2007. <*If appropriate*> The European Investment Bank was represented at these discussions by <*name and title*>.

During these discussions, the Regional Strategy Paper including an Indicative Programme of Community Aid in favour of <*name of the region*> was drawn up in accordance with the provisions of Articles 8 and 10 of Annex IV to the ACP-EC Partnership Agreement, signed in Cotonou on 23 June 2000. These discussions complete the programming process in <*name of the region*>.

The <name of the region> includes the following countries:

<*name of ACP countries*>

....

....

The Regional Strategy Paper and the Indicative Programme are annexed to the present document.

(2) As regards the indicative programmable financial resources which the Community envis-ages to make available to <*name of the region*> for the period <*year of signature*> –2007, an amount of € .... million is foreseen for the allocation referred to in Article 9 of Annex IV of the ACP-EU Partnership Agreement. This allocation is not an entitlement and may be revised by the Community, following the completion of mid-term and end-of-term reviews, in accordance with Article 11 of Annex IV. Balances remaining from previous EDFs at the date of entry into force of the Financial Protocol as well as decommitments made at a later stage, will be added to this indicative allocation, in accordance with Paragraph 5 of Annex 1 of the ACP-EU Partnership Agreement.

(3) The Indicative Programme under chapter 6 concerns the resources of the allocation. This allocation is destined to cover economic integration and trade support, sectoral policies,

---

1 (GENERAL PROVISIONS) is the title of Appendix B and should not be added as title to the provisions.

2 Text parts in italic characters are to be completed or deleted for the final drafting.

programmes and projects at the regional level in support of the focal or non-focal areas of Community Assistance. It does not pre-empt financing decisions by the Commission.

(4) The European Investment Bank may contribute to the present Regional Strategy paper by operations financed from the Investment Facility and/or from its own resources, in accordance with Articles 3 and 4 of the Financial Protocol of the ACP-EU Partnership agreement <(*see paragraph ... for further details*)>.

(5) In accordance with Article 11 of Annex IV to the ACP-EU Partnership Agreement, the signatories will undertake a mid-term and end-of-term review of the Regional Strategy Paper and the Indicative Programme in the light of current needs and performance. The mid-term review shall be undertaken within two years and the end-of-term review shall be undertaken within four years from the date of signature of the Regional Strategy Paper and the Regional Indicative Programme. Following the completion of the mid- and end-of-term reviews, the Community may revise the resource allocation in the light of current needs and performance.

(6) The agreement of the two parties on this Regional Strategy Paper and Regional Indicative Programme, subject to the ratification and entry into force of the ACP-EU Partnership Agreement, will be regarded as definitive within eight weeks of the date of the signature, unless either party communicates the contrary before the end of this period.

Signatures

For the Region of ....   For the Commission

Annex 3

The European Commission's Regional Co-operation Principles and Objectives

In accordance with Article 177 of the Treaty Establishing the European Community, development cooperation policy shall foster:

- The sustainable economic and social development of the developing countries, and more particularly the most disadvantaged among them;

- The smooth and gradual integration of the developing countries into the world economy;

- The campaign against poverty in the developing countries.

These objectives have been confirmed and reinforced in Article 1 of the ACP-EC Partnership Agreement, signed in Cotonou on 23 June 2000, which puts main emphasis on the objective of reducing and eventually eradicating poverty. Cooperation between the Community and <*name of the region*> shall pursue these objectives, taking into account fundamental principles laid down in Article 2 of the Agreement and essential and fundamental elements as defined in Article 9.

Furthermore, in their Statement on the European Community's Development Policy of 10 November 2000, the Council of the European Union and the European Commission determined a limited number of areas selected on the basis of their contribution towards reducing poverty and for which Community action provides added value: link between trade and development; support for regional integration and co-operation; support for macro-economic policies; transport; food security and sustainable rural development; institutional capacity-building, particularly in the area of good governance and the rule of law.

In the regional context, Article 28 of the Agreement presents the general approach for regional cooperation and integration. "Cooperation shall provide effective assistance to achieve the objectives and priorities, which the ACP countries have set themselves in the context of regional and sub-regional cooperation and integration (...). In this context cooperation support shall aim to: a) foster the gradual integration of the ACP States into the world economy; b) accelerate economic cooperation and development both within and between the regions of the ACP States; c) promote the free movement of persons, goods, capital services, labour and technology among ACP countries; d) accelerate diversification of the economies of the ACP States; and coordination and harmonisation of regional and sub-regional cooperation policies; and e) promote and expand inter and intra-ACP trade and with third countries".

Cooperation in the area of regional economic integration and regional cooperation should support the main fields identified in articles 29 and 30 of the Cotonou Agreement. Furthermore, it is stated in article 35 that "economic and trade cooperation shall build on regional integration initiatives of ACP States, bearing in mind that regional integration is a key instrument for the integration of ACP countries into the world economy".

The Treaty establishing the EC foresees that the Community and the Member States shall co-ordinate their policies on development cooperation and shall consult each other on their aid programmes, including in international organisations and during international conferences. Efforts must be made to ensure that Community development policy objectives are taken into account in the formulation and implementation of other policies affecting the developing countries. Furthermore, as laid down in Article 20 of the Agreement, systematic account shall be taken in mainstreaming into all areas of cooperation the following thematic or cross-cutting themes: gender issues, environmental issues and institutional development and capacity building.

The above objectives and principles together with the policy agenda for the region constitute the starting point for the formulation of the RSP, in accordance with the principle of ownership of development strategies.

Annex 4

Presentation of the Indicative Programme

6.1. Introduction

Within the general framework of the present Regional Strategy Paper, and in accordance with provisions of Article 10 of Annex IV to the Cotonou agreement, the Parties have agreed on the main priorities for their cooperation and on the sector(s) on which the support of the Community will be concentrated. A detailed Indicative Programme is presented in this chapter, followed by annexes containing a series of tables presenting the intervention frameworks for each focal sector, an activity pipeline chronogramme and the indicative commitment and expenditure schedules.

Amounts mentioned in this chapter indicate the global distribution of funds between economic integration and trade support, other focal sector(s) and other programmes. This distribution can be modified in the context of mid- and end-of-term reviews.

6.2. Financial instruments

This Indicative Programme is based on the indicative allocation for *<name of the region>* amounting to *<amount of the allocation in €>*. The indicative allocation will be distributed as follows:

<Focal sector 1: Economic Integration and Trade Support>   *<amount>* *<% of total>*

<Focal sector 2>   *<amount>* *<% of total>*

<Other programmes>   *<amount>* *<% of total>*

   <of which support to non state actors' initiatives, if appropriate> *<amount>*

Balances remaining from previous EDFs at the date of entry into force of the Financial Protocol as well as decommitments made at a later stage, will be added to the above mentioned indicative allocation. These funds will be used for projects and programmes already identified under indicative programmes of preceding EDFs, for which no financial decision was taken before the entry into force of the 9th EDF. Remaining balances should be used to support projects and programmes in line with the priorities set out in this indicative programme.

6.3. Focal sector(s)

XXX *<Economic Integration and Trade Support>*

The following specific objective shall be pursued:

For indicative purposes, approximately .... € shall be reserved for this sector.

The major interventions foreseen are:

The major policy measures to be taken by the Region as a contribution to the implementation of the response strategy in this sector are:

XXX <name of the second focal sector> (if appropriate)

The following specific objective shall be pursued:

For indicative purposes, approximately .... € shall be reserved for this sector.

The major interventions foreseen are:

The major policy measures to be taken by the Region as a contribution to the implementation of the response strategy in this sector are:

6.4. Other programmes

An indicative amount of .... € has been reserved for the following purposes:

- <non-focal sector: formulate the specific objective and major interventions>
- Institutional support for non-state actors <if appropriate> (indicate the eligibility criteria for non-state actors to be involved, taking into account Article 6 of the Cotonou Agreement)
- A reserve for insurance against possible claims and to cover cost increases and contingencies.

6.5. Duly mandated organisations

For the purpose of the implementation of this Indicative Programme the duly mandated regional organisations are <list of organisations>.

Optional: The following Governments of the ACP states of the region <list of governments> are also mandated for the implementation of the Indicative Programme.

Optional: <organisation A> is mandated to implement activities in <area of co-operation>, <organisation B> is. ....

<country A> is mandated to implement activities in <area of co-operation>, <country B> is. ....

Optional: The duly mandated regional organisations will set up the following co-ordination mechanism for the implementation of the Indicative Programme: <description of co-ordination mechanism>.

In order to implement the activities set out in the present Indicative Programme, the duly mandated regional organisations and Governments shall appoint Regional Authorising Officers. The function of Regional Authorising Officer is defined by analogy to the description of the function of National Authorising Officer in the Cotonou agreement (Annex IV, Articles 14.3 and 35).

The list of duly mandated organisations and Governments of ACP States, as well as their respective responsibilities in the implementation of the Indicative Programme can be amended by exchange of letters between the Regional Authorising Officer(s) and the Chief Authorising Officer.

Annex 5

EIB Desk Officers and Contact Details

European Investment Bank
100, bd Konrad Adenauer
L – 2950 Luxembourg
Tel: (+352) 43 79 –1
Fax (+352) 43 77 04
e-mail: info@eib.org

Mr. Martin CURWEN
Director lending operations in ACP countries
e-mail: m.curwen@eib.org
Fax: (+352) 43 77 04

Mr. Guus HEIM
Head of Division; lending operations in West Africa
e-mail: g.heim@eib.org
Fax: (+352) 43 79 72 74

Mr. Tassilo HENDUS
Head of Division; lending operations in Central and East Africa
e-mail: t.hendus@eib.org
Fax: (+352) 43 79 72 76

Mr. Justin LOASBY
Head of Division; lending operations in Southern Africa and the Indian Ocean
region and South Africa
e-mail: j.loasby@eib.org
Fax: (+352) 43 79 72 70

Mr. Stephen McCARTHY
Head of Division; lending operations in the Caribbean and the Pacific region
Fax: (+352) 43 79 72 72

Mr. Bram SCHIM VAN DER LOEFF
Information and Communications Officer for the ACP region
e-mail: a.schimvanderloeff@eib.org
Fax: (+352) 43 79 31 89

Annex 6

Applying for EIB Funding

Details to be submitted to the European Investment Bank

The layout and contents of documents to be submitted to the EIB are the responsibility of the project promoter. Given the range and diversity of potential projects there is no standard documentation and the Bank does not require its borrowers to complete set forms or questionnaires. As a general rule, it would expect to receive a comprehensive feasibility study. Where this has not been prepared, the project promoter may use its own discretion in compiling as detailed information as possible to permit the technical, environmental, economic, financial and legal appraisal of projects. The following documentation list is intended as a guideline:

A. THE PROMOTER

1. **General information about the enterprise, its legal status, principal partners and shareholders, organizational structure:**

- The enterprise: legal documents covering incorporation, statutes, activities, accounting policies, management, audited financial statements (balance sheets, profit and loss accounts, cashflow statements) for the last three financial years, details of short, medium and long-term liabilities, dividend distribution policy.

- Promoters and principal partners: articles of association, shareholders, activities and audited financial statements for the last three financial years.

- Legal status of the proposed project, relationship with the promoter's other activities, licences and concessions obtained.

B. THE PROJECT

2. **Technical and environmental data:**

- General purpose, justification and location, (rated and forecast capacity).

- Technical description: technology, site and site development, buildings. production and storage plant, general services, transport systems and equipment.

- Environmental impact assessment, where relevant and appropriate, including reference to relevant laws, mitigating measures to protect the environment, specific studies.

- Engineering studies and implementation: consultants (if any), procedures for tendering and awarding contracts, supervision, works schedule and implementation timetable.

- Detailed cost estimate itemising site and plant expenditure, provision for physical and price contingencies, interest during construction, initial and start-up expenses, together with a breakdown in foreign and local currencies.

- Operation: raw materials and products, flowcharts, consumption and output levels, managerial staff and workers, management organisation, technical assistance where applicable.

3. Socio-economic data:

- Market: statistics showing present and forecast trends in supply, demand and prices for project output and significant raw material inputs.

- Marketing: sales policy and organisation, position of company in relation to main competitors, domestic and export sales, pricing policy.

- Jobs created or maintained by the project: permanent and seasonal jobs, professional training, replacement of expatriate staff (if any).

- Data used for calculating the economic rate of return of the project and assessing its contribution to the economic development of the country concerned (balance of payments, public finance, etc.).

- Social impact of the project, availability and type of workforce, salary level, social benefits, security, working conditions. Conformity to national labour, health and safety regulations and to local regulatory requirements.

4. Financial data:

- Breakdown of project operating and maintenance costs, depreciation and overheads.

- Financing plan for the project and schedule of projected expenditure.

- Projected cashflows, profit and loss accounts, and balance sheets until the project comes fully on stream.

- Estimate of working capital needed and changing requirements over time incorporating the project.

- Calculation of the project's IRR.

- Security and guarantees offered.

Annex 7

What Intermediate Financial Institutions Currently Manage EIB Global Loans?

Status quo January 2003

- **Caribbean Development Bank (CDB)**

- **Ecobank Bénin**
  Mr. Christophe Jocktane Lawson
  Directeur Général
  Rue du Gouverneur Bayol
  01 BP 1280
  Cotonou
  Tel: +229 31 40 23
  Fax: +229 31 33 85

- **Financial Bank Bénin**
  Mr. Pierre Leclaire
  Directeur Général
  Immeuble Adjibi
  Rue Cdt. Decoeur
  01 BP 2700
  Cotonou
  Tel: +229 31 31 00
  Fax: +229 31 31 02

- **Finadev**
  Mr. Patrick Lelong
  Directeur Général
  01 BP 2700
  Cotonou
  Tel: +229 31 31 00
  Fax: +229 31 31 02

- **Bank of Africa**
  Mr. Alain Chapuis
  Directeur Général
  Boulevard Jean Paul II
  08 BP 0879
  Cotonou
  Tel: +229 31 32 28
  Fax: +229 31 31 17

- **Société Générale de Banques au Burkina (SGBB)**
  M. Emile Pare
  Président Directeur Générale
  01 BP 585
  Ouagadougou 01
  Tel: +226 30 60 34
  Fax: +226 31 05 61

- **Bank of Africa (BOA)**
  M. José Espeillac
  Directeur Général
  Avenue de la Résistance du 17 mai
  01 BP 1319
  Ouagadougou 01
  Tel: +226 30 88 70 (-73)
  Fax: +226 30 88 74

- **Burkina Bail**
  M. Abdoulaye K. Sory
  Directeur Général
  1340 avenue Dimdolobsom
  01 BP 1913
  Ouagadougou 01
  Tel: +226 30 69 85 (-87)
  Fax: +226 30 70 02

- **Credit Lyonnais Cameroon (SCB)**

- **Standard Chartered Bank Cameroon**

- **Banque Internationale du Cameroon pour l'Epargne et le Crédit (BICEC)**

- **Caixa Economica de Cabo Verde**
  M. A.C. Moreira Semedo
  Administrateur
  Avenida Cidade de Lisboa
  CP 199, Praia
  Tel: +238 60 36 03
  Fax: +238 61 55 60

- **Banco Commercial do Atlantico**
  M. Miguel Alfonso
  Directeur
  Avenida Amilcar Cabral
  CP 474, Praia
  Tel: +238 61 55 28
  Fax: +238 61 30 00

- **Banco Interatlantico**
  Mme. Adalgisa Barbosa Vaz
  Administrateur
  Avenida Cidade de Lisboa
  CP 131 A
  Praia
  Tel: +238 61 35 04/61 40 08
  Fax: +238 61 47 52/61 47 12

- **Agricultural, Industrial and Development Bank (AID Bank)**

- **Banco ADEMI de Desarrollo S.A.**

- **Banco Intercontinental S.A. (BANINTER)**

- **Development Bank of Ethiopia (DBE)**

Ghana Leasing Sector Global Loan:

- **General Leasing & Finance Company**
  1. Mr. Daiel Ofori-Dankwa
     Head of the Marketing and Portfolio
     Administration Department
     e-mail: dodankwa@glfcgh.com
  2. Mr. Godwill Nigel Akrong
     Manager, Finance and Accounts
     e-mail: gnakrong@glfcgh.com
  3. Mr. Kofi I. Andah
     Managing Director
     e-mail: kiandah@glfcgh.com
  Mary Dee House Hse no. C124/3
  Sobukwe Road
  Off Farrar Av.
  P O Box CT 1967 Cantonments
  Accra – Ghana
  Tel: +233 21 231 844
  Fax: +233 21 233 636

- **Ghana Leasing Company Ltd**
  1. Kwame Owusu
     kowusu@ghanaleasing.com
     Finance Manager
  2. Sam Darkwa
     samdarkwa@ghanaleasing.com
     Snr. Marketing Officer
  45 Independence Avenue
  PO Box 14295
  Accra – Ghana
  Tel: +233 21 667 218
  Fax: +233 21 668 553

- **Leasafric**
  Mr. Seth K. Dei
  Managing Director
  Mr. Mathais Dorfe
  General Manager
  Nr. 7 Main Street – Tesano
  PO Box CT 2430 Cantonments
  Accra – Ghana
  Tel: +233 21 230 280
  Fax: +233 21 223 942

Ghana Financial Sector Global Loan:

- **Ecobank Ghana Limited**
  Mr. Albert K. Essien
  aessien@ecobank.com
  Deputy Managing Director
  Mr. Daniel Sackey
  Country Risk Manager
  19, Seventh Avenue/Ridge West
  P.M.B., G.P.O.
  Accra – Ghana
  Tel: +233 21 231 936
  Tel: +233 21 221 103
  Fax: +233 21 232 096
  Fax: +233 21 232 091

- **Social Security Bank (SSB) Limited**
  Mr P. K. Thompson
  thompson@ghana.com
  Managing Director
  PO Box 13119
  Accra – Ghana

Tel:. +233 21 225 313
Tel:. +233 21 221 726
Fax +233 21 225 313

- **Institute of Private Enterprise Development (IPED)**

- **Sofihdes**

- **Jamaica Venture Fund Ltd (JVF)**

- **National Development Bank of Jamaica Ltd (NDB)**

- **Trafalgar Development Bank (TDB)**

- **Development Bank of Kenya Ltd**

- **Kenya Commercial Bank Ltd**

- **National Bank of Kenya Ltd**

- **Barclays Bank of Kenya Ltd**

- **Industrial Development Bank Ltd**

- **Kenya Equity Management Ltd**

- **Standard Chartered Bank Kenya Ltd**

- **East African Development Bank**

- **Crédit Agrlcole Indosuez**

- **ABN/AMRO Bank**

- **Stanbic Bank Kenya Ltd**

- **Development Bank of Kiribati**

- **Lesotho National Development Corporation (LNDC)**
  Mrs. Sophia Mohapi
  ce@ilesotho.org.ls
  Chief Executive
  Private Bag A96
  100 Maseru
  Tel: +266 22 315 096
  Fax: +266 22 310 038

- **FIARO – Financière d'Investissement ARO**
  M. Patrick W. Razafindrafito

Immeuble ARO FIARO
Rue Jules Ranaivo
Ampefiloha
Antananarivo
Tel: + 261 20 22 342 60
Fax: + 261 20 22 221 47

- **BMOI – Banque Malgache de l'Océan Indien**
  M. Robert Durbec
  Place de l'Indépendance
  B.P. 25 Bis – Antaninarenina
  Antananarivo
  Tel: + 261 20 22 346 09
  Fax: + 261 20 22 346 10

- **BFV – Société Générale**
  M. A. Catalano
  14, Làlana Jeneraly Rabehevitra
  B.P. 196
  Antananarivo 101
  Tel: + 261 20 22 264 24
  Fax: +261 20 22 235 40

- **BNI – Crédit Lyonnais Madagascar**
  M. Daniel Bourgery
  74, rue du 26 juin 1960
  B.P. 174
  Antananarivo 101
  Tel: + 261 20 22 228 00
  Fax: + 261 20 22 337 49

- **Union Commercial Bank (UCB)**
  M. Paul Giblin
  Rue Solombavambahoaka Frantsay, 77
  B.P. 197 – Antsahavola
  Antananarivo 101
  Tel: +261 20 22 272 62
  Fax: +261 20 22 287 40

- **Indebank**
  Mrs. A. J. Varela
  General Manager
  Indebank House
  Kaushong Road
  Top Mandala

P.O. Box 358
Blantyre
Tel: +265 1 620 055
Fax: +265 1 623 353

- **Générale de Banque de Mauritanie (GBM)**
M. Mohamed Hamyen Bouamatou
Directeur Général
BP 5558
Nouakchott
Tel: +222 525 36 36
Fax: +222 525 46 47

- **Mauritanie Leasing**
M. Limame Ould Ebnou
Administrateur Directeur Général
Avenue Charles de Gaulle Socogim
Tefragh Zeina Lot n° 100
BP 3842
Nouakchott
Tel: +222 529 05 69
Fax: +222 529 05 71

- **Banque Mauritanienne pour le Commerce International (BMCI)**
Isselmou Ould Didi Ould Tajedin
Président Directeur Général
BP 5050
Nouakchott
Tel: +222 529 28 76
Fax: +222 529 28 77

- **Banque pour le Commerce et l'Industrie**
Isselmou Ould Didi Ould Tajedin
Président Directeur Général
BP 5050
Nouakchott
Tel: +222 529 28 76
Fax: +222 529 28 77

- **Banco Comercial e de Investimentos, SARL**
M. Abdul Magid Osman
Av. 25 de Setembro

Prédio John Orr's, n° 1465
Maputo
Moçambique
Tel: +258 1 30 77 77
Fax: +258 1 30 71 52

- **UULC Moçambique**
M. Victor VISEU
Edificio 33 andares
Rua da Impensa 256
7 Andar
Caixa Postal 4447
Maputo
Mozambique
Tel: + 258 1 42 31 08
Fax: +258 1 43 12 90

- **Banco Austral**
M. Johan Stander
Av. 25 de Setembro, 1184
Maputo
Moçambique
Tel: +258 1 42 89 42
Fax: +258 1 42 90 32

- **Banco Internaçional de Moçambique**
M. José Mandlate
Av. 25 de Setembro, 1800, 8° andar
Maputo
Mozambique
Tel: +258 1 30 74 81
Fax: +258 1 30 88 08

- **Banco Standard Totta**
M. Carlos Ramalho
Praça 25 de Junho, 1 – 1° andar
P.O. Box 2086
Maputo
Mozambique
Tel: +258 1 42 30 42
Fax: +258 1 42 69 67

- **Banco de Fomento**
M. Diogo Quental
Av. Julius Nyerere, 210

Maputo
Mozambique
Tel: +258 1 49 34 43
Fax: +258 1 49 44 01

- **Commercial Bank of Namibia**
Mr. Martin Moeller
MoellerM@C-Bank.com.na
Senior Manager International Trade
Service
P.O. Box 1
12–20 Bülow Street
Windhoek
Tel: +264 61 295 2014
Fax: +264 61 295 2046

- **First National Bank Namibia**
Mr. F. Botha
fbotha@fnbnamibia.com.na
Departmental Head
4th floor, First National Building
211 Independence Avenue
P.O. Box 195
Windhoek
Tel: +264 61 299 2178
Fax: +264 61 299 2125

- **Standard Bank Namibia**
Mr. James Hill
hillj@standardbank.com.na
Executive Director
4th Floor
Mutual Platz
PO Box 3327
Windhoek
Tel: +264 61 294 2302
Fax: +264 61 294 2409

- **Bank Windhoek**
Mr. Wilhelm Mosehuus
wilhelm@bankwindhoek.com.na
Manager Corporate Banking Services
Bank Windhoek Building
P.O. Box 15
262 Independence Avenue, Windhoek

Tel: +264 61 299 1214
Fax: +264 61 299 1480

- **Bank of Namibia**
Mr. Kuruvilla Mathew
Kuruvilla.mathew@bon.com.na
Financial Manager
71 Robert Mugabe Avenue
PO Box 2882
Windhoek
Tel: +264 61 283 5148/9
Fax: +264 61 283 5067

- **NIB Namibia**
Mr. Steve Galloway
steve@nibnamibia.com
Managing Director
3 Schützen Avenue
PO Box 25576
Windhoek
Tel: +264 61 227 950
Fax: +264 61 259 701

- **Banque Internationale pour l'Afrique au Niger (BIA)**
M. Daniel Hasser
Directeur Général
Avenue de la Mairie
BP 10350
Niamey
Tel: +227 73 31 01
Fax: +227 73 35 95

- **Bank of Africa Niger (BOA Niger)**
M. Bernard Puechaldou
Directeur Général
Immeuble Sonara II
BP 10973
Niamey
Tel: +227 73 36 20
Fax: +227 73 38 18

- **Ecobank Niger**
M. Jean-Jacques Kodjo
Directeur Général
Angle Bld. de la Liberté et Rue des

Bâtisseurs
BP 13804
Niamey
Tel: +227 73 71 81
Fax: +227 73 72 04

- **Société Nigérienne de Banque (Sonibank)**
  M. Haitou Moussa
  Directeur Général
  Avenue de la Mairie
  BP 891
  Niamey
  Tel: +227 73 48 54
  Fax: +227 73 46 93

- Ventures & Trusts Ltd
  M. Femi Akingbe
  Managing Director
  5a, Adeyemo Alakija Street
  PO Box 53659 Falomo
  Victoria Island, Lagos
  Tel: +234 1 262 06 02 (-3)
  Fax: +234 1 262 03 03

- **Banque Commerciale du Rwanda**

- **Banque de Kigali**

- **Banque Rwandaise de Développement**

- **Development Bank of St Kitts and Nevis**

- **Development Bank of Samoa**

- **Banque Sénégalo-Tunisienne (BST)**
  M. Abdoul Mbaye
  Administrateur Directeur Général
  97, avenue André Peytavin
  BP 4111, Dakar
  Tel: +221 849 60 71
  Fax: +221 823 82 37

- **Société Générale de Banques au Sénégal**
  M. Bernard Labadens
  Administrateur, Directeur Général

19, Av. Pdt L. S. Senghor
BP 232
Dakar
Tel: +2218395500
Fax: +221 823 90 36

- **Compagnie Bancaire de l'Afrique Occidentale**
  M. Patrick Mestrallet
  Administrateur, Directeur Général
  Place de l'Indépendance
  BP 129
  Dakar
  Tel: +221 823 30 85 / 823 52 79
  Fax: +221 823 83 90

- **Crédit Lyonnais Sénégal**
  M. J. C. Dubois
  Administrateur, Directeur Général
  Bd El H. Djily Mbaye X Rue Huart
  BP 56
  Dakar
  Tel: +221 823 10 08
  Fax: +221 823 84 30

- **Banque Internationale pour le Commerce et l'Industrie du Sénégal (BICIS)**
  M. Amadou Kane
  Directeur Général
  2, Av. Pdt L.. S. Senghor
  BP 392
  Dakar
  Tel: +221 823 92 18 / 839 03 00
  Fax: +221 823 47 21 / 823 37 07

- **Development Bank of Seychelles (DBS)**
  M. Simon Hoareau
  Independence Avenue
  P.O. Box 217
  Victoria
  Mahe
  Swaziland
  Tel: +248 22 44 71
  Fax: +248 22 42 74

- Development Bank of Solomon Islands (DBSI)

- Swaziland Industrial Development Corporation Ltd (SIDC)
  Dr T. Gina
  sidc@dial.pipex.sz
  Managing Director
  Swaziland Industrial Development Company Ltd.
  Dhlan'Ubeka House
  5th Floor
  P.O. Box 866
  Mbabane
  Tel: +268 40 43391-3
  Fax: +268 40 45619

- Tanzania Development Finance Company Ltd (TDFC)

- CRDB (1996) Ltd

- Stanbic Bank Tanzania Ltd

- East African Development Bank (EADB)

- Tonga Development Bank (TDB)

- Development Finance Ltd (DFL)

- Development Bank of Tuvalu (DBT)

- Bank of Uganda

- Bank of Baroda

- Barclays Bank

- Development Finance Cy of Uganda

- East Africa Development Bank

- Industrial Promotion Services

- Stanbic Bank

- Standard Chartered Bank

- Gold Trust Bank

- Orient Bank

- African Banking Corporation Zambia Ltd
  Abdul Munshi
  amunshi@abcz.co.zm
  Managing Director
  4th Floor, National Savings & Credit Bank Building, Cairo Road, North End
  Lusaka
  P.O. Box 39501
  Tel: +260 1 234 541
  Fax: +260 1 234 542

- Barclays Bank of Zambia Ltd
  Yusuf Koya
  yusuf.koya@barclays.com
  Head of Corporate Relationship Support Team
  Head Office
  Kafue House, Cairo Road
  P.O. Box 31936
  Lusaka
  Tel: +260 1 229709
  Fax: +260 1 223519

- Indo-Zambia Bank Ltd
  Alok K. Misra
  izb@zamnet.zm
  Managing Director
  Head Office
  Mezzanine Floor
  Cairo Road
  P.O. Box 35411
  Lusaka
  Tel: +260 1 224979
  Fax: +260 1 225090

- Industrial Credit Company Ltd
  Charles H Sichangwa
  charles@microlink.zm
  Managing Director
  44 Buteko Avenue
  P.O. Box 70742
  Ndola
  Tel: +260 2 236173
  Fax: +260 2 618621

- **Stanbic Bank Zambia Ltd**
  Jordan Soko
  Stanbic1@zamnet.zm
  General Manager of Financial Services
  Woodgate House
  Cairo Road
  P.O. Box 31955
  Lusaka
  Tel: +260 1 22 48 06/09
  Fax: +260 1 22 48 24/22 11 52

- **Standard Chartered Bank Zambia**
  Joseph Chikolwa
  Joe.Chikolwa@zm.standardchartered.
  com
  Head of Corporate & Institutional
  Banking
  Standard Chartered House
  Cairo Road
  P.O. Box 32238
  10101 Lusaka
  Tel: +260 1 22 29 83
  Fax: +260 1 22 51 48

Financial Intermediaries of the European
Investment Bank in the Republic of South
Africa

Status quo November 2002

- **Development Bank of South Africa
  (DBSA)**
  Mandla Gantsho
  mandlag@dbsa.org
  Chief Executive
  P.O. Box 1234
  Headway Hill, Midrand
  Gauteng
  Tel: +27 11 313 3319
  Fax: +27 11 313 3401

- **Industrial Development Corporation of
  South Africa (IDC)**
  Jeff Midzuk
  jeffm@idc.co.za
  19 Fredman Drive
  P.O. Box 784055
  Sandton 2146
  Tel: +27 11 269 3035
  Fax: +27 11 269 3230

- **Infrastructure Finance Corporation Ltd
  (INCA)**
  Johan Kruger
  johankruger@inca.co.za
  Managing Director
  4th Floor, 1 First Place Bankcity
  Cnr Simmonds and Pritchard Streets
  Johannesburg 2001
  Tel: +27 11 352 34 55
  Fax: +27 11 352 96 78

- **Nedbank Bank**
  Mr David N. Fienberg
  davidfi@nedcor.co.za
  Head: International Specialised Finance
  135 Rivonia Road
  Sandton 2196
  South Africa
  Tel: +27 11 294 3140
  Fax: +27 11 294 8140

- **First Rand Bank Limited**
  (Rand Merchant Bank)
  Gert-Jan Scholtz
  gertjan.scholtz@rmb.co.za
  1 Merchant Place
  Cnr Fredman Drive and Rivonia Road
  P.O. Box 786273
  Sandton 2146
  Tel: +27 11 282 8000/8392
  Fax: +27 11 282 8318

Annex 8

CTA Application for Seminar Support Programme

CTA (ACP-EU Technical Centre for Agricultural and Rural Cooperation)
Post bus 380
NL 6700 AJ Wageningen
The Netherlands
Tel: +31 317 467137
Fax: +31 317 460067
Email: traore@cta.int

Application for Seminar Support Program

Part A: To be completed by applicant (Please type or print in block letters)

1. Personal Details

1. Family name ....

2. First name ....

3. Date of Birth ..../ ..../ ....
   Day   Mo.   Yr

4. Sex: M / F ....

5. Nationality ....

6. Official address for correspondence ....
   ....

7. City ....   8. Country ....

9. Telephone ....   10. Fax ....

11. E-mail ....

2. Your Organization, Work Experience & Skills

12. Full Name of your organization ....

13. Type of Organisation   14. Sector

    ☐ Farmers' Association   ☐ public

    ☐ Non-governmental Organisation   ☐ private

    ☐ Research institution

    ☐ Other, please specify

15. Main activities of your Organisation:
   ....

16. Your current job title ....

17. Date appointed ....

18. List your major duties and responsibilities in an order of priority.
   ....
   ....
   ....

19. List any professional experience prior to your present job.
   ....
   ....

20. Your level of training
   ☐ PhD   ☐ MSc   ☐ MA   ☐ BSc   ☐ BA
   Other, please specify ....

21. Language competence: Please indicate your language ability using:
   slight = S, fair = F, good = G.
   English: S/F/G .... French: S/F/G .... Portuguese: S/F/G ....
   Other: ....

3. **Your Expectations**

22. What role are you going to play in the meeting?
   ☐ Keynote Speaker   ☐ Communication   ☐ Poster Presentation
   ☐ Chairman of Session
   ☐ Other, please specify ....

23. What are your personal expectations of the conference?
   ....
   ....
   ....

Part B: Conference details

24. Conference title ....

25. Conference venue (city) ....

26. Conference venue (country) ....

27. Conference Language ....

28. Start date   /   /   29. End date   /   /

30. Conference organisers (name, address) ....
....

31. Contact person of the conference organizers ....

5. Accommodation (per person)

32. Conference registration fee ....

33. Hotel rate per day ....

34. Transport cost ....

35. In case of favourable decision, the conference organisers accept to manage the funds allocated by CTA and pre-finance the participation of the applicants.
    If yes, please attach evidence of the acceptance ....
    If no, could you pre-finance your participation?
    Otherwise please suggest alternative solution ....

6. Conference Themes

36. Please indicate, among the following, the main theme(s) and sub-theme (s) of the conference. Select a maximum of 2 main themes and 3 sub-themes.

☐ **MARKET-ORIENTED PRODUCTION AND TRADE**
Activities aimed to adapt agricultural production to market demand at local, regional, national and international level. It includes:

☐ Rural credit, banking and finance

☐ Enterprises & agro-industry development

☐ Trade & marketing at national, regional and international level

☐ Business intelligence

☐ Consumer/demand side

☐ Handling, transport, storage

☐ Processing of agricultural products

☐ Agricultural prices

☐ Other, please specify ....

☐ **ENVIRONMENTAL PROTECTION & NATURAL RESOURCES MANAGEMENT**
Natural resources management in relation to agriculture, including wildlife, conservation of plants and land resources. It includes:

☐ Environmental policies and management

☐ Forest policies and management

☐ Energy policies and management

☐ Water policies and management

☐ Soil and land management

☐ Agro-climatology

☐ Pollution

☐ Waste management

☐ Environmental monitoring

☐ Agricultural engineering (e.g. irrigation and water harvesting equipments)

☐ Other, please specify ....

☐ **AGRICULTURAL SOCIO-ECONOMICS AND POLICIES**
Multi-disciplinary approach to agricultural systems analysis, design, planning, policies and strategies. Consider this subject only when it deals with its impact on agricultural and rural policies and activities. It includes:

☐ Strengthening formulation of national, regional, and international policies and programmes

☐ Structural adjustment policies

☐ Strengthening economic planning, economic analysis and econometrics

☐ Labour and employment (policies, administration, organisation and management)

☐ Development economics and policies, rural development planning, programmes, policies

☐ International co-operation for development

☐ Integration of the independent sector with the governmental sector

☐ Other, please specify ....

☐ **ANIMAL PRODUCTION AND HEALTH**
Animal production systems (dairy farming, aviculture, apiculture, sericulture)

☐ Animal feeding

☐ Genetics, biotechnologies, breeding and taxonomy

☐ Veterinary medicine, surgery, dentistry and obstetrics

☐ Veterinary organisations and services

☐ Animal health inspection and hygiene

☐ Animal pests and diseases and other disorders

☐ Aquaculture and fisheries

☐ Other, please specify ....

☐ **CROP PRODUCTION AND PROTECTION**
Production techniques and systems including plant propagation, seed production and processing, plant nutrition and fertilisers.

☐ Integrated pest management (including chemical, biological and natural control)

☐ Identification and taxonomy of pests, plant pathologies, weeds and other factors

☐ Agricultural machinery, equipment and engineering

☐ Biotechnologies and GMOs

☐ Other, please specify ....

☐ **INFORMATION AND COMMUNICATION**
Strengthening information networks and systems with a particular emphasis on ICTs pertaining to agriculture and rural development. It includes:

☐ Collect and storage methods

☐ Information and communication media (including conventional media and ICTs)

☐ National and regional information policies and strategies

☐ Knowledge and content management

☐ Communication techniques and methods

☐ Other, please specify ....

☐ **RURAL DYNAMICS**
Greater community participation in the formulation of development policies. It includes:

☐ Social organisation of rural communities

☐ Gender issues

☐ Rural-urban relations

☐ Strengthening local NGOs, farmer co-operatives, farmer associations and private sector

☐ Rural legislation

☐ Other, please specify ....

Signature of the Applicants .... Date ....

Annex 9

Contact Details of CDE Headquarters and Caribbean Regional Office

Director, CDE
52 avenue Herrmann-Debroux
1160 Brussels
Belgium
Tel: + 32 2 679
Fax: 32 2 675 26 03 and 32 2 679 18 31

CDE Caribbean Regional Office
Gary AYLMER
CDE Caribbean Regional Office
Calli 6 number 10 Ensanche Paraiso
Santo Domingo
Republique Dominicaine/ Dominican Republic
Tel: + 1 809 683 47 72
Fax: + 1 809 375 05 81
Cde.co@codetel.net.do

Annex 10

Contact Details of CDE Decentralised Management Units

BENIN
Centre de promotion et d'encadrement des
petites et moyennes entreprises (CEPEPE)
B.P. 2093
Cotonou
Tel: +229 31 44 47
Fax: +229 31 59 50
cepepe@firstnet.bj

DOMINIQUE/ DOMINICA
The Organisation of the Eastern Caribbean
States/ Export Development Unit
(OECS/ EDU)
Prevo Cinamall, Kennedy Avenue
PO Box 769
Roseau
Tel: + 1 767 448 22 40
Fax: + 1 767 448 55 54
oecsdu@cwdom.dm

CÔTE D'IVOIRE
Appui et Service aux Entreprises (A.S.E.)
01 B.P. 8081
Abidjan 01
Tel: +225 22 44 66 39
Fax: +225 22 48 70 09
ase@.africaonline.co.ci

GHANA
Empretec Ghana Foundation
36 Ringway Crescent, Osu
Accra
Tel: +233 (021) 701 0203
Fax: +233 (021) 231 239
ykwarteeng@mpretecgh.org

JAMAÎQUE/ JAMAICA
JAMPRO Corporation
35 Trafalgar Road
Kingston 10, Jamaica

Tel: +1 876 978 33 37
Fax: + 1 876 978 22 67
jampro@investjamaica.com

KENYA
Karumasi Consultancy Ltd (KCL)
Finance House 10th Floor
Loita Street
PO Box 51270
Nairobi
Tel: + 254 2 21 39 14
Fax: + 254 2 24 09 21
mth@karumasi.com

MADAGASCAR
Cabinet Cadic Gombert
Océan Indien Sarl (CGOI)
BP 3859
101 Antananarivo
Tel: + 261 320 71 15 42
Tel:/ Fax: + 261 202 25 67 31
cgoimcar@dts.mg
Cgoi2@ds.mg

MAURICE/ MAURITIUS
Chambre de Commerce et d'Industrie
3 Rue Royale, Port Louis
Tel: +230 208 3301
Fax: +230 208 0076
mcci@intnet.mu

MOZAMBIQUE
CPI (Investment Promotion Centre)
Rue de Imprensa 332, R/ C
Predio 33 Andares
C.P. 4635
Maputo
Tel: +258 1 31 32 95
Fax: +258 1 31 33 25
staibo@cpi.co.mz

SÉNÉGAL
SODIDA
Rue 14X Bourguiba
B.P. 4112
Dakar
Tel: + 221 865 20 60
Fax: + 221 824 14 33
sodidamail@sodida.sn

TANZANIE/TANZANIA
KANGAROO Limited
P.O. Box 76565
Dar es Salaam
Tel: + 255 222 119 001
Mob: +255 741601104
issltd@intafrica.com

TRINITÉ ET TOBAGO/
TRINIDAD AND TOBAGO
Caribbean Business Services Limited (CBSL)
Development Finance Building
10 Cipriani Boulevard
Port of Spain
Tel: + 1 868 625 9542
Fax: + 1 868 625 9532
cbser@tstt.net.tt
info@cbser.com

VANUATU
VIPA – Vanuatu Investment Promotion
Authority
Level 1
Pioloko House
Port Vila
Tel: + 678 24096
Fax: + 678 25216

Annex 11

Contact Details of CDE Antennae Network

1. SOUTHERN AFRICA

ANGOLA
Ministerio da Industria
Direcçao Nacional de Industria
Rua Cerqueira Lukoki 25
Caixa Postal 594
Luanda
Tel: +244 2 33 70 55
Fax: +244 2 39 24 00
gvmi-ag@ebonet.net

LESOTHO
Lesotho National Development Corporation
(LNDC)
Development House
Kingsway Street Private Bag A96
Maseru 100
Tel: +266 31 20 12
Fax: +266 31 00 38
Lndc@pixie.co.za

MOZAMBIQUE
Mr. Neves Correia
R/C ICL-Mozambique
Bairro Coop – PH9 R/C
Maputo
Tel: +258 1 416 023
Fax: +258 1 417 329
neves@iclmoz.com

NAMIBIA
Namibia Investment Centre
Ministry of Trade and Industry
Brendan Simbwaye Square
Goethe Street
Windhoek
Tel: +264 61 2837324
Fax: +264 61 22 02 78
zaire@mti.gov.na

Chamber of Commerce and Industry
PO Box 191
Windhoek
Tel: +264 61 22 20 00
Fax: +264 61 33 690

SWAZILAND
Swaziland Industrial Development
Company
PO Box 866
Mbabane
Tel: +268 40 43391
Fax: +268 45 619
sidc@iafrica.sz

ZAMBIA
Zambia Investment Centre
6457 Los Angeles Boulevard
PO Box 34580
Lusaka
Tel: +260 1 25 52 41
Fax: +260 1 25 21 50
www.zic.org

ZIMBABWE
Zimbabwe Investment Centre
109 Rotten Row
PO Box 5950
Harare
Tel: +263 4 757931
Fax: +263 4 757937
makurumidze@zic.co.zm

2. CENTRAL AFRICA

BURUNDI
Banque Nationale de Développement
Économique (BNDE)
BP 1620
Bujumbura

Tel: +257 22 28 88
Fax: +257 22 37 75
bnde@cbinfo.com

CAMEROON
Beta Conseil
BP 1731
Douala
Tel: +237 343 25 85
Fax: +237 343 16 91
beta@camnet.cn

CENTRAL AFRICAN REPUBLIC
CCIMA
BP 252 et BP 813
Bangui
Tel: +236 61 16 68/61 15 76
Fax: s/c +236 61 35 61

CONGO
Banque de Développement des États de
l'Afrique Centrale (BDEAC)
Place du Gouvernement
BP 1177
Brazzaville
Tel: +242 81 18 85
Fax: +242 81 18 80

Chambre de Commerce et d'Agriculture
du Kouilou
Boulevard Général de Gaulle 3
Pointe Noire
Tel/Fax: +242 94 44 75

African Management Corporation
(AMC Consulting)
Hôtel Saphir
BP 1307
Brazzaville
Tel: +242 67 35 91
Fax: +242 81 15 35

Société de Développement Régional
Cuvettes/Plateaux (SDRCP)
BP 2769
Brazzaville

Courrier via la Belgique:
Otraci
21, Marche en Pré
5300 Sclayn
Tel: +32 081 58 04 34
Fax: +32 081 58 04 34

DEMOCRATIC REPUBLIC OF THE CONGO
Beetor Bureau
80, avenue Marine
Binza/lpn-Commune de Ngaliema
BP 16653
Kinshasa 1
Tel: +243 99 07 761 (Mob)
+243 91 12 952
Fax: +1 801 697 33 27 (via USA)
beetor33@hotmail.com

Congo Trading & Engineering (CTE)
BP 12401
Kinshasa
Tel: +243 12 45 499/49 175
Fax: +1 212 3769259 (via USA)
Contact en Belgique
GEDIF division EARTH
Rue Maurice Liétart, 66
1150 Bruxelles
Tel: +32 2 772 4555
Fax: +32 2 772 1799
earth@pophost.eunet.be

Fédération des Entreprises du Congo (FEC)
10, Avenue des Aviateurs
BP 7247
Kinshasa
Tel: +243 12 22 565
Telecel: 8800751
Fax: +377 97 00 60

GABON
ISTA
BP 3910
Libreville
Tel/Fax: +241 74 42 46

PROMOGABON
BP 2111
Libreville
Tel: +241 26 79 19
Fax: +241 74 89 59
promogabon@inet.ga

CHAD
BAT
BP 5159
N'djaména
Tel: +235 51 97 45
Fax: +235 51 57 80

3. EAST AFRICA

COMOROS
Association pour la Promotion du Secteur
Privé (APSP)
BP 1337
Moroni
Tel: +269 730338
Fax: +269 730313
apsp@snpt.km

DJIBOUTI
Chambre Internationale de Commerce et
d'Industrie de Djibouti (CICID)
BP 84
Djibouti
Tel: +253 351070
Fax: +253 350096

ERITREA
Eritrean National Chamber of Commerce
PO Box 856
Asmara
Tel: +291 112 1589
Fax: +291 112 0138
encc@eol.com.er

ETHIOPIA
Zewde and Associates PLC
PO Box 62109
Addis Abeba

Tel: +251 162 3419
Fax: +251 161 5386
ewde&asso@telecom.net.et

Berhane Ghebray & Associates
PO Box 5786
Addis Abeba
Tel: +251 1 61 07 58
Fax: +251 1 61 26 69
Mob. +251 1 (09) 20 18 97
berhaneg@telecom.net.et

KENYA
ASIS Development Company Ltd
PO Box 10902
Nairobi
Tel: +254 2 246 726
Mobile: +254 2 733 753 139
Fax: +254 2 247 992
asisdevelopment@hotmail.com

UGANDA
ACE Quality Assurance Consultants Ltd.
PO Box 4520
Kampala
Tel: :+256 414445826
Fax: +256 41254188
bts-sebunya@africaonline.co.ug

RWANDA
Bureau d'Etudes AVENIR
BP 4248
Kigali
Tel: +250 74108
Fax: +250 74108
Mob : +241 26 79 19
avenir@rwanda1.com

Centre d'Appui Petites et Moyennes
Entreprises au Rwanda (CAPMER)
BP 5019
Kigali
Tel: +250 586119
Fax: +250 586113
capmer@rwdate11.rwanda.com

SEYCHELLES
Ministry of Industries and International
Business
BP Box 648, Latanier Road
Victoria, Mahé
Tel: +248 61 12 00
Fax: +248 22 50 86
miib@seychelles.net

SUDAN
Sudan Development Corporation
PO Box 710
Khartoum
Tel: +249 11 47 21 51
Fax: +249 11 4721 48

4. WEST AFRICA

BURKINA FASO
Projet D'Appui à La Création de Petites et
Moyennes Entreprises (PAPME)
01 BP 1777 Ouagadougou 01
Tel: +226 31 83 11
Fax: +226 31 83 14
papmedg@fasonet.bf

CAPE VERDE
IADE
Av. Cidade de Lisboa
CX P. 581
Praia
Tel: +236 61 44 44
Fax: +236 61 24 34
iade@cvtelecom.cv

Câmara de Comercio
Agricultura Industria e Serviços do
Barlavento (CCIASB)
Rua da Luz 31
CP 728
Mindelo
Tel: +238 32 84 95
Fax: + 238 32 84 96
camara.com@cvtelecom.cv

CÔTE D'IVOIRE
Chambre de Commerce et de l'Industrie de
Côte d'Ivoire
01 BP 1758
Abidjan 01
Tel: +225 324 700
Fax: +225 272 117

GAMBIA
Sahel Investment Management
International
2 Sahel Drive
Bakau Newtown
PO Box 1411
Banjul
Tel: +220 49 78 56
Fax: +220 49 79 51
sahel@qanet.gm

GHANA
Mr. E. Y. Bonso
27 Cocoa Street
PO Box TN 2137
Teshie Nungua Estates
Accra
Tel: +233 21 71 26 57
eybonso@yahoo.com

GUINEA
Office de Promotion des Investissements
Privés
BP 2024
Conakry
Tel: +224 44 34 36
Fax: +224 41 31 61
cdi@opip.org.gn

GUINEA BISSAU
Fundei
Rua General Omar Torrijos 49
Caixa Postal 839
Bissau
Tel: +245 20 2470
Fax: +245 20 2209
loja4@sol.gtelecom.gw

MALI
Centre National de Promotion Industrielle
(CNPI)
BP 1980
Bamako
Tel: +223 22 80 85
Fax: +223 22 80 85
capes@capes.capes.ml

MAURITANIA
Fédération des Industries et des Mines
(FIM)
BP 3475
Nouakchott
Tel: +222 2 53974
Fax: +222 25 95 83

Association Professionnelle Promotion de La
Pêche Artisanale et du Crédit Maritime
Mutuel en Mauritanie
BP 08
Nouadhibou
Tel: +222 7 46030
Fax: +222 7 46003
fnp@toptechnology.mr

Banque Mauritanienne pour le Commerce
International (BMCI)
Avenue Général Abdel Naser
BP 622
Nouakchott
Tel: +222 525 24 69
Fax: +222 525 20 45

NIGERIA
Nigeria Industrial Development Bank Ltd.
(NIDB)
PO Box 2357
NIDB House
63–71 Broad Street
Lagos
Tel: +234 1 266 3470
Fax: +234 1 266 6733

New Nigeria Development Co. Ltd. (NNDC)
PMB 2120 – Ahmed Talib House
18/19 Amhadu Bello Way
Kaduna
Lagos
Tel: +234 62 20 02 50
Fax: +234 62 35 482
nndc@skannet.com

Mitecs Ltd.
30–32 Ojuelegba Road
Surulere, Lagos
GPO Box 1221
Tel: +234 18 34 108
Fax: +234 12614496
MITECS@infoweb.abs.net

Grid Consulting Ltd.
3A, Eko Akete Clos
PO Box 52453 Ikoyi
Lagos
Tel: +234 1 773 93 09
Fax: +234 1 266 79 05
Mobile: +234 0802 290 0403
gridcon@compuserve.com

SÉNÉGAL
Performances Management Consulting
43 Boulevard Djilly Mbaye
BP 22352
Dakar
Tel: +221 8219747
Fax: +221 8229710

SIERRA LEONE
Sierra Leone Development Investment
Corporation (SLDIC)
18/20 Walpole Street
PMB 6 – Freetown
Tel: +232 22 229760
Fax: +232 22 229097
sledic@sierratel.sl

TOGO
Chambre de Commerce d'Agriculture et
d'Industrie du Togo (CCAI)
BP 360
Lomé, Togo
Tel: +228 21 20 65
Fax: +228 21 47 30
coamega@hotmail.com

5. CARIBBEAN

ANTIGUA AND BARBUDA
Antigua Chamber of Commerce and
Industry Ltd.
PO Box 774
North and Popeshead Streets St. John's
Antigua et Barbude
Tel: +1268-462 0743
Fax: +1268-462 4575
chamcom@candw.ag

BAHAMAS
Bahamas Chamber of Commerce
PO Box N-665
BS – Nassau
Tel: +1 242 322 21 45/33 20
Fax: +1 242 322 46 49
www.tropitec.net/bahama-schamber

BARBADOS
Barbados Investment and Development
Corporation (BIDC)
Pelican House-Princess Alice Highway
PO Box 1250
BDS – Bridgetown
Tel: +1 246 427 53 50
Fax: +1 246 426 78 02
bidc@bidc.org

Casse Consultants Ltd.
3, Holders Plantation
St. James
PO Box 194 G.P.O.
BDS-Bridgetown
Tel: +1 246 432 5880/1

Fax: +1 246 432 5882
casse@caribsurf.com

BELIZE
Belize Chamber of Commerce and Industry
63 Regent Street
PO Box 291
BH – Belize City
Tel: +501 2 731 48
Fa : +501 2 749 84
bcci@btl.net

Ministry of Natural Resources, the
Environment & Industry
East Block Building
Independence Hill
Belmopan City
Tel: +501 8 222 199
Fax: +501 8 222 923
psindustry@btl.net

DOMINICA
National Development Corporation
Valley Road – PO Box 293
Roseau
Tel: +1 767 448 20 45
Fax: +1 767 448 58 40
ndcindustry@cwdom.dm

GRENADA
Industrial Development Corporation (IDC)
Frequente Industrial Park
St. Georges
Tel: +1 476 444 10 35
Fax: +1 476 444 48 28
gidc@caribsurf.com

GUYANA
The Private Sector Commission of
Guyana Ltd.
157 Waterloo Street
North Cummingsburg
Georgetown
Tel: +592 2 509 77
Fax: +592 2 509 78
pscentre@guyana.net.gy

HAITI
Association des industries d'Haiti (ADIH)
PO Box 2568
Port au Prince

REPUBLIQUE DOMINICAINE/
DOMINICAN REPUBLIC
Mr. Eduardo Beauchamp
Av. Sarasota No 117
Bella Vista
Santo Domingo
Tel: +1 809 532 1737
ordl.lome4@codetel.net.do

SAINT KITTS AND NEVIS
Chamber of Industry and Commerce
PO Box 332
Basse-Terre
Tel: +1 869 465 29 80/ 39 67
Fax: +1 869 465 44 90
sknchamber@caribsurf.com

ST. LUCIA
St. Lucia National Development Corporation
Block B. Waterfront
PO Box 495, Castries
Tel: +1 758 452 36 14
Fax: +1 758 452 18 41
devcorp@candw.lc

ST VINCENT & THE GRENADINES
The Development Corporation (DEVCO)
PO Box 841
Kingstown
Tel: +1 784 457 13 58
Fax: +1 784 457 28 38
devco@caribsurf.com

SURINAME
Chamber of Commerce and Industry
PO Box 149
Mr. Dr. J.C. de Mirandastraat 10
Paramaribo
Tel: +597 474 536
Fax: +597 474 779
chamber@sr.net

6. PACIFIC

COOK ISLANDS
Mr. Nooroa Bim TOU
PO Box 461
Nikao
Rarotonga
Tel: +682 21 352
Fax: +682 27 207

FIJI
Fiji Trade and Investment Board
6th Floor Civic Tower
Victoria Parade
PO Box 2303, Suva
Tel: +679 31 59 88
Fax: +679 30 17 83
frances@ftib.org.fj

KIRIBATI
Development Bank of Kiribati
PO Box 33
KIR – Bairiki, Tarawa
Tel: +686 210 80
Fax: +686 21 297

MARSHALL ISLANDS
Trade and Investment Services Department
Ministry of Resources and Development
PO Box 1727
Majuro, MH 96960
Tel: +692 625 3206
Fax: +692 625 3821

SAMOA ISLANDS
Department of Trade, Commerce & Industry
PO Box 862
Apia
Tel: +685 20471
Fax: +685 21646
tipu@tci.gov.ws

SOLOMON ISLANDS
National Planning and Human
Resources Development
PO Box G30

Honiara
Tel: +677 38336
Fax: +677 30163

NIUE
Mr. Tongiavalu Pitigia
Gutuma, Tuapa
Tel: +683 4148
Fax: +683 4232

PAPUA NEW GUINEA
Investment Promotion Authority
PO Box 5053
Boroko, NCD
Tel: +675 321 73 11
Fax: +675 321 2819
iepd@ipa.gov.pg

TONGA
Tonga Development Bank
PO Box 126
Nuku'alofa
Tel: +676 213 33
Fax: +676 237 75
tdb@kalianet.to

TUVALU
Development Bank of Tuvalu
GPO Box 9 – Vaiaku, Funafuti
Atoll
Tel: +688 20 850
Fax: +688 20 850

Annex 12

Contact Details of CDE EU Network

GERMANY
Afrika-Verein e.V.
Neuer Jungfernstieg, 21
Hamburg 20354
Tel: +49 (40) 4191330
post@afrikaverein.de

DEG-Deutsche Investitions und
Entwicklungsgesellschaft mbH
Belvederestrasse 40
50933 Cologne
Tel: +49 (221) 498 63 64
businessrelations@deginvest.de

AUSTRIA
Federal Economic Chamber of Austria
Wiedner Hauptstrasse 63
Postfach 150
Vienna 1045
Tel: +43 (1) 50105

Austria Wirtschaftsservice
Gesellschaft
Taborstrasse 10
Vienna 1020
Tel: +43 (1) 2147574229

Ministry for Foreign Affairs
(Department for Development Cooperation)
Minoritenplatz 9
Vienna 1014
Tel: +43 (1) 53115 /4526

BELGIUM
Chambre de Commerce d'Industrie et
d'Agriculture Belgique-Luxembourg-ACP
Avenue Marnix 30
Bruxelles 1000
Tel: +32 (2) 512 99 50

Comité Belge du Forum
Francophone des Affaires

Avenue d'Auderghem 63
Bruxelles 1050
Tel: +32 (81) 582855
siffa@skynet.be

Ministère de la Région Bruxelles
Capitale (Service Investissements
Étrangers)
Rue du Champ de Mars 25
Bruxelles 1050
Tel: +32 (2) 513 97 00

Ministère de la Région Wallonne
(DGRE/ AWEX)
2 Place Sainctelette
Bruxelles 1080
Tel: +32 (2) 421 82 11
p.suinen@awex.wallonie.be

DENMARK
Industrialisation Fund for Developing
Countries (IFU)
Bremerholm 4
Copenhagen 1069
Tel: +45 (33) 637500
ifu@ifu.dk

SPAIN
Compania Espanola de Financión del
Desarrollo (Cofides)
C/ Principe de Vergara 132
Planta 12
Madrid 28002
Tel: +34 (91) 5626008
cofides@cofides.es

Consorci de Promocio Comercial de
Catalunya (COPCA)
Pg. de Gràcia 94
Barcelona 08008
Tel: +34 (93) 4849605
coopercio@copca.com

Instituto Galego de Promoción
Económica (IGAPE)
Complexo Administrativo San Lazaro
Santiago de Compostela 15703
Tel: +34 (981) 541162
cvg@igape.es

Instituto de Fomento de Andalucia (IFA)
Avda. Republica Argentina 24
5a Planta
Sevilla
Tel: +34 (95) 4280227
alvaro@cdea.es

Instituto Valenciano de la Exportación
(IVEX)
Pl. de América 2–7
Valencia 46004
Tel: +34 (96) 3952001
cmiguel@ivex.es

Instituto Espanol de Comercio Exterior
(ICEX)
Paseo de la Castellana 14
Madrid 28046
Tel: +34 (91) 3496206
Fernando.Acena@icex.es

Promociones Exteriores de Canarias
(PROEXCA)
c/Emilio Castelar 4–5 Planta
Las Palmas de Gran Canaria 35007
Tel: +34 (928) 472400

Sociedad Para La Promoción Y
Reconversión Industrial (SPRI)
Gran Via 65–3°
Bilbao 48009
Tel: +34 (94) 4037000

FINLAND
FINNFUND
PO Box 391
Helsinki 00121
Tel: +358 (9) 348434
finnfund@finnfund.fi

FINPRO
PO Box 908
Helsinki 00101
Tel: +358 (204) 695455
marianne.koski@finpro.fi

Ministry for Foreign Affairs
Department for Development Cooperation
Katajanokanlaituri 3
PO Box 127
Helsinki 00160
Tel: +358 (9) 13416366
laura.kakko@formin.fi

FRANCE
Agence française de Développement (AfD)
Proparco
5, rue Roland Barthes
75598 Paris cedex 12
Tel: +33 (1) 53443131
Tel: +33 (1) 53443737
balc@afd.fr
beudind@afd.fr

Assemblée des Chambres Françaises
Commerce et d'Industrie (ACFCI)
45, Av. d'Iéna
BP 448–16
Tel: +32 (2) 221 04 20
o.lemerle@acfci.cci.fr
Tel: +33 (1) 40693700
f.duverge@acfci.cci.fr

Ministère des Affaires étrangères
Association Régionale pour le
Développement et la Coopération
Industrielle Internationale
20, rue Monsieur
Paris 75700, France
Tel: + 33 (1) 53694224
Marc.basquin@diplomatie.gouv.fr

Chambre de Commerce et d'Industrie de
Rouen (CCIR)
Centre d'Affaires Rouen International

4, rue du docteur Rambert
Palais des Consuls – BP641
Rouen Cedex 76007
Tel: +33 (2) 35143887
ipad@rouen.cci.fr

Entreprise Rhône Alpes International (ERAI)
104 route de Paris
Charbonnières Les Bains 69620
Tel: +33 (4) 72383361

Interco Aquitaine
Agence de Coopération Internationale
Cité Mondiale, Bureaux de la Cité
23 Parvis des Chartrons
Bordeaux 33074
Tel: +33 (5) 5601 7834
Gilles.roulland@interco.cr-aquitaine.fr

Institut Régional de Coopération-
Développement (IRCOD)
2 Rue de l'Olican
Chalons-en-Champagne 51037
Tel: +33 (3) 26 692475
ircod@wanadoo.fr

GREECE
Hellenic Organisation of Small & Medium
Sized Industries & Handicrafts (EOMMEX)
Xenias 16
Athènes 11528
Tel: +30 (1) 7491287
interel@eommex.gr

Hellenic Foreign Trade Board (HEPO)
86–88 M. Antypa Str
16346 Ilioupolis, Athènes
Tel: +30 (1) 9950980/9982220

IRELAND
Enterprise Ireland
Glasnevin
Dublin 9
Tel: +353 (1) 8082035
charles.kelly@enterpriseireland.com

ITALY
Instituto Nazionale per il Commercio Estero
(ICE)
Via Liszt 21
Rome 00144
Tel: +39 (06) 59929516
i.aronadio@ice.it

Politiche per le Imprese SPA-ERVET
Via Morgagni 6
Bologna 40122
Tel: +39 (051) 6450411
politicheue@ervet.it

LUXEMBOURG
Lux-Development SA
1 rue Emile Bian
BP 2273
Luxembourg 1022
Tel: +352 4782362
ask@lux-development.lu

Minstère des Affaires étrangères
(Service de la Coopération)
6 rue de la Congrégation
Luxembourg 2911
Tel: +352 4782362

NETHERLANDS
FMO-Netherlands Development
Finance Co.
Koningskade 40
PO Box 93060
La Haye 2509 AB
Te : +31 (70) 3149636
t.van.den.elsken@fmo.nl

PORTUGAL
Instituto Portugues de Apoio ao
Desenvolvimento (IPAD)
Av. Da Liberdade 258–5°
Lisboa 1200
Tel: +351 021 3177300
isabel@apad.pt

BCP Atlântico
Av. José Malhoa – Lote 1686
Lisboa 1070
Tel: +351 (21) 7218400

Banco Português de Investimento, SA
Largo Jean Monnet, 1
Piso 9°
Lisboa 1200
Tel: +351 (21) 3226577
Vitorino_Conceicao_Caeiro@BancoBPI.PT

Investimentos, Comercio e Turismo
De Portugal (ICEP)
101, Av. 5 de Outubro
Lisboa 1050–051
Tel: +351 (21) 7909578
rutegir@icep.pt

UNITED KINGDOM
CDC Capital Partners
Business Development Dept.
1 Bessborough Gardens
London SW1V 2JQ
Tel: +44 (0)20 7828 4488

Trade Partners UK-British Trade
International
Kingsgate House
66–74 Victoria Street
London SW1E 65W
Tel: +44 (0)20 7215 4450
David.Elliott@tradepartners.gov.uk

SWEDEN
Swedfund International AB
Sveavâgen 24–26
PO Box 3286
10365 Stockholm
Tel: +46 (8) 725 9400
info@swedfund.se

Swedish International Development
Cooperation Agency (SIDA)
Sveavâgen 20
10525 Stockolm
Tel: +46 (8) 698 5036
bo.dan.bergman@sida.se

Annex 13

The Tasks of the Inter-service Quality Support Group

The **Inter-service Quality Support-Group** is required to:

> *examine the strategies and programming of the Community's external assistance both to improve the efficiency, coherence and co-ordination of the various community co-operation strategies and to ensure that the relevant strategy and programming documents reach the high standard required of reform.*

The role of the **Inter-service Quality Support Group** is to:

> *provide help, support and guidance, particularly as regards best practice techniques, in the preparation of strategies and programme.*

The **Inter-service Quality Support Group** examines:

> *the most important strategy and planning documents, and in particular CSPs and National Indicative Programmes (NIPs), at an early stage.*

On the basis of this examination the **Inter-service Quality Support Group** then makes:

> *comments and suggestions for improvements, if the high standards required by the reform has not been reached.*

Annex 14

The Tasks of the Office Quality Support Group

The main purpose of the **Office Quality Support Group** is to contribute to:

improving the quality system of the Office, in order to promote a gradual development of a coherent Office quality approach in all the thematic and cross cutting areas.

The **Office Quality Support Group** will:

- set the minimum common procedures and criteria for the 'quality assessment' of measures;

- gradually improve and harmonise common procedures and criteria, through the use of the scoring system being put in place by the Evaluation Unit and the use of indicators and benchmarks developed by the thematic networks.

The **Office Quality Support Group** is responsible for the quality assessment of a *limited number* of *proposals for identification* and proposals for measures. The **Office Quality Support Group** will review all Proposals for Identification which have to be submitted for projects over Euro 2 million. Each Proposal for Identification will then be assessed with reference to:

- its coherence with wider programme objectives;

- the conduct and timing of the planned identification and appraisal process;

- the need for a feasibility analysis of the key policy and operational elements of the proposal;

- the wider relevance of the proposal in terms of the internal learning process within the Commission;

- the scope for cross fertilisation of other operations.

The work of the **Office Quality Support Group** should be carefully co-ordinated with the work of the **Directorate Quality Support Group**.

In reviewing the Proposal for Identification each operation will be allocated to a 'thematic' rapporteur to facilitate identification of best practices and internal learning processes (cross fertilisation).

Where it is deemed appropriate the **Office Quality Support Group** will:

make specific recommendations aiming at improving the identification/appraisal process, at better incorporating the feasibility techniques and sector guidelines or exploiting synergies with other donors.

Conclusions and recommendation from the **Office Quality Support Group** are passed on to the concerned operational Directorate of the European Commission with the Director concerned taking the final decision on whether or not to go ahead with the identification and appraisal of the proposed project or programme.

Each Proposal for Identification has a 'quality-rating sheet' compiled on it. Each *quality-rating sheet* compiled by the **Office Quality Support Group** will need to be signed off on by the Deputy Director General. The *quality-rating sheet* is completed by a staff member that is not directly involved in the management of the project. This is intended to promote an objective assessment of the project and programme proposals being reviewed for their quality. It is foreseen that improved *quality-rating sheets* will be progressively introduced in response to on-going work on improving assessments.

Annex 15

The Tasks of the Directorate Quality Support Group

The **Directorate Quality Support Group** is established in each of the operational Directorates of AIDCO, is chaired by the Director of each respective Directorate and consists of experienced staff members. The task of the **Directorate Quality Support Group** is to:

deliver the 'quality assessment' for the majority of the measures that will eventually be approved by the Commission.

It will be responsible for establishing minimal common procedures and criteria for use in the quality assessments in various geographic and thematic areas of the Commission's work in ACP countries. It will review all proposals for identification, in collaboration with the Secretariat to the Quality Support Group and examine the proposed measures which are not examined by the Office Quality Support Group structures. Where the **Directorate Quality Support Group** examines a proposed measure it will deliver the quality assessment. In these cases where appropriate the **Directorate Quality Support Group** will make specific recommendation aimed at improving the identification and appraisal process. Where the **Directorate Quality Support Group** is responsible for compiling the *quality rating sheet* the concerned Director will sign off on the sheet.

The opinion of one of the structures of the Quality Support Group on the Proposal for Identification is a necessary pre-condition for the actual commitment of funds for any operation, this includes funds for initial identification and feasibility studies.

In the Commission's view this whole process of assessment by the Quality Support Group, including approval by the Geographical Director, should not take more than one month.

Annex 16

Declaration XXII, Joint Declaration Concerning Agricultural Products Referred to in Article 1(2)(A) of Annex V

Joint Declaration concerning agricultural products referred to in Article 1(2)(a) of Annex V

The Parties have taken note that the Community intends to take the measures mentioned in the Annex, and which are laid down at the date of signing of the Agreement, with a view to granting ACP States the preferential treatment provided for in Article 1(2)(a), for certain agricultural and processed products.

They have taken note that the Community declares that it will take all the measures required to ensure that the corresponding agricultural regulations are adopted in good time and that, wherever possible, they come into force at the same time as the interim arrangements which will be introduced after the signing of the successor Agreement to the Fourth ACP-EC Convention signed in Lomé on 15 December 1989.

Preferential treatment applicable to agricultural products and foodstuffs originating in the ACP States

01 LIVE ANIMALS

0101	LIVE HORSES, ASSES, MULES AND HINNIES
0101	exemption
0102	LIVE BOVINE ANIMALS
01029005	reduction 100% ad valorem customs duties
01029021	reduction 100% ad valorem customs duties
01029029	reduction 100% ad valorem customs duties
01029041	reduction 100% ad valorem customs duties
01029049	reduction 100% ad valorem customs duties
01029051	reduction 100% ad valorem customs duties
01029059	reduction 100% ad valorem customs duties
01029061	reduction 100% ad valorem customs duties
01029069	reduction 100% ad valorem customs duties
01029071	reduction 100% ad valorem customs duties
01029079	reduction 100% ad valorem customs duties
0103	LIVE SWINES
01039110	reduction 16%
01039211	reduction 16%
01039219	reduction 16%
0104	LIVE SHEEP AND GOATS
01041030	reduction 100% customs duties within the limit of the quota (ctg 1)
01041080	reduction 100% customs duties within the limit of the quota (ctg 1)
01042010	exemption
01042090	reduction 100% customs duties within the limit of the quota (ctg 1)
0105	LIVE POULTRY, FOWLS OF THE SPECIES GALLUS DOMESTICUS, DUCKS. GEESE, TURKEYS AND GUINEA FOWLS
0105	reduction 16%
0106	LIVE ANIMALS (EXCL HORSES, ASSES, MULES, MINNIES, BOVINE ANIMALS, SWINE. SHEEP, GOATS, POULTRY, FISH. CRUSTACEANS, MOLLUSCS AND OTHER AQUATIC INVERTEBRATES, AND MICRO-ORGANIC CULTURES, ETC.)
0106	exemption

02 MEAT AND EDIBLE MEAT OFFAL

0201	MEAT OF BOVINE ANIMALS, FRESH OR CHILLED
0201	reduction 100% ad valorem customs duties (1)
0202	MEAT OF BOVINE ANIMALS, FROZEN
0202	reduction 100% ad valorem customs duties (1)
0203	MEAT OF SWINE, FRESH, CHILLED OR FROZEN
02031110	within the limit of the quota (ctg 7) reduction 50%
02031190	exemption
02031211	within the limit of the quota (ctg 7) reduction 50%
02031219	within the limit of the quota (ctg 7) reduction 50%
02031290	exemption
02031911	within the limit of the quota (ctg 7) reduction 50%
02031913	within the limit of the quota (ctg 7) reduction 50%

02031915	within the limit of the quota (ctg 7) reduction 50%
ex 02031955	within the limit of the quota (ctg 7) reduction 50% (excluding tenderloin presented separately)
02031959	within the limit of the quota (ctg 7) reduction 50%
02031990	exemption
02032110	within the limit of the quota (ctg 7) reduction 50%
02032190	exemption
02032211	within the limit of the quota (ctg 7) reduction 50%
02032219	within the limit of the quota (ctg 7) reduction 50%
02032290	exemption
02032911	within the limit of the quota (ctg 7) reduction 50%
02032913	within the limit of the quota (ctg 7) reduction 50%
02032915	within the limit of the quota (ctg 7) reduction 50%
ex 02032955	within the limit of the quota (ctg 7) reduction 50% (excluding the tenderioin in one piece)
02032959	within the limit of the quota (ctg 7) reduction 50%
02032990	exemption
0204	MEAT OF SHEEP OR GOATS, FRESH, CHILLED OR FROZEN
0204	reduction 100% ad valorem customs duties; domestic sheep: within the limit of the quota (quota 2) reduction 65% specific duties; ind foodstuffs originating in the ACP States other species: within the limit of the quota (quota 1) reduction 100% specific duties
0205	MEAT OF HORSES, ASSES, MULES OR HINNIES, FRESH, CHILLED OR FROZEN
0205	exemption
0206	EDIBLE OFFAL OF BOVINE ANIMALS, SWINE, SHEEP. GOATS, HORSES. ASSES, MULES OR HINNIES, FRESH, CHILLED OR FROZEN
02061091	exemption
02061095	reduction 100% ad valorem customs duties (1)
02061099	exemption
020621	exemption
020622	exemption
02062991	reduction 100% ad valorem customs duties (1)
02062999	exemption
02063021	within the limit of the quota (ctg 7) reduction 50%
02063031	within the limit of the quota (ctg 7) reduction 50%
02063090	exemption
02064191	within the limit of the quota (ctg 7) reduction 50%
02064199	exemption
02064991	within the limit of the quota (ctg 7) reduction 50%

Preferential treatment applicable to agricultural products and foodstuffs originating in the ACP States

02064999	exemption
020680	exemption
020690	exemption
0207	MEAT AND EDIBLE OFFAL OF FOWLS OF THE SPECIES QALLUS DOMESTICUS, DUCKS, GEESE, TURKEYS AND GUINEA FOWLS, FRESH, CHILLED OR FROZEN
0207	within the limit of the quota (ctg 3) reduction 65%
0206	MEAT AND EDIBLE OFFAL OF RABBITS, HARES, PIGEONS AND OTHER ANIMALS NOT ELSEWHERE SPECIFIED OR INCLUDED, FRESH,CHILLED OR FROZEN
0208	exemption
0209	PIG FAT, FREE OF LEAN MEAT AND POULTRY FAT NOT RENDERED, FRESH, CHILLED, FROZEN, SALTED, IN BRINE, DRIED OR SMOKED
02090011	within the limit of the quota (ctg 7) reduction 50%
02090019	within the limit of the quota (ctg 7) reduction 50%
02090030	within the limit of the quota (ctg 7) reduction 50%
02090090	reduction 16%
0210	MEAT AND EDIBLE OFFAL, SALTED, IN BRINE, DRIED OR SMOKED; EDIBLE FLOURS AND MEALS OF MEAT OR MEAT OFFAL
02101111	within the limit of the quota (ctg 7) reduction 50%
02101119	within the limit of the quota (ctg 7) reduction 50%
02101131	within the limit of the quota (ctg 7) reduction 50%
02101139	within the limit of the quota (ctg 7) reduction 50%
02101190	exemption
02101211	within the limit of the quota (ctg 7) reduction 50%
02101219	within the limit of the quota (ctg 7) reduction 50%
02101290	exemption
02101910	within the limit of the quota (ctg 7) reduction 50%
02101920	within the limit of the quota (ctg 7) reduction 50%
02101930	within the limit of the quota (ctg 7) reduction 50%
02101940	within the limit of the quota (ctg 7) reduction 50%
02101951	within the limit of the quota (ctg 7) reduction 50%
02101959	within the limit of the quota (ctg 7) reduction 50%
02101960	within the limit of the quota (ctg 7) reduction 50%
02101970	within the limit of the quota (ctg 7) reduction 50%
02101981	within the limit of the quota (ctg 7) reduction 50%
02101989	within the limit of the quota (ctg 7) reduction 50%
02101990	exemption
021020	reduction 100% ad valorem customs duties
02109010	exemption
02109011	reduction 100% ad valorem customs duties; domestic sheep: within the limit of the quota (quota 2) reduction 65% specific duties; other species: within the limit of the quota (quota 1) reduction 100% specific duties
02109019	reduction 100% ad valorem customs duties; domestic sheep: within the limit of the quota (quota 2) reduction 65% specific duties; other species: within the limit of the quota (quota 1) reduction 100% specific duties
02109021	exemption
02109029	exemption
02109031	within the limit of the quota (ctg 7) reduction 50%
02109039	within the limit of the quota (ctg 7) reduction 50%"
02109041	reduction 100% ad valorem customs duties
02109049	exemption
02109060	exemption
02109071	reduction 16%
02109079	reduction 16%
02109080	exemption
02109090	reduction 100% ad valorem customs duties

03 FISH AND CRUSTACEANS, MOLLUSCS AND OTHER AQUATIC INVERTEBRATES

03	exemption

04 DAIRY PRODUCE; BIRDS' EGGS; NATURAL HONEY; EDIBLE PRODUCTS OF ANIMAL ORIGIN, NOT ELSEWHERE SPECIFIED OR INCLUDED

0401	MILK AND CREAM, NOT CONCENTRATED NOR CONTAINING ADDED SUGAR OR OTHER SWEETENING MATTER
0401	reduction 16%
0402	MILK AND CREAM, CONCENTRATED OR CONTAINING ADDED SUGAR OR OTHER SWEETENING MATTER
0402	within the limit of the quota (ctg 5) reduction 65%
0403	BUTTERMILK, CURDLED MILK AND CREAM YOGURT, KEPHIR AND OTHER FERMENTED OR ACIDIFIED MILK AND CREAM, WHETHER OR NOT CONCENTRATED OR FLAVOURED OR CONTAINING ADDED SUGAR OR OTHER SWEETENING MATTER, FRUITS, NUTS OR COCOA
04031011	reduction 16%
04031013	reduction 16%
04031019	reduction 16%
04031031	reduction 16%
04031033	reduction 16%
04031051	reduction 100% ad valorem customs duties
04031053	reduction 100% ad valorem customs duties
04031059	reduction 100% ad valorem customs duties

Preferential treatment applicable to agricultural products and foodstuffs originating in the ACP States

04031091	reduction 100% ad valorem customs duties
04031093	reduction 100% ad valorem customs duties
04031099	reduction 100% ad valorem customs duties
04039011	reduction 16%
04039013	reduction 16%
04039019	reduction 16%
04039031	reduction 16%
04039033	reduction 16%
04039039	reduction 16%
04039051	reduction 16%
04039053	reduction 16%
04039059	reduction 16%
04039061	reduction 16%
04039063	reduction 16%
04039069	reduction 16%
04039071	reduction 100% ad valorem customs duties
04039073	reduction 100% ad valorem customs duties
04039079	reduction 100% ad valorem customs duties
04039091	reduction 100% ad valorem customs duties
04039093	reduction 100% ad valorem customs duties
04039099	reduction 100% ad valorem customs duties
0404	WHEY, WHETHER OR NOT CONCENTRATED OR CONTAINING ADDED SUGAR OR OTHER SWEETENING MATTER; PRODUCTS CONSISTING OF NATURAL MILK CONSTITUENTS, WHETHER OR NOT CONTAINING ADDED SUGAR OR OTHER SWEETENING MATTER, NOT ELSEWHERE SPECIFIED OR INCLUDED
0404	reduction 16%
0405	BUTTER AND OTHER FATS AND OILS DERIVED FROM MILK
0405	reduction 16%
0406	CHEESE AND CURD
0406	within the limit of the quota (ctg 6) reduction 65%
0407	BIRDS' EGGS, IN SHELL, FRESH, PRESERVED OR COOKED
04070011	reduction 16%
04070019	reduction 16%
04070030	reduction 16%
04070090	exemption
0408	BIRDS' EGGS, NOT IN SHELL, AND EGG YOLKS, FRESH, DRIED, COOKED BY STEAMING OR BY BOILING IN WATER, MOULDED, FROZEN OR OTHERWISE PRESERVED, WHETHER OR NOT CONTAINING ADDED SUGAR OR OTHER SWEETENING MATTER
04081180	reduction 16%
04081981	reduction 16%
04081989	reduction 16%
04089180	reduction 16%
04089980	reduction 16%
0409	NATURAL HONEY
0409	exemption

0410	TURTLES' EGGS, BIRDS' NESTS AND OTHER EDIBLE PRODUCTS OF ANIMAL ORIGIN NOT ELSEWHERE SPECIFIED OR INCLUDED
0410	exemption

05 PRODUCTS OF ANIMAL ORIGIN NOT ELSEWHERE SPECIFIED OR INCLUDED

05	exemption

06 LIVE TREES AND OTHER PLANTS; BULBS, ROOTS AND THE LIKE; CUT FLOWERS AND ORNAMENTAL FOLIAGE

06	exemption

07 EDIBLE VEGETABLES AND CERTAIN ROOTS AND TUBERS

0701	POTATOES, FRESH OR CHILLED
0701	exemption
0702	TOMATOES, FRESH OR CHILLED
0702	tomatoes other than cherry tomatoes 15/11–30/4: reduction 60% ad valorem customs duties within the limit of the quota (quota 13a); cherry tomatoes 15/11–30/4: reduction 100% ad valorem customs duties within the limit of the quota (quota 13b)
0703	ONIONS, SHALLOTS, GARLIC. LEEKS AND OTHER ALLIACEOUS VEGETABLES, FRESH OR CHILLED
07031019	reduction 15% from 16/5–31/1, exemption 1/2–15/5
07031090	reduction 16%
070320	reduction 15% from 1/6–31/1, exemption 1/2–31/5
070390	reduction 16%
0704	CABBAGES, CAULIFLOWERS, KOHLRABI, KALE AND SIMILAR EDIBLE BRASSICAS, FRESH OR CHILLED
070410	reduction 16%
070420	reduction 16%
07049010	reduction 16%
07049090	Chinese cabbage: reduction 15% 1/1–30/10, exemption 1/11–31/12; other cabbages: reduction 16%
0705	LETTUCE 'LACTUCA SATIVA' AND CHICORY 'CICHORIUM SPP', FRESH OR CHILLED
070511	Iceberg salad: reduction 15% 1/11–30/6, exemption 1/7–31/10; other salads: reduction 16%
070519	reduction 16%
070521	reduction 16%
070529	reduction 16%
0706	CARROTS, TURNIPS, SALAD BEETROOT, SALSIFY, CELERIAC, RADISHES AND SIMILAR EDIBLE ROOTS, FRESH OR CHILLED
070610	carrots: reduction 15% 1/4–31/12, exemption 1/1–31/3; turnips: reduction 16%
07069005	reduction 16%
07069011	reduction 16%
07069017	reduction 16%
07069030	exemption
ex 07069090	salad beetroot and radishes (raphanus sativus): exemption

Preferential treatment applicable to agricultural products and foodstuffs originating in the ACP States

0707	CUCUMBERS AND GHERKINS, FRESH OR CHILLED		071110	exemption
			071130	exemption
ex 07070005	small winter cucumbers 1/11–15/5: reduction 100% ad valorem customs duties; winter cucumbers other than small cucumbers: reduction 16% ad valorem customs duties		071140	exemption
			07119010	exemption
			07119030	reduction 100% ad valorem customs duties
			07119040	exemption
			07119060	exemption
07070090	reduction 16%		07119070	exemption
			07119090	exemption
0708	LEGUMINOUS VEGETABLES, SHELLED OR UNSHELLED, FRESH OR CHILLED		0712	DRIED VEGETABLES, WHOLE, CUT, SLICED, BROKEN OR IN POWDER, BUT NOT FURTHER PREPARED
0708	exemption			
0709	OTHER VEGETABLES, FRESH OR CHILLED		071220	exemption
070910	reduction 15% from 1/1–30/9, reduction 100% ad valorem customs duties 1/10–31/12		071230	exemption
			07129005	exemption
			07129019	reduction 1.81 EUR/t
070920	reduction 15% from 1/2–14/8, reduction 40% from 16/1–31/1, exemption 15/8–15/1		07129030	exemption
			07129050	exemption
			07129090	exemption except olives
070930	exemption			
070940	exemption		0713	DRIED LEGUMINOUS VEGETABLES, SHELLED, WHETHER OR NOT SKINNED OR SPLIT
07095110	reduction 16%			
0095130	reduction 16%			
07095150	reduction 16%		0713	exemption
07095190	exemption			
070952	reduction 16%		0714	MANIOC, ARROWROOT, SALEP, JERUSALEM ARTICHOKES, SWEET POTATOES AND SIMILAR ROOTS AND TUBERS WITH HIGH STARCH OR INULIN CONTENT, FRESH OR DRIED, WHETHER OR NOT SLICED OR IN THE FORM OF PELLETS; SAGO PITH
070960	exemption			
070970	reduction 16%			
07099010	reduction 16%			
07099020	reduction 16%			
07099040	reduction 16%			
07099050	reduction 16%		07141010	reduction 8.38 EUR/t
07099060	eduction 1,81 EUR/t		07141091	exemption
07099070	reduction 100% ad valorem customs duties		07141099	reduction 6.19 EUR/t
07099090	exemption		071420	exemption
			07149011	exemption
0710	VEGETABLES, UNCOOKED OR COOKED BY STEAMING OR BOILING IN WATER, FROZEN		07149019	reduction 6.19 EUR/t; arrow-root: exemption
			07149090	exemption
071010	exemption			

071021	exemption		0801	COCONUTS, BRAZIL NUTS AND CASHEW NUTS, FRESH OR DRIED, WHETHER OR NOT SHELLED OR PEELED
071022	exemption			
071029	exemption			
071030	exemption		0801	exemption
071040	reduction 100% ad valorem customs duties			
07108051	exemption		0802	OTHER NUTS, FRESH OR DRIED, WHETHER OR NOT SHELLED OR PEELED (EXCL. COCONUTS, BRAZIL NUTS AND CASHEW NUTS)
07108059	exemption			
0710806	exemption			
07108069	exemption			
07108070	exemption		08021190	reduction 16%
07108080	exemption		08021290	reduction 16%
07108085	exemption		080221	reduction 16%
07108095	exemption		080222	reduction 16%
071090	exemption		080231	exemption
			080232	exemption
0711	VEGETABLES PROVISIONALLY PRESERVED, E.G. BY SULPHUR DIOXIDE GAS, IN BRINE, IN SULPHUR WATER OR IN OTHER PRESERVATIVE SOLUTIONS, BUT UNSUITABLE IN THAT STATE FOR IMMEDIATE CONSUMPTION		080240	reduction 16%
			080250	exemption
			080290	exemption

Preferential treatment applicable to agricultural products and foodstuffs originating in the ACP States

0803	BANANAS, INCL. PLANTAINS, FRESH OR DRIED
08030011	exemption
08030019	The Community import regime for bananas is presently under review. The Parties agree to provide appropriate preferential access for ACP bananas in the context of the Community's future banana regime
08030090	exemption
0804	DATES, FIGS, PINEAPPLES, AVOCADOS, GUAVAS, MANGOES AND MANGOSTEENS, FRESH OR DRIED
080410	exemption
08042010	exemption from 1/11–30/4 within the limit of the ceiling (ceiling 3)
08042090	exemption
080430	exemption
080440	exemption
080450	exemption
0805	CITRUS FRUIT, FRESH OR DRIED
080510	reduction 80% ad valorem customs duties; within the framework of the reference quantity (rq 1) 15/5–30/9 reduction 100% ad valorem customs duties (4)
080520	reduction 80% ad valorem customs duties; within the framework of the reference quantity (rq 2) 15/5–30/9 reduction 100% ad valorem customs duties (4)
08053090	exemption
080540	exemption
080590	exemption
0806	GRAPES, FRESH OR DRIED
ex 08061010	seedless table grapes: within the limit of the quota (quota 14) 1/12–31/1 exemption; within the framework of the reference quantity (rq 3) 1/2–31/3 exemption (4) from 1/2–31/3 exemption (4)
080620	exemption
0807	MELONS, INCL. WATERMELONS, AND PAPAW 'PAPAYAS', FRESH
0807	exemption
0808	APPLES, PEARS AND QUINCES, FRESH
080810	within the limit of the quota (ctg 15) reduction 50% ad valorem customs duties
08082010	within the limit of the quota (ctg 16) reduction 65% ad valorem customs duties
08082050	within the limit of the quota (ctg 16) reduction 65% ad valorem customs duties
08082090	reduction 16%
0809	APRICOTS, CHERRIES, PEACHES INCL. NECTARINES, PLUMS AND SLOES, FRESH
080910	from 1/5–31/8 reduction 15% ad valorem custom duties, 1/9–30/4 exemption
08092005	from 1/11–31/3: exemption
080930	from 1/4–30/11 reduction 15% ad valorem customs duties, 1/12–31/3 exemption
08094005	from 1/4–14/12 reduction 15% ad valorem customs duties, 15/12–31/3 exemption
08094090	exemption

0810	STRAWBERRIES, RASPBERRIES, BLACKBERRIES, BLACK. WHITE OR RED CURRANTS, GOOSEBERRIES AND OTHER EDIBLE FRUIT, NOT ELSEWHERE SPECIFIED OR INCLUDED, FRESH
08101005	within the limit of the quota (ctg 17) from 1/11–29/2 exemption
08101080	within the limit of the quota (ctg 17) from 1/11–29/2 exemption
081020	reduction 16%
081030	reduction 16%
08104030	exemption
08104050	duty = 3%
08104090	duty = 5%
081090	exemption
0811	FRUIT AND NUTS, UNCOOKED OR COOKED STEAMING OR BOILING IN WATER, FROZEN WHETHER OR NOT CONTAINING ADDED SUGAR OR OTHER SWEETENING MATTER
08111011	reduction 100% ad valorem customs duties
08111019	exemption
08111090	exemption
08112011	reduction 100% ad valorem customs duties
08112019	exemption
08112031	exemption
08112039	exemption
08112051	exemption
08112059	exemption
08112090	exemption
08119011	reduction 100% ad valorem customs duties
08119019	reduction 100% ad valorem customs duties
08119031	exemption
08119039	exemption
08119050	exemption
08119070	exemption
08119075	exemption
08119080	exemption
08119085	exemption
08119095	exemption
0812	FRUIT AND NUTS, PROVISIONALLY PRESERVED, E.G. BY SULPHUR DIOXIDE GAS, IN BRINE, IN SULPHUR WATER OR IN OTHER PRESERVATIVE SOLUTIONS, BUT UNSUITABLE IN THAT STATE FOR IMMEDIATE CONSUMPTION
081210	exemption
081220	exemption
08129010	exemption
08129020	exemption
08129030	exemption
08129040	exemption
08129050	exemption
08129060	exemption
08129070	exemption
08129095	exemption
0813	APRICOTS, PRUNES, APPLES, PEACHES, PEARS, PAWPAWS, TAMARINDS AND OTHER DRIED FRUIT NOT ELSEWHERE SPECIFIED OR INCLUDED; MIXTURES OF EDIBLE NUTS OR DRIED FRUITS
0813	exemption

Preferential treatment applicable to agricultural products and foodstuffs originating in the ACP States

0814	PEEL OF CITRUS FRUIT OR MELONS, INCL. WATERMELONS, FRESH, FROZEN, DRIED OR PROVISIONALLY PRESERVED IN BRINE OR IN WATER WITH OTHER ADDITIVES	
0814	exemption	

09 COFFEE, TEA, MATE AND SPICES

09	exemption

10 CEREALS

1001	WHEAT AND MESLIN	
100110	within the limit of the quota (ctg 10) reduction 50%	
10019010	exemption	
10019091	within the limit of the quota (ctg 10) reduction 50%	
10019099	within the limit of the quota (ctg 10) reduction 50%	
1002	RYE	
1002	within the limit of the quota (ctg 10) reduction 50%	
1003	BARLEY	
1003	within the limit of the quota (ctg 10) reduction 50%	
1004	OATS	
1004	within the limit of the quota (ctg 10) reduction 50%	
1005	MAIZE OR CORN	
10051090	reduction 1.81 EUR/t	
100590	reduction 1.81 EUR/t	
1006	RICE	
10061010	exemption	
10061021	within the limit of the quota (ctg 11) reduction 65% and 4.34 EUR/t (2)	
10061023	within the limit of the quota (ctg 11) reduction 65% and 4.34 EUR/t (2)	
10061025	within the limit of the quota (ctg 11) reduction 65% and 4.34 EUR/t (2)	
10061027	within the limit of the quota (ctg 11) reduction 65% and 4.34 EUR/t (2)	
10061092	within the limit of the quota (ctg 11) reduction 65% and 4.34 EUR/t (2)	
10061094	within the limit of the quota (ctg 11) reduction 65% and 4.34 EUR/t (2)	
10061096	within the limit of the quota (ctg 11) reduction 65% and 4.34 EUR/t (2)	
10061098	within the limit of the quota (ctg 11) reduction 65% and 4.34 EUR/t (2)	
100620	within the limit of the quota (ctg 11) reduction 65% and 4.34 EUR/t (2)	
100630	within the limit of the quota (ctg 11) reduction of 16.78 EUR/t, then reduced by 65% and 6.52 EUR/t (2)	
100640	within the limit of the quota (ctg 12) reduction 65% and 3.62 EUR/t (2)	
1007	GRAIN SORGHUM	
1007	reduction 60% within the limit of the ceiling (ceiling 3) (3)	

1008	BUCKWHEAT, MILLET, CANARY SEED AND OTHER CEREALS (EXCL. WHEAT AND MESLIN RYE, BARLEY, OATS, MAIZE, RICE AND GRAIN SORGHUM)
100810	within the limit of the quota (ctg 10) reduction 50%
100820	reduction 100% within the limit of the ceiling (ceiling 2) (3)
100890	within the limit of the quota (ctg 10) reduction 50%

11 PRODUCTS OF THE MILLING INDUSTRY; MALT; STARCHES; INULIN; WHEAT GLUTEN

1101	WHEAT OR MESLIN FLOUR
1101	reduction 16%
1102	CEREAL FLOURS (EXCL. WHEAT OR MESLIN)
110210	reduction 16%
11022010	reduction 7.3 EUR/t
11022090	reduction 3.6 EUR/t
110230	reduction 3.6 EUR/t
11029010	reduction 7.3 EUR/t
11029030	reduction 7.3 EUR/t
11029090	reduction 3.6 EUR/t
1103	CEREAL GROATS, MEAL AND PELLETS
110311	reduction 16%
110312	reduction 7.3 EUR/t
11031310	reduction 7.3 EUR/t
1031390	reduction 3.6 EUR/t
110314	reduction 3.6 EUR/t
11031910	reduction 7.3 EUR/t
11031930	reduction 7.3 EUR/t
11031990	reduction 3.6 EUR/t
110321	reduction 7.3 EUR/t
11032910	reduction 7.3 EUR/t
11032920	reduction 7.3 EUR/t
11032930	reduction 7.3 EUR/t
11032940	reduction 7.3 EUR/t
11032950	reduction 3.6 EUR/t
11032990	reduction 3.6 EUR/t
1104	CEREAL GRAINS OTHERWISE WORKED E.G. HULLED, ROLLED, FLAKED, PEARLED, SLICED OR KEBBLED; GERM OF CEREALS, WHOLE, ROLLED, FLAKED OR GROUND (EXCL. CEREAL FLOURS, AND HUSKED AND SEMI- OR WHOLLY MILLED RICE AND BROKEN RICE)
11041110	reduction 3.6 EUR/t
11041190	reduction 7.3 EUR/t
11041210	reduction 3.6 EUR/t
11041290	reduction 7.3 EUR/t
110419	reduction 7.3 EUR/t
11042110	reduction 3.6 EUR/t
11042130	reduction 3.6 EUR/t
11042150	reduction 7.3 EUR/t
11042190	reduction 3.6 EUR/t
11042199	reduction 3.6 EUR/t
110422	reduction 3.6 EUR/t
110423	reduction 3.6 EUR/t
110429	reduction 3.6 EUR/t
110430	reduction 7.3 EUR/t

Preferential treatment applicable to agricultural products and foodstuffs originating in the ACP States

1105	FLOUR, MEAL, FLAKES, GRANULES AND PELLETS OF POTATOES	
1105	exemption	
1106	FLOUR, MEAL AND POWDER OF THE DRIED LEGUMINOUS VEGETABLES OF HEADING 0713, OF SAGO OR OF ROOTS AND TUBERS OF HEADING 0714 OR OF THE PRODUCTS OF CHAPTER 8	
110610	exemption	
11062010	reduction 7.98 EUR/t; arrow-root; exemption	
11062090	reduction 29.18 EUR/t; arrow-root; exemption	
110630	exemption	
1108	STARCHES; INULIN	
110811	reduction 24.8 EUR/t	
110812	reduction 24.8 EUR/t	
110813	reduction 24.8 EUR/t	
110814	reduction 50% + reduction 24.8 EUR/t	
11081910	reduction 37.2 EUR/t	
11081990	reduction 50% + reduction 24.8 EUR/t; arrow-root; exemption	
110820	exemption	
1109	WHEAT GLUTEN, WHETHER OR NOT DRIED	
1109	reduction 219 EUR/t	

12 OIL SEEDS AND OLEAGINOUS FRUITS; MISCELLANEOUS GRAINS, SEEDS AND FRUIT; INDUSTRIAL OR MEDICAL PLANTS; STRAW AND FODDER

1208	FLOURS AND MEALS OF OIL SEEDS OR OLEAGINOUS FRUITS (EXCL. MUSTARD)	
120810	exemption	
1209	SEEDS, FRUITS AND SPORES, FOR SOWING (EXCL. LEGUMINOUS VEGETABLES AND SWEETCORN, COFFEE, TEA, MATE AND SPICES, CEREALS, OIL SEEDS AND OLEAGINOUS FRUITS, AND SEEDS AND FRUIT USED PRIMARILY IN PERFUMERY	
1209	exemption	
1210	HOP CONES, FRESH OR DRIED, WHETHER OR NOT GROUND, POWDERED OR IN THE FORM OF PELLETS; LUPULIN	
1210	exemption	
121	PLANTS AND PARTS OF PLANTS, INCL. SEEDS AND FRUITS OF A KIND USED PRIMARILY IN PERFUMERY, MEDICAMENTS OR FOR INSECTICIDAL, FUNGICIDAL OR SIMILAR PURPOSES, FRESH OR DRIED, WHETHER OR NOT CUT, CRUSHED OR POWDERED	
1211	exemption	
1212	LOCUST BEANS, SEAWEEDS AND OTHER ALQAE, SUGAR BEET AND SUGAR CANE, FRESH OR DRIED, WHETHER OR NOT GROUND; FRUIT STONES AND KERNELS AND OTHER VEGETABLE PRODUCTS, INCL. UNROASTED CHICORY ROOTS OF THE VARIETY CICHORIUM INTYBU	
121210	exemption	

121230	exemption	
121291	reduction 16% (5)	
121292	reduction 16% (5)	
12129910	exemption	
1214	SWEDES, MANGOLDS, FODDER ROOTS, HAY, ALFALFA, CLOVER, SAINFOIN, FORAGE KALE, LUPINES, VETCHES AND SIMILAR FORAGE PRODUCTS, WHETHER OR NOT IN THE FORM OF PELLETS	
12149010	exemption	

13 LACS; GUMS, RESINS AND OTHER VEGETABLE SAPS AND EXTRACTS

13	exemption	

15 ANIMAL OR VEGETABLE FATS AND OILS AND THEIR CLEAVAGE PRODUCTS; PREPARED EDIBLE FATS; ANIMAL OR VEGETABLE WAXES

1501	LARD; OTHER PIG FAT AND POULTRY FAT, RENDERED, WHETHER OR NOT PRESSED OR SOLVENT-EXTRACTED	
1501	reduction 16%	
1502	FATS OF BOVINE ANIMALS, SHEEP OR GOATS, RAW OR RENDERED, WHETHER OR NOT PRESSED OR SOLVENT-EXTRACTED	
1502	exemption	
1503	LARD STEARIN, LARD OIL, OLEOSTEARIN, OLEO-OIL AND TALLOW OIL (EXCL. EMULSIFIED, MIXED OR OTHERWISE PREPARED)	
1503	exemption	
1504	FATS AND OILS AND THEIR FRACTIONS OF FISH OR MARINE MAMMALS, WHETHER OR NOT REFINED (EXCL. CHEMICALLY MODIFIED)	
1504	exemption	
1505	WOOL GREASE AND FATTY SUBSTANCES DERIVED THEREFROM, INCL. LANOLIN	
1505	exemption	
1506	OTHER ANIMAL FATS AND OILS AND THEIR FRACTIONS, WHETHER OR NOT REFINED, BUT NOT CHEMICALLY MODIFIED (EXCL. PIG FAT, POULTRY FAT, FATS OF BOVINE ANIMALS, SHEEP AND GOATS, FATS OF FISH AND OTHER MARINE ANIMALS, LARD STEARIN	
1506	exemption	
1507	SOYA-BEAN OIL AND ITS FRACTIONS, WHETHER OR NOT REFINED (EXCL. CHEMICALLY MODIFIED)	
1507	exemption	
1508	GROUND-NUT OIL AND ITS FRACTIONS, WHETHER OR NOT REFINED, BUT NOT CHEMICALLY MODIFIED	
1508	exemption	
1511	PALM OIL AND ITS FRACTIONS, WHETHER OR NOT REFINED (EXCL. CHEMICALLY MODIFIED)	
1511	exemption	

Preferential treatment applicable to agricultural products and foodstuffs originating in the ACP States

1512	SUNFLOWER-SEED, SAFFLOWER OR COTTON SEED OIL AND FRACTIONS THEREOF, WHETHER OR NOT REFINED, BUT NOT CHEMICALLY MODIFIED
1512	exemption
1513	COCONUT 'COPRA', PALM KERNEL OR BABASSU OIL AND FRACTIONS THEREOF, WHETHER OR NOT REFINED, BUT NOT CHEMICALLY MODIFIED
1513	exemption
1514	RAPE, COLZA OR MUSTARD OIL AND FRACTIONS THEREOF, WHETHER OR NOT REFINED, BUT NOT CHEMICALLY MODIFIED
1514	exemption
1515	OTHER FIXED VEGETABLE FATS AND OILS, INCL. JOJOBA OIL, AND THEIR FRACTIONS, WHETHER OR NOT REFINED, BUT NOT CHEMICALLY MODIFIED
1515	exemption
1516	ANIMAL OR VEGETABLE FATS AND OILS AND THEIR FRACTIONS, PARTLY OR WHOLLY HYDROGENATED, INTER-ESTERIFIED, RE-ESTERIFIED OR ELAIDINISED, WHETHER OR NOT REFINED, BUT NOT FURTHER PREPARED
1516	exemption
1517	MARGARINE, OTHER EDIBLE MIXTURES OR PREPARATIONS OF ANIMAL OR VEGETABLE FATS OR OILS AND EDIBLE FRACTIONS OF DIFFERENT FATS OR OILS
15171010	reduction 100% ad valorem customs duties
15171090	exemption
15179010	reduction 100% ad valorem customs duties
15179091	exemption
15179093	exemption
15179099	exemption
1518	ANIMAL OR VEGETABLE FATS AND OILS AND THEIR FRACTIONS, BOILED, OXIDISED, DEHYDRATED, SULPHURISED, BLOWN, POLYMERISED BY HEAT IN VACUUM OR IN INERT GAS OR OTHERWISE CHEMICALLY MODIFIED; INEDIBLE MIXTURES OR PREPARATIONS OF ANIMAL OR VEGETABLE FATS OR OILS OR FRACTIONS OF DIFFERENT FATS OR OILS, NOT ELSEWHERE SPECIFIED OR INCLUDED
1518	exemption
1520	GLYCEROL 'GLYCERINE', WHETHER OR NOT PURE; GLYCEROL WATERS AND GLYCEROL LYES
1520	exemption
1521	VEGETABLE WAXES, BEESWAX, OTHER INSECT WAXES AND SPERMACETI, WHETHER OR NOT REFINED OR COLOURED (EXCL. TRIGLYCERIDES)
1521	exemption
1522	DEGRAS; RESIDUES RESULTING FROM THE TREATMENT OF FATTY SUBSTANCES OR ANIMAL OR VEGETABLE WAXES
15220010	exemption
15220091	exemption
15220099	exemption

16 PREPARATIONS OF MEAT, FISH OR CRUSTACEANS, MOLLUSCS OR OTHER AQUATIC INVERTEBRATES

1601	SAUSAGES AND SIMILAR PRODUCTS, OF MEAT, OFFAL OR BLOOD; FOOD PREPARATIONS BASED ON THESE PRODUCTS
1601	within the limit of the quota (ctg 8) reduction 65%
1602	PREPARED OR PRESERVED MEAT, OFFAL OR BLOOD (EXCL. SAUSAGES AND SIMILAR PRODUCTS, AND MEAT EXTRACTS AND JUICES)
160210	reduction 16%
16022011	exemption
16022019	exemption
16022090	reduction 16%
160231	within the limit of the quota (ctg 4) reduction 65%
160232	within the limit of the quota (ctg 4) reduction 65%
160239	within the limit of the quota (ctg 4) reduction 65%
16024110	reduction 16%
16024190	exemption
16024210	reduction 16%
16024290	exemption
160249	reduction 16%
16025031	exemption
16025039	exemption
16025080	exemption
16029010	reduction 16%
16029031	exemption
16029041	exemption
16029051	reduction 16%
16029069	exemption
16029072	exemption
16029074	exemption
16029076	exemption
16029078	exemption
16029098	exemption
1603	EXTRACTS AND JUICES OF MEAT, FISH OR CRUSTACEANS, MOLLUSCS AND OTHER AQUATIC INVERTEBRATES
1603	exemption
1604	PREPARED OR PRESERVED FISH; CAVIAR AND CAVIAR SUBSTITUTES PREPARED FROM FISH EGGS
1604	exemption
1605	CRUSTACEANS, MOLLUSCS AND OTHER AQUATIC INVERTEBRATES, PREPARED OR PRESERVED
1605	exemption

Preferential treatment applicable to agricultural products and foodstuffs originating in the ACP States

17 SUGARS AND SUGAR CONFECTIONERY

1702	OTHER SUGARS, INCL. CHEMICALLY PURE LACTOSE, MALTOSE, GLUCOSE AND FRUCTOSE, IN SOLID FORM; SUGAR SYRUPS NOT CONTAINING ADDED FLAVOURING OR COLOURING MATTER; ARTIFICIAL HONEY, WHETHER OR NOT MIXED WITH NATURAL HONEY; CARAMEL
170211	reduction 16%
170219	reduction 16%
170220	reduction 16% (5)
17023010	reduction 16% (5)
17023051	reduction 117 EUR/t
17023059	reduction 81 EUR/t
17023091	reduction 117 EUR/t
17023099	reduction 81 EUR/t
17024010	reduction 16% (5)
17024090	reduction 81 EUF/t
170250	exemption
170260	reduction 16% (5)
17029010	exemption
17029030	reduction 16% (5)
17029050	reduction 81 EUR/t
17029060	reduction 16% (5)
17029071	eduction 16% (5)
17029075	reduction 117 EUR/t
17029079	reduction 81 EUR/t
17029080	reduction 16% (5)
17029099	reduction 16% (5)
1703	MOLASSES RESULTING FROM THE EXTRACTION OR REFINING OF SUGAR
1703	within the limit of the quota (ctg 9) reduction 100%
1704	SUGAR CONFECTIONERY NOT CONTAINING COCOA, INCL. WHITE CHOCOLATE
170410	reduction 100% ad valorem customs duties
17049010	exemption
17049030	exemption
17049051	reduction 100% ad valorem customs dirties ,
17049055	reduction 100% ad valorem customs duties
17049061	reduction 100% ad valorem customs duties
17049065	reduction 100% ad valorem customs duties
17049071	reduction 100% ad valorem customs dirties
17049075	reduction 100% ad valorem customs duties
17049081	reduction 100% ad valorem customs duties
17049099	reduction 100% ad valorem customs duties

18 COCOA AND COCOA PREPARATIONS

1801	COCOA BEANS, WHOLE OR BROKEN, RAW OR ROASTED
1801	exemption
1802	COCOA SHELLS, HUSKS, SKINS AND OTHER COCOA WASTE
1802	exemption
1803	COCOA PASTE, WHETHER OR NOT DEFATTED
1803	exemption
1804	COCOA BUTTER, FAT AND OIL
1804	exemption

1805	COCOA POWDER, NOT CONTAINING ADDED SUGAR OR OTHER SWEETENING MATTER
1805	exemption
1806	CHOCOLATE AND OTHER FOOD PREPARATIONS CONTAINING COCOA
18061015	exemption
18061020	reduction 100% ad valorem customs duties
18061030	reduction 100% ad valorem customs duties
18061090	reduction 100% ad valorem customs duties
180620	exemption
180631	exemption
180632	exemption
18069011	exemption
18069019	exemption
18069031	exemption
18069039	exemption
18069050	exemption
18069060	reduction 100% ad valorem customs duties
18069070	reduction 100% ad valorem customs duties
18069090	reduction 100% ad valorem customs duties

19 PREPARATIONS OF CEREALS, FLOUR, STARCH OR MILK-PASTRYCOOKS' PRODUCTS

1901	MALT EXTRACT; FOOD PREPARATIONS OF FLOUR, MEAL, STARCH OR MALT EXTRACT, NOT CONTAINING COCOA POWDER OR CONTAINING COCOA POWDER IN A PROPORTION BY WEIGHT OF < 40% NOT ELSEWHERE SPECIFIED OR INCLUDED; FOOD PREPARATIONS OF GOODS OF HEADINGS 04 01 TO 04 04
190110	reduction 100% ad valorem customs duties; exemption EA under the condition (c 1)
190120	reduction 100% ad valorem customs duties; exemption EA under the condition (c 1)
19019011	reduction 100% ad valorem customs duties
19019019	reduction 100% ad valorem customs duties
19019091	exemption
19019099	reduction 100% ad valorem customs duties; exemption EA under the condition (c 1)
1902	PASTA, WHETHER OR NOT COOKED OR STUFFED WITH MEAT OR OTHER SUBSTANCES OR OTHERWISE PREPARED, SUCH AS SPAGHETTI, MACARONI, NOODLES, LASAGNE, GNOCCHI, RAVIOLI, CANNELLONI; COUSCOUS, WHETHER OR NOT PREPARED
190211	reduction 100% ad valorem customs duties
190219	reduction 100% ad valorem customs duties
19022010	exemption
19022030	reduction 16%
19022091	reduction 100% ad valorem customs duties
19022099	reduction 100% ad valorem customs duties
190230	reduction 100% ad valorem customs duties
190240	reduction 100% ad valorem customs duties
1903	TAPIOCA AND SUBSTITUTES THEREFOR PREPARED FROM STARCH, IN THE FORM OF FLAKES, GRAINS, PEARLS, SIFTINGS OR SIMILAR FORMS
1903	exemption

Preferential treatment applicable to agricultural products and foodstuffs originating in the ACP States

1904	PREPARED FOODS OBTAINED BY THE SWELLING OR ROASTING OF CEREALS OR CEREAL PRODUCTS, E.G. CORN FLAKES; CEEALS, OTHER THAN MAIZE 'CORN', IN GRAIN FORM, PRE-COOKED OR OTHERWISE PREPARED	
1904	reduction 100% ad valorem customs duties	
1905	BREAD, PASTRY CAKES, BISCUITS AND OTHER BAKERS' WARES, WHETHER OR NOT CONTAINING COCOA; COMMUNION WAFERS, EMPTY CACHETS OF A KIND SUITABLE FOR PHARMACEUTICAL USE, SEALING WAFERS, RICE PAPER AND SIMILAR PRODUCTS	
190510	reduction 100% ad valorem customs duties	
190520	reduction 100% ad valorem customs duties	
19053011	reduction 100% d valorem customs duties; biscuits: exemption	
19053019	reduction 100% ad valorem customs duties; biscuits: exemption	
19053030	reduction 100% ad valorem customs duties	
19053051	reduction 100% ad valorem customs duties	
19053059	reduction 100% ad valorem customs duties	
19053091	reduction 100% ad valorem customs duties	
19053099	reduction 100% ad valorem customs duties	
190540	reduction 100% ad valorem customs duties	
190590	reduction 100% ad valorem customs duties	

20 PREPARATIONS OF VEGETABLES, FRUIT, NUTS OR OTHER PARTS OF PLANTS

2001	VEGETABLES, FRUIT, NUTS AND OTHER EDIBLE PARTS OF PLANTS, PREPARED OR PRESERVED BY VINEGAR OR ACETIC ACID	
200110	exemption	
200120	exemption	
20019020	exemption	
20019030	reduction 100% ad valorem customs duties	
20019040	reduction 100% ad valorem customs duties	
20019050	exemption	
20019060	exemption	
20019065	exemption	
20019070	exemption	
20019075	exemption	
20019085	exemption	
20019091	exemption	
ex 20019096	exemption except vine leaves	
2002	TOMATOES, PREPARED OR PRESERVED OTHERWISE THAN BY VINEGAR OR ACETIC ACID	
2002	exemption	
2003	MUSHROOMS AND TRUFFLES, PREPARED OR PRESERVED OTHERWISE THAN BY VINEGAR OR ACETIC ACID	
2003	exemption	
2004	OTHER VEGETABLES, PREPARED OR PRESERVED OTHERWISE THAN BY VINEGAR OR ACETIC ACID, FROZEN (EXCL. TOMATOES, MUSHROOMS AND TRUFFLES)	
20041010	exemption	

20041091	reduction 100% ad valorem customs duties
20041099	exemption
20049010	reduction 100% ad valorem customs duties
ex 20049030	exemption except olives
20049050	exemption
20049091	exemption
20049098	exemption
2005	OTHER VEGETABLES PREPARED OR PRESERVED OTHERWISE THAN BY VINEGAR OR ACETIC ACID (EXCL. FROZEN AND TOMATOES, MUSHROOMS AND TRUFFLES)
200510	exemption
20052010	reductlon 100% ad valorem customs duties
20052020	reduction 16%
20052080	reduction 16%
200540	exemption
200551	exemption
200559	exemption
200560	exemption
200570	exemption
200580	reduction 100% ad valorem customs duties
200590	exemption
2006	FRUIT, NUTS, FRUIT-PEEL AND OTHER PARTS OF PLANTS, PRESERVED BY SUGAR, DRAINED GLACE OR CRYSTALLIZED
20060031	reductlon 100% ad valorem customs duties
20060035	reduction 100% ad valorem customs duties
20060038	reduction 100% ad valorem customs duties
20060091	exemption
20060099	exemption
2007	JAMS, FRUIT JELLIES, MARMALADES, FRUIT OR NUT PUREE AND FRUIT OR NUT PASTES BEING COOKED PREPARATIONS, WHETHER OR NOT CONTAINING ADDED SUGAR OR OTHER SWEETENING MATTER
20071010	exemption
20071091	exemption
20071099	exemption
20079110	reduction 1000/0 ad valorem customs duties
20079130	reduction 1000/0 ad valorem customs duties
20079190	exemption
20079910	exemption
20079920	exemption
20079931	exemption
20079933	exemption
20079935	exemption
20079939	exemption
20079951	exemption
20079955	exemption
20079958	exemption
20079991	exemption
20079993	exemption
20079998	exemption
2008	FRUITS, NUTS AND OTHER EDIBLE PARTS OF PLANTS, PREPARED OR PRESERVED, WHETHER OR NOT CONTAINING ADDED SUGAR OR OTHER SWEETENING MATTER OR SPIRIT, NOT ELSEWHERE SPECIFIED OR INCLUDED

Preferential treatment applicable to agricultural products and foodstuffs originating in the ACP States

200811	exemption
200819	exemption
200820	exemption
20083011	exemption
20083019	reduction 100% ad valorem customs duties; grapefruit: exemption
20083031	exemption
20083039	exemption
20083051	exemption
20083055	exemption
20083059	exemption
20083071	exemption
20083075	exemption
20083079	exemption
20083091	exemption
20083099	exemption
200840	exemption
20085011	exemption
20085019	reduction 100% ad valorem customs duties
20085031	exemption
20085039	exemption
20085051	reduction 100% ad valorem customs duties
20085059	exemption
20085061	exemption
20085069	exemption
20085071	exemption
20085079	exemption
20085092	exemption
20085094	exemption
20085099	exemption
20086011	exemption
20086019	reduction 100% ad valorem customs duties
20086031	exemption
20086039	exemption
20086051	exemption
20086059	exemption
20086061	exemption
20086069	exemption
20086071	exemption
20086079	exemption
20086091	exemption
20086099	exemption
20087011	exemption
20087019	reduction 100% ad valorem customs duties
20087031	exemption
20087039	exemption
20087051	reduction 100% ad valorem customs duties
20087059	exemption
20087061	exemption
20087069	exemption
20087071	exemption
20087079	exemption
20087092	exemption
20087094	exemption
20087099	exemption
200880	exemption
200891	exemption
20089212	exemption
20089214	exemption
20089216	exemption
20089218	exemption

20089232	exemption
20089234	exemption
20089236	exemption
20089238	exemption
20089251	exemption
20089259	exemption
20089272	exemption
20089274	exemption
20089276	exemption
20089278	exemption
20089292	exemption
20089293	exemption
20089294	exemption
20089296	exemption
20089297	exemption
20089298	exemption
20089911	exemption
20089919	exemption
20089921	exemption
20089923	exemption
20089925	exemption
20089926	exemption
20089928	exemption
20089932	exemption
20089933	reduction 100% ad valorem customs duties
20089934	reduction 100% ad valorem customs duties
20089936	exemption
20089937	exemption
20089938	exemption
20089940	exemption
20089943	exemption
20089945	exemption
20089946	exemption
20089947	exemption
20089949	exemption
20089953	exemption
20089955	exemption
20089961	exemption
20089962	exemption
20089968	exemption
20089972	exemption
20089974	exemption
20089979	exemption
20089985	exemption except sweet corn
20089991	reduction 100% ad valorem customs duties
20089999	exemption except vine leaves
2009	FRUIT JUICES, INCL. GRAPE MUST AND VEGETABLE JUICES, UNFERMENTED NOT CONTAINING ADDED SPIRIT, WHETHER OR NOT CONTAINING ADDED SUGAR OR OTHER SWEETENING MATTER
20091111	reduction 100% ad valorem customs duties
20091119	exemption
20091191	reduction 100% ad valorem customs duties
20091199	exemption
20091911	reduction 100% ad valorem customs duties
20091919	exemption
20091991	reduction 100% ad valorem customs duties
20091999	exemption
200920	exemption

Preferential treatment applicable to agricultural products and foodstuffs originating in the ACP States

20093011	reduction 100% ad valorem customs duties
20093019	exemption
20093031	exemption
20093039	exemption
20093051	reduction 100% ad valorem customs duties
20093055	exemption
20093059	exemption
20093091	reduction 100% ad valorem customs duties
20093095	exemption
20093099	exemption
200940	exemption
200950	exemption
200960	exemption
20097011	reduction 100% ad valorem customs duties
20097019	exemption
20097030	exemption
20097091	reduction 100% ad valorem customs duties
20097093	exemption
20097099	exemption
20098011	reduction 100% ad valorem customs duties
20098019	exemption
20098032	exemption
20098033	reduction 100% ad valorem customs duties
20098035	reduction 100% ad valorem customs duties
20098036	exemption
20098038	exemption
20098050	exemption
20098061	reduction 100% ad valorem customs duties
20098063	exemption
20098069	exemption
20098071	exemption
20098073	exemption
20098079	exemption
20098083	exemption
20098084	reduction 100% ad valorem customs duties
20098086	reduction 100% ad valorem customs duties
20098088	exemption
20098089	exemption
20098095	exemption
20098096	exemption
20098097	exemption
20098099	exemption
20099041	exemption
20099049	exemption
20099051	exemption
20099059	exemption
20099071	reduction 100% ad valorem customs duties
20099073	exemption
20099079	exemption
20099092	exemption
20099094	reduction 100% ad valorem customs duties
20099095	exemption
20099096	exemption
20099097	exemption
20099098	exemption

21 MISCELLANEOUS EDIBLE PREPARATIONS

2101	EXTRACTS, ESSENCES AND CONCENTRATES OF COFFEE, TEA OR MATE AND PREPARATIONS WITH A BASIS OF THESE PRODUCTS OR WITH A BASIS OF COFFEE, TEA OR MATE; ROASTED CHICORY AND OTHER ROASTED COFFEE SUBSTITUTES, AND EXTRACTS, ESSENCE
210111	exemption
210112	exemption
210120	exemption
21013011	exemption
21013019	reduction 100% ad valorem customs duties
21013091	exemption
21013099	reduction 100% ad valorem customs duties
2102	YEASTS, ACTIVE OR INACTIVE, OTHER DEAD SINGLE-CELL MICRO-ORGANISMS, PREPARED BAKING POWDERS (EXCL. SINGLE-CELL MICRO-ORGANISMS PACKAGED AS MEDICAMENTS)
21021010	exemption
21021031	reduction 100% ad valorem customs duties
21021039	reduction 100% ad valorem customs duties
21021090	exemption
210220	exemption
210230	exemption
2103	SAUCE AND PREPARATIONS THEREFOR; MIXED CONDIMENTS AND MIXED SEASONINGS; MUSTARD FLOUR AND MEAL, WHETHER OR NOT PREPARED, AND MUSTARD
2103	exemption
2104	SOUPS AND BROTHS AND PREPARATIONS THEREFOR; FOOD PREPARATIONS CONSISTING OF FINELY HOMOGENIZED MIXTURES OF TWO OR MORE BASIC INGREDIENTS, SUCH AS MEAT, FISH, VEGETABLES OR FRUIT, PUT UP FOR RETAIL SALE AS INFANT FOOD
2104	exemption
2105	ICE CREAM AND OTHER EDIBLE ICE, WHETHER OR NOT CONTAINING COCOA
2105	reduction 100% ad valorem customs duties
2106	FOOD PREPARATIONS NOT ELSEWHERE SPECIFIED OR INCLUDED
210610	reduction 100% ad valorem customs duties
21069020	exemption
21069030	reduction 16% (5)
21069051	reduction 16%
21069055	reduction 81 EUR/t
21069059	reduction 16% (5)
21069092	exemption
21069098	reduction 100% ad valorem customs duties

Preferential treatment applicable to agricultural products and foodstuffs originating in the ACP States

22 BEVERAGES, SPIRITS AND VINEGAR		
2201	WATERS, INCL. NATURAL OR ARTIFICIAL MINERAL WATERS AND AERATED WATERS, NOT CONTAINING ADDED SUGAR, OTHER SWEETENING MATTER OR FLAVOURED; ICE AND SNOW	
2201	exemption	
2202	WATERS INCL. MINERAL WATERS AND AERATED WATERS, CONTAINING ADDED SUGAR OR OTHER SWEETENING MATTER OR FLAVOURED, AND OTHER NON-ALCOHOLIC BEVERAGES (EXCLUDING FRUIT OR VEGETABLE JUICES AND MILK)	
200210	exemption	
22029010	exemption	
22029091	reduction 100% ad valorem customs duties	
22029095	reduction 100% ad valorem customs duties	
22029099	reduction 100% ad valorem customs duties	
2203	BEER MADE FROM MALT	
2203	exemption	
2204	WINE OF FRESH GRAPES, INCL. FORTIFIED WINES; GRAPE MUST, PARTLY FERMENTED OF ACTUAL ALCOHOLIC STRENGTH OF > 0.5% VOL, WHETHER OR NOT WITH ADDED ALCOHOL	
22043092	exemption	
22043094	exemption	
22043096	exemption	
22043098	exemption	
2205	VERMOUTH AND OTHER WINE OF FRESH GRAPES, FLAVOURED WITH PLANTS OR AROMATIC SUBSTANCES	
2205	exemption	
2206	OTHER FERMENTED BEVERAGES AND MIXTURES OF FERMENTED BEVERAGES (CIDER, PERRY, MEAD); MIXTURES OF FERMENTED BEVERAGES AND NON-ALCOHOLIC BEVERAGES NOT ELSEWHERE SPECIFIED OR INCLUDED	
22060031	exemption	
22060039	exemption	
22060051	exemption	
22060059	exemption	
22060081	exemption	
22060089	exemption	
2207	UNDENATURED ETHYL ALCOHOL OF AN ALCOHOLIC STRENGTH BY VOLUME OF 80%; ETHYL ALCOHOL AND OTHER SPIRITS, DENATURED, OF ANY STRENGTH	
2207	exemption	
2208	UNDENATURED ETHYL ALCOHOL OF AN ALCOHOLIC STRENGTH BY VOLUME OF 80%; SPIRITS, LIQUEURS AND OTHER SPIRITUOUS BEVERAGES; COMPOUND ALCOHOLIC PREPARATIONS OF A KIND USED FOR THE MANUFACTURE OF BEVERAGES	
2208	exemption	
2209	VINEGAR AND SUBSTITUTES FOR VINEGAR OBTAINED FROM ACETIC ACID	
22090091	exemption	
22090099	exemption	
23 RESIDUES AND WASTE FROM THE FOOD INDUSTRIES; PREPARED ANIMAL FODDER		
2302	BRAN, SHARPS AND OTHER RESIDUES DER1VED FROM THE SIFTING, MILLING OR OTHER WORKING OF CEREALS OR OF LEGUMINOUS PLANTS	
230210	reduction 7.2 EUR/t	
230220	reduction 7.2 EUR/t	
230230	reduction 7.2 EUR/t	
230240	reduction 7.2 EUR/t	
230250	exemption	
2303	RESIDUES OF STARCH MANUFACTURE AND SIMILAR RESIDUES, BEET-PULP, BAGASSE AND OTHER WASTE OF SUGAR MANUFACTURE, BREWING OR DISTILLING DREGS AND WASTE, WHETHER OR NOT IN THE FORM OF PELLETS	
23031011	reduction 219 EUR/t	
2308	ACORNS, HORSE-CHESTNUTS, MARC AND OTHER VEGETABLE MATERIALS AND VEGETABLE WASTE, VEGETABLE RESIDUES AND BY-PRODUCTS OF A KIND USED IN ANIMAL FEEDING, WHETHER OR NOT IN THE FORM OF PELLETS, NOT ELSEWHERE SPECIFIED OR INCLUDED	
23089090	exemption	
2309	PREPARATIONS OF A KIND USED IN ANIMAL FEEDING	
23091013	reduction 10.9 EUR/t	
23091015	reduction 16%	
23091019	reduction 16%	
23091033	reduction 10.9 EUR/t	
23091039	reduction 16%	
23091051	reduction 10.9 EUR/t	
23091053	reduction 10.9 EUR/t	
23091059	reduction 16%	
23091070	reduction 16%	
23091090	exemption	
23099010	exemption	
23099031	reduction 10.9 EUR/t	
23099033	reduction 10.9 EUR/t	
23099035	reduction 16%	
23099039	reduction 16%	
23099041	reduction 10.9 EUR/t	
23099043	reduction 10.9 EUR/t	
23099049	reduction 16%	
23099051	reduction 10.9 EUR/t	
23099053	reduction 10.9 EUR/t	
23099059	reduction 16%	
23099070	reduction 16%	
23099091	exemption	

Preferential treatment applicable to agricultural products and foodstuffs originating in the ACP States

24 TOBACCO AND MANUFACTURED TOBACCO SUBSTITUTES
24   exemption (6)

29 ORGANIC CHEMICALS
290   ACYCLIC ALCOHOLS AND THEIR HALOGENATED, SULPHONATED, NITRATED OR NITROSATED DERIVATIVES
2905   reduction 100% ad valorem customs duties

33 ESSENTIAL OILS AND RESINOIDS; PERFUMERY, COSMETIC OR TOILET PREPARATIONS COSMÉTIQUES
3301   ESSENTIAL OILS, WHETHER OR NOT TERPENELESS, INCL. CONCRETES AND ABSOLUTES; RESINOIDS; CONCENTRATES OR ESSENTIAL OILS IN FATS, FIXED OILS, WAXES OR THE LIKE, OBTAINED BY ENFLEURAGE OR MACERATION; TERPENIC BY-PRODUCTS
3301   exemption

3302   MIXTURES OF ODORIFEROUS SUBSTANCES AND MIXTURES, INCL. ALCOHOLIC SOLUTIONS, BASED ON ONE OR MORE OF THESE SUBSTANCES, OF A KIND USED AS RAW MATERIALS IN INDUSTRY
33021029   exemption

35 ALBUMINOUS SUBSTANCES; MODIFIED STARCHES; GLUES; ENZYMES
3501   CASEIN, CASEINATES AND OTHER CASEIN DERIVATIVES: CASEIN GLUES (EXCL. THOSE PACKAGED AS GLUE FOR RETAIL SALE AND WEIGHING = < 1 KG)
3501   exemption

3502   ALBUMINS, INCL. CONCENTRATES OF TWO OR MORE WHEY PROTEINS CONTAINING BY WEIGHT > 80% WHEY PROTEINS, CALCULATED ON THE DRY MATTER, ALBUMINATES AND OTHER ALBUMIN DERIVATIVES
35021190   reduction 100% ad valorem customs duties
35021990   reduction 100% ad valorem customs duties
35022091   reduction 100% ad valorem customs duties
35022099   reduction 100% ad valorem customs duties

3503   GELATIN, WHETHER OR NOT IN SQUARE OR RECTANGULAR SHEETS. WHETHER OR NOT SURFACE-WORKED OR COLOURED AND GELATIN DERIVATIVES; ISINGLASS; OTHER GLUES OF ANIMAL ORIGIN (EXCL. CASEIN GLUES OF HEADING No 3501)

350   exemption

3504   PEPTONES AND THEIR DERIVATIVES; OTHER ALBUMINOUS SUBSTANCES AND THEIR DERIVATIVES NOT ELSEWHERE SPECIFIED OR INCLUDED; HIDE POWDER, WHETHER OR NOT CHROMED
3504   exemption

3505   DEXTRINS AND OTHER MODIFIED STARCHES E.G. PRE-GELATINISED OR ESTERIFIED STARCHES; GLUES BASED ON STARCHES DEXTRINS OR OTHER MODIFIED STARCHES (EXCL. THOSE PUT UP FOR RETAIL SALE AND WEIGHING = < 1 KG)
35051010   reduction 100% ad valorem customs duties
35051050   exemption
35051090   reduction 100% ad valorem customs duties
350520   reduction 100% ad valorem customs duties

38 MISCELLANEOUS CHEMICAL PRODUCTS
3809   FINISHING AGENTS. DYE CARRIERS TO ACCELERATE THE DYEING OR FIXING OF DYES AND OTHER PRODUCTS AND PREPARATIONS SUCH AS DRESSINGS AND MORDANTS OF A KIND USED IN THE TEXTILE, PAPER, LEATHER OR LIKE INDUSTRIES NOT ELSEWHERE SPECIFIED OR INCLUDED
380910   reduction 100% ad valorem customs duties

3824   PREPARED BINDERS FOR FOUNDRY MOULDS OR CORES; CHEMICAL PRODUCTS AND PREPARATIONS FOR THE CHEMICAL OR ALLIED INDUSTRIES, INCL. MIXTURES OF NATURAL PRODUCTS NOT ELSEWHERE SPECIFIED OR INCLUDED; RESIDUAL PRODUCTS OF THE CHEMICAL OR ALLIED INDUSTRIES
382460   reduction 100% ad valorem customs duties

50 SILK
50   exemption

52 COTTON
52   exemption

Annex 17

Rules of Origin Applied to ACP Fisheries Products

Title II
Article 2
General Requirements

1. For the purpose of implementing the trade co-operation provisions of ANNEX V, the following products shall be considered as originating in the ACP States:

(a)   products wholly obtained in the ACP States within the meaning of Article 3 of this Protocol;

(b)   products obtained in the ACP States incorporating materials which have not been wholly obtained there, provided that such materials have under-gone sufficient working or processing in the ACP States within the meaning of Article 4 of this Protocol.

2.   For the purpose of implementing paragraph 1, the territories of the ACP States shall be considered as being one territory.

Originating products made up of materials wholly obtained or sufficiently worked or processed in two or more ACP Sates shall be considered as products originating in the ACP State where the last working or processing took place, provided the working or processing carried out there goes beyond that referred to in Article 5 of this protocol.

Article 3
Wholly Obtained Products

1.   The following shall be considered as wholly obtained, the ACP States or in the Community, or in the overseas countries and territories defined in Annex III, hereafter referred to as the OCT:

(f)   Products of sea fishing and other products taken from the sea outside the territorial waters by their vessels;

(g)   products made aboard their factory ships exclusively from products referred to in sub-paragraph (f);

2.   The Terms 'their vessels' and 'their factory ships' in paragraph 1(f) and (g) shall apply only to vessels and factory ships:

(a)   Which are registered or recorded in an EC Member State, in an ACP State or in an OCT;

(b)   Which sail under the flag of an EC Member State, of an ACP State or of an OCT;

(c)   Which are owned to an extent of at least 50% by nationals of States party to the Agreement, or of an OCT, or by a company with its head office in one of these States or OCT, of which the Chairman of the Board of Directors or the Supervisory Board, and the majority of the members of such boards are nationals of State party to the Agreement, or of an OCT, and of which, in addition, in the case of partnerships or limited companies, at least half the capital belongs to those States party to the Agreement or to public bodies or nationals of the said States, or of an OCT:

(d) Of which at least 50% of the crew, master and officers included, are nationals of States party to the Agreement, or of an OCT.

3. Notwithstanding the provisions of paragraph 2, the Community shall recognise, upon request of an ACP State, that vessels chartered or leased by the ACP State be treated as 'their vessels' to undertake fisheries activities in its exclusive economic zone under the following conditions:

- That the ACP offered the Community the opportunity to negotiate a fisheries agreement and the Community did not accept this offer;

- That at least 50% of the crew, master and officers included are national of States party to the Agreement, or of an OCT;

- That the charter or lease contract has been accepted by the ACP-EC Customs Cooperation Committee as providing adequate opportunities for developing the capacity of the ACP State to fish on its own account and in particular as conferring on the ACP State the responsibility for the nautical and commercial management of the vessel placed at its disposal for a significant period of time.

Article 4
Sufficiently Worked or Processed Products

1. For the purposes of this Protocol, products which are not wholly obtained are considered to be sufficiently worked or processed in the ACP States, or in the Community or in the OCT, when the conditions set out in the list in Annex II are fulfilled.

The conditions referred to above indicate, for all products covered by this Agreement, the working or processing which must be carried out on non-originating materials used in manufacturing and apply only in relation to such materials. Accordingly, it follows that if a product, which has acquired originating status by fulfilling the conditions set out in the list is used in the manufacture of another product, the conditions applicable to the product in which it is incorporated do not apply to it, and no account shall be taken of the non-originating materials which may have been used in its manufacture.

2. Notwithstanding paragraph 1, non-originating materials which, according to the conditions set out in the list, should not be used in the manufacture of a given product may nevertheless be used provided that:

(a) Their total value does not exceed 15 per cent of the ex-works price product;

(b) Any of the percentages given in the list for the maximum value of non-originating materials are not exceeded through the application of this paragraph.

3. Paragraphs 1 and 2 shall apply except as provided in Article 5.

Annex 18

List of Workings or Processing Required to be Carried Out on Non-originating Materials in order that the Product Manufactured Can Obtain Originating Status

Annex II to Protocol 1

The products mentioned in the list may not all be covered by this Agreement. It is therefore necessary to consult the other parts of this Agreement.

HS heading No	Description of product	Working or processing carried out on non-originating materials that confers originating status
(1)	(2)	(3) or (4)
Chapter 01	Live animals	All the animals of Chapter 1 used must be wholly obtained
Chapter 02	Meat and edible meat offal	Manufacture in which all the materials of Chapters 1 and 2 used must be wholly obtained
Chapter 03	Fish and crustaceans, molluscs and other aquatic invertebrates	Manufacture in which all the materials of Chapter 3 used must be wholly obtained
ex Chapter 04	Dairy produce; birds' eggs; natural honey; edible products of animal origin, not elsewhere specified or included; except for:	Manufacture in which all the materials of Chapter 4 used must be wholly obtained
0403	Buttermilk, curdled milk and cream, yoghurt, kephir and other fermented or acidified milk and cream, whether or not concentrated or containing added sugar or other sweetening matter or flavoured or containing added fruit, nuts or cocoa	Manufacture in which: – all the materials of Chapter 4 used must be wholly obtained; – any fruit juice (except those of pineapple, lime or grapefruit) of heading No 2009 used must already be originating; – the value of any materials of Chapter 17 used does not exceed 30% of the ex-works price of the product
ex Chapter 05	Products of animal origin, not elsewhere specified or included; except for:	Manufacture in which all the materials of Chapter 5 used must be wholly obtained
ex 0502	Prepared pigs', hogs' or boars' bristles and hair	Cleaning, disinfecting, sorting and straightening of bristles and hair
Chapter 06	Live trees and other plants; bulbs, roots and the like; cut flowers and ornamental foliage	Manufacture in which: – all the materials of Chapter 6 used must be wholly obtained; – the value of all the materials used does not exceed 50% of the ex-works price of the product

HS heading No	Description of product	Working or processing carried out on non-originating materials that confers originating status
(1)	(2)	(3) or (4)
Chapter 07	Edible vegetables and certain roots and tubers	Manufacture in which all the materials of Chapter 7 used must be wholly obtained
Chapter 08	Edible fruit and nuts; peel of citrus fruits or melons	Manufacture in which: – all the fruit and nuts used must be wholly obtained; – the value of any materials of Chapter 17 used does not exceed 30% of the value of the ex-works price of the product
ex Chapter 09	Coffee, tea, maté and spices; except for:	Manufacture in which all the materials of Chapter 9 used must be wholly obtained
0901	Coffee, whether or not roasted or decaffeinated; coffee husks and skins; coffee substitutes containing coffee in any proportion	Manufacture from materials of any heading
0902	Tea, whether or not flavoured	Manufacture from materials of any heading
ex 0910	Mixtures of spices	Manufacture from materials of any heading
Chapter 10	Cereals	Manufacture in which all the materials of Chapter 10 used must be wholly obtained
ex Chapter 11	Products of the milling industry; malt; starches; inulin; wheat gluten; except for:	Manufacture in which all the cereals, edible vegetables, roots and tubers of heading No 0714 or fruit used must be wholly obtained
ex 1106	Flour, meal and powder of the dried, shelled leguminous vegetables of heading No 0713	Drying and milling of leguminous vegetables of heading No 0708
Chapter 12	Oil seeds and oleaginous fruits; miscellaneous grains, seeds and fruit; industrial or medicinal plants; straw and fodder	Manufacture in which all the materials of Chapter 12 used must be wholly obtained
1301	Lac; natural gums, resins, gum-resins and oleoresins (for example, balsams)	Manufacture in which the value of any materials of heading No 1301 used may not exceed 50% of the ex-works price of the product
1302	Vegetable saps and extracts; pectic substances, pectinates and pectates; agar-agar and other mucilages and thickeners, whether or not modified, derived from vegetable products:	

HS heading No	Description of product	Working or processing carried out on non-originating materials that confers originating status
(1)	(2)	(3) or (4)
	– Mucilages and thickeners, modified, derived from vegetable products	Manufacture from non-modified mucilages and thickeners
	– Other	Manufacture in which the value of all the materials used does not exceed 50% of the ex-works price of the product
Chapter 14	Vegetable plaiting materials; vegetable products not elsewhere specified or included	Manufacture in which all the materials of Chapter 14 used must be wholly obtained
ex Chapter 15	Animal or vegetable fats and oils and their cleavage products; prepared edible fats; animals or vegetable waxes; except for:	Manufacture in which all the materials used are classified within a heading other than that of the product
1501	Pig fat (including lard) and poultry fat, other than that of heading No 0209 or 1503:	
	– Fats from bones or waste	Manufacture from materials of any heading except those of heading Nos 0203, 0206 or 0207 or bones of heading No 0506
	– Other	Manufacture from meat or edible offal of swine of heading No 0203 or 0206 or of meat and edible offal of poultry of heading No 0207
1502	Fats of bovine animals, sheep or goats, other than those of heading No 1503	
	– Fats from bones or waste	Manufacture from materials of any heading except those of heading Nos 0201, 0202, 0204 or 0206 or bones of heading No 0506
	– Other	Manufacture in which all the materials of Chapter 2 used must be wholly obtained
1504	Fats and oils and their fractions, of fish or marine mammals, whether or not refined, but not chemically modified:	
	– Solid fractions	Manufacture from materials of any heading including other materials of heading No 1504
	– Other	Manufacture in which all the materials of Chapters 2 and 3 used must be wholly obtained
ex 1505	Refined lanolin	Manufacture from crude wool grease of heading No 1505

HS heading No	Description of product	Working or processing carried out on non-originating materials that confers originating status
(1)	(2)	(3) or (4)
1506	Other animals fats and oils and their fractions, whether or not refined, but not chemically modified:	
	– Solid fractions	Manufacture from materials of any heading including other materials of heading No 1506
	– Other	Manufacture in which all the materials of Chapter 2 used must be wholly obtained
1507 to 1515	Vegetable oils and their fractions:	
	– Soya, ground nut, palm, copra, palm kernel, babassu, tung and oiticica oil, myrtle wax and Japan wax, fractions of jojoba oil and oils for technical or industrial uses other than the manufacture of foodstuffs for human consumption	Manufacture in which all the materials used are classified within a heading other than that of the product
	– Solid fractions, except for that of jojoba oil	Manufacture from other materials of heading Nos 1507 to 1515
	– Other	Manufacture in which all the vegetable materials used must be wholly obtained
1516	Animal or vegetable fats and oils and their fractions, partly or wholly hydrogenated, inter-esterified, re-esterified or elaidinized, whether or not refined, but not further prepared	Manufacture in which: – all the materials of Chapter 2 used must be wholly obtained; – all the vegetable materials used must be wholly obtained. However, materials of headings 1507, 1508, 1511 and 1513 may be used
1517	Margarine; edible mixtures or preparations of animal or vegetable fats or oils or of fractions of different fats or oils of this Chapter, other than edible fats or oils or their fractions of heading No 1516	Manufacture in which: – all the materials of Chapters 2 and 4 used must be wholly obtained; – all the vegetable materials used must be wholly obtained. However, materials of headings 1507, 1508, 1511 and 1513 may be used
Chapter 16	Preparations of meat, of fish or of crustaceans, molluscs or other aquatic invertebrates	Manufacture from animals of Chapter 1. All the materials of Chapter 3 used must be wholly obtained
ex Chapter 17	Sugars and sugar confectionery; except for:	Manufacture in which all the materials used are classified within a heading other than that of the product
ex 1701	Cane or beet sugar and chemically pure sucrose, in solid form, flavoured or coloured	Manufacture in which the value of any materials of Chapter 17 used does not exceed 30% of the ex-works price of the product

HS heading No	Description of product	Working or processing carried out on non-originating materials that confers originating status
(1)	(2)	(3) or (4)
1702	Other sugars, including chemically pure lactose, maltose, glucose and fructose, in solid form; sugar syrups not containing added flavouring or colouring matter; artificial honey, whether or not mixed with natural honey; caramel:	
	– Chemically pure maltose and fructose	Manufacture from materials of any heading including other materials of heading No 1702
	– Other sugars in solid form, flavoured or coloured	Manufacture in which the value of any materials of Chapter 17 used does not exceed 30% of the ex-works price of the product
	– Other	Manufacture in which all the materials used must already be originating
ex 1703	Molasses resulting from the extraction or refining of sugar, flavoured or coloured	Manufacture in which the value of any materials of Chapter 17 used does not exceed 30% of the ex-works price of the product
1704	Sugar confectionery (including white chocolate), not containing cocoa	Manufacture in which: – all the materials used are classified within a heading other than that of the product; – the value of any materials of Chapter 17 used does not exceed 30% of the ex-works price of the product
Chapter 18	Cocoa and cocoa preparations	Manufacture in which: – all the materials used are classified within a heading other than that of the product; – the value of any materials of Chapter 17 used does not exceed 30% of the ex-works price of the product
1901	Malt extract; food preparations of flour, meal, starch or malt extract, not containing cocoa or containing less than 40% by weight of cocoa calculated on a totally defatted basis, not elsewhere specified or included; food preparations of goods of heading Nos. 0401 to 0404, not containing cocoa or containing less than 5% by weight of cocoa calculated on a totally defatted basis, not elsewhere specified or included:	

HS heading No	Description of product	Working or processing carried out on non-originating materials that confers originating status
(1)	(2)	(3) or (4)
	– Malt extract	Manufacture from cereals of Chapter 10
	– Other	Manufacture in which: – all the materials used are classified within a heading other than that of the product; – the value of any materials of Chapter 17 used does not exceed 30% of the ex-works price of the product
1902	Pasta, whether or not cooked or stuffed (with meat or other substances) or otherwise prepared, such as spaghetti, macaroni, noodles, lasagne, gnocchi, ravioli, cannelloni; couscous, whether or not prepared:	
	– Containing 20% or less by weight of meat, meat offal, fish, crustaceans or molluscs	Manufacture in which all the cereals and derivatives (except durum wheat and its derivatives) used must be wholly obtained
	– Containing more than 20% by weight of meat, meat offal, fish, crustaceans or molluscs	Manufacture in which: – all cereals and derivatives (except durum wheat and its derivatives) used must be wholly obtained; – all the materials of Chapters 2 and 3 used must be wholly obtained
1903	Tapioca and substitutes therefor prepared from starch, in the form of flakes, grains, pearls, siftings or in similar forms	Manufacture from materials of any heading except potato starch of heading No 1108
1904	Prepared foods obtained by the swelling or roasting of cereals or cereal products (for example, corn flakes); cereals (other than maize (corn)) in grain form or in the form of flakes or other worked grains (except flour and meal), pre-cooked, or otherwise prepared, not elsewhere specified or included	Manufacture: – from materials not classified within heading No 1806; – in which all the cereals and flour – (except durum wheat and its – derivates and Zea indurata maize) – used must be wholly obtained[1]; – in which the value of any materials of Chapter 17 used does not exceed 30% of the ex-works price of the product
1905	Bread, pastry, cakes, biscuits and other bakers' wares, whether or not containing cocoa; communion wafers, empty cachets of a kind suitable for pharmaceutical use, sealing wafers, rice paper and similar products	Manufacture from materials of any heading except those of Chapter 11

HS heading No	Description of product	Working or processing carried out on non-originating materials that confers originating status
(1)	(2)	(3) or (4)
ex Chapter 20	Preparations of vegetables, fruit, nuts or other parts of plants; except for:	Manufacture in which all the fruit, nuts or vegetables used must be wholly obtained
ex 2001	Yams, sweet potatoes and similar edible parts of plants containing 5% or more by weight of starch, prepared or preserved by vinegar or acetic acid	Manufacture in which all the materials used are classified within a heading other than that of the product
ex 2004 and ex 2005	Potatoes in the form of flour, meal or flakes, prepared or preserved otherwise than by vinegar or acetic acid	Manufacture in which all the materials used are classified within a heading other than that of the product
2006	Vegetables, fruit, nuts, fruit-peel and other parts of plants, preserved by sugar (drained, glacé or crystallized)	Manufacture in which the value of any materials of Chapter 17 used does not exceed 30% of the ex-works price of the product
2007	Jams, fruit jellies, marmalades, fruit or nut purée and fruit or nut pastes, being cooked preparations, whether or not containing added sugar or other sweetening matter	Manufacture in which: – all the materials used are classified within a heading other than that of the product; – the value of any materials of Chapter 17 used does not exceed 30% of the ex-works price of the product
ex 2008	– Nuts, not containing added sugar or spirit	Manufacture in which the value of the originating nuts and oil seeds of heading Nos 0801, 0802 and 1202 to 1207 used exceeds 60% of the ex-works price of the product
	– Peanut butter; mixtures based on cereals; palm hearts; maize (corn)	Manufacture in which all the materials used are classified within a heading other than that of the product
	– Other except for fruit and nuts cooked otherwise than by steaming or boiling in water, not containing added sugar, frozen	Manufacture in which: – all the materials used are classified within a heading other than that of the product;
	– the value of any materials of Chapter 17 used does not exceed 30% of the ex-works price of the product	
2009	Fruit juices (including grape must) and vegetable juices, unfermented and not containing added spirit, whether or not containing added sugar or other sweetening matter	Manufacture in which: – all the materials used are classified within a heading other than that of the product; – the value of any materials of Chapter 17 used does not exceed 30% of the ex-works price of the product

HS heading No	Description of product	Working or processing carried out on non-originating materials that confers originating status
(1)	(2)	(3) or (4)
ex Chapter 21	Miscellaneous edible preparations; except for:	Manufacture in which all the materials used are classified within a heading other than that of the product
2101	Extracts, essences and concentrates, of coffee, tea or maté and preparations with a basis of these products or with a basis of coffee, tea or maté; roasted chicory and other roasted coffee substitutes, and extracts, essences and concentrates thereof	Manufacture in which: – all the materials used are classified within a heading other than that of the product; – all the chicory used must be wholly obtained
2103	Sauces and preparations therefor; mixed condiments and mixed seasonings; mustard flour and meal and prepared mustard:	
	– Sauces and preparations therefor; mixed condiments and mixed seasonings	Manufacture in which all the materials used are classified within a heading other than that of the product. However, mustard flour or meal or prepared mustard may be used
	– Mustard flour and meal and prepared mustard	Manufacture from materials of any heading
ex 2104	Soups and broths and preparations therefor	Manufacture from materials of any heading except prepared or preserved vegetables of heading Nos 2002 to 2005
2106	Food preparations not elsewhere specified or included	Manufacture in which: – all the materials used are classified within a heading other than that of the product; – the value of any materials of Chapter 17 used does not exceed 30% of the ex-works price of the product
ex Chapter 22	Beverages, spirits and vinegar; except for:	Manufacture in which: – all the materials used are classified within a heading other than that of the product; – all the grapes or any material derived from grapes used must be wholly obtained

HS heading No	Description of product	Working or processing carried out on non-originating materials that confers originating status
(1)	(2)	(3) or (4)
2202	Waters, including mineral waters and aerated waters, containing added sugar or other sweetening matter or flavoured, and other non-alcoholic beverages, not including fruit or vegetable juices of heading No 2009	Manufacture in which: – all the materials used are classified within a heading other than that of the product; – the value of any materials of Chapter 17 used does not exceed 30% of the ex-works price of the product; – any fruit juice used (except for pineapple, lime and grapefruit juices) must already be originating
2207	Undenatured ethyl alcohol of an alcoholic strength by volume of 80% vol or higher; ethyl alcohol and other spirits, denatured, of any strength.	Manufacture: – using materials not classified in headings 2207 or 2208, – in which all the grapes or any materials derived from grapes used must be wholly obtained or if all the other materials used are already originating, arrack may be used up to a limit of 5% by volume
2208	Undenatured ethyl alcohol of an alcoholic strength by volume of less than 80% vol; spirits, liqueurs and other spirituous beverages	Manufacture: – from materials not classified within heading Nos 2207 or 2208, – in which all the grapes or any material derived from grapes used must be wholly obtained or if all the other materials used are already originating, arrack may be used up to a limit of 5% by volume
ex Chapter 23	Residues and waste from the food industries; prepared animal fodder; except for:	Manufacture in which all the materials used are classified within a heading other than that of the product
ex 2301	Whale meal; flours, meals and pellets of fish or of crustaceans, molluscs or other aquatic invertebrates, unfit for human consumption	Manufacture in which all the materials of Chapters 2 and 3 used must be wholly obtained
ex 2303	Residues from the manufacture of starch from maize (excluding concentrated steeping liquors), of a protein content, calculated on the dry product, exceeding 40% by weight	Manufacture in which all the maize used must be wholly obtained
ex 2306	Oil cake and other solid residues resulting from the extraction of olive oil, containing more than 3% of olive oil	Manufacture in which all the olives used must be wholly obtained

HS heading No	Description of product	Working or processing carried out on non-originating materials that confers originating status
(1)	(2)	(3) or (4)
2309	Preparations of a kind used in animal feeding	Manufacture in which: – all the cereals, sugar or molasses, meat or milk used must already be originating; – all the materials of Chapter 3 used must be wholly obtained
ex Chapter 24	Tobacco and manufactured tobacco substitutes; except for:	Manufacture in which all the materials of Chapter 24 used must be wholly obtained
2402	Cigars, cheroots, cigarillos and cigarettes, of tobacco or of tobacco substitutes	Manufacture in which at least 70% by weight of the unmanufactured tobacco or tobacco refuse of heading No 2401 used must already be originating
ex 2403	Smoking tobacco	Manufacture in which at least 70% by weight of the unmanufactured tobacco or tobacco refuse of heading No 2401 used must already be originating
ex Chapter 25	Salt; sulphur; earths and stone; plastering materials, lime and cement; except for:	Manufacture in which all the materials used are classified within a heading other than that of the product
ex 2504	Natural crystalline graphite, with enriched carbon content, purified and ground	Enriching of the carbon content, purifying and grinding of crude crystalline graphite
ex 2515	Marble, merely cut, by sawing or otherwise, into blocks or slabs of a rectangular (including square) shape, of a thickness not exceeding 25 cm	Cutting, by sawing or otherwise, of marble (even if already sawn) of a thickness exceeding 25 cm
ex 2516	Granite, porphyry, basalt, sandstone and other monumental and building stone, merely cut, by sawing or otherwise, into blocks or slabs of a rectangular (including square) shape, of a thickness not exceeding 25 cm	Cutting, by sawing or otherwise, of stone (even if already sawn) of a thickness exceeding 25 cm
ex 2518	Calcined dolomite	Calcination of dolomite not calcined
ex 2519	Crushed natural magnesium carbonate (magnesite), in hermetically-sealed containers, and magnesium oxide, whether or not pure, other than fused magnesia or dead-burned (sintered) magnesia	Manufacture in which all the materials used are classified within a heading other than that of the product. However, natural magnesium carbonate (magnesite) may be used
ex 2520	Plasters specially prepared for dentistry	Manufacture in which the value of all the materials used does not exceed 50% of the ex-works price of the product

HS heading No	Description of product	Working or processing carried out on non-originating materials that confers originating status
(1)	(2)	(3) or (4)
ex 2524	Natural asbestos fibres	Manufacture from asbestos concentrate
ex 2525	Mica powder	Grinding of mica or mica waste
ex 2530	Earth colours, calcined or powdered	Calcination or grinding of earth colours
Chapter 26	Ores, slag and ash	Manufacture in which all the materials used are classified within a heading other than that of the product
ex Chapter 27	Mineral fuels, mineral oils and products of their distillation; bituminous substances; mineral waxes; except for:	Manufacture in which all the materials used are classified within a heading other than that of the product
ex 2707	Oils in which the weight of the aromatic constituents exceeds that of the non-aromatic constituents, being oils similar to mineral oils obtained by distillation of high temperature coal tar, of which more than 65% by volume distils at a temperature of up to 250°C (including mixtures of petroleum spirit and benzole), for use as power or heating fuels	Operations of refining and/or one or more specific process(es)[1] or Other operations in which all the materials used are classified within a heading other than that of the product. However, materials classified within the same heading may be used provided their value does not exceed 50% of the ex-works price of the product
ex 2709	Crude oils obtained from bituminous minerals	Destructive distillation of bituminous materials
2710	Petroleum oils and oils obtained from bituminous materials, other than crude; preparations not elsewhere specified or included, containing by weight 70% or more of petroleum oils or of oils obtained from bituminous materials, these oils being the basic constituents of the preparations	Operations of refining and/or one or more specific process(es)[2] or Other operations in which all the materials used are classified within a heading other than that of the product. However, materials classified within the same heading may be used provided their value does not exceed 50% of the ex-works price of the product
2711	Petroleum gases and other gaseous hydrocarbons	Operations of refining and/or one or more specific process(es)[2] or Other operations in which all the materials used are classified within a heading other than that of the product. However, materials classified within the same heading may be used provided their value does not exceed 50% of the ex-works price of the product

[1]For the special conditions to 'specific processes' see Introductory Notes 7.1 and 7.3.
[2]For the special conditions to 'specific processes' see Introductory Note 7.2.

HS heading No	Description of product	Working or processing carried out on non-originating materials that confers originating status
(1)	(2)	(3) or (4)
2712	Petroleum jelly; paraffin wax, microcrystalline petroleum wax, slack wax, ozokerite, lignite wax, peat wax, other mineral waxes and similar products obtained by synthesis or by other processes, whetheror not coloured	Operations of refining and/or one or more specific process(es)[1] or Other operations in which all the materials used are classified within a heading other than that of the product. However, materials classified within the same heading may be used provided their value does not exceed 50% of the ex-works price of the product
2713	Petroleum coke, petroleum bitumen and other residues of petroleum oils or of oils obtained from bituminous materials	Operations of refining and/or one or more specific process(es)[1] or Other operations in which all the materials used are classified within a heading other than that of the product. However, materials classified within the same heading may be used provided their value does not exceed 50% of the ex-works price of the product
2714	Bitumen and asphalt, natural; bituminous or oil shale and tar sands; asphaltites and asphaltic rocks	Operations of refining and/or one or more specific process(es)[1] or Other operations in which all the materials used are classified within a heading other than that of the product. However, materials classified within the same heading may be used provided their value does not exceed 50% of the ex-works price of the product
2715	Bituminous mixtures based on natural asphalt, on natural bitumen, on petroleum bitumen, on mineral tar or on mineral tar pitch (for example, bituminous mastics, cut-backs)	Operations of refining and/or one or more specific process(es)[1] or Other operations in which all the materials used are classified within a heading other than that of the product. However, materials classified within the same heading may be used provided their value does not exceed 50% of the ex-works price of the product
ex Chapter 28	Inorganic chemicals; organic or inorganic compounds of precious metals, of rare-earth metals, of radioactive elements or of isotopes; except for:	Manufacture in which all the materials used are classified within a heading other than that of the product. However, materials classified within the same heading may be used provided their value does not exceed 20% of the ex-works price of the product

[1]For the special conditions to 'specific processes' see Introductory Note 7.2.

284

HS heading No	Description of product	Working or processing carried out on non-originating materials that confers originating status
(1)	(2)	(3) or (4)
		Manufacture in which the value of all the materials used does not exceed 40% of the ex-works price of the product
ex 2805	'Mischmetall'	Manufacture by electrolytic or thermal treatment in which the value of all the materials used does not exceed 50% of the ex-works price of the product
ex 2811	Sulphur trioxide	Manufacture from sulphur dioxide Manufacture in which the value of all the materials used does not exceed 40% of the ex-works price of the product
ex 2833	Aluminium sulphate	Manufacture in which the value of all the materials used does not exceed 50% of the ex-works price of the product
ex 2840	Sodium perborate	Manufacture from disodium tetraborate pentahydrate Manufacture in which the value of all the materials used does not exceed 40% of the ex-works price of the product
ex Chapter 29	Organic chemicals; except for:	Manufacture in which all the materials used are classified within a heading other than that of the product. However, materials classified within the same heading may be used provided their value does not exceed 20% of the ex-works price of the product Manufacture in which the value of all the materials used does not exceed 40% of the ex-works price of the product
ex 2901	Acyclic hydrocarbons for use as power or heating fuels	Operations of refining and/or one or more specific process(es)[1] or Other operations in which all the materials used are classified within a heading other than that of the product. However, materials classified within the same heading may be used provided their value does not exceed 50% of the ex-works price of the product

[1]For the special conditions to 'specific processes' see Introductory Notes 7.1 and 7.3.

HS heading No	Description of product	Working or processing carried out on non-originating materials that confers originating status
(1)	(2)	(3) or (4)
ex 2902	Cyclanes and cyclenes (other than azulenes), benzene, toluene, xylenes, for use as power or heating fuels	Operations of refining and/or one or more specific process(es)[1] or Other operations in which all the materials used are classified within a heading other than that of the product. However, materials classified within the same heading may be used, provided their value does not exceed 50% of the ex-works price of the product
ex 2905	Metal alcoholates of alcohols of this heading and of ethanol	Manufacture from materials of any heading, including other materials of heading No 2905. However, metal alcoholates of this heading may be used, provided their value does not exceed 20% of the ex-works price of the product Manufacture in which the value of all the materials used does not exceed 40% of the ex-works price of the product
2915	Saturated acyclic monocarboxylic acids and their anhydrides, halides, peroxides and peroxyacids; their halogenated, sulphonated, nitrated or nitrosated derivatives	Manufacture from materials of any heading. However, the value of all the materials of headings Nos 2915 and 2916 used may not exceed 20% of the ex–works price of the product Manufacture in which the value of all the materials used does not exceed 40% of the ex-works price of the product
ex 2932	– Internal ethers and their halogenated, sulphonated, nitrated or nitrosated derivatives	Manufacture from materials of any heading. However, the value of all the materials of heading No 2909 used may not exceed 20% of the ex-works price of the product
	– Cyclic acetals and internal hemiacetals and their halogenated, sulphonated, nitrated or nitrosated derivatives	Manufacture from materials of any heading Manufacture in which the value of all the materials used does not exceed 40% of the ex-works price of the product Manufacture in which the value of all the materials used does not exceed 40% of the ex-works price of the product

HS heading No	Description of product	Working or processing carried out on non-originating materials that confers originating status
(1)	(2)	(3) or (4)
2933	Heterocyclic compounds with nitrogen hetero-atom(s) only	Manufacture from materials of any heading. However, the value of all the materials of headings Nos 2932 and 2933 used may not exceed 20% of the ex-works price of the product Manufacture in which the value of all the materials used does not exceed 40% of the ex-works price of the product
2934	Nucleic acids and their salts; other heterocyclic compounds	Manufacture from materials of any heading. However, the value of all the materials of headings Nos 2932, 2933 and 2934 used may not exceed 20% of the ex-works price of the product Manufacture in which the value of all the materials used does not exceed 40% of the ex-works price of the product
ex Chapter 30	Pharmaceutical products; except for:	Manufacture in which all the materials used are classified within a heading other than that of the product. However, materials classified within the same heading may be used provided their value does not exceed 20% of the ex-works price of the product
3002	Human blood; animal blood prepared for therapeutic, prophylactic or diagnostic uses; antisera and other blood fractions and modified immunological products, whether or not obtained by means of biotechno-logical processes; vaccines, toxins, cultures of micro-organisms (excluding yeasts) and similar products:	
	– Products consisting of two or more constituents which have been mixed together for therapeutic or prophylactic uses or unmixed products for these uses, put up in measured doses or in forms or packings for retail sale	Manufacture from materials of any heading, including other materials of heading No 3002. The materials of this description may also be used, provided their value does not exceed 20% of the ex-works price of the product
	– Other:	
	– human blood	Manufacture from materials of any heading, including other materials of heading No 3002. The materials of this description may also be used, provided their value does not exceed 20% of the ex-works price of the product

HS heading No	Description of product	Working or processing carried out on non-originating materials that confers originating status	
(1)	(2)	(3) or (4)	
	– animal blood prepared for therapeutic or prophylactic uses	Manufacture from materials of any heading, including other materials of heading No 3002. The materials of this description may also be used, provided their value does not exceed 20% of the ex-works price of the product	
	– blood fractions other than antisera, haemoglobin, blood globulins and serum globulins	Manufacture from materials of any heading, including other materials of heading No 3002. The materials of this description may also be used, provided their value does not exceed 20% of the ex-works price of the product	
	– haemoglobin, blood globulins and serum globulins	Manufacture from materials of any heading, including other materials of heading No 3002. The materials of this description may also be used, provided their value does not exceed 20% of the ex-works price of the product	
	– other	Manufacture from materials of any heading, including other materials of heading No 3002. The materials of this description may also be used, provided their value does not exceed 20% of the ex-works price of the product	
3003 and 3004	Medicaments (excluding goods of heading No 3002, 3005 or 3006):		
	– Obtained from amikacin of heading No 2941	Manufacture in which all the materials used are classified within a heading other than that of the product. However, materials of heading No 3003 or 3004 may be used provided their value, taken together, does not exceed 20% of the ex-works price of the product	
	– Other	Manufacture in which: – all the materials used are classified within a heading other than that of the product. However, materials of heading No 3003 or 3004 may be used provided their value, taken together, does not exceed 20% of the ex-works price of the product; – the value of all the materials used does not exceed 50% of the ex-works price of the product	

HS heading No	Description of product	Working or processing carried out on non-originating materials that confers originating status
(1)	(2)	(3) or (4)
ex Chapter 31	Fertilisers; except for:	Manufacture in which all the materials used are classified within a heading other than that of the product. However, materials classified within the same heading may be used provided their value does not exceed 20% of the ex-works price of the product Manufacture in which the value of all the materials used does not exceed 40% of the ex-works price of the product
ex 3105	Mineral or chemical fertilizers containing two or three of the fertilizing elements nitrogen, phosphorous and potassium; other fertilizers; goods of this Chapter, in tablets or similar forms or in packages of a gross weight not exceeding 10 kg, except for: – sodium nitrate – calcium cyanamide – potassium sulphate – magnesium potassium sulphate	Manufacture in which: – all the materials used are classified within a heading other than that of the product. However, materials classified within the same heading may be used provided their value does not exceed 20% of the ex-works price of the product; – the value of all the materials used does not exceed 50% of the ex-works price of the product Manufacture in which the value of all the materials used does not exceed 40% of the ex-works price of the product
ex Chapter 32	Tanning or dyeing extracts; tannins and their derivatives; dyes, pigments and other colouring matter; paints and varnishes; putty and other mastics; inks; except for:	Manufacture in which all the materials used are classified within a heading other than that of the product. However, materials classified within the same heading may be used provided their value does not exceed 20% of the ex-works price of the product Manufacture in which the value of all the materials used does not exceed 40% of the ex-works price of the product
ex 3201	Tannins and their salts, ethers, esters and other derivatives	Manufacture from tanning extracts of vegetable origin Manufacture in which the value of all the materials used does not exceed 40% of the ex-works price of the product
3205	Colour lakes; preparations as specified in Note 3 to this Chapter based on colour lakes[1]	Manufacture from materials of any heading, except headings Nos 3203, 3204 and 3205. However, materials from heading No 3205 may be used provided their value does not exceed 20% of the ex-works price of the product Manufacture in which the value of all the materials used does not exceed 40% of the ex-works price of the product

[1]Note 3 to Chapter 32 says that these preparations are those of a kind used for colouring any material or used as ingredients in the manufacturing of colouring preparations, provided they are not classified in another heading in Chaper 32.

HS heading No	Description of product	Working or processing carried out on non-originating materials that confers originating status
(1)	(2)	(3) or (4)
ex Chapter 33	Essential oils and resinoids; perfumery, cosmetic or toilet preparations; except for:	Manufacture in which all the materials used are classified within a heading other than that of the product. However, materials classified within the same heading may be used provided their value does not exceed 20% of the ex-works price of the product Manufacture in which the value of all the materials used does not exceed 40% of the ex-works price of the product
3301	Essential oils (terpeneless or not), including concretes and absolutes; resinoids; extracted oleoresins; concentrates of essential oils in fats, in fixed oils, in waxes or the like, obtained by enfleurage or maceration; terpenic by-products of the deterpenation of essential oils; aqueous distillates and aqueous solutions of essential oils	Manufacture from materials of any heading, including materials of a different 'group'[1] in this heading. However, materials of the same group may be used, provided their value does not exceed 20% of the ex-works price of the product Manufacture in which the value of all the materials used does not exceed 40% of the ex-works price of the product
ex Chapter 34	Soap, organic surface-active agents, washing preparations, lubricating preparations, artificial waxes, prepared waxes, polishing or scouring preparations, candles and similar articles, modelling pastes, 'dental waxes' and dental preparations with a basis of plaster; except for:	Manufacture in which all the materials used are classified within a heading other than that of the product. However, materials classified within the same heading may be used provided their value does not exceed 20% of the ex-works price of the product Manufacture in which the value of all the materials used does not exceed 40% of the ex-works price of the product
ex 3403	Lubricating preparations containing petroleum oils or oils obtained from bituminous minerals, provided they represent less than 70% by weight	Operations of refining and/or one or more specific process(es);[2] or Other operations in which all the materials used are classified within a heading other than that of the product. However, materials classified within the same heading may be used provided their value does not exceed 50% of the ex-works price of the product
3404	Artificial waxes and prepared waxes: – With a basis of paraffin, petroleum waxes, waxes obtained from bituminous minerals, slack wax or scale wax	Manufacture in which all the materials used are classified within a heading other than that of the product. However, materials classified within the same heading may be used provided their value does not exceed 50% of the ex-works price of the product

[1]A 'group' is regarded as any part of the heading separated from the rest by a semi-colon.
[2]For the special conditions to 'specific processes' see Introductory Notes 7.1 and 7.3.

HS heading No	Description of product	Working or processing carried out on non-originating materials that confers originating status
(1)	(2)	(3) or (4)
	– Other	Manufacture from materials of any heading, except: – hydrogenated oils having the character of waxes of heading No 1516; Manufacture in which the value of all the materials used does not exceed 40% of the ex-works price of the product – fatty acids not chemically defined or industrial fatty alcohols having the character of waxes of heading No 3823; – materials of heading No 3404 However, these materials may be used provided their value does not exceed 20% of the ex-works price of the product
ex Chapter 35	Albuminoidal substances; modified starches; glues; enzymes; except for:	Manufacture in which all the materials used are classified within a heading other than that of the product. However, materials classified within the same heading may be used provided their value does not exceed 20% of the ex-works price of the product Manufacture in which the value of all the materials used does not exceed 40% of the ex-works price of the product
3505	Dextrins and other modified starches (for example, pregelatinised or esterified starches); glues based on starches, or on dextrins or other modified starches:	
	– Starch ethers and esters	Manufacture from materials of any heading, including other materials of heading No 3505 Manufacture in which the value of all the materials used does not exceed 40% of the ex-works price of the product
	– Other	Manufacture from materials of any heading, except those of heading No
1108		Manufacture in which the value of all the materials used does not exceed 40% of the ex-works price of the product
ex 3507	Prepared enzymes not elsewhere specified or included	Manufacture in which the value of all the materials used does not exceed 50% of the ex-works price of the product

HS heading No (1)	Description of product (2)	Working or processing carried out on non-originating materials that confers originating status (3) or (4)
Chapter 36	Explosives; pyrotechnic products; matches; pyrophoric alloys; certain combustible preparations	Manufacture in which all the materials used are classified within a heading other than that of the product. However, materials classified within the same heading may be used provided their value does not exceed 20% of the ex-works price of the product Manufacture in which the value of all the materials used does not exceed 40% of the ex-works price of the product
ex Chapter 37	Photographic or cinematographic goods; except for:	Manufacture in which all the materials used are classified within a heading other than that of the product. However, materials classified within the same heading may be used provided their value does not exceed 20% of the ex-works price of the product Manufacture in which the value of all the materials used does not exceed 40% of the ex-works price of the product
3701	Photographic plates and film in the flat, sensitized, unexposed, of any material other than paper, paper-board or textiles; instant print film in the flat, sensitized, unexposed, whether or not in packs:	
	– Instant print film for colour photography, in packs	Manufacture in which all the materials used are classified within a heading other than heading Nos 3701 or 3702. However, materials from heading No 3702 may be used provided their value does not exceed 30% of the ex-works price of the product Manufacture in which the value of all the materials used does not exceed 40% of the ex-works price of the product
	– Other	Manufacture in which all the materials used are classified within a heading other than heading No 3701 or 3702. However, materials from heading Nos 3701 and 3702 may be used provided their value taken together, does not exceed 20% of the ex-works price of the product Manufacture in which the value of all the materials used does not exceed 40% of the ex-works price of the product

HS heading No	Description of product	Working or processing carried out on non-originating materials that confers originating status
(1)	(2)	(3) or (4)
3702	Photographic film in rolls, sensitized, unexposed, of any material other than paper, paperboard or textiles; instant print film in rolls, sensitized, unexposed	Manufacture in which all the materials used are classified within a heading other than heading Nos 3701 or 3702 Manufacture in which the value of all the materials used does not exceed 40% of the ex-works price of the product
3704	Photographic plates, film paper, paperboard and textiles, exposed but not developed	Manufacture in which all the materials used are classified within a heading other than heading Nos 3701 to 3704 Manufacture in which the value of all the materials used does not exceed 40% of the ex-works price of the product
ex Chapter 38	Miscellaneous chemical products; except for:	Manufacture in which all the materials used are classified within a heading other than that of the product. However, materials classified within the same heading may be used provided their value does not exceed 20% of the ex-works price of the product Manufacture in which the value of all the materials used does not exceed 40% of the ex-works price of the product
ex 3801	– Colloidal graphite in suspension in oil and semi-colloidal graphite; carbonaceous pastes for electrodes	Manufacture in which the value of all the materials used does not exceed 50% of the ex-works price of the product
	– Graphite in paste form, being a mixture of more than 30% by weight of graphite with mineral oils	Manufacture in which the value of all the materials of heading No 3403 used does not exceed 20% of the ex-works price of the product Manufacture in which the value of all the materials used does not exceed 40% of the ex-works price of the product
ex 3803	Refined tall oil	Refining of crude tall oil Manufacture in which the value of all the materials used does not exceed 40% of the ex-works price of the product
ex 3805	Spirits of sulphate turpentine, purified	Purification by distillation or refining of raw spirits of sulphate turpentine Manufacture in which the value of all the materials used does not exceed 40% of the ex-works price of the product
ex 3806	Ester gums	Manufacture from resin acids Manufacture in which the value of all the materials used does not exceed 40% of the ex-works price of the product

HS heading No	Description of product	Working or processing carried out on non-originating materials that confers originating status
(1)	(2)	(3) or (4)
ex 3807	Wood pitch (wood tar pitch)	Distillation of wood tar Manufacture in which the value of all the materials used does not exceed 40% of the ex-works price of the product
3808	Insecticides, rodenticides, fungicides, herbicides, anti-sprouting products and plant-growth regulators, disinfectants and similar products, put up in forms or packings for retail sale or as preparations or articles (for example, sulphur-treated bands, wicks and candles, and fly-papers)	Manufacture in which the value of all the materials used does not exceed 50% of the ex-works price of the products
3809	Finishing agents, dye carriers to accelerate the dyeing or fixing of dyestuffs and other products and preparations (for example, dressings and mordants), of a kind used in the textile, paper, leather or like industries, not elsewhere specified or included	Manufacture in which the value of all the materials used does not exceed 50% of the ex-works price of the products
3810	Pickling preparations for metal surfaces; fluxes and other auxiliary preparations for soldering, brazing or welding; soldering, brazing or welding powders and pastes consisting of metal and other materials; preparations of a kind used as cores or coatings for welding electrodes or rods	Manufacture in which the value of all the materials used does not exceed 50% of the ex-works price of the products
3811	Anti-knock preparations, oxidation inhibitors, gum inhibitors, viscosity improvers, anti-corrosive preparations and other prepared additives, for mineral oils (including gasoline) or for other liquids used for the same purposes as mineral oils:	
	– Prepared additives for lubricating oil, containing petroleum oils or oils obtained from bituminous minerals	Manufacture in which the value of all the materials of heading No 3811 used does not exceed 50% of the ex-works price of the product
	– Other	Manufacture in which the value of all the materials used does not exceed 50% of the ex-works price of the product

HS heading No	Description of product	Working or processing carried out on non-originating materials that confers originating status
(1)	(2)	(3) or (4)
3812	Prepared rubber accelerators; compound plasticizers for rubber or plastics, not elsewhere specified or included; anti-oxidizing preparations and other compound stabilizers for rubber or plastics	Manufacture in which the value of all the materials used does not exceed 50% of the ex-works price of the product
3813	Preparations and charges for fire-extinguishers; charged fire-extinguishing grenades	Manufacture in which the value of all the materials used does not exceed 50% of the ex-works price of the product
3814	Organic composite solvents and thinners, not elsewhere specified or included; prepared paint or vanish removers	Manufacture in which the value of all the materials used does not exceed 50% of the ex-works price of the product
3818	Chemical elements doped for use in electronics, in the form of discs, wafers or similar forms; chemical compounds doped for use in electronics	Manufacture in which the value of all the materials used does not exceed 50% of the ex-works price of the product
3819	Hydraulic brake fluids and other prepared liquids for hydraulic transmission, not containing or containing less than 70% by weight of petroleum oils or oils obtained from bituminous minerals	Manufacture in which the value of all the materials used does not exceed 50% of the ex-works price of the product
3820	Anti-freezing preparations and prepared de-icing fluids	Manufacture in which the value of all the materials used does not exceed 50% of the ex-works price of the product
3822	Diagnostic or laboratory reagents on a backing and prepared diagnostic or laboratory reagents, whether or not on a backing, other than those of heading No 3002 or 3006	Manufacture in which the value of all the materials used does not exceed 50% of the ex-works price of the product
3823	Industrial monocarboxylic fatty acids; acid oils from refining; industrial fatty alcohols.	
	– Industrial monocarboxylic fatty acids, acid oils from refining	Manufacture in which all the materials used are classified within a heading other than that of the product
	– Industrial fatty alcohols	Manufacture from materials of any heading including other materials of heading No 3823

HS heading No	Description of product	Working or processing carried out on non-originating materials that confers originating status
(1)	(2)	(3) or (4)
3824	Prepared binders for foundry moulds or cores; chemical products and preparations of the chemical or allied industries (including those consisting of mixtures of natural products), not elsewhere specified or included; residual products of the chemical or allied industries, not elsewhere specified or included:	
	– The following of this heading: Prepared binders for foundry moulds or cores based on natural resinous products Naphthenic acids, their water insoluble salts and their esters	
	Sorbitol other than that of heading No 2905 Petroleum sulphonates, excluding petroleum sulphonates of alkali metals, of ammonium or of ethanolamines; thiophenated sulphonic acids of oils obtained from bituminous minerals, and their salts Ion exchangers Getters for vacuum tubes	Manufacture in which all the materials used are classified within a heading other than that of the product. However, materials classified within the same heading may be used provided their value does not exceed 20% of the ex-works price of the product Manufacture in which the value of all the materials used does not exceed 40% of the ex-works price of the product
	Alkaline iron oxide for the purification of gas Ammoniacal gas liquors and spent oxide produced in coal gas purification Sulphonaphthenic acids, their water insoluble salts and their esters Fusel oil and Dippel's oil Mixtures of salts having different anions Copying pastes with a basis of gelatin, whether or not on a paper or textile backing	
	– Other	Manufacture in which the value of all the materials used does not exceed 50% of the ex-works price of the product

HS heading No	Description of product	Working or processing carried out on non-originating materials that confers originating status
(1)	(2)	(3) or (4)
3901 to 3915	Plastics in primary forms, waste, parings and scrap, of plastic; except for heading Nos ex 3907 and 3912 for which the rules are set out below:	
	– Addition homopolymerization products in which a single monomer contributes more than 99% by weight to the total polymer content	Manufacture in which: – the value of all the materials used does not exceed 50% of the ex-works price of the product; – the value of any materials of Chapter 39 used does not exceed 20% of the ex-works price of the product[1] Manufacture in which the value of all the materials used does not exceed 25% of the ex-works price of the product
	– Other	Manufacture in which the value of the materials of Chapter 39 used does not exceed 20% of the ex-works price of the product[1] Manufacture in which the value of all the materials used does not exceed 25% of the ex-works price of the product
ex 3907	– Copolymer, made from poly-carbonate and acrylonitrile-butadiene-styrene copolymer (ABS)	Manufacture in which all the materials used are classified within a heading other than that of the product. However, materials classified within the same heading may be used provided their value does not exceed 50% of the ex-works price of the product[1]
	– Polyester	Manufacture in which the value of any materials of Chapter 39 used does not exceed 20% of the ex-works price of the product and/or manufacture from poly-carbonate of tetrabromo-(bisphenol A)
3912	Cellulose and its chemical derivatives, not elsewhere specified or included, in primary forms	Manufacture in which the value of any materials classified in the same heading as the product does not exceed 20% of the ex-works price of the product
3916 to 3921	Semi-manufactures and articles of plastics; except for headings Nos ex 3916, ex 3917, ex 3920 and ex 3921, for which the rules are set out below:	

[1]In the case of the products composed of materials classified within both headings 3901 to 3906, on the one hand, and within headings Nos 3907 to 3911, on the other hand, this restriction only applies to that group of materials which predominates by weight in the product.

HS heading No	Description of product	Working or processing carried out on non-originating materials that confers originating status
(1)	(2)	(3) or (4)
	– Flat products, further worked than only surface-worked or cut into forms other than rectangular (including square); other products, further worked than only surface-worked	
	– Other:	Manufacture in which the value of any materials of Chapter 39 used does not exceed 50% of the ex-works price of the product Manufacture in which the value of all the materials used does not exceed 25% of the ex-works price of the product
	– Addition homopolymerization products in which a single monomer contributes more than 99% by weight to the total polymer content	Manufacture in which: – the value of all the materials used does not exceed 50% of the ex-works price of the product; – the value of any materials of Chapter – 39 used does not exceed 20% of – the ex-works price of the product[1] Manufacture in which the value of all the materials used does not exceed 25% of the ex-works price of the product
	– Other	Manufacture in which the value of any materials of Chapter 39 used does not exceed 20% of the ex-works price of the product[1] Manufacture in which the value of all the materials used does not exceed 25% of the ex-works price of the product
ex 3916 and ex 3917	Profile shapes and tubes	Manufacture in which: – the value of all the materials used does not exceed 50% of the ex-works price of the product; – the value of any materials classified within the same heading as the product does not exceed 20% of the ex-works price of the product Manufacture in which the value of all the materials used does not exceed 25% of the ex-works price of the product

[1]In the case of the products composed of materials classified within both headings 3901 to 3906, on the one hand, and within headings Nos 3907 to 3911, on the other hand, this restriction only applies to that group of materials which predominates by weight in the product.

HS heading No	Description of product	Working or processing carried out on non-originating materials that confers originating status
(1)	(2)	(3) or (4)
ex 3920	– Ionomer sheet or film	Manufacture from a thermoplastic partial salt which is a copolymer of ethylene and metacrylic acid partly neutralized with metal ions, mainly zinc and sodium Manufacture in which the value of all the materials used does not exceed 25% of the ex-works price of the product
	– Sheets of regenerated cellulose, polyamides or polyethylene	Manufacture in which the value of any materials classified in the same heading as the product does not exceed 20% of the ex-works price of the product
ex 3921	Foils of plastic, metallized	Manufacture from highly transparent polyester foils with a thickness of less than 23 micron[1] Manufacture in which the value of all the materials used does not exceed 25% of the ex-works price of the product
3922 to 3926	Articles of plastics	Manufacture in which the value of all the materials used does not exceed 50% of the ex-works price of the product
ex Chapter 40	Rubber and articles thereof; except for:	Manufacture in which all the materials used are classified within a heading other than that of the product
ex 4001	Laminated slabs of crepe rubber for shoes	Lamination of sheets of natural rubber
4005	Compounded rubber, unvulcanised, in primary forms or in plates, sheets or strip	Manufacture in which the value of all the materials used, except natural rubber, does not exceed 50% of the ex-works price of the product
4012	Retreaded or used pneumatic tyres of rubber; solid or cushion tyres, interchangeable tyre treads and tyre flaps, of rubber:	
	– Retreaded pneumatic, solid or cushion tyres, of rubber	Retreading of used tyres
	– Other	Manufacture from materials of any heading, except those of heading Nos 4011 or 4012
ex 4017	Articles of hard rubber	Manufacture from hard rubber
ex Chapter 41	Raw hides and skins (other than furskins) and leather; except for:	Manufacture in which all the materials used are classified within a heading other than that of the product

HS heading No	Description of product	Working or processing carried out on non-originating materials that confers originating status
(1)	(2)	(3) or (4)
ex 4102	Raw skins of sheep or lambs, without wool on	Removal of wool from sheep or lamb skins, with wool on
4104 to 4107	Leather, without hair or wool, other than leather of heading Nos 4108 or 4109	Retanning of pre-tanned leather or Manufacture in which all the materials used are classified within a heading other than that of the product
4109	Patent leather and patent laminated leather; metallized leather	Manufacture from leather of heading Nos 4104 to 4107 provided its value does not exceed 50% of the ex-works price of the product
Chapter 42	Articles of leather; saddlery and harness; travel goods, handbags and similar containers; articles of animal gut (other than silk worm gut)	Manufacture in which all the materials used are classified within a heading other than that of the product
ex Chapter 43	Furskins and artificial fur; manufactures thereof; except for:	Manufacture in which all the materials used are classified within a heading other than that of the product
ex 4302	Tanned or dressed furskins, assembled:	
	– Plates, crosses and similar forms	Bleaching or dyeing, in addition to cutting and assembly of non-assembled tanned or dressed furskins
	– Other	Manufacture from non-assembled, tanned or dressed furskins
4303	Articles of apparel, clothing accessories and other articles of furskin	Manufacture from non-assembled tanned or dressed furskins of heading No 4302
ex Chapter 44	Wood and articles of wood; wood charcoal; except for:	Manufacture in which all the materials used are classified within a heading other than that of the product
ex 4403	Wood roughly squared	Manufacture from wood in the rough, whether or not stripped of its bark or merely roughed down
ex 4407	Wood sawn or chipped lengthwise, sliced or peeled, of a thickness exceeding 6 mm, planed, sanded or finger-jointed	Planing, sanding or finger-jointing
ex 4408	Veneer sheets and sheets for plywood, of a thickness not exceeding 6 mm, spliced, and other wood sawn lengthwise, sliced or peeled of a thickness not exceeding 6 mm, planed, sanded or finger-jointed	Splicing, planing, sanding or finger-jointing

HS heading No	Description of product	Working or processing carried out on non-originating materials that confers originating status
(1)	(2)	(3) or (4)
ex 4409	Wood continuously shaped along any of its edges or faces, whether or not planed, sanded or finger-jointed:	
	– Sanded or finger-jointed	Sanding or finger-jointing
	– Beadings and mouldings	Beading or moulding
ex 4410 to ex 4413	Beadings and mouldings, including moulded skirting and other moulded boards	Beading or moulding
ex 4415	Packing cases, boxes, crates, drums and similar packings, of wood	Manufacture from boards not cut to size
ex 4416	Casks, barrels, vats, tubs and other coopers' products and parts thereof, of wood	Manufacture from riven staves, not further worked than sawn on the two principal surfaces
ex 4418	– Builders' joinery and carpentry of wood	Manufacture in which all the materials used are classified within a heading other than that of the product. However, cellular wood panels, shingles and shakes may be used
	– Beadings and mouldings	Beading or moulding
ex 4421	Match splints; wooden pegs or pins for footwear	Manufacture from wood of any heading except drawn wood of heading No 4409
ex Chapter 45	Cork and articles of cork; except for:	Manufacture in which all the materials used are classified within a heading other than that of the product
4503	Articles of natural cork	Manufacture from cork of heading No 4501
Chapter 46	Manufactures of straw, of esparto or of other plaiting materials; basketware and wickerwork	Manufacture in which all the materials used are classified within a heading other than that of the product
Chapter 47	Pulp of wood or of other fibrous cellulosic material; recovered (waste and scrap) paper or paperboard	Manufacture in which all the materials used are classified within a heading other than that of the product
ex Chapter 48	Paper and paperboard; articles of paper pulp, of paper or of paperboard; except for:	Manufacture in which all the materials used are classified within a heading other than that of the product
ex 4811	Paper and paperboard, ruled, lined or squared only	Manufacture from paper-making materials of Chapter 47
4816	Carbon paper, self-copy paper and other copying papers (other than those of heading No 4809), duplicator stencils and offset plates, of paper, whether or not put up in boxes	Manufacture from paper-making materials of Chapter 47

HS heading No	Description of product	Working or processing carried out on non-originating materials that confers originating status
(1)	(2)	(3) or (4)
4817	Envelopes, letter cards, plain post-cards and correspondence cards, of paper or paperboard; boxes, pouches, wallets and writing compendiums, of paper or paperboard, containing an assortment of paper stationery	Manufacturing in which: – all the materials used are classified within a heading other than that of the product; – the value of all the materials used does not exceed 50% of the ex-works price of the product
ex 4818	Toilet paper	Manufacture from paper-making materials of Chapter 47
ex 4819	Cartons, boxes, cases, bags and other packing containers, of paper, paperboard, cellulose wadding or webs of cellulose fibres	Manufacture in which: – all the materials used are classified within a heading other than that of the product; – the value of all the materials used does not exceed 50% of the ex-works price of the product
ex 4820	Letter pads	Manufacture in which the value of all the materials used does not exceed 50% of the ex-works price of the product
ex 4823	Other paper, paperboard, cellulose wadding and webs of cellulose fibres, cut to size or shape	Manufacture from paper-making materials of Chapter 47
ex Chapter 49	Printed books, newspapers, pictures and other products of the printing industry; manuscripts, typescripts and plans; except for:	Manufacture in which all the materials used are classified within a heading other than that of the product
4909	Printed or illustrated postcards; printed cards bearing personal greetings, messages or announce-ments, whether or not illustrated, with or without envelopes or trimmings	Manufacture from materials not classified within heading Nos 4909 or 4911
4910	Calendars of any kind, printed, including calendar blocks:	
	– Calendars of the 'perpetual' type or with replaceable blocks mounted on bases other than paper or paperboard	Manufacture in which: – all the materials used are classified within a heading other than that of the product; – the value of all the materials used does not exceed 50% of the ex-works price of the product
	– Other	Manufacture from materials not classified in heading Nos 4909 or 4911

HS heading No	Description of product	Working or processing carried out on non-originating materials that confers originating status
(1)	(2)	(3) or (4)
ex Chapter 50	Silk; except for:	Manufacture in which all the materials used are classified within a heading other than that of the product
ex 5003	Silk waste (including cocoons unsuitable for reeling, yarn waste and garnetted stock), carded or combed	Carding or combing of silk waste
5004 to ex 5006	Silk yarn and yarn spun from silk waste	Manufacture from:[1] – raw silk or silk waste carded or combed or otherwise prepared for spinning, – other natural fibres not carded or combed or otherwise prepared for spinning, – chemical materials or textile pulp, or – paper-making materials
5007	Woven fabrics of silk or of silk waste:	
	– Incorporating rubber thread	Manufacture from single yarn[1]
	– Other	Manufacture from[1]: – coir yarn, – natural fibres, – man-made staple fibres not carded or combed or otherwise prepared for spinning, – chemical materials or textile pulp, or – paper or Printing accompanied by at least two preparatory or finishing operations (such as scouring, bleaching, mercerizing, heat setting, raising, calendering, shrink resistance processing, permanent finishing, decatizing, impregnating, mending and burling) where the value of the unprinted fabric used does not exceed 47.5% of the ex-works price of the product
ex Chapter 51	Wool, fine or coarse animal hair; horsehair yarn and woven fabric; except for:	Manufacture in which all the materials used are classified within a heading other than that of the product

[1]For special conditions relating to products made of mixture of textile materials, see Introductory Note 5.

HS heading No	Description of product	Working or processing carried out on non-originating materials that confers originating status
(1)	(2)	(3) or (4)
5106 to 5110	Yarn of wool, of fine or coarse animal hair or of horsehair	Manufacture from:[1] – raw silk or silk waste carded or combed or otherwise prepared for spinning, – natural fibres not carded or combed or otherwise prepared for spinning, – chemical materials or textile pulp, or – paper-making materials
5111 to 5113	Woven fabrics of wool, of fine or coarse animal hair or of horsehair:	
	– Incorporating rubber thread	Manufacture from single yarn[1]
	– Other	Manufacture from:[1] – coir yarn, – natural fibres, – man-made staple fibres not carded or combed or otherwise prepared for spinning, – chemical materials or textile pulp, or – paper or printing accompanied by at least two preparatory or finishing operations (such as scouring, bleaching, mercerizing, heat setting, raising, calendering, shrink resistance processing, permanent finishing, decatizing, impregnating, mending and burling) where the value of the unprinted fabric used does not exceed 47.5% of the ex-works price of the product
ex Chapter 52	Cotton; except for:	Manufacture in which all the materials used are classified within a heading other than that of the product
5204 to 5207	Yarn and thread of cotton	Manufacture from:[1] – raw silk or silk waste carded or combed combed or otherwise prepared for spinning, – natural fibres not carded or combed or otherwise prepared for spinning, – chemical materials or textile pulp, or – paper-making materials
5208 to 5212	Woven fabrics of cotton:	
	– Incorporating rubber thread	Manufacture from single yarn[1]

[1]For special conditions relating to products made of mixture of textile materials, see Introductory Note 5.

HS heading No	Description of product	Working or processing carried out on non-originating materials that confers originating status
(1)	(2)	(3) or (4)
	– Other	Manufacture from:[1] – coir yarn, – natural fibres, – man-made staple fibres not carded or combed or otherwise prepared for spinning, – chemical materials or textile pulp, or – paper; or Printing accompanied by at least two preparatory or finishing operations (such as scouring, bleaching, mercerizing, heat setting, raising, calendering, shrink resistance processing, permanent finishing, decatizing, impregnating, mending and burling) where the value of the unprinted fabric used does not exceed 47.5% of the ex-works price of the product
ex Chapter 53	Other vegetable textile fibres; paper yarn and woven fabrics of paper yarn; except for:	Manufacture in which all the materials used are classified within a heading other than that of the product
5306 to 5308	Yarn of other vegetable textile fibres; paper yarn	Manufacture from:[1] – raw silk or silk waste carded or combed or otherwise prepared for spinning, – natural fibres not carded or combed or otherwise prepared for spinning, – chemical materials or textile pulp, or – paper-making materials
5309 to 5311	Woven fabrics of other vegetable textile fibres; woven fabrics of paper yarn:	
	– Incorporating rubber thread	Manufacture from single yarn[1]
	– Other	Manufacture from:[1] – coir yarn, – natural fibres, – man-made staple fibres not carded or combed or otherwise prepared for spinning, – chemical materials or textile pulp, or – paper

[1] For special conditions relating to products made of mixture of textile materials, see Introductory Note 5.

HS heading No	Description of product	Working or processing carried out on non-originating materials that confers originating status
(1)	(2)	(3) or (4)
		or Printing accompanied by at least two preparatory or finishing operations (such as scouring, bleaching, mercerizing, heat setting, raising, calendering, shrink resistance processing, permanent finishing, decatizing, impregnating, mending and burling) where the value of the unprinted fabric used does not exceed 47.5% of the ex-works price of the product
5401 to 5406	Yarn, monofilament and thread of man-made filaments	Manufacture from:[1] – raw silk or silk waste carded or combed or otherwise prepared for spinning, – natural fibres not carded or combed or otherwise prepared for spinning, – chemical materials or textile pulp, or – paper-making materials
5407 and 5408	Woven fabrics of man-made filament yarn:	
	– Incorporating rubber thread	
	– Other	Manufacture from:[1] – coir yarn, – natural fibres, – man-made staple fibres not carded or combed or otherwise prepared for spinning, – chemical materials or textile pulp, or – paper; or Printing accompanied by at least two preparatory or finishing operations (such as scouring, bleaching, mercerizing, heat setting, raising, calendering, shrink resistance processing, permanent finishing, decatizing, impregnating, mending and burling) where the value of the unprinted fabric used does not exceed 47.5% of the ex-works price of the product
5501 to 5507	Man-made staple fibres	Manufacture from chemical materials or textile pulp

[1]For special conditions relating to products made of mixture of textile materials, see Introductory Note 5.

HS heading No	Description of product	Working or processing carried out on non-originating materials that confers originating status
(1)	(2)	(3) or (4)
5508 to 5511	Yarn and sewing thread of man-made staple fibres	Manufacture from:[1] – raw silk or silk waste carded or combed or otherwise prepared for spinning, – natural fibres not carded or combed or otherwise prepared for spinning, – chemical materials or textile pulp, or – paper-making materials
5512 to 5516	Woven fabrics of man-made staple fibres:	
	– Incorporating rubber thread	Manufacture from single yarn[1]
	– Other	Manufacture from:[1] – coir yarn, – natural fibres, – man-made staple fibres not carded or combed or otherwise prepared for spinning, – chemical materials or textile pulp, or – paper; or Printing accompanied by at least two preparatory or finishing operations (such as scouring, bleaching, mercerizing, heat setting, raising, calendering, shrink resist ance processing, permanent finishing-decatising, impregnating, mending and burling) where the value of the unprinted fabric used does not exceed 47.5% of the ex-works price of the product
ex Chapter 56	Wadding, felt and non-wovens; special yarns; twine, cordage, ropes and cables and articles thereof; except for:	Manufacture from:[1] – coir yarn, – natural fibres, – chemical materials or textile pulp, or – paper-making materials
5602	Felt, whether or not impregnated, coated, covered or laminated:	
	– Needleloom felt	Manufacture from:[1] – natural fibres, – chemical materials or textile pulp However: – polypropylene filament of heading No 5402, – polypropylene fibres of heading No 5503 or 5506 or

[1]For special conditions relating to products made of mixture of textile materials, see Introductory Note 5.

HS heading No	Description of product	Working or processing carried out on non-originating materials that confers originating status
(1)	(2)	(3) or (4)
		– polypropylene filament tow of heading No 5501, of which the denomination in all cases of a single filament or fibre is less than 9 decitex may be used provided their value does not exceed 40% of the ex-works price of the product
	– Other	Manufacture from:[1] – natural fibres, – man-made staple fibres made from casein, or – chemical materials or textile pulp
5604	Rubber thread and cord, textile covered; textile yarn, and strip and the like of heading No 5404 or 5405, impregnated, coated, covered or sheathed with rubber or plastics:	
	– Rubber thread and cord, textile covered	Manufacture from rubber thread or cord, not textile covered
	– Other	Manufacture from:[1] – natural fibres not carded or combed or – otherwise processed for spinning – chemical materials or textile pulp, or – paper-making materials
5605	Metallized yarn, whether or not gimped, being textile yarn, or strip or the like of heading No 5404 or 5405, combined with metal in the form of thread, strip or powder or covered with metal	Manufacture from:[1] – natural fibres, – man-made staple fibres not carded or combed or otherwise processed for spinning, – chemical materials or textile pulp, or – paper-making materials
5606	Gimped yarn, and strip and the like of heading No 5404 or 5405, gimped (other than those of heading No 5605 and gimped horsehair yarn); chenille yarn (including flock chenille yarn; loop wale-yarn	Manufacture from:[1] – natural fibres, – man-made staple fibres not carded or combed or otherwise processed for spinning, – chemical materials or textile pulp, or – paper-making materials

[1]For special conditions relating to products made of mixture of textile materials, see Introductory Note 5.

HS heading No	Description of product	Working or processing carried out on non-originating materials that confers originating status
(1)	(2)	(3) or (4)
Chapter 57	Carpets and other textile floor coverings:	
	– Of needleloom felt	Manufacture from:[1] – natural fibres, or – chemical materials or textile pulp However: – polypropylene filament of heading No 5402, – polypropylene fibres of heading No 5503 or 5506 or – polypropylene filament tow of heading No 5501, of which the denomination in all cases of a single filament or fibre is less than 9 decitex may be used provided their value does not exceed 40% of the ex-works price of the product – jute fabric may be used as backing
	– Of other felt	Manufacture from:[1] – natural fibres not carded or combed or otherwise processed for spinning, or – chemical materials or textile pulp
	– Other	Manufacture from:[1] – coir or jute yarn, – synthetic or artificial filament yarn, – natural fibres, or – man-made staple fibres not carded or combed or otherwise processed for spinning Jute fabric may be used as backing
ex Chapter 58	Special woven fabrics; tufted textile fabrics; lace; tapestries; trimmings; embroidery; except for:	
	– Combined with rubber thread	Manufacture from single yarn[1]
	– Other	Manufacture from:[1] – natural fibres, – man-made staple fibres not carded or combed or otherwise processed for spinning, or – chemical materials or textile pulp,

[1]For special conditions relating to products made of mixture of textile materials, see Introductory Note 5.

HS heading No	Description of product	Working or processing carried out on non-originating materials that confers originating status
(1)	(2)	(3) or (4)
		or; Printing accompanied by at least two preparatory or finishing operations (such as scouring, bleaching, mercerizing, heat setting, raising, calendering, shrink resistance processing, permanent finishing, decatizing, impregnating, mending and burling) where the value of the unprinted fabric used does not exceed 47.5% of the ex-works price of the product
5805	Hand-woven tapestries of the types gobelins, flanders, aubusson, beauvais and the like, and needle-worked tapestries (for example, petit point, cross stitch), whether or not made up	Manufacture in which all the materials used are classified within a heading other than that of the product
5810	Embroidery in the piece, in strips or in motifs	Manufacture in which: – all the materials used are classified within a heading other than that of the product; – the value of all the materials used does not exceed 50% of the ex-works price of the product
5901	Textile fabrics coated with gum or amylaceous substances, of a kind used for the outer covers of books or the like; tracing cloth; prepared painting canvas; buckram and similar stiffened textile fabrics of a kind used for hat foundations	Manufacture from yarn
5902	Tyre cord fabric of high tenacity yarn of nylon or other polyamides, polyesters or viscose rayon:	
	– Containing not more than 90% by weight of textile materials	Manufacture from yarn
	– Other	Manufacture from chemical materials or textile pulp
5903	Textile fabrics impregnated, coated, covered or laminated with plastics, other than those of heading No 5902	Manufacture from yarn or Printing accompanied by at least two preparatory or finishing operations (such as scouring, bleaching, mercerising, heat setting, rasing, calendering, shrink resist ance processing, permanent finishing, decatising, impregnating, mending and burling) where the value of the unprinted fabric used does not exceed 47.5% of the ex-works price of the product

HS heading No	Description of product	Working or processing carried out on non-originating materials that confers originating status
(1)	(2)	(3) or (4)
5904	Linoleum, whether or note cut to shape; floor coverings consisting of a coating or covering applied on a textile backing, whether or not cut to shape	Manufacture from single yarn[1]
5905	Textile wall coverings:	
	– Impregnated, coated, covered or laminated with rubber, plastics or other materials	Manufacture from yarn
	– Other	Manufacture from single yarn[1] – coir yarn, – natural fibres, – man-made staple fibres not carded or combed or otherwise processed for spinning, or – chemical materials or textile pulp, or Printing accompanied by at least two preparatory or finishing operations (such as scouring, bleaching, mercerizing, heat setting, raising, calendering, shrink resistance processing, permanent finishing, decatizing, impregnating, mending and burling) where the value of the unprinted fabric used does not exceed 47.5% of the ex-works price of the product
5906	Rubberized textile fabrics, other than those of heading No 5902:	
	– Knitted or crocheted fabrics	Manufacture from:[1] – natural fibres, – man-made staple fibres not carded or combed or otherwise processed for spinning, or – chemical materials or textile pulp
	– Other fabrics made of synthetic filament yarn, containing more than 90% by weight of textile materials	Manufacture from chemical materials
	– Other	Manufacture from yarn

[1]For special conditions relating to products made of mixture of textile materials, see Introductory Note 5.

HS heading No	Description of product	Working or processing carried out on non-originating materials that confers originating status
(1)	(2)	(3) or (4)
5907	Textile fabrics otherwise impregnated, coated or covered; painted canvas being theatrical scenery, studio back-cloths or the like	Manufacture from yarn; or Printing accompanied by at least two preparatory or finishing operations (such as scouring, bleaching, mercerising, heat setting, rasing, calendering, shrink resist ance processing, permanent finishing, decatising, impregnating, mending and burling) where the value of the unprinted fabric used does not exceed 47.5% of the ex-works price of the product
5908	Textile wicks, woven, plaited or knitted, for lamps, stoves, lighters, candles or the like; incandescent gas mantles and tubular knitted gas mantle fabric therefor, whether or not impregnated:	
	– Incandescent gas mantles, impregnated	Manufacture from tubular knitted gas mantle fabric
	– Other	Manufacture in which all the materials used are classified within a heading other than that of the product
5909 to 5911	Textile articles of a kind suitable for industrial use: – Polishing discs or rings other than of felt of heading No 5911 – Woven fabrics, of a kind commonly used in papermaking or other technical uses, felted or not, whether or not impregnated or coated, tubular or endless with single or multiple warp and/or weft, or flat woven with multiple warp and/or weft of heading No 5911	Manufacture from yarn or waste fabrics or rags of heading No 6310 Manufacture from:[1] – coir yarn, – the following materials: – yarn of polytetrafluoroethylene,[2] – yarn, multiple, of polyamide, coated impregnated or covered with a phenolic resin, – yarn of synthetic textile fibres of aromatic polyamides, obtained by poly-condensation of m-phenylenediamine and isophthalic acid, – monofil of polytetrafluoroethylene[2] – yarn of synthetic textile fibres of poly-phenylene terephthalamide, – glass fibre yarn, coated with phenol resin and gimped with acrylic yarn[2] – copolyester monofilaments of a polyester and a resin of terephthalic acid and 1,4 – cyclohexanediethanol and isophthalic acid,

[1]For special conditions relating to products made of mixture of textile materials, see Introductory Note 5.

[2]The use of this material is restricted to the manufacture of woven fabrics of a kind used in paper-making machinery.

HS heading No	Description of product	Working or processing carried out on non-originating materials that confers originating status
(1)	(2)	(3) or (4)
5909 to 5911 (contin.)		– natural fibres, – man-made staple fibres not carded or combed or otherwise processed for spinning, or – chemical materials or textile pulp
	– Other	Manufacture from:[1] – coir yarn, – natural fibres, – man-made staple fibres not carded or combed or otherwise processed for spinning, or – chemical materials or textile pulp
Chapter 60	Knitted or crocheted fabrics	Manufacture from:[1] – natural fibres, – man-made staple fibres not carded or combed or otherwise processed for spinning, or – chemical materials or textile pulp
Chapter 61	Articles of apparel and clothing accessories, knitted or crocheted:	
	– Obtained by sewing together or otherwise assembling, two or more pieces of knitted or crocheted fabric which have been either cut to form or obtained directly to form	Manufacture from yarn[1,2]
	– Other	Manufacture from:[1] – natural fibres, – man-made staple fibres not carded or combed or otherwise processed for spinning, or – chemical materials or textile pulp
ex Chapter 62	Articles of apparel and clothing accessories, not knitted or crocheted; except for:	Manufacture from yarn[3,1]
ex 6202, ex 6204, ex 6206, ex 6209 and ex 6211	Women's, girls' and babies' clothing and clothing accessories for babies, embroidered	Manufacture from yarn[3] or Manufacture from unembroidered fabric provided the value of the unembroidered fabric used does not exceed 40% of the ex-works price of the product[3]

[1] For special conditions relating to products made of mixture of textile materials, see Introductory Note 5.

[2] The use of this material is restricted to the manufacture of woven fabrics of a kind used in paper-making machinery.

[3] See Introductory Note 6.

HS heading No (1)	Description of product (2)	Working or processing carried out on non-originating materials that confers originating status (3) or (4)
ex 6210 and ex 6216	Fire-resistant equipment of fabric covered with foil of aluminized polyester	Manufacture from yarn[1] or Manufacture from uncoated fabric provided the value of the uncoated fabric used does not exceed 40% of the ex-works price of the product[1]
6213 and 6214	Handkerchiefs, shawls, scarves, mufflers, mantillas, veils and the like:	
	– Embroidered	Manufacture from unbleached single yarn;[1,2] or Manufacture from unembroidered fabric provided the value of the unembroidered fabric used does not exceed 40% of the ex-works price of the product[1]
	– Other	Manufacture from unbleached single yarn;[1,2] or Making up followed by printing accompanied by at least two preparatory or finishing operations (such as scouring, bleaching, mercerizing, heat setting, raising, calendering, shrink resist ance processing, permanent finishing, decatizing, impregnating, mending and burling) where the value of the unprinted goods of heading Nos 6213 and 6214 used does not exceed 47.5% of the ex-works price of the product
6217	Other made up clothing accessories; parts of garments or of clothing accessories, other than those of heading No 6212:	
	– Embroidered	Manufacture from yarn[1] or Manufacture from unembroidered fabric provided the value of the unembroidered fabric used does not exceed 40% of the ex-works price of the product[1]
	– Fire-resistant equipment of fabric covered with foil of aluminized polyester	Manufacture from yarn[1] or Manufacture from uncoated fabric provided the value of the uncoated fabric used does not exceed 40% of the ex-works price of the product[1]

[1]See Introductory Note 6.
[2]For special conditions relating to products made of mixture of textile materials, see Introductory Note 5.

HS heading No	Description of product	Working or processing carried out on non-originating materials that confers originating status
(1)	(2)	(3) or (4)
6217 (contin.)	– Interlinings for collars and cuffs, cut out	Manufacture in which: – all the materials used are classified within a heading other than that of the product; – the value of all the materials used does not exceed 40% of the ex-works price of the product
	– Other	Manufacture from yarn[1]
ex Chapter 63	Other made-up textile articles; sets; worn clothing and worn textile articles; rags; except for:	Manufacture in which all the materials used are classified within a heading other than that of the product
6301 to 6304	Blankets, travelling rugs, bed linen etc.; curtains etc.; other furnishing articles:	
	– Of felt, of nonwovens	Manufacture from:[2] – natural fibres, or – chemical materials or textile pulp
	– Other:	
	– Embroidered	Manufacture from unbleached single yarn[2,3] or Manufacture from unembroidered fabric (other than knitted or crocheted) provided the value of the unembroidered fabric used does not exceed 40% of the ex-works price of the product
	– Other	Manufacture from unbleached single yarn[1,2]
6305	Sacks and bags, of a kind used for the packing of goods	Manufacture from:[2] – natural fibres, – man-made staple fibres not carded or combed or otherwise processed for spinning, or – chemical materials or textile pulp
6306	Tarpaulins, awnings and sunblinds; tents; sails for boats, sailboards or landcraft; camping goods:	
	– Of nonwovens	Manufacture from:[1,2] – natural fibres, or – chemical materials or textile pulp

[1]See Introductory Note 6.

[2]For special conditions relating to products made of mixture of textile materials, see Introductory Note 5.

[3]For knitted or crocheted articles, not elastic or rubberized, obtained by sewing or assembly pieces of knitted or crocheted fabrics (cut out or knitted directly to shape), see Introductory Note 6.

HS heading No	Description of product	Working or processing carried out on non-originating materials that confers originating status
(1)	(2)	(3) or (4)
6306 (contin.)	– Other	Manufacture from unbleached single yarn[1,2]
6307	Other made-up articles, including dress patterns	Manufacture in which the value of all the materials used does not exceed 40% of the ex-works price of the product
6308	Sets consisting of woven fabric and yarn, whether or not with accessories, for making up into rugs, tapestries, embroidered table cloths or serviettes,or similar textile articles, put up in packings for retail sale	Each item in the set must satisfy the rule which would apply to it if it were not included in the set. However, non-originating articles may be incorporated provided their total value does not exceed 15% of the ex-works price of the set
ex Chapter 64	Footwear, gaiters and the like; except for:	Manufacture from materials of any heading except for assemblies of uppers affixed to inner soles or to other sole components of heading No 6406
6406	Parts of footwear (including uppers whether or not attached to soles other than outer soles); removable in-soles, heel cushions and similar articles; gaiters, leggings and similar articles, and parts thereof	Manufacture in which all the materials used are classified within a heading other than that of the product
ex Chapter 65	Headgear and parts thereof, except for:	Manufacture in which all the materials used are classified within a heading other than that of the product
6503	Felt hats and other felt headgear, made from the hat bodies, hoods or plateaux of heading No 6501, whether or not lined or trimmed	Manufacture from yarn or textile fibres[1]
6505	Hats and other headgear, knitted or crocheted, or made up from lace, felt or other textile fabric, in the piece (but not in strips), whether or not lined or trimmed; hair-nets of any material, whether or not lined or trimmed	Manufacture from yarn or textile fibres[1]
ex Chapter 66	Umbrellas, sun umbrellas, walking-sticks, seat-sticks, whips, riding-crops, and parts thereof; except for:	Manufacture in which all the materials used are classified within a heading other than that of the product
6601	Umbrellas and sun umbrellas (including walking-stick umbrellas, garden umbrellas and similar umbrellas)	Manufacture in which the value of all the materials used does not exceed 50% of the ex-works price of the product

[1]For special conditions relating to products made of mixture of textile materials, see Introductory Note 5.
[2]See Introductory Note 6.

HS heading No	Description of product	Working or processing carried out on non-originating materials that confers originating status
(1)	(2)	(3) or (4)
Chapter 67	Prepared feathers and down and articles made of feathers or of down; artificial flowers; articles of human hair	Manufacture in which all the materials used are classified within a heading other than that of the product
ex Chapter 68	Articles of stone, plaster, cement, asbestos, mica or similar materials; except for:	Manufacture in which all the materials used are classified within a heading other than that of the product
ex 6803	Articles of slate or of agglomerated slate	Manufacture from worked slate
ex 6812	Articles of asbestos; articles of mixtures with a basis of asbestos or of mixtures with a basis of asbestos and magnesium carbonate	Manufacture from materials of any heading
ex 6814	Articles of mica, including agglomerated or reconstituted mica, on a support of paper, paperboard or other materials	Manufacture from worked mica (including agglomerated or reconstituted mica)
Chapter 69	Ceramic products	Manufacture in which all the materials used are classified within a heading other than that of the product
ex Chapter 70	Glass and glassware; except for :	Manufacture in which all the materials used are classified within a heading other than that of the product
ex 7003 ex 7004 and ex 7005	Glass with a non-reflecting layer	Manufacture from materials of heading No 7001
7006	Glass of heading No 7003, 7004 or 7005, bent, edgeworked, engraved, drilled, enamelled or otherwise worked, but not framed or fitted with other materials:	
	– glass plate substrate coated with dielectric thin film, semi-conductor grade, in accordance with SEMII standards[1]	Manufacture from non-coated glass plate substrate of heading No 7006
	– other	Manufacture from materials of heading No 7001
7007	Safety glass, consisting of toughened (tempered) or laminated glass	Manufacture from materials of heading No 7001
7008	Multiple-walled insulating units of glass	Manufacture from materials of heading No 7001
7009	Glass mirrors, whether or not framed,including rear-view mirrors	Manufacture from materials of heading No 7001

[1]SEMI – Semiconductor Equipment and Materials Incorporated.

HS heading No	Description of product	Working or processing carried out on non-originating materials that confers originating status
(1)	(2)	(3) or (4)
7010	Carboys, bottles, flasks, jars, pots, phials, ampoules and other containers, of glass, of a kind used for the conveyance or packing of goods; preserving jars of glass; stoppers, lids and other closures, of glass	Manufacture in which all the materials used are classified within a heading other than that of the product or Cutting of glassware, provided the value of the uncut glassware does not exceed 50% of the ex-works price of the product
7013	Glassware of a kind used for table, kitchen, toilet, office, indoor decoration or similar purposes (other than that of heading No 7010 or 7018)	Manufacture in which all the materials used are classified within a heading other than that of the product or Cutting of glassware, provided the value of the uncut glassware does not exceed 50% of the ex-works price of the product or Hand-decoration (with the exception of silk-screen printing) of hand-blown glassware, provided the value of the hand-blown glassware does not exceed 50% of the ex-works price of the product
ex 7019	Articles (other than yarn) of glass fibres	Manufacture from: – uncoloured slivers, rovings, yarn or chopped strands, or – glass wool
ex Chapter 71	Natural or cultured pearls, precious or semi-precious stones, precious metals, metals clad with precious metal, and articles thereof; imitation jewellery; coin; except for:	Manufacture in which all the materials used are classified within a heading other than that of the product
ex 7101	Natural or cultured pearls, graded and temporarily strung for convenience of transport	Manufacture in which the value of all the materials used does not exceed 50% of the ex-works price of the product
ex 7102, ex 7103 and ex 7104	Worked precious or semi-precious stones (natural, synthetic or reconstructed)	Manufacture from unworked precious or semi-precious stones
7106, 7108 and 7110	Precious metals: – Unwrought	Manufacture from materials not classified within heading No 7106, 7108 or 7110 or Electrolytic, thermal or chemical separation of precious metals of heading No 7106, 7108 or 7110 or Alloying of precious metals of heading No 7106, 7108 or 7110 with each other or with base metals

HS heading No	Description of product	Working or processing carried out on non-originating materials that confers originating status
(1)	(2)	(3) or (4)
	– Semi-manufactured or in powder form	Manufacture from unwrought precious metals
ex 7107, ex 7109 and ex 7111	Metals clad with precious metals, semi-manufactured	Manufacture from metals clad with precious metals, unwrought
7116	Articles of natural or cultured pearls, precious or semi-precious stones (natural, synthetic or reconstructed)	Manufacture in which the value of all the materials used does not exceed 50% iof the ex-works price of the product
7117	Imitation jewellery	Manufacture in which all the materials used are classified within a heading other than that of the product or Manufacture from base metal parts, not plated or covered with precious metals, provided the value of all the materials used does not exceed 50% of the ex-works price of the product
ex Chapter 72	Iron and steel; except for:	Manufacture in which all the materials used are classified within a heading other than that of the product
7207	Semi-finished products of iron or non-alloy steel	Manufacture from materials of heading No 7201, 7202, 7203, 7204 or 7205
7208 to 7216	Flat-rolled products, bars and rods, angles, shapes and sections of iron or non-alloy steel	Manufacture from ingots or other primary forms of heading No 7206
7217	Wire of iron or non-alloy steel	Manufacture from semi-finished materials of heading No 7207
ex 7218, 7219 to 7222	Semi-finished products, flat-rolled products, bars and rods, angles, shapes and sections of stainless steel	Manufacture from ingots or other primary forms of heading No 7218
7223	Wire of stainless steel	Manufacture from semi-finished materials of heading No 7218
ex 7224, 7225 to 7228	Semi-finished products, flat-rolled products, hot-rolled bars and rods, in irregularly wound coils; angles, shapes and sections, of other alloy steel; hollow drill bars and rods, of alloy or non-alloy steel	Manufacture from ingots or other primary forms of heading No 7206, 7218 or 7224
7229	Wire of other alloy steel	Manufacture from semi-finished materials of heading No 7224
ex Chapter 73	Articles of iron or steel; except for:	Manufacture in which all the materials used are classified within a heading other than that of the product

HS heading No	Description of product	Working or processing carried out on non-originating materials that confers originating status	
(1)	(2)	(3) or (4)	
ex 7301	Sheet piling	Manufacture from materials of heading No 7206	
7302	Railway or tramway track construction materials of iron or steel, the following: rails, checkrails and rackrails, switch blades, crossing frogs, point rods and other crossing pieces, sleepers (cross-ties), fish-plates, chairs, chair wedges, sole pates (base plates), rail clips, bedplates, ties and other material specialized for jointing or fixing rails	Manufacture from materials of heading No 7206	
7304, 7305 and 7306	Tubes, pipes and hollow profiles, of iron (other than cast iron) or steel	Manufacture from materials of heading No 7206, 7207, 7218 or 7224	
ex 7307	Tube or pipe fittings of stainless steel (ISO No X5CrNiMo 1712), consisting of several parts	Turning, drilling, reaming, threading, deburring and sandblasting of forged blanks the value of which does not exceed 35% of the ex-works price of the product	
7308	Structures (excluding prefabricated buildings of heading No 9406) and parts of structures (for example, bridges and bridge-sections, lock-gates, towers, lattice masts, roofs, roofing frame-works, doors and windows and their frames and thresholds for doors, shutters, balustrades, pillars and columns), of iron or steel; plates, rods, angles, shapes, sections, tubes and the like, prepared for use in structures, of iron or steel	Manufacture in which all the materials used are classified within a heading other than that of the product. However, welded angles, shapes and sections of heading No 7301 may not be used	
ex 7315	Skid chain	Manufacture in which the value of all the materials of heading No 7315 used does not exceed 50% of the ex-works price of the product	
ex Chapter 74	Copper and articles thereof; except for:	Manufacture in which: – all the materials used are classified within a heading other than that of the product; – the value of all the materials used does not exceed 50% of the ex-works price of the product	
7401	Copper mattes; cement copper (precipitated copper)	Manufacture in which all the materials used are classified within a heading other than that of the product	

HS heading No	Description of product	Working or processing carried out on non-originating materials that confers originating status
(1)	(2)	(3) or (4)
7402	Unrefined copper; copper anodes for electrolytic refining	Manufacture in which all the materials used are classified within a heading other than that of the product
7403	Refined copper and copper alloys, unwrought:	
	– Refined copper	Manufacture in which all the materials used are classified within a heading other than that of the product
	– Copper alloys and refined copper containing other elements	Manufacture from refined copper, unwrought, or waste and scrap of copper
7404	Copper waste and scrap	Manufacture in which all the materials used are classified within a heading other than that of the product
7405	Master alloys of copper	Manufacture in which all the materials used are classified within a heading other than that of the product
ex Chapter 75	Nickel and articles thereof; except for:	Manufacture in which: – all the materials used are classified within a heading other than that of the product; – the value of all the materials used does not exceed 50% of the ex-works price of the product
7501 to 7503	Nickel mattes, nickel oxide sinters and other intermediate products of nickel metallurgy; unwrought nickel; nickel waste and scrap	Manufacture in which all the materials used are classified within a heading other than that of the product
ex Chapter 76	Aluminium and articles thereof; except for:	Manufacture in which: – all the materials used are classified within a heading other than that of the product; – the value of all the materials used does not exceed 50% of the ex-works price of the product
7601	Unwrought aluminium	Manufacture in which: – all the materials used are classified within a heading other than that of the product; and – the value of all the materials used does not exceed 50% of the ex-works price of the product or Manufacture by thermal or electrolytic treatment from unalloyed aluminium or waste and scrap of aluminium

HS heading No	Description of product	Working or processing carried out on non-originating materials that confers originating status
(1)	(2)	(3) or (4)
7602	Aluminium waste or scrap	Manufacture in which all the materials used are classified within a heading other than that of the product
ex 7616	Aluminium articles other than gauze, cloth, grill, netting, fencing, reinforcing fabric and similar materials (including endless bands) of aluminium wire, and expanded metal of aluminium	Manufacture in which: – all the materials used are classified – within a heading other than that of – the product. However, gauze, cloth, – grill netting, fencing, reinforcing fabric – and similar materials (including – endless bands) of aluminium wire, or – expanded metal of aluminium may – be used; – the value of all the materials used – does not exceed 50% of the ex-works – price of the product
Chapter 77		Reserved for possible future use in HS
ex Chapter 78	Lead and articles thereof; except for:	Manufacture in which: – all the materials used are classified – within a heading other than that of – the product; – the value of all the materials used – does not exceed 50% of the ex-works – price of the product
7801	Unwrought lead:	
	– Refined lead	Manufacture from 'bullion' or 'work' lead
	– Other	Manufacture in which all the materials used are classified within a heading other than that of the product. However, waste and scrap of heading No 7802 may not be used
7802	Lead waste and scrap	Manufacture in which all the materials used are classified within a heading other than that of the product
ex Chapter 79	Zinc and articles thereof; except for:	Manufacture in which: – all the materials used are classified within a heading other than that of the product; – the value of all the materials used does not exceed 50% of the ex-works price of the product
7901	Unwrought zinc	Manufacture in which all the materials used are classified within a heading other than that of the product. However, waste and scrap of heading No 7902 may not be used

HS heading No	Description of product	Working or processing carried out on non-originating materials that confers originating status
(1)	(2)	(3) or (4)
7902	Zinc waste and scrap	Manufacture in which all the materials used are classified within a heading other than that of the product
ex Chapter 80	Tin and articles thereof; except for:	Manufacture in which: – all the materials used are classified within a heading other than that of the product; – the value of all the materials used does not exceed 50% of the ex-works price of the product
8001	Unwrought tin	Manufacture in which all the materials used are classified within a heading other than that of the product. However, waste and scrap of heading No 8002 may not be used
8002 and 8007	Tin waste and scrap; other articles of tin	Manufacture in which all the materials used are classified within a heading other than that of the product
Chapter 81	Other base metals; cermets; articles thereof:	
	– Other base metals, wrought; articles thereof	Manufacture in which the value of all the materials classified within the same heading as the product used does not exceed 50% of the ex-works price of the product
	– Other	Manufacture in which all the materials used are classified within a heading other than that of the product
ex Chapter 82	Tools, implements, cutlery, spoons and forks, of base metal; parts thereof of base metal; except for:	Manufacture in which all the materials used are classified within a heading other than that of the product
8206	Tools of two or more of the heading Nos 8202 to 8205, put up in sets for retail sale	Manufacture in which all the materials used are classified within a heading other than heading Nos 8202 to 8205. However, tools of heading Nos 8202 to 8205 may be incorporated into the set provided their value does not exceed 15% of the ex-works price of the set
8207	Interchangeable tools for hand tools, whether or not power-operated, or for machine-tools (for example, for pressing, stamping, punching, tapping, threading, drilling, boring, broaching, milling, turning, or screw-driving), including dies for drawing or extruding metal, and rock drilling or earth boring tools	Manufacture in which: – all the materials used are classified within a heading other than that of the product; – the value of all the materials used does not exceed 40% of the ex-works price of the product

HS heading No	Description of product	Working or processing carried out on non-originating materials that confers originating status
(1)	(2)	(3) or (4)
8208	Knives and cutting blades, for machines or for mechanical appliances	Manufacture in which: – all the materials used are classified within a heading other than that of the product; – the value of all the materials used does not exceed 40% of the ex-works price of the product
ex 8211	Knives with cutting blades, serrated or not (including pruning knives), other than knives of heading No 8208	Manufacture in which all the materials used are classified within a heading other than that of the product. However, knife blades and handles of base metal may be used
8214	Other articles of cutlery (for example, hair clippers, butchers' or kitchen cleavers, choppers and mincing knives, paper knives); manicure or pedicure sets and instruments (including nail files)	Manufacture in which all the materials used are classified within a heading other than that of the product. However, handles of base metal may be used
8215	Spoons, forks, ladles, skimmers, cake-servers, fish-knives, butter-knives, sugar tongs and similar kitchen or tableware	Manufacture in which all the materials used are classified within a heading other than that of the product. However, handles of base metal may be used
ex Chapter 83	Miscellaneous articles of base metal; except for:	Manufacture in which all the materials used are classified within a heading other than that of the product
ex 8302	Other mountings, fittings and similar articles suitable for buildings, and automatic door closers	Manufacture in which all the materials used are classified within a heading other than that of the product. However, the other materials of heading No 8302 may be used provided their value does not exceed 20% of the ex-works price of the product
ex 8306	Statuettes and other ornaments, of base metal	Manufacture in which all the materials used are classified within a heading other than that of the product. However, the other materials of heading No 8306 may be used provided their value does not exceed 30% of the ex-works price of the product
ex Chapter 84	Nuclear reactors, boilers, machinery and mechanical appliances; parts thereof; except for:	Manufacture in which: – all the materials used are classified within a heading other than that of the product; – the value of all the materials used does not exceed 40% of the ex-works price of the product

HS heading No	Description of product	Working or processing carried out on non-originating materials that confers originating status
(1)	(2)	(3) or (4)
		Manufacture in which the value of all the materials used does not exceed 30% of the ex-works price of the product
ex 8401	Nuclear fuel elements	Manufacture in which all the materials used are classified within a heading other than that of the product[1] Manufacture in which the value of all the materials used does not exceed 30% of the ex-works price of the final product
8402	Steam or other vapour generating boilers (other than central heating hot water boilers capable also of producing low pressure steam); super heated water boilers	Manufacture in which: – all the materials used are classified within a heading other than that of the product; – the value of all the materials used does not exceed 40% of the ex-works price of the product Manufacture in which the value of all the materials used does not exceed 25% of the ex-works price of the product
8403 and ex 8404	Central heating boilers other than those of heading No 8402 and auxiliary plant for central heating boilers	Manufacture in which all the materials used are classified within a heading other than heading No 8403 or 8404 Manufacture in which the value of all the materials used does not exceed 40% of the ex-works price of the product
8406	Steam turbines and other vapour turbines of the ex-works price of the product	Manufacture in which the value of all the materials used does not exceed 40%
8407	Spark-ignition reciprocating or rotary internal combustion piston engines	Manufacture in which the value of all the materials used does not exceed 40% of the ex-works price of the product
8408	Compression-ignition internal combustion piston engines (diesel or semi-diesel engines)	Manufacture in which the value of all the materials used does not exceed 40% of the ex-works price of the product
8409	Parts suitable for use solely or principally with the engines of heading No 8407 or 8408 of the product	Manufacture in which the value of all the materials used does not exceed 40% of the ex-works price
8411	Turbo-jets, turbo propellers and other gas turbines	Manufacture in which: – all the materials used are classified within a heading other than that of the product;

[1]This rule shall apply until 31 December 2005.

HS heading No	Description of product	Working or processing carried out on non-originating materials that confers originating status
(1)	(2)	(3) or (4)
8411 (contin.)		– the value of all the materials used does not exceed 40% of the ex-works price of the product Manufacture in which the value of all the materials used does not exceed 25% of the ex-works price of the product
8412	Other engines and motors	Manufacture in which the value of all the materials used does not exceed 40% of the ex-works price of the product
ex 8413	Rotary positive displacement pumps	Manufacture in which: all the materials used are classified within a heading other than that of the product; – the value of all the materials used does not exceed 40% of the ex-works price of the product Manufacture in which the value of all the materials used does not exceed 25% of the ex-works price of the product
ex 8414	Industrial fans, blowers and the like	Manufacture in which: – all the materials used are classified within a heading other than that of the product; – the value of all the materials used does not exceed 40% of the ex-works price of the product Manufacture in which the value of all the materials used does not exceed 25% of the ex-works price of the product
8415	Air conditioning machines, comprising a motor-driven fan and elements for changing the temperature and humidity, including those machines in which the humidity cannot be separately regulated	Manufacture in which the value of all the materials used does not exceed 40% of the ex-works price of the product
8418	Refrigerators, freezers and other refrigerating or freezing equipment, electric or other; heat pumps other than air conditioning machines of heading No 8415	Manufacture in which: – all the materials used are classified within a heading other than that of the product; – the value of all the materials used does not exceed 40% of the ex-works price of the product; – the value of all the non-originating materials used does not exceed the value of the originating materials used

HS heading No	Description of product	Working or processing carried out on non-originating materials that confers originating status
(1)	(2)	(3) or (4)
8418 (contin.)		Manufacture in which the value of all the materials used does not exceed 25% of the ex-works price of the product
ex 8419	Machines for wood, paper pulp and paperboard industries	Manufacture: – in which the value of all the materials used does not exceed 40% of the ex-works price of the product; – where, within the above limit, the materials classified within the same heading as the product are only used up to a value of 25% of the ex-works price of the product Manufacture in which the value of all the materials used does not exceed 30% of the ex-works price of the product
8420	Calendering or other rolling machines, other than for metals or glass, and cylinders therefore of the ex-works price of the product;	Manufacture: – in which the value of all the materials used does not exceed 40% of the ex-works price of the product; – where, within the above limit, the materials classified within the same heading as the product are only used up to a value of 25% of the ex-works price of the product Manufacture in which the value of all the materials used does not exceed 30% of the ex-works price of the product
8423	Weighing machinery (excluding balances of a sensitivity of 5 cg or better), including weight operated counting or checking machines; weighing machine weights of all	Manufacture in which: – all the materials used are classified within a heading other than that of the product; – the value of all the materials used does kinds not exceed 40% of the ex-works price of the product Manufacture in which the value of all the materials used does not exceed 25% of the ex-works price of the product
8425 to 8428	Lifting, handling, loading or unloading machinery	Manufacture: – in which the value of all the materials used does not exceed 40% of the ex-works price of the product; – where, within the above limit, the materials classified within heading No 8431 are only used up to a value of 10% of the ex-works price of the product

HS heading No	Description of product	Working or processing carried out on non-originating materials that confers originating status
(1)	(2)	(3) or (4)
		Manufacture in which the value of all the materials used does not exceed 30% of the ex-works price of the product
8429	Self-propelled bulldozers, angledozers, graders, levellers, scrapers, mechanical shovels, excavators, shovel loaders, tamping machines and road rollers:	
	– Road rollers	Manufacture in which the value of all the materials used does not exceed 40% of the ex-works price of the product
	– Other	Manufacture: – in which the value of all the materials used does not exceed 40% of the ex-works price of the product; – where, within the above limit, the materials classified within heading No 8431 are only used up to a value of 10% of the ex-works price of the product Manufacture in which the value of all the materials used does not exceed 30% of the ex-works price of the product
8430	Other moving, grading, levelling, scraping, excavating, tamping, compacting, extracting or boring machinery, for earth, minerals or ores; pile-drivers and pile-extractors; now-ploughs and snow-blowers	Manufacture: – in which the value of all the materials used does not exceed 40% of the ex-works price of the product; – where, within the above limit, the value of the materials classified within heading No 8431 are only used up to a value of 10% of the ex-works price of the product Manufacture in which the value of all the materials used does not exceed 30% of the ex-works price of the product
ex 8431	Parts suitable for use solely or principally with road rollers	Manufacture in which the value of all the materials used does not exceed 40% of the ex-works price of the product
8439	Machinery for making pulp of fibrous cellulosic material or for making or finishing paper or paperboard	Manufacture: – in which the value of all the materials used does not exceed 40% of the ex-works price of the product; – where, within the above limit, the materials classified within the same heading as the product are only used up to a value of 25% of the ex-works price of the product

HS heading No	Description of product	Working or processing carried out on non-originating materials that confers originating status
(1)	(2)	(3) or (4)
8439 (contin.)		Manufacture in which the value of all the materials used does not exceed 30% of the ex-works price of the product
8441	Other machinery for making up paper pulp, paper or paperboard, including cutting machines of all kinds	Manufacture: – in which the value of all the materials used does not exceed 40% of the ex-works price of the product; – where, within the above limit, the materials classified within the same heading as the product are only used up to a value of 25% of the ex-works price of the product Manufacture in which the value of all the materials used does not exceed 30% of the ex-works price of the product
8444 to 8447	Machines of these headings for use in the textile industry	Manufacture in which the value of all the materials used does not exceed 40% of the ex-works price of the product
ex 8448 8445	Auxiliary machinery for use with machines of headings Nos 8444 and	Manufacture in which the value of all the materials used does not exceed 40% of the ex-works price of the product
8452	Sewing machines, other than book-sewing machines of heading No 8440; furniture, bases and covers specially designed for sewing machines; sewing machine needles:	
	Sewing machines (lock stitch only) with heads of a weight not exceeding 16 kg without motor or 17 kg with motor	Manufacture: – in which the value of all the materials used does not exceed 40% of the ex-works price of the product; – where the value of all the non-originating materials used in assembling the head (without motor) does not exceed the value of the originating materials used; – the thread tension, crochet and zigzag mechanisms used are already originating
	– Other	Manufacture in which the value of all the materials used does not exceed 40% of the ex-works price of the product
8456 to 8466	Machine-tools and machines and their parts and accessories of headings Nos 8456 to 8466	Manufacture in which the value of all the materials used does not exceed 40% of the ex-works price of the product

HS heading No	Description of product	Working or processing carried out on non-originating materials that confers originating status	
(1)	(2)	(3) or (4)	
8469 to 8472	Office machines (for example, typewriters, calculating machines, automatic data processing machines, duplicating machines, stapling machines)	Manufacture in which the value of all the materials used does not exceed 40% of the ex-works price of the product	
8480	Moulding boxes for metal foundry; mould bases; moulding patterns; moulds for metal (other than ingot moulds), metal carbides, glass, mineral materials, rubber or plastics	Manufacture in which the value of all the materials used does not exceed 50% of the ex-works price of the product	
8482	Ball or roller bearings	Manufacture in which: – all the materials used are classified within a heading other than that of the product; – the value of all the materials used does not exceed 40% of the ex-works price of the product	Manufacture in which the value of all the materials used does not exceed 25% of the ex-works price of the product
8484	Gaskets and similar joints of metal sheeting combined with other material or of two or more layers of metal; sets or assortments of gaskets and similar joints, dissimilar in composition, put up in pouches, envelopes or similar packings; mechanical seals	Manufacture in which the value of all the materials used does not exceed 40% of the ex-works price of the product	
8485	Machinery parts, not containing electrical connectors, insulators, coils, contacts or other electrical features, not specified or included elsewhere in this Chapter	Manufacture in which the value of all the materials used does not exceed 40% of the ex-works price of the product	
ex Chapter 85	Electrical machinery and equipment and parts thereof; sound recorders and reproducers, television image and sound recorders and reproducers, and parts and accessories of such articles; except for:	Manufacture in which – all the materials used are classified within a heading other than that of the product; – the value of all the materials used does not exceed 40% of the ex-works price of the product	Manufacture in which the value of all the materials used does not exceed 30% of the ex-works price of the product

HS heading No	Description of product	Working or processing carried out on non-originating materials that confers originating status
(1)	(2)	(3) or (4)
8501	Electric motors and generators (excluding generating sets)	Manufacture: – in which the value of all the materials used does not exceed 40% of the ex-works price of the product; – where, within the above limit, the materials classified within heading No 8503 are only used up to a value of 10% of the ex-works price of the product
8501 (contin.)		Manufacture in which the value of all the materials used does not exceed 30% of the ex-works price of the product
8502	Electric generating sets and rotary converters	Manufacture: – in which the value of all the materials used does not exceed 40% of the ex-works price of the product; – where, within the above limit, the materials classified within heading No 8501 or 8503, taken together, are only used up to a value of 10% of the ex-works price of the product Manufacture in which the value of all the materials used does not exceed 30% of the ex-works price of the product
ex 8504	Power supply units for automatic data-processing machines	Manufacture in which the value of all the materials used does not exceed 40% of the ex-works price of the product
ex 8518	Microphones and stands therefor; loudspeakers, whether or not mounted in their enclosures; audio-frequency electric amplifiers; electric sound amplifier sets	Manufacture: – in which the value of all the materials used does not exceed 40% of the ex-works price of the product; – where the value of all the non-originating materials used does not exceed the value of the originating materials used Manufacture in which the value of all the materials used does not exceed 25% of the ex-works price of the product
8519	Turntables (record-decks), record-players, cassette-players and other sound reproducing apparatus, not	Manufacture: – in which the value of all the materials used does not exceed 40% of the ex-works incorporating a sound recording device price of the product; – where the value of all the non-originating materials used does not exceed the value of the originating materials used

HS heading No	Description of product	Working or processing carried out on non-originating materials that confers originating status
(1)	(2)	(3) or (4)
8519 (contin.)		Manufacture in which the value of all the materials used does not exceed 30% of the ex-works price of the product
8520	Magnetic tape recorders and other sound recording apparatus, whether or not incorporating a sound reproducing device	Manufacture: – in which the value of all the materials used does not exceed 40% of the ex-works price of the product;
8520		– where the value of all the non-originating materials used does not exceed the value of the originating materials used Manufacture in which the value of all the materials used does not exceed 30% of the ex-works price of the product
8521	Video recording or reproducing apparatus, whether or not incorporating a video tuner	Manufacture: – in which the value of all the materials used does not exceed 40% of the ex-works price of the product; – where the value of all the non-originating materials used does not exceed the value of the originating materials used Manufacture in which the value of all the materials used does not exceed 30% of the ex-works price of the product
8522	Parts and accessories suitable for use solely or principally with the apparatus of heading Nos 8519 to 8521	Manufacture in which the value of all the materials used does not exceed 40% of the ex-works price of the product
8523	Prepared unrecorded media for sound recording or similar recording of other phenomena, other than products of Chapter 37	Manufacture in which the value of all the materials used does not exceed 40% of the ex-works price of the product
8524	Records, tapes and other recorded media for sound or other similarly recorded phenomena, including matrices and masters for the production of records, but excluding products of Chapter 37:	
	– Matrices and masters for the production of records	Manufacture in which the value of all the materials used does not exceed 40% of the ex-works price of the product

HS heading No	Description of product	Working or processing carried out on non-originating materials that confers originating status
(1)	(2)	(3) or (4)
8524 (contin.)	– Other	Manufacture: – in which the value of all the materials used does not exceed 40% of the ex-works price of the product; – where, within the above limit, the materials classified within heading No 8523 are only used up to a value of 10% of the ex-works price of the product Manufacture in which the value of all the materials used does not exceed 30% of the ex-works price of the product
8525	Transmission apparatus for radio-telephony, radio-telegraphy, radio-broadcasting or television, whether or not incorporating reception apparatus or sound recording or reproducing apparatus; television cameras; still image video cameras and other video camera recorders	Manufacture: – in which the value of all the materials used does not exceed 40% of the ex-works price of the product; – where the value of all the non-originating materials used does not exceed the value of the originating materials used Manufacture in which the value of all the materials used does not exceed 25% of the ex-works price of the product
8526	Radar apparatus, radio navigational aid apparatus and radio remote control apparatus	Manufacture: – in which the value of all the materials used does not exceed 40% of the ex-works price of the product; – where the value of all the non-originating materials used does not exceed the value of the originating materials used Manufacture in which the value of all the materials used does not exceed 25% of the ex-works price of the product
8527	Reception apparatus for radio-telephony, radio-telegraphy or radio broadcasting, whether or not combined, in the same housing, with sound recording or reproducing apparatus or a clock	Manufacture: – in which the value of all the materials used does not exceed 40% of the ex-works price of the product; – where the value of all the non-originating materials used does not exceed the value of the originating materials used Manufacture in which the value of all the materials used does not exceed 25% of the ex-works price of the product

HS heading No	Description of product	Working or processing carried out on non-originating materials that confers originating status
(1)	(2)	(3) or (4)
8528	Reception apparatus for television, whether or not incorporating radio broadcast receivers or sound or video recording or reproducing apparatus; video monitors and video projectors	Manufacture: – in which the value of all the materials used does not exceed 40% of the ex-works price of the product; – where the value of all the non-originating materials used does not exceed the value of the originating materials used Manufacture in which the value of all the materials used does not exceed 25% of the ex-works price of the product
8529	Parts suitable for use solely or principally with the apparatus of heading Nos 8525 to 8528:	
	– Suitable for use solely or principally with video recording or reproducing apparatus	Manufacture in which the value of all the materials used does not exceed 40% of the ex-works price of the product
	– Other	Manufacture: – in which the value of all the materials used does not exceed 40% of the ex-works price of the product; – where the value of all the non-originating materials used does not exceed the value of the originating materials used Manufacture in which the value of all the materials used does not exceed 25% of the ex-works price of the product
8535 and 8536	Electrical apparatus for switching or protecting electrical circuits, or for making connections to or in	Manufacture: – in which the value of all the materials used does not exceed 40% of the ex-works electrical circuits price of the product; – where, within the above limit, the materials classified within heading No 8538 are only used up to a value of 10% of the ex-works price of the product Manufacture in which the value of all the materials used does not exceed 30% of the ex-works price of the product

HS heading No	Description of product	Working or processing carried out on non-originating materials that confers originating status
(1)	(2)	(3) or (4)
8537	Boards, panels, consoles, desks, cabinets and other bases, equipped with two or more apparatus of heading No 8535 or 8536, for electric control or the distribution of electricity, including those incorporating instruments or apparatus of Chapter 90, and numerical control apparatus, other than switching apparatus of heading No 8517	Manufacture: – in which the value of all the materials used does not exceed 40% of the ex-works price of the product; – where, within the above limit, the materials classified within heading No 8538 are only used up to a value of 10% of the ex-works price of the product Manufacture in which the value of all the materials used does not exceed 30% of the ex-works price of the product
ex 8541	Diodes, transistors and similar semi-conductor devices, except wafers not yet cut into chips	Manufacture in which: – all the materials used are classified within a heading other than that of the product;
ex 8541		– the value of all the materials used does not exceed 40% of the ex-works price of the product Manufacture in which the value of all the materials used does not exceed 25% of the ex-works price of the product
8542	Electronic integrated circuits and microassemblies	Manufacture: – in which the value of all the materials used does not exceed 40% of the ex–works price of the product; – where, within the above limit, the materials classified within heading No 8541 or 8542, taken together, are only used up to a value of 10% of the ex-works price of the product Manufacture in which the value of all the materials used does not exceed 25% of the ex-works price of the product
8544	Insulated (including enamelled or anodised) wire, cable (including coaxial cable) and other insulated electric conductors, whether or not fitted with connectors; optical fibre cables, made up of individually sheathed fibres, whether or not assembled with electric conductors or fitted with connectors	Manufacture in which the value of all the materials used does not exceed 40% of the ex-works price of the product
8545	Carbon electrodes, carbon brushes, lamp carbons, battery carbons and other articles of graphite or other carbon, with or without metal, of a kind used for electrical purposes	Manufacture in which the value of all the materials used does not exceed 40% of the ex-works price of the product

HS heading No	Description of product	Working or processing carried out on non-originating materials that confers originating status	
(1)	(2)	(3)	or (4)
8546	Electrical insulators of any material	Manufacture in which the value of all the materials used does not exceed 40% of the ex-works price of the product	
8547	Insulating fittings for electrical machines, appliances or equipment, being fittings wholly of insulating materials apart from any minor components of metal (for example, threaded sockets) incorporated during moulding solely for purposes of assembly other than insulators of heading No 8546; electrical conduit tubing and joints therefor, of base metal lined with insulating material	Manufacture in which the value of all the materials used does not exceed 40% of the ex-works price of the product	
8548	Waste and scrap of primary cells, primary batteries and electric accumulators; spent primary cells, spent primary batteries and spent electric accumulators; electrical parts of machinery or apparatus, not specified or included elsewhere in this Chapter	Manufacture in which the value of all the materials used does not exceed 40% of the ex-works price of the product	
ex Chapter 86	Railway or tramway locomotives, rolling-stock and parts thereof; railway or tramway track fixtures and fittings and parts thereof; mechanical (including electro-mechanical) traffic signaling equipment of all kinds; except for:	Manufacture in which the value of all the materials used does not exceed 40% of the ex-works price of the product	
8608	Railway or tramway track fixtures and fittings; mechanical (including electro-mechanical) signalling, safety or traffic control equipment for railways, tramways, roads, inland waterways, parking facilities, port installations or airfields; parts of the foregoing	Manufacture in which: – all the materials used are classified within a heading other than that of the product; – the value of all the materials used does not exceed 40% of the ex-works price of the product	Manufacture in which the value of all the materials used does not exceed 30% of the ex-works price of the product
ex Chapter 87	Vehicles other than railway or tramway rolling-stock, and parts and accessories thereof; except for:	Manufacture in which the value of all the materials used does not exceed 40% of the ex-works price of the product	

HS heading No	Description of product	Working or processing carried out on non-originating materials that confers originating status
(1)	(2)	(3) or (4)
8709	Works trucks, self-propelled, not fitted with lifting or handling equipment, of the type used in factories, warehouses, dock areas or airports for short distance transport of goods; tractors of the type used on railway station platforms; parts of the foregoing vehicles	Manufacture in which: – all the materials used are classified within a heading other than that of the product; – the value of all the materials used does not exceed 40% of the ex-works price of the product Manufacture in which the value of all the materials used does not exceed 30% of the ex-works price of the product
8710	Tanks and other armoured fighting vehicles, motorized, whether or not fitted with weapons, and parts of such vehicles	Manufacture in which: – all the materials used are classified within a heading other than that of the product; – the value of all the materials used does not exceed 40% of the ex-works price of the product Manufacture in which the value of all the materials used does not exceed 30% of the ex-works price of the product
8711	Motorcycles (including mopeds) and cycles fitted with an auxiliary motor, with or without side-cars; side-cars: – With reciprocating internal combustion piston engine of a cylinder capacity:	
	– Not exceeding 50 cc	Manufacture: – in which the value of all the materials used does not exceed 40% of the ex- works price of the product; – where the value of all the non-originating materials used does not exceed the value of the originating materials used Manufacture in which the value of all the materials used does not exceed 20% of the ex-works price of the product
	– Exceeding 50 cc	Manufacture: – in which the value of all the materials used does not exceed 40% of the ex-works price of the product; – where the value of all the non-originating materials used does not exceed the value of the originating materials used Manufacture in which the value of all the materials used does not exceed 25% of the ex-works price of the product

HS heading No	Description of product	Working or processing carried out on non-originating materials that confers originating status
(1)	(2)	(3) or (4)
8711 (contin.)	– Other	Manufacture: – in which the value of all the materials used does not exceed 40% of the ex-works price of the product; – where the value of all the non-originating materials used does not exceed the value of the originating materials used Manufacture in which the value of all the materials used does not exceed 30% of the ex-works price of the product
ex 8712	Bicycles without ball bearings	Manufacture from materials not classified in heading No 8714 Manufacture in which the value of all the materials used does not exceed 30% of the ex-works price of the product
8715	Baby carriages and parts thereof	Manufacture in which: – all the materials used are classified within a heading other than that of the product; – the value of all the materials used does not exceed 40% of the ex-works price of the product Manufacture in which the value of all the materials used does not exceed 30% of the ex-works price of the product
8716	Trailers and semi-trailers; other vehicles, not mechanically propelled; parts thereof	Manufacture in which: – all the materials used are classified within a heading other than that of the product; – the value of all the materials used does not exceed 40% of the ex-works price of the product Manufacture in which the value of all the materials used does not exceed 30% of the ex-works price of the product
ex Chapter 88	Aircraft, spacecraft, and parts thereof; except for:	Manufacture in which all the materials used are classified within a heading other than that of the product Manufacture in which the value of all the materials used does not exceed 40% of the ex-works price of the product
ex 8804	Rotochutes	Manufacture from materials of any heading including other materials of heading No 8804 Manufacture in which the value of all the materials used does not exceed 40% of the ex-works price of the product

HS heading No	Description of product	Working or processing carried out on non-originating materials that confers originating status
(1)	(2)	(3) or (4)
8805	Aircraft launching gear; deck-arrestor or similar gear; ground flying trainers; parts of the foregoing articles	Manufacture in which all the materials used are classified within a heading other than that of the product Manufacture in which the value of all the materials used does not exceed 30% of the ex-works price of the product
Chapter 89	Ships, boats and floating structures	Manufacture in which all the materials used are classified within a heading other than that of the product. However, hulls of heading No 8906 may not be used Manufacture in which the value of all the materials used does not exceed 40% of the ex-works price of the product
ex Chapter 90	Optical, photographic, cinemato-graphic, measuring, checking, precision, medical or surgical instruments and apparatus; parts and accessories thereof; except for:	Manufacture in which: – all the materials used are classified within a heading other than that of the product; – the value of all the materials used does not exceed 40% of the ex-works price of the product Manufacture in which the value of all the materials used does not exceed 30% of the ex-works price of the product
9001	Optical fibres and optical fibre bundles; optical fibre cables other than those of heading No 8544; sheets and plates of polarizing material; lenses (including contact lenses), prisms, mirrors and other optical elements, of any material, unmounted, other than such elements of glass not optically worked	Manufacture in which the value of all the materials used does not exceed 40% of the ex-works price of the product
9002	Lenses, prisms, mirrors and other optical elements, of any material, mounted, being parts of or fittings for instruments or apparatus, other than such elements of glass not optically worked	Manufacture in which the value of all the materials used does not exceed 40% of the ex-works price of the product
9004	Spectacles, goggles and the like, corrective, protective or other	Manufacture in which the value of all the materials used does not exceed 40% of the ex-works price of the product

HS heading No	Description of product	Working or processing carried out on non-originating materials that confers originating status
(1)	(2)	(3) or (4)
ex 9005	Binoculars, monoculars, other optical telescopes, and mountings therefor, except for astronomical refracting telescopes and mountings therefor	Manufacture in which: – all the materials used are classified within a heading other than that of the product; – the value of all the materials used does not exceed 40% of the ex-works price of the product; – the value of all the non-originating materials used does not exceed the value of the originating materials used Manufacture in which the value of all the materials used does not exceed 30% of the ex-works price of the product
ex 9006	Photographic (other than cinemato-graphic) cameras; photographic flashlight apparatus and flashbulbs other than electrically ignited flash-bulbs	Manufacture in which: – all the materials used are classified within a heading other than that of the product; – the value of all the materials used does not exceed 40% of the ex-works price of the product; – the value of all the non-originating materials used does not exceed the value of the originating materials used Manufacture in which the value of all the materials used does not exceed 30% of the ex-works price of the product
9007	Cinematographic cameras and projectors, whether or not incorporating sound recording or reproducing apparatus	Manufacture in which: – all the materials used are classified within a heading other than that of the product; – the value of all the materials used does not exceed 40% of the ex-works price of the product; – the value of all the non-originating materials used does not exceed the value of the originating materials used Manufacture in which the value of all the materials used does not exceed 30% of the ex-works price of the product
9011	Compound optical microscopes, including those for photomicrography, cinephotomicrography or micro-projection	Manufacture in which: – all the materials used are classified within a heading other than that of the product; – the value of all the materials used does not exceed 40% of the ex-works price of the product;

HS heading No	Description of product	Working or processing carried out on non-originating materials that confers originating status
(1)	(2)	(3) or (4)
9011 (contin.)		– the value of all the non-originating materials used does not exceed the value of the originating materials used Manufacture in which the value of all the materials used does not exceed 30% of the ex-works price of the product
ex 9014	Other navigational instruments and appliances	Manufacture in which the value of all the materials used does not exceed 40% of the ex-works price of the product
9015	Surveying (including photo-grammetrical surveying), hydrographic, oceanographic, hydrological, meteorological or geophysical instruments and appliances, excluding compasses; rangefinders	Manufacture in which the value of all the materials used does not exceed 40% of the ex-works price of the product
9016	Balances of a sensitivity of 5 cg or better, with or without weights	Manufacture in which the value of all the materials used does not exceed 40% of the ex-works price of the product
9017	Drawing, marking-out or mathematical calculating instruments (for example, drafting machines, pantographs, protractors, drawing sets, slide rules, disc calculators); instruments for measuring length, for use in the hand (for example, measuring rods and tapes, micrometers, callipers), not specified or included elsewhere in this Chapter	Manufacture in which the value of all the materials used does not exceed 40% of the ex-works price of the product
9018	Instruments and appliances used in medical, surgical, dental or veterinary sciences, including scintigraphic apparatus, other electro-medical apparatus and sight-testing instruments:	
	– Dentists' chairs incorporating dental appliances or dentists' spittoons	Manufacture from materials of any heading, including other materials of heading No 9018 Manufacture in which the value of all the materials used does not exceed 40% of the ex-works price of the product
	– Other	Manufacture in which: – all the materials used are classified within a heading other than that of the product;

HS heading No	Description of product	Working or processing carried out on non-originating materials that confers originating status
(1)	(2)	(3) or (4)
		– the value of all the materials used does not exceed 40% of the ex-works price of the product Manufacture in which the value of all the materials used does not exceed 25% of the ex-works price of the product
9019	Mechano-therapy appliances; massage apparatus; psychological aptitude-testing apparatus; ozone therapy, oxygen therapy, aerosol therapy, artificial respiration or other therapeutic respiration apparatus	Manufacture in which: – all the materials used are classified within a heading other than that of the product; – the value of all the materials used does not exceed 40% of the ex-works price of the product Manufacture in which the value of all the materials used does not exceed 25% of the ex-works price of the product
9020	Other breathing appliances and gas masks, excluding protective masks having neither mechanical parts nor replaceable filters	Manufacture in which: – all the materials used are classified within a heading other than that of the product; – the value of all the materials used does not exceed 40% of the ex-works price of the product Manufacture in which the value of all the materials used does not exceed 25% of the ex-works price of the product
9024	Machines and appliances for testing the hardness, strength, compressibility, elasticity or other mechanical properties of materials (for example, metals, wood, textiles, paper, plastics)	Manufacture in which the value of all the materials used does not exceed 40% of the ex-works price of the product
9025	Hydrometers and similar floating instruments, thermometers, pyrometers, barometers, hygrometers and psychrometers, recording or not, and any combination of these instruments	Manufacture in which the value of all the materials used does not exceed 40% of the ex-works price of the product
9026	Instruments and apparatus for measuring or checking the flow, level, pressure or other variables of liquids or gases (for example, flow meters, level gauges, manometers, heat meters), excluding instruments and apparatus of heading No 9014, 9015, 9028 or 9032	Manufacture in which the value of all the materials used does not exceed 40% of the ex-works price of the product

HS heading No	Description of product	Working or processing carried out on non-originating materials that confers originating status
(1)	(2)	(3) or (4)
9027	Instruments and apparatus for physical or chemical analysis (for example, polarimeters, refractometers, spectrometers, gas or smoke analysis apparatus); instruments and apparatus for measuring or checking viscosity, porosity, expansion, surface tension or the like; instruments and apparatus for measuring or checking quantities of heat, sound or light (including exposure meters); microtomes	Manufacture in which the value of all the materials used does not exceed 40% of the ex-works price of the product
9028	Gas, liquid or electricity supply or production meters, including calibrating meters therefor:	
	– Parts and accessories	Manufacture in which the value of all the materials used does not exceed 40% of the ex-works price of the product
	– Other	Manufacture: – in which the value of all the materials used does not exceed 40% of the ex-works price of the product; – where the value of all the non-originating materials used does not exceed the value of the originating materials used Manufacture in which the value of all the materials used does not exceed 30% of the ex-works price of the product
9029	Revolution counters, production counters, taximeters, mileometers, pedometers and the like; speed indicators and tachometers, other than those of heading Nos 9014 or 9015; stroboscopes	Manufacture in which the value of all the materials used does not exceed 40% of the ex-works price of the product
9030	Oscilloscopes, spectrum analysers and other instruments and apparatus for measuring or checking electrical quantities, excluding meters of heading No 9028; instruments and apparatus for measuring or detecting alpha, beta, gamma, X-ray, cosmic or other ionizing radiations	Manufacture in which the value of all the materials used does not exceed 40% of the ex-works price of the product
9031	Measuring or checking instruments, appliances and machines, not specified or included elsewhere in this Chapter; profile projectors	Manufacture in which the value of all the materials used does not exceed 40% of the ex-works price of the product

HS heading No	Description of product	Working or processing carried out on non-originating materials that confers originating status	
(1)	(2)	(3) or (4)	
9032	Automatic regulating or controlling instruments and apparatus	Manufacture in which the value of all the materials used does not exceed 40% of the ex-works price of the product	
9033	Parts and accessories (not specified or included elsewhere in this Chapter) for machines, appliances, instruments or apparatus of Chapter 90	Manufacture in which the value of all the materials used does not exceed 40% of the ex-works price of the product	
ex Chapter 91	Clocks and watches and parts thereof; except for:	Manufacture in which the value of all the materials used does not exceed 40% of the ex-works price of the product	
9105	Other clocks	Manufacture: – in which the value of all the materials used does not exceed 40% of the ex-works price of the product;	
9105		– where the value of all the non-originating materials used does not exceed the value of the originating materials used Manufacture in which the value of all the materials used does not exceed 30% of the ex-works price of the product	
9109	Clock movements, complete and assembled	Manufacture: – in which the value of all the materials used does not exceed 40% of the ex-works price of the product; – where the value of all the non-originating materials used does not exceed the value of the originating materials used Manufacture in which the value of all the materials used does not exceed 30% of the ex-works price of the product	
9110	Complete watch or clock movements, unassembled or partly assembled (movement sets); incomplete watch or clock movements, assembled; rough watch or clock movements	Manufacture: – in which the value of all the materials used does not exceed 40% of the ex-works price of the product; – where, within the above limit, the materials classified within heading No 9114 are only used up to a value of 10% of the ex-works price of the product Manufacture in which the value of all the materials used does not exceed 30% of the ex-works price of the product	

HS heading No	Description of product	Working or processing carried out on non-originating materials that confers originating status
(1)	(2)	(3) or (4)
9111	Watch cases and parts thereof	Manufacture in which: – all the materials used are classified within a heading other than that of the product; – the value of all the materials used does not exceed 40% of the ex-works price of the product Manufacture in which the value of all the materials used does not exceed 30% of the ex-works price of the product
9112	Clock cases and cases of a similar type for other goods of this Chapter, and parts thereof	Manufacture in which: – all the materials used are classified within a heading other than that of the product; – the value of all the materials used does not exceed 40% of the ex-works price of the product
	Manufacture in which the value of all the materials used does not exceed 30% of the ex-works price of the product	
9113	Watch straps, watch bands and watch bracelets, and parts thereof:	
	– Of base metal, whether or not gold- or silver-plated, or of metal clad with precious metal	Manufacture in which the value of all the materials used does not exceed 40% of the ex-works price of the product
	– Other	Manufacture in which the value of all the materials used does not exceed 50% of the ex-works price of the product
Chapter 92	Musical instruments; parts and accessories of such articles	Manufacture in which the value of all the materials used does not exceed 40% of the ex-works price of the product
Chapter 93	Arms and ammunition; parts and accessories thereof	Manufacture in which the value of all the materials used does not exceed 50% of the ex-works price of the product
ex Chapter 94	Furniture; bedding, mattresses, mattress supports, cushions and similar stuffed furnishings; lamps and lighting fittings, not elsewhere specified or included; illuminated signs, illuminated name-plates and the like; prefabricated buildings; except for:	Manufacture in which all the materials used are classified within a heading other than that of the product Manufacture in which the value of all the materials used does not exceed 40% of the ex works price of the product

HS heading No	Description of product	Working or processing carried out on non-originating materials that confers originating status	
(1)	(2)	(3) or (4)	
ex 9401 and ex 9403	Base metal furniture, incorporating unstuffed cotton cloth of a weight of 300 g/m2 or less	Manufacture in which all the materials used are classified in a heading other than that of the product; or Manufacture from cotton cloth already made up in a form ready for use of heading No 9401 or 9403, provided:	Manufacture in which the value of all the materials used does not exceed 40% of the ex-works price of the product
		– its value does not exceed 25% of the ex-works price of the product;	
		– all the other materials used are already originating and are classified in a heading other than heading No 9401 or 9403	
9405	Lamps and lighting fittings including searchlights and spotlights and parts thereof, not elsewhere specified or included; illuminated signs, illuminated name-plates and the like, having a permanently fixed light source, and parts thereof not elsewhere specified or included	Manufacture in which the value of all the materials used does not exceed 50% of the ex-works price of the product	
9406	Prefabricated buildings	Manufacture in which the value of all the materials used does not exceed 50% of the ex-works price of the product	
ex Chapter 95	Toys, games and sports requisites; parts and accessories thereof; except for:	Manufacture in which all the materials used are classified within a heading other than that of the product	
9503	Other toys; reduced-size ('scale') models and similar recreational models, working or not; puzzles of all kinds	Manufacture in which: – all the materials used are classified within a heading other than that of the product; – the value of all the materials used does not exceed 50% of the ex-works price of the product	
ex 9506	Golf clubs and parts thereof	Manufacture in which all the materials used are classified within a heading other than that of the product. However, roughly shaped blocks for making golf club heads may be used	
ex Chapter 96	Miscellaneous manufactured articles; except for:	Manufacture in which all the materials used are classified within a heading other than that of the product	
ex 9601 and ex 9602	Articles of animal, vegetable or mineral carving materials	Manufacture from 'worked' carving materials of the same heading	

HS heading No	Description of product	Working or processing carried out on non-originating materials that confers originating status
(1)	(2)	(3) or (4)
ex 9603	Brooms and brushes (except for besoms and the like and brushes made from marten or squirrel hair), hand-operated mechanical floor sweepers, not motorized, paint pads and rollers, squeegees and mops	Manufacture in which the value of all the materials used does not exceed 50% of the ex-works price of the product
9605	Travel sets for personal toilet, sewing or shoe or clothes cleaning	Each item in the set must satisfy the rule, which would apply to it if it were not included in the set. However, non-originating articles may be incorporated, provided their total value does not exceed 15% of the ex-works price of the set
9606	Buttons, press-fasteners, snap-fasteners and press-studs, button moulds and other parts of these articles; button blanks	Manufacture in which: – all the materials used are classified within a heading other than that of the product; – the value of all the materials used does not exceed 50% of the ex-works price of the product
9608	Ball-points pens; felt-tipped and other porous-tipped pens and markers; fountain pens, stylograph pens and other pens; duplicating stylos; propelling or sliding pencils; penholders, pencil-holders and similar holders; parts (including caps and clips) of the foregoing articles, other than those of heading No 9609	Manufacture in which all the materials used are classified within a heading other than that of the product. However, nibs or nib-points classified within the same heading may be used
9612	Typewriter or similar ribbons, inked or otherwise prepared for giving impressions, whether or not on spools or in cartridges; ink-pads, whether or not inked, with or without boxes	Manufacture in which: – all the materials used are classified within a heading other than that of the product; – the value of all the materials used does not exceed 50% of the ex-works price of the product
ex 9613	Lighters with piezo-igniter	Manufacture in which the value of all the materials of heading No 9613 used does not exceed 30% of the ex-works price of the product
ex 9614	Smoking pipes and pipe bowls	Manufacture from roughly shaped blocks
Chapter 97	Works of art, collectors' pieces and antiques	Manufacture in which all the materials used are classified within a heading other than that of the product

Annex 19

List of Working or Processing Conferring the Character of ACP Origin on a Product Obtained When Working or Processing is Carried Out on Textile Materials Originating in Developing Countries Referred to in Article 6(11) of this Protocol

Textiles and textile articles falling within Section XI

CN Code	Description of product	Working or processing carried out on non-originating materials that confers the status of originating products
(1)	(2)	(3)
ex 5101	Wool, not carded or combed	
	– degreased, not carbonized	Manufacture from greasy, including piece-wasted wool, the value of which does not exceed 50% of the ex-works price of the product
	– carbonized	Manufacture from degreased wool, not carbonized the value of which does not exceed 50% of the ex-works price of the product
ex 5103	Waste of wool or of fine or coarse animal hair, carbonized	Manufacture from non-carbonized waste, the value of which does not exceed 50% of the ex-works price of the product
ex 5201	Cotton, not carded or combed, bleached	Manufacture from raw cotton, the value of which does not exceed 50% of the ex-works price of the product
5501 to 5507	Man-made staple fibres	
	– not carded or combed or otherwise processed for spinning	Manufacture from chemical materials or textile pulp
	– carded or combed or other	Manufacture from chemical materials or textile pulp or waste falling within CN code 5505
ex Chapter 50 to Chapter 55	Yarn, monofilament and thread, other than paper yarn:	Manufacture from: – natural fibres not carded or combed or otherwise processed for spinning, – chemical materials or textile pulp, or – paper making materials

CN Code	Description of product	Working or processing carried out on non-originating materials that confers the status of originating products
(1)	(2)	(3)
ex Chapter 50 to Chapter 55 (contin.)	– printed or dyed	Manufacture from: – natural fibres not carded or combed or otherwise processed for spinning, – grege silk or silk waste – chemical materials or textile pulp, or man-made staple fibres, filament tow or waste of fibres, not carded or combed or otherwise prepared for spinning or Printing or dyeing of yarn or monofilaments, unbleached or prebleached (1), accompanied by preparatory or finishing operations, twisting or texturizing not being considered as such, the value of the non-originating material (including yarn), not exceeding 48% of the ex-works price of the product
	– other	Manufacture from: – natural fibres not carded or combed or otherwise processed for spinning, – grege silk or silk waste – chemical materials or textile pulp, or – man-made staple fibres, filament tow – or waste of fibres, not carded or – combed or otherwise prepared for – spinning
	Woven fabrics, other than fabrics of paper yarn:	
	– printed or dyed	Manufacture from yarn; or Printing or dyeing of unbleached or prebleached fabrics, accompanied by preparatory or finishing operations (1) (2)
	– other	Manufacture from yarn
5601	Wadding of textile materials and articles therof; textile fibres not exceeding 5 mm in length (flock), textile dust and mill neps	Manufacture from fibres
5602	Felt, whether or not impregnated, coated, covered or laminated:	
	– printed or dyed	Manufacture from fibres; or Printing or dyeing of unbleached or prebleached fabrics, accompanied by preparatory or finishing operations (1) (2)

CN Code	Description of product	Working or processing carried out on non-originating materials that confers the status of originating products
(1)	(2)	(3)
5602 (contin.)	– impregnated, coated, covered or laminated	Impregnation, coating, covering or laminating of non-wovens, unbleached (3)
	– other	Manufacture from fibres
5603	Non- wovens, whether or not impregnated, coated, covered or laminated	
	– Printed or dyed	Manufacture from fibres or Printing or dyeing of unbleached or prebleached fabrics, accompanied by preparatory or finishing operations (1) (2)
	– impregnated, coated, covered or laminated	Impregnation, coating, covering or laminating of non-wovens, unbleached (3)
	– other	Manufacture from fibres
5604	Rubber thread and cord, textile covered; textile yarn, and strip and the like of heading No 5404 or 5405, impregnated, coated, covered or sheathed with rubber or plastics:	
	Rubber thread and cord, textile covered	Manufacture from rubber thread or cord, not textile covered
	– other	Impregnation, coating, covering or sheathing of textile yarn and strip and the like, unbleached
5607	Twine cordage, rope and cables, whether or not plaited or braided and whether or not impregnated, coated, covered or sheathed with rubber or plastics	Manufacture from fibres, coir yarn, synthetic or artificial filament yarn or monofilament
5609	Articles of yarn, strip or the like falling with CN codes 5404 or 5405, twine, cordage, rope or cables, not elsewhere specified or included	Manufacture from fibres, coir yarn, synthetic or artificial filament yarn or monofilament
5704	Carpets and other textile floor coverings:	Manufacture from fibres
ex Chapter 58	Special woven fabrics; tufted textile fabrics; lace; tapestries; trimmings; embroidery;	
	– embroidery in the piece, in strips or in motifs (CN code 5810)	Manufacture in which the value of the materials used does not exceed 50% of the ex-works price of the product

CN Code	Description of product	Working or processing carried out on non-originating materials that confers the status of originating products
(1)	(2)	(3)
ex Chapter 58 (contin.)	– printed or dyed	Manufacture from yarn or Printing or dyeing of unbleached or prebleached fabrics, accompanied by preparatory or finishing operations (1) (2)
	– impregnated, coated or covered	Manufacture from unbleached fabrics, felt or non-wovens
	– other	Manufacture from yarn
5901	Textile fabrics coated with gum or amylaceous substances, of a kind used for the outer covers of books or the like; tracing cloth; prepared painting canvas; buckram and similar stiffened textile fabrics of a kind used for hat foundations	Manufacture from unbleached fabrics
5902	Tyre cord fabric of high tenacity yarn of nylon or other polyamides, polyesters or viscose rayon:	Manufacture from yarn
5903	Textile fabrics impregnated, coated, covered or laminated with plastics, other than those falling within CN code 5902	Manufacture from unbleached fabrics or Printing or dyeing of unbleached or prebleached fabrics, accompanied by preparatory or finishing operations (1) (2)
5904	Linoleum, whether or not cut to shape; floor coverings consisting of a coating or covering applied on a textile backing, whether or not cut to shape	Manufacture from unbleached fabrics, felt or non-wovens
5905	Textile wall coverings	Manufacture from unbleached fabrics or Printing or dyeing of unbleached or prebleached fabrics, accompanied by preparatory or finishing operations (1) (2)
5906	Rubberized textile fabrics, other than those of heading No 5902:	Manufacture from bleached knitted or crocheted fabrics, or from other unbleached fabrics
5907	Textile fabrics otherwise impregnated, coated or covered; painted canvas, being theatrical scenery, studio backcloths or the like	Manufacture from unbleached fabrics or Printing or dyeing of unbleached or prebleached fabrics, accompanied by preparatory or finishing operations (1) (2)

CN Code	Description of product	Working or processing carried out on non-originating materials that confers the status of originating products
(1)	(2)	(3)
5908	Textile wicks, woven, plaited or knitted, for lamps, stoves, lighters, candles and the like; incandescent gas mantles and tubular knitted gas mantle fabric therefor, whether or not, impregnated	Manufacture from yarn
5909	Textile hosepiping and similar textile tubing with or without lining, amour or accessories or other materials	Manufacture from yarn or fibres
5910	Transmission or conveyor belts or belting, of textile material, whether or not reinforced with metal or other materials	Manufacture from yarn or fibres
5911	Textile products and articles, for technical uses, specified in Note 7 to Chapter 59 of the combined nomenclature::	
	polishing discs or rings other than of felt	Manufacture from yarn, waste fabrics or rags falling within CN code 6310
	other	Manufacture from yarn or fibres
*Chapter 60	Knitted or crocheted fabrics	
	– printed or dyed	Manufacture from yarn; or Printing or dyeing of unbleached or prebleached fabrics, accompanied by preparatory or finishing operations (1) (2)
	– other	Manufacture from yarn
Chapter 61	Articles of apparel and clothing accessories, knitted or crocheted:	Complete making up (4)
	– obtained by sewing together or otherwise assembling, two or more pieces of knitted or crocheted fabric which have been either cut to form or obtained directly to form	
	– other	Manufacture from yarn
*ex Chapter 62	Articles of apparel and clothing accessories, not knitted or crocheted; except those falling within CN codes 6213 and 6214 for which the rules are set out below:	Manufacture from yarn
	– finished or complete	Complete making up (4)
	– unfinished or incomplete	Manufacture from yarn

*See also the products excluded from the derogation procedure listed in Annex X.

CN Code	Description of product	Working or processing carried out on non-originating materials that confers the status of originating products
(1)	(2)	(3)
6213 and 6214	Handkerchiefs, shawls, scarves, mufflers, mantillas, veils and the like:	
-	– embroidered	Manufacture from yarn or Manufacture from unembroidered fabric provided the value of the unembroidered fabric used does not exceed 40% of the ex-works price of the product*
-	– other	Manufacture from yarn
6301 to ex 6306	Blankets and travelling rugs, bed linen, table linen, toilet linen and kitchen linen; curtains (including drapes) and interior blinds; curtain and bed valances; other furnishing articles (excluding those falling within CN code 9494); sacks and bags of a kind used for the packing of goods; tarpaulins, awnings, and camping goods;	
	Of felt, of non-wovens: – not impregnated, coated, covered or laminated	Manufacture from fibres
	– impregnated, coated, covered or laminated	Impregnation, coating, covering or laminating of felt or non-wovens, unbleached (3)
	– other	
	– knitted or crocheted – unembroidered – embroidered	 Complete making up (4) Complete making up (4) or Manufacture from unembroidered knitted or crocheted fabric provided the value of the unembroidered knitted or crocheted fabric used does not exceed 40% of the ex-works price of the product
	– not knitted or crocheted – unembroidered – embroidered	 Manufacture from yarn Manufacture from yarn or Manufacture from unembroidered fabric provided the value of the unembroidered fabric used does not exceed 40% of the ex-works price of the product

CN Code	Description of product	Working or processing carried out on non-originating materials that confers the status of originating products
(1)	(2)	(3)
6307	Other made-up textile articles, (including dress patterns), except for fans and hand screens, non-mechanical, frames and handles therefor and parts of such frames and handles	
	– floor cloths, dish cloths, dusters and the like	Manufacture from yarn
	– other	Manufacture in which the value of all the materials used does not exceed 40% of the ex-works price of the product
6308	Sets consisting of woven fabric and yarn, whether or not with accessories, for making up into rugs, tapestries, embroidered table cloths or serviettes or similar textile articles, put up in packings for retail sale	Incorporation in a set in which the total value of all the non-originating articles incorporated does not exceed 25% of the ex-works price of the set.

Notes

(1) The term 'prebleached', used in the list in Annex IX to characterize the level of manufacture required when certain non-originating materials are used, applies to certain yarns, woven fabrics and knitted or crocheted fabrics which have only been washed after the spinning or weaving operation.

(2) However, to be regarded as a working or processing conferring origin, thermoprinting has to be accompanied by printing of the transfer paper.

(3) The term 'Impregnation, coating, covering or laminating' does not cover those operations designed to bind fabrics together.

(4) The term 'complete making-up' used in the list in Annex IX means that all the operations following cutting of the fabric or knitting or crocheting of the fabric directly to shape have to be performed. However, making-up shall not necessarily be considered as incomplete where one or more finishing operations have not been carried out. The following is a list of examples of finishing operations: fitting of buttons and/or other types of fastenings, making of button-holes, finishing off the ends of trouser legs and sleeves or the bottom hemming of skirts and dresses, fitting of trimmings and accessories such as pockets, labels, badges, etc, ironing and other preparations of garments for sale 'ready made'.

Remarks concerning finishing operations – special cases

It is possible that in particular manufacturing operations, the accomplishment of finishing operations, especially in the case of a combination of operations, is of such importance that these operations must be considered as going beyond simple finishing. In these particular cases, the non-accomplishing of finishing operations will deprive the making-up of its complete nature.

Annex 20

Textile Products Excluded from the Cumulation Procedure with Certain Developing Countries Referred to in Article 6 (11) of the Protocol

6101 10 90 6101 20 90 6101 30 90	Jerseys, pullovers, slip-overs, waistcoats, twinsets, cardigans, bed-jackets and jumpers (other than jackets and blazers), anoraks, windcheaters, waister jackets and the like, knitted or crocheted
6102 10 90 6102 20 90 6102 30 90	
6110 10 10 6110 10 31 6110 10 35 6110 10 38 6110 10 91 6110 10 95 6110 10 98 6110 20 91 6110 20 99 6110 30 91 6110 30 99	
6203 41 10 6203 41 90 6203 42 31 6203 42 33 6203 42 35 6203 42 90 6203 43 19 6203 43 90 6203 49 19 6203 49 50	Men's or boys' woven breeches, shorts other than swimwear and trousers (including slacks); women's or girls' woven trousers and slacks, of wool, of cotton or of man-made fibres, lower parts of tracksuits with lining, other than category 16 or 29, of cotton or of man-made fibres
6204 61 10 6204 62 31 6204 62 33 6204 62 39 6204 63 18 6204 69 18	
6211 32 42 6211 33 42 6211 42 42 6211 43 42	

Annex 21

Products for Which the Cumulation Provisions with South Africa Referred to in Article 6(3) Apply after 3 Years from the Provisional Application of the Agreement on Trade, Development and Co-operation between the European Community and the Republic of South Africa

Industrial Products	Chlorides, chloride oxides and chloride hydroxides:	Hydrides, nitrides, azides, silicides and borides:
CN code 96	28271000	28500070
Salt (including table salt and denatured salt):	**Sulphides; polysulphides:**	**Cyclic hydrocarbons:**
25010051	28301000	29025000
25010091	**Phosphinates (hypophosphites), phosphonates:**	**Halogenated derivatives of hydrocarbons:**
25010099	28351000	29031100
Alkali or alkaline-earth metals; rare-earth metals:	28352200	29031200
28051100	28352300	29031300
28051900	28352400	29031400
28052100	28352510	29031500
28052200	28352590	29031600
28053010	28352610	29031910
28053090	28352690	29031990
28054010	28352910	29032100
Ammonia, anhydrous or in aqueous solution:	28352990	29032300
28141000	28353100	29032900
28142000	28353910	29033010
Sodium hydroxide (caustic soda):	28353930	29033031
28151100	28353970	29033033
28151200	**Carbonates; peroxocarbonates (percarbonates):**	29033038
Zinc oxide; zinc peroxide:	28362000	29033090
28170000	28364000	29034100
Artificial corundum:	28366000	29034200
28181000	**Salts of oxometallic or peroxometallic acids:**	29034300
28182000	28416100	29034410
28183000	**Radioactive chemical elements:**	29034490
Chromium oxides and hydroxides:	28443011	29034510
28191000	28443019	29034515
28199000	28443051	29034520
Manganese oxides:	**Isotopes other than those of heading No 2844:**	29034525
28201000	28451000	29034530
28209000	28459010	29034535
Titanium oxides:	**Carbides, whether or not chemically defined:**	29034540
28230000	28492000	29034545
Hydrazine and hydroxylamine:	28499030	29034550
28258000		29034555
		29034590
		29034610
		29034620
		29034690
		29034700
		29034910
		29034920

29034990
29035190
29035910
29035930
29035990
29036100
29036200
29036910
29036990

Acyclic alcohols and their halogenated, sulphonated derivatives:
29051100
29051200
29051300
29051410
29051490
29051500
29051610
29051690
29051700
29051910
29051990
29052210
29052290
29052910
29052990
29053100
29053200
29053910
29053990
29054100
29054200
29054910
29054951
29054959
29054990
29055010
29055030
29055099

Phenols; phenol-alcohols:
29071100
29071500
29072210

Ethers, ether-alcohols, ether-phenols:
29091100
29091900
29092000
29093031
29093039
29093090
29094100
29094200
29094300
29094400
29094910
29094990
29095010

29095090
29096000

Epoxides, epoxyalcohols, epoxyphenols and epoxyethols:
29102000

Aldehydes, whether or not with other oxygen functions:
29124100
29126000

Ketones and quinones, whether or not with other oxygen functions:
29141100
29142100

Saturated acyclic monocarboxylic acids:
29151100
29151200
29151300
29152100
29152200
29152300
29152400
29152900
29153100
29153200
29153300
29153400
29153500
29153910
29153930
29153950
29153990
29154000
29155000
29156010
29156090
29157015
29157020
29157025
29157030
29157080
29159010
29159020
29159080

Unsaturated acyclic monocarboxylic acids:
29161210
29161220
29161290
29161410
29161490

Polycarboxylic acids, their anhydrides, halides:
29171100
29171400
29173500

29173600
29173700

Carboxylic acids with additional oxygen function:
29181400
29181500
29182200
29189000

Amino-function compounds:
29211110
29211190
29211200
29211910
29211930
29211990
29212100
29212200
29212900
29213010
29213090
29214100
29214210
29214290
29214310
29214390
29214400
29214500
29214910
29214990
29215110
29215190
29215900
Oxygen-function amino-compounds:
29221100
29221200
29221300
29221900
29222100
29222200
29222900
29223000
29224210
29224300
29224980
29225000

Carboxyamide-function compounds:
29242110
29242190
29242930

Nitrile-function compounds:
29261000
29269090

Organo-sulphur compounds:
29302000
29309012

29309014
29309016

Other organo-inorganic compounds:
29310040

Heterocyclic compounds with oxygen hetero-atom(s):
29321200
29321300
29322100

Heterocyclic compounds with nitrogen hetero-atom(s):
29336100

Sulphonamides:
29350000

Mineral or chemical fertilizers, nitrogenous:
31021010
31021090
31022100
31022900
31023010
31023090
31024010
31024090
31025090
31026000
31027090
31028000
31029000

Mineral or chemical fertilizers, phosphatic:
31031010
31031090

Mineral or chemical fertilizers:
31051000
31052010
31052090
31053010
31053090
31054010
31054090
31055100
31055900
31056010
31056090
31059091
31059099

Tanning extracts of vegetable origin:
32012000
32019020

Other colouring matter:
32061100
32061900
32062000

32063000
32064100
32064200
32064300
32064990
32065000

Activated carbon; activated natural mineral products:
38021000
38029000

Insecticides, rodenticides, fungicides, herbicides:
38081020
38081030
38083011
38083013
38083015
38083017
38083021
38083023
38083027
38083030
38083090

Prepared rubber accelerators; compound plasticiser:
38123020

Organic composite solvents and thinners:
38140090

Mixed alkylbenzenes and mixed alkylnaphthalenes:
38171010
38171050
38171080
38172000

Prepared binders for foundry moulds or cores:
38249090

Polymers of ethylene, in primary forms:
39011010
39011090
39012000
39013000
39019000

Polymers of propylene or of other olefins:
39021000
39022000
39023000
39029000

Polymers of styrene, in primary forms:
39031100
39031900
39032000

39033000
39039000

Polymers of vinyl chloride:
39041000
39042100
39042200
39043000
39044000
39045000
39046190
39046900
39049000

Polymers of vinyl acetate:
39051200

Polyacetals, other polyethers and epoxide resins:
39072019
39072090
39076090
39079110
39079190
39079910
39079990

Other plates, sheets, film, foil and strip:
39201022
39201028
39201040
39201080
39202021
39202029
39202071
39202079
39202090
39203000
39204111
39204119
39204191
39204199
39204211
39204219
39204291
39204299
39205100
39205900
39206100
39206210
39206290
39206300
39206900
39207111
39207119
39207190
39207200
39207310
39207350
39207390
39207900
39209100

39209200
39209300
39209400
39209911
39209919
39209950
39209990

Other plates, sheets, film, foil and strip:
39219019

Articles for the conveyance or packing of goods:
39232100

Retreaded or used pneumatic tyres of rubber:
40121030
40121050
40121080
40122090
40129010
40129090

Inner tubes, of rubber:
40131010
40131090
40132000
40139010
40139090

Leather of bovine or equine animals, without hair:
41041091
41041095
41041099
41042100
41042290
41042900
41043111
41043119
41043130
41043190
41043910
41043990

Sheep or lamb skin leather, without wool on:
41052000

Leather of other animals, without hair on:
41071010
41072910
41079010
41079090

Chamois (including combination chamois) leather:
41080010
41080090

Patent leather and patent laminated leather:
41090000

Composition leather with a basis of leather or leather:
41110000

Articles of apparel and clothing accessories:
42031000
42032100
42032910
42032991
42032999
42033000
42034000

Particle board and similar board of wood:
44101100
44101910
44101930
44101950
44101990
44109000

Fibreboard of wood or other ligneous materials:
44111100
44111900
44112100
44112900
44113100
44113900
44119100
44119900

Plywood, veneered panels and similar laminated wood:
44121311
44121319
44121390
44121400
44121900
44122210
44122291
44122299
44122300
44122920
44122980
44129210
44129291
44129299
44129300
44129920
44129980

Builders' joinery and carpentry of wood:
44181010
44181050
44181090
44182010
44182050
44182080
44183010
44189010

Wood marquetry and inlaid wood; caskets and cases:
44209011
44209019

Articles of natural cork:
45031010
45031090
45039000

Plaits and similar products of plaiting materials:
46019910

Basketwork, wickerwork and other articles:
46029010

Registers, account books, note books, order books:
48201030

Children's picture, drawing or colouring books:
49030000

Maps and hydrographic or similar charts of all kinds:
49051000

Transfers (decalcomanias):
49081000
49089000

Printed or illustrated postcards: printed cards:
49090010
49090090

Calendars of any kind, printed, including calendars:
49100000

Other printed matter, including printed pictures:
49111010
49111090
49119180
49119900

Silk yarn (other than yarn spun from silk waste):
50040010
50040090

Yarn spun from silk waste, not put up for retail sale:
50050010
50050090

Silk yarn and yarn spun from silk waste, put up for retail sale:
50060010
50060090

Woven fabrics of silk or of silk waste:

50071000
50072011
50072019
50072021
50072031
50072039
50072041
50072051
50072059
50072061
50072069
50072071
50079010
50079030
50079050
50079090

Yarn of carded wool, not put up for retail sale:

51061010
51061090
51062011
51062019
51062091
51062099

Yarn of combed wool, not put up for retail sale:

51071010
51071090
51072010
51072030
51072051
51072059
51072091
51072099

Yarn of fine animal hair (carded or combed), not put up for retail sale:

51081010
51081090
51082010
51082090

Yarn of wool or of fine animal hair, put up for retail sale:

51091010
51091090
51099010
51099090

Yarn of coarse animal hair or of horsehair:

51100000

Woven fabrics of carded wool or of carded fine animal hair:

51111111
51111119
51111191
51111199
51111911
51111919
51111931
51111939
51111991
51111999
51112000
51113010
51113030
51113090
51119010
51119091
51119093
51119099

Woven fabrics of combed wool or of combed fine animal hair:

51121110
51121190
51121911
51121919
51121991
51121999
51122000
51123010
51123030
51123090
51129010
51129091
51129093
51129099

Woven fabrics of coarse animal hair or of horsehair:

51130000

Cotton sewing thread, whether or not put up for retail sale:

52041100
52041900
52042000

Cotton yarn (other than sewing thread):

52051100
52051200
52051300
52051400
52051510
52051590
52052100
52052200
52052300
52052400
52052600
52052700
52052800
52053100
52053200
52053300
52053400
52053510
52053590
52054100
52054200
52054300
52054400
52054600
52054700
52054800

Cotton yarn (other than sewing thread):

52061100
52061200
52061300
52061400
52061510
52061590
52062100
52062200
52062300
52062400
52062510
52062590
52063100
52063200
52063300
52063400
52063510
52063590
52064100
52064200
52064300
52064400
52064510
52064590

Cotton yarn (other than sewing thread) put up for retail sale:

52071000
52079000

Flax yarn:

53061011
530610191
53061031
53061039
53061050
53061090
53062011
53062019
53062090

Yarn of other vegetable textile fibres; paper yarn:

53082010
53082090
53083000
53089011
53089013
53089019
53089090

Woven fabrics of flax:

53091111

53091119
53091190
53091910
53091990
53092110
53092190
53092910
53092990

Woven fabrics of jute or of other textile bast fibres:
53101010
53101090
53109000

Woven fabrics of other vegetable textile fibres:
53110010
53110090

Sewing thread of man-made filaments:
54011011
54011019
54011090
54012010
54012090

Synthetic filament yarn (other than sewing thread):
54021010
54021090
54022000
54023110
54023130
54023190
54023200
54023310
54023390
54023910
54023990
54024110
54024130
54024190
54024200
54024310
54024390
54024910
54024991
54024999
54025110
54025130
54025190
54025210
54025290
54025910
54025990
54026110
54026130
54026190
54026210
54026290

54026910
54026990

Artificial filament yarn (other than sewing thread):
54031000
54032010
54032090
54033100
54033200
54033310
54033390
54033900
54034100
54034200
54034900

Synthetic monofilament of 67 decitex or more:
54041010
54041090
54049011
54049019
54049090

Artificial monofilament of 67 decitex or more:
54050000

Man-made filament yarn (other than sewing thread):
54061000
54062000

Woven fabrics of synthetic filament yarn:
54071000
54072011
54072019
54072090
54073000
54074100
54074200
54074300
54074400
54075100
54075200
54075300
54075400
54076110
54076130
54076150
54076190
54076910
54076990
54077100
54077200
54077300
54077400
54078100
54078200
54078300

54078400
54079100
54079200
54079300
54079400

Woven fabrics of artificial filament yarn:
54081000
54082100
54082210
54082290
54082310
54082390
54082400
54083100
54083200
54083300
54083400

Synthetic filament tow:
55011000
55012000
55013000
55019000

Artificial filament tow:
55020010
55020090

Synthetic staple fibres, not carded, combed or otherwise:
55031011
55031019
55031090
55032000
55033000
55034000
55039010
55039090

Artificial staple fibres, not carded, combed or otherwise:
55041000
55049000

Waste (including noils, yarn waste):
55051010
55051030
55051050
55051070
55051090
55052000

Synthetic staple fibres, carded, combed or otherwise:
55061000
55062000
55063000
55069010
55069091
55069099

Artificial staple fibres, carded, combed or otherwise:
55070000

Sewing thread of man-made staple fibres:
55081011
55081019
55081090
55082010
55082090

Yarn (other than sewing thread) of synthetic staple fibres:
55091100
55091200
55092110
55092190
55092210
55092290
55093110
55093190
55093210
55093290
55094110
55094190
55094210
55094290
55095100
55095210
55095290
55095300
55095900
55096110
55096190
55096200
55096900
55099110
55099190
55099200
55099900

Yarn (other than sewing thread) of artificial smtaple fibres:
55101100
55101200
55102000
55103000
55109000

Yarn (other than sewing thread) of man-made staple fibres:
55111000
55112000
55113000

Wadding of textile materials and articles thereof:
56011010
56011090
56012110
56012190
56012210

56012291
56012299
56012900
56013000

Felt, whether or not impregnated:
56021011
56021019
56021031
56021035
56021039
56021090
56022100
56022910
56022990
56029000

Nonwovens, whether or not impregnated:
56031110
56031190
56031210
56031290
56031310
56031390
56031410
56031490
56039110
56039190
56039210
56039290
56039310
56039390
56039410
56039490

Rubber thread and cord, textile covered:
56041000
56042000
56049000

Metallised yarn, whether or not gimped:
56050000

Gimped yarn, and strip:
56060010
56060091
56060099

Articles of yarn, strip:
56090000

Carpets and other textile floor coverings:
57011010
57011091
57011093
57011099
57019010
57019090

Woven pile fabrics and chenille fabrics:
58011000
58012100
58012200
58012300
58012400
58012500
58012600
58013100
58013200
58013300
58013400
58013500
58013600
58019010
58019090

Terry towelling and similar woven terry fabrics:
58021100
58021900
58022000
58023000

Gauze, other than narrow fabrics:
58031000
58039010
58039030
58039050
58039090

Tulles and other net fabrics, not including woven:
58041011
58041019
58041090
58042110
58042190
58042910
58042990
58043000

Hand-woven tapestries of the type Gobelins:
58050000

Narrow woven fabrics:
58061000
58062000
58063110
58063190
58063210
58063290
58063900
58064000

Labels, badges and similar articles of textile matter:
58071010
58071090
58079010
58079090

Braids in the piece; ornamental trimmings:
58081000
58089000

Woven fabrics of metal thread and woven fabrics:
58090000

Embroidery in the piece, in strips or in motifs:
58101010
58101090
58109110
58109190
58109210
58109290
58109910
58109990

Quilted textile products in the piece:
58110000

Textile fabrics coated with gum:
59011000
59019000

Tyre cord fabric of high tenacity yarn of nylon:
59021010
59021090
59022010
59022090
59029010
59029090

Textile fabrics impregnated, coated, covered:
59031010
59031090
59032010
59032090
59039010
59039091
59039099

Linoleum, whether or not cut to shape:
59041000
59049110
59049190
59049200

Textile wall coverings:
59050010
59050031
59050039
59050050
59050070
59050090

Rubberized textile fabrics:
59061010
59061090

59069100
59069910
59069990

Textile fabrics otherwise impregnated, coated or covered:
59070010
59070090

Textile wicks, woven, plaited or knitted:
59080000

Textile hosepiping and similar textile tubing:
59090010
59090090

Transmission or conveyor belts or belting:
59100000

Textile products and articles, for technical uses:
59111000
59112000
59113111
59113119
59113190
59113210
59113290
59114000
59119010
59119090

Pile fabrics, including "long pile" fabrics:
60011000
60012100
60012200
60012910
60012990
60019110
60019130
60019150
60019190
60019210
60019230
60019250
60019290
60019910
60019990

Men's or boys' overcoats, car-coats, capes, cloaks:
61011010
61011090
61012010
61012090
61013010
61013090
61019010
61019090

Women's or girls' overcoats, car-coats, capes, cloaks:
61021010
61021090
61022010
61022090
61023010
61023090
61029010
61029090

Men's or boys' suits, ensembles, jackets, blazers:
61034110
61034190
61034210
61034290
61034310
61034390
61034910
61034991
61034999

Women's or girls' suits, ensembles, jackets, blazers:
61045100
61045200
61045300
61045900
61046110
61046190
61046210
61046290
61046310
61046390
61046910
61046991
61046999

Men's or boys' underpants, briefs, nightshirts, pyjamas:
61071100
61071200
61071900
61072100
61072200
61072900
61079110
61079190
61079200
61079900

Women's or girls' slips, petticoats, briefs, panties:
61081110
61081190
61081910
61081990
61082100
61082200
61082900
61083110
61083190

61083211
61083219
61083290
61083900
61089110
61089190
61089200
61089910
61089990

T-shirts, singlets and other vests, knitted or crocheted:
61091000
61099010
61099030

Track suits, ski suits and swimwear, knitted or crocheted:
61121100
61121200
61121900
61122000
61123110
61123190
61123910
61123990
61124110
61124190
61124910
61124990

Garments, made up of knitted or crocheted fabrics:
61130010
61130090

Other garments, knitted or crocheted:
61141000
61142000
61143000
61149000

Panty hose, tights, stockings, socks and other hosiery:
61151100
61151200
61151910
61151990
61152011
61152019
61152090
61159100
61159200
61159310
61159330
61159391
61159399
61159900

Gloves, mittens and mitts, knitted or crocheted:
61161020
61161080

61169100
61169200
61169300
61169900

Other made up clothing accessories, knitted or crocheted:
61171000
61172000
61178010
61178090
61179000

Men's or boys' overcoats, car-coats, capes, cloaks:
62011100
62011210
62011290
62011310
62011390
62011900
62019100
62019200
62019300
62019900

Women's or girls' overcoats, car-coats, capes, cloaks:
62021100
62021210
62021290
62021310
62021390
62021900
62029100
62029200
62029300
62029900

Men's or boys' suits, ensembles, jackets, blazers:
62034110
62034130
62034190
62034211
62034231
62034233
62034235
62034251
62034259
62034290
62034311
62034319
62034331
62034339
62034390
62034911
62034919
62034931
62034939
62034950
62034990

Women's or girls' suits, ensembles, jackets, blazers:
62045100
62045200
62045300
62045910
62045990
62046110
62046180
62046190
62046211
62046231
62046233
62046239
62046251
62046259
62046290
62046311
62046318
62046331
62046339
62046390
62046911
62046918
62046931
62046939
62046950
62046990

Men's or boys' shirts:
62051000
62052000
62053000
62059010
62059090

Men's or boys' singlets and other vests, underpants:
62071100
62071900
62072100
62072200
62072900
62079110
62079190
62079200
62079900

Women's or girls' singlets and other vests, slips:
62081100
62081910
62081990
62082100
62082200
62082900
62089111
62089119
62089190
62089210
62089290
62089900

Brassières, girdles, corsets, braces, suspenders:
62121000
62122000
62123000
62129000

Handkerchiefs:
62131000
62132000
62139000

Shawls, scarves, mufflers, mantillas, veils:
62141000
62142000
62143000
62144000
62149010
62149090

Ties, bow ties and cravats:
62151000
62152000
62159000

Gloves, mittens and mitts:
62160000

Other made up clothing accessories:
62171000
62179000

Blankets and travelling rugs:
63011000
63012010
63012091
63012099
63013010
63013090
63014010
63014090
63019010
63019090

Sacks and bags:
63051010
63051090
63052000
63053211
63053281
63053289
63053290
63053310
63053391
63053399
63053900
63059000

Tarpaulins, awnings and sunblinds; tents; sails:
63061100
63061200
63061900

63062100
63062200
63062900
63063100
63063900
63064100
63064900
63069100
63069900

Other made up articles, including dress patterns:
63071010
63071030
63071090
63072000
63079010
63079091
63079099

Sets consisting of woven fabric and yarn:
63080000

Worn clothing and other worn articles:
63090000

Waterproof footwear with outer soles and uppers of rubber:
64011010
64011090
64019110
64019190
64019210
64019290
64019910
64019990

Other footwear with outer soles and uppers of rubber:
64021210
64021290
64021900
64022000
64023000
64029100
64029910
64029931
64029939
64029950
64029991
64029993
64029996
64029998

Footwear with outer soles of rubber, plastics, leather:
64031200
64031900
64032000
64033000
64034000
64035111

64035115
64035119
64035191
64035195
64035199
64035911
64035931
64035935
64035939
64035950
64035991
64035995
64035999
64039111
64039113
64039116
64039118
64039191
64039193
64039196
64039198
64039911
64039931
64039933
64039936
64039938
64039950
64039991
64039993
64039996
64039998

Footwear with outer soles of rubber, plastics, leather:
64041100
64041910
64041990
64042010
64042090

Other footwear:
64051010
64051090
64052010
64052091
64052099
64059010
64059090

Parts of footwear (including uppers):
64061011
64061019
64061090
64062010
64062090
64069100
64069910
64069930
64069950
64069960
64069980

Unglazed ceramic flags and paving, hearth or wall tiles:
- 69071000
- 69079010
- 69079091
- 69079093
- 69079099

Glazed ceramic flags and paving, hearth or wall tiles:
- 69081010
- 69081090
- 69089011
- 69089021
- 69089029
- 69089031
- 69089051
- 69089091
- 69089093
- 69089099

Tableware, kitchenware, other household articles:
- 69111000
- 69119000

Ceramic tableware, kitchenware, other household articles:
- 69120010
- 69120030
- 69120050
- 69120090

Statuettes and other ornamental ceramic articles:
- 69131000
- 69139010
- 69139091
- 69139093
- 69139099

Glassware of a kind used for table, kitchen:
- 70131000
- 70132111
- 70132119
- 70132191
- 70132199
- 70132910
- 70132951
- 70132959
- 70132991
- 70132999
- 70133110
- 70133190
- 70133200
- 70133910
- 70133991
- 70133999
- 70139110
- 70139190
- 70139910
- 70139990

Glass fibres (including glass wool):
- 70191100
- 70191200
- 70191910
- 70191990
- 70193100
- 70193200
- 70193910
- 70193990
- 70194000
- 70195110
- 70195190
- 70195200
- 70195910
- 70195990
- 70199010
- 70199030
- 70199091
- 70199099

Other articles of precious metal:
- 71159010
- 71159090

Ferro-alloys:
- 72025000
- 72027000
- 72029100
- 72029200
- 72029930
- 72029980

Copper bars, rods and profiles:
- 74071000
- 74072110
- 74072190
- 74072210
- 74072290
- 74072900

Copper wire:
- 74081100
- 74081910
- 74081990
- 74082100
- 74082200
- 74082900

Copper plates, sheets and strip:
- 74091100
- 74091900
- 74092100
- 74092900
- 74093100
- 74093900
- 74094010
- 74094090
- 74099010
- 74099090

Copper foil (whether or not printed or backed with)
- 74101100

- 74101200
- 74102100
- 74102200

Copper tubes and pipes:
- 74111011
- 74111019
- 74111090
- 74112110
- 74112190
- 74112200
- 74112910
- 74112990

Copper tube or pipe fittings:
- 74121000
- 74122000

Stranded wire, cables, plaited bands and the like:
- 74130091
- 74130099

Cloth (including endless bands), grill and netting:
- 74142000
- 74149000

Nails, tacks, drawing pins, staples:
- 74151000
- 74152100
- 74152900
- 74153100
- 74153200
- 74153900

Copper springs:
- 74160000

Cooking or heating apparatus
- 74170000

Table, kitchen or other household articles:
- 74181100
- 74181900
- 74182000

Other articles of copper:
- 74191000
- 74199100
- 74199900

Aluminium bars, rods and profiles:
- 76041010
- 76041090
- 76042100
- 76042910
- 76042990

Aluminium wire:
- 76051100
- 76051900
- 76052100
- 76052900

Aluminium plates, sheets and strip:
76061110
76061191
76061193
76061199
76061210
76061250
76061291
76061293
76061299
76069100
76069200

Aluminium foil:
76071110
76071190
76071910
76071991
76071999
76072010
76072091
76072099

Aluminium tubes and pipes:
76081090
76082030
76082091
76082099

Aluminium tube or pipe fittings:
76090000

Aluminium structures:
76101000
76109010
76109090

Aluminium reservoirs, tanks, vats:
76110000

Aluminium casks, drums, cans, boxes:
76121000
76129010
76129020
76129091
76129098

Aluminium containers for compressed or liquefied:
76130000

Stranded wire, cables, plaited bands and the like:
76141000
76149000

Table, kitchen or other household articles:
76151100
76151910
76151990
76152000

Other articles of aluminium:
76161000
76169100
76169910
76169990

Unwrought lead:
78011000
78019100
78019991
78019999

Tungsten (wolfram) and articles thereof, including waste:
81011000
81019110

Molybdenum and articles thereof, including waste:
81021000
81029110
81029300

Magnesium and articles thereof, including waste:
81041100
81041900

Cadmium and articles thereof, including waste:
81071010

Titanium and articles thereof, including waste:
81081010
81081090
81089030
81089050
81089070
81089090

Zirconium and articles thereof, including waste:
81091010
81099000

Antimony and articles thereof, including waste:
81100011
81100019

Beryllium, chromium, germanium, vanadium, gallium:
81122031
81123020
81123090
81129110
81129131
81129930

Cermets and articles thereof, including waste:
81130020
81130040

Nuclear reactors; fuel elements (cartridges):
84011000
84012000
84013000
84014010
84014090

Hydraulic turbines, water wheels, and regulators:
84101100
84101200
84101300
84109010
84109090

Turbo-jets, turbo-propellers and other gas turbines:
84111190
84111290
84112190
84112290
84118190
84118291
84118293
84118299
84119190
84119990

Air or vacuum pumps, air or other gas compressors:
84141030
84141050
84141090
84142091
84142099
84143030
84143091
84143099
84144010
84144090
84145190
84145930
84145950
84145990
84146000
84148021
84148029
84148031
84148039
84148041
84148049
84148060
84148071
84148079
84148090
84149090

Fork-lift trucks; other works trucks
84271010
84271090
84272011

367

84272019
84272090
84279000

Sewing machines, other than book-sewing machines:
84521011
84521019
84521090
84522100
84522900
84523010
84523090
84524000
84529000

Electro-mechanical domestic appliances:
85091010
85091090
85092000
85093000
85094000
85098000
85099010
85099090

Electric instantaneous or storage water heaters:
85162991
85163110
85163190
85164010
85164090
85165000
85166070
85167100
85167200
85167980

Turntables (record-decks), record-players, cassette-players:
85191000
85192100
85192900
85193100
85193900
85194000
85199331
85199339
85199381
85199389
85199912
85199918
85199990

Magnetic tape recorders and other sound recording:
85201000
85203219
85203250
85203291
85203299

85203319
85203390
85203910
85203990
85209090

Video recording or reproducing apparatus:
85211030
85211080
85219000

Parts and accessories:
85221000
85229030
85229091
85229098

Prepared unrecorded media for sound recording:
85233000

Records, tapes and other recorded media:
85241000
85243200
85243900
85245100
85245200
85245300
85246000
85249900

Reception apparatus for radio-telephony:
85271210
85271290
85271310
85271391
85271399
85272120
85272152
85272159
85272170
85272192
85272198
85272900
85273111
85273119
85273191
85273193
85273198
85273290
85273910
85273991
85273999
85279091
85279099

Reception apparatus for television:
85281214
85281216
85281218

85281222
85281228
85281252
85281254
85281256
85281258
85281262
85281266
85281272
85281276
85281281
85281289
85281291
85281298
85281300
85282114
85282116
85282118
85282190
85282200
85283010
85283090

Parts suitable for use solely or principally with:
85291020
85291031
85291039
85291040
85291050
85291070
85291090
85299051
85299059
85299070
85299081
85299089

Electric sound or visual signalling apparatus:
85311020
85311030
85311080
85318090
85319090

Thermionic, cold cathode or photocathode valves:
85401111
85401113
85401115
85401119
85401191
85401199
85401200
85402010
85402030
85402090
85404000
85405000
85406000
85407100
85407200

85407900
85408100
85408911
85408919
85408990
85409100
85409900

Electronic integrated circuits and microassemblies:
85421425

Insulated (including enamelled or anodised) wire:
85441110
85441190
85441910
85441990
85442000
85443090
85444110
85444190
85444920
85444980
85445100
85445910
85445920
85445980
85446010
85446090
85447000

Motor vehicles for the transport of ten or more persons:
87021091
87021099
87029031
87029039
87029090

Motor vehicles for the transport of goods:
87041011
87041019
87041090
87042110
87042191
87042199
87042210
87042310
87043110
87043191
87043199
87043210
87049000

Special purpose motor vehicles:
87051000
87052000
87053000
87054000
87059010
87059030

87059090

Works trucks, self-propelled, not fitted with lift:
87091110
87091190
87091910
87091990
87099010
87099090

Motor-cycles (including mopeds):
87111000
87112010
87112091
87112093
87112098
87113010
87113090
87114000
87115000
87119000

Bicycles and other cycles:
87120010
87120030
87120080

Photocopying apparatus:
90091100
90091200
90092100
90092210
90092290
90093000
90099010
90099090

Liquid crystal devices:
90131000
90132000
90138011
90138019
90138030
90138090
90139010
90139090

Wrist-watches, pocket-watches and other watches:
91011100
91011200
91011900
91012100
91012900
91019100
91019900

Wrist-watches, pocket-watches and other watches:
91021100
91021200
91021900
91022100

91022900
91029100
91029900

Clocks with watch movements:
91031000
91039000

Other clocks:
91051100
91051900
91052100
91052900
91059100
91059910
91059990

Pianos, including automatic pianos; harpsichords:
92011010
92011090
92012000
92019000

Revolvers and pistols:
93020010
93020090

Other firearms and similar devices:
93031000
93032030
93032080
93033000
93039000

Other arms (for example, spring, air or gas guns:
93040000

Parts and accessories of articles of heading Nos 9:
93051000
93052100
93052910
93052930
93052980
93059090

Bombs, grenades, torpedoes, mines, missiles:
93061000
93062100
93062940
93062970
93063010
93063091
93063093
93063098
93069090

Seats (other than those of heading No 9402):
94012000
94019010

94019030
94019080

Other furniture and parts thereof:
94034010
94034090
94039010
94039030
94039090

Mattress supports; articles of bedding:
94041000
94042110
94042190
94042910
94042990
94043010
94043090
94049010
94049090

Lamps and lighting fittings including searchlights:
94051021
94051029
94051030
94051050
94051091
94051099
94052011
94052019
94052030
94052050
94052091
94052099
94053000
94054010
94054031
94054035
94054039
94054091
94054095
94054099
94055000
94056091
94056099
94059111
94059119
94059190
94059290
94059990

Prefabricated buildings:
94060010
94060031
94060039
94060090

Other toys; reduced-size ('scale') models:
95031010

95031090
95032010
95032090
95033010
95033030
95033090
95034100
95034910
95034930
95034990
95035000
95036010
95036090
95037000
95038010
95038090
95039010
95039032
95039034
95039035
95039037
95039051
95039055
95039099

Brooms, brushes:
96031000
96032100
96032910
96032930
96032990
96033010
96033090
96034010
96034090
96035000
96039010
96039091
96039099

Agricultural Products

Live horses, asses, mules and hinnies:
01011990
01012090

Other live animals:
01060020

Edible offal of bovine animals, swine, sheep, goat:
02063021
02064191
02068091
02069091

Meat and edible offal:
02071391
02071491
02072691
02072791
02073591

02073689

Other meat and edible meat offal, fresh, chilled:
02081011
02081019
02089010
02089050
02089060
02089080

Meat and edible meat offal, salted, in brine, dried:
02109010
02109060
02109079
02109080

Birds' eggs, in shell, fresh, preserved or cooked:
04070090

Edible products of animal origin, not elsewhere sp ·
04100000

Bulbs, tubers, tuberous roots, corms, crowns:
06012030
06012090

Other live plants (including their roots), cutting:
06022090
06023000
06024010
06024090
06029010
06029030
06029041
06029045
06029049
06029051
06029059
06029070
06029091
06029099

Foliage, branches and other parts of plants:
06049121
06049129
06049149
06049990

Potatoes, fresh or chilled:
07019059
07019090

Onions, shallots, garlic, leeks:
07032000

Other vegetables, fresh or chilled:
07091040

07095130
07095200
07096099
07099031
07099071
07099073

Vegetables (uncooked or cooked by steaming or boiling:
07108059

Vegetables provisionally preserved:
07119010

Dried vegetables, whole, cut, sliced, broken:
07129005

Other nuts, fresh or dried, whether or not shelled:
08021290

Dates, figs, pineapples, avocados, guavas, mangoes:
08041000

Citrus fruit, fresh or dried:
08054095

Grapes, fresh or dried:
08062091
08062092
08062098

Apricots, cherries, peaches (including nectarines):
08094010
08094090

Other fruit, fresh:
08104050

Fruit and nuts, uncooked or cooked by steaming:
08112019
08112051
08112090
08119031
08119050
08119085

Fruit and nuts, provisionally preserved:
08129040

Fruit, dried:
08131000
08133000
08134030
08134095

Coffee, whether or not roasted or decaffeinated:
09011200
09012100

09012200
09019090

Cloves (whole fruit, cloves and stems):
09070000

Ginger, saffron, turmeric (curcuma), thyme, bay leaf:
09104013
09104019
09104090
09109190
09109999

Seeds, fruit and spores, of a kind used for sowing:
12091100
12091900

Locust beans, seaweeds and other algae, sugar beet:
12129200

Pig fat (including lard) and poultry fat:
15010090

Lard stearin, lard oil, oleostearin, oleo-oil:
15030090

Ground-nut oil and its fractions, whether or not refined:
15081090
15089090

Palm oil and its fractions, whether or not refined:
15119011
15119019
15119099

Coconut (copra), palm kernel or babassu oil:
15131191
15131199
15131911
15131919
15131991
15131999
15132130
15132190
15132911
15132919
15132950
15132991
15132999

Other fixed vegetable fats and oils:
15151990
15152190
15152990
15155019

15155099
15159029
15159039
15159051
15159059
15159091
15159099

Animal or vegetable fats and oils:
15161010
15161090
15162091
15162096
15162098

Margarine; edible mixtures:
15171090
15179091
15179099

Animal or vegetable fats and oils:
15180010
15180091
15180099

Sausages and similar products, of meat, meat offal:
16010010

Extracts and juices of meat, fish or crustaceans:
16030010

Molasses:
17031000
17039000

Cocoa paste, whether or not defatted:
18031000
18032000

Cocoa butter, fat and oil:
18040000

Cocoa powder, not containing added sugar or other:
18050000

Vegetables, fruit, nuts and other edible parts:
20019060
20019070
20019075
20019085
20019091

Other vegetables prepared or preserved otherwise:
20049030

Other vegetables prepared or preserved otherwise:
20057010

20057090
20059010
20059030
20059050
20059060
20059070
20059075
20059080

Vegetables, fruit, nuts, fruit-peel and other parts:
20060091

Fruit, nuts and other edible parts of plants:
20081110
20081192
20081196
20081911
20081913
20081951
20081993
20083071
20089100
20089212
20089214
20089232
20089234
20089236
20089238
20089911
20089919
20089938
20089940
20089947

Fruit juices (including grape must):
20098036
20098038
20098088
20098089
20098095
20098096

Yeasts (active or inactive):
21023000

Sauces and preparations therefor:
21031000
21033090
21039090

Soups and broths and preparations therefor:
21041010
21041090
21042000

Food preparations not elsewhere specified:
21069092

Waters, including mineral waters and aerated water:
22021000
22029010

Other fermented beverages (for example, cider):
22060031
22060039
22060051
22060059
22060081
22060089

Undenatured ethyl alcohol of an alcoholic strength:
22085011
22085019
22085091
22085099
22086011
22086091
22086099
22087010
22087090
22089011
22089019
22089057
22089069
22089074
22089078

Preparations of a kind used in animal feeding:
23091090
23099091
23099093
23099098

Unmanufactured tobacco; tobacco refuse:
24011030
24011050
24011070
24011080
24011090
24012030
24012049
24012050
24012080
24012090
24013000

Cigars, cheroots, cigarillos and cigarettes:
24021000
24022010
24022090
24029000

Other manufactured tobacco and manufactured tobacco:
24031010
24031090
24039100
24039910
24039990

Casein, caseinates and other casein derivatives:
35011090
35019010
35019090

Albumins:
35029070

Industrial monocarboxylic fatty acids; acid oils:
38231200
38237000

Annex 22

Products for Which the Cumulation Provisions with South Africa Referred to in Article 6(3) Apply after 6 Years from the Provisional Application of the Agreement on Trade, Development and Co-operation between the European Community and the Republic of South Africa

Industrial Products (1)

CN code 96

Woven fabrics of cotton, containing 85% or more:

52081110
52081190
52081211
52081213
52081215
52081219
52081291
52081293
52081295
52081299
52081300
52081900
52082110
52082190
52082211
52082213
52082215
52082219
52082291
52082293
52082295
52082299
52082300
52082900
52083100
52083211
52083213
52083215
52083219
52083291
52083293
52083295
52083299
52083300
52083900
52084100
52084200
52084300
52084900
52085100

52085210
52085290
52085300
52085900

Woven fabrics of cotton, containing 85% or more:

52091100
52091200
52091900
52092100
52092200
52092900
52093100
52093200
52093900
52094100
52094200
52094300
52094910
52094990
52095100
52095200
52095900

Woven fabrics of cotton, containing less than 85%:

52101110
52101190
52101200
52101900
52102110
52102190
52102200
52102900
52103110
52103190
52103200
52103900
52104100
52104200
52104900
52105100
52105200
52105900

Woven fabrics of cotton, containing less than 85%:

52111100
52111200
52111900
52112100
52112200
52112900
52113100
52113200
52113900
52114100
52114200
52114300
52114910
52114990
52115100
52115200
52115900

Other woven fabrics of cotton:

52121110
52121190
52121210
52121290
52121310
52121390
52121410
52121490
52121510
52121590
52122110
52122190
52122210
52122290
52122310
52122390
52122410
52122490
52122510
52122590

Woven fabrics of synthetic staple fibres:

55121100
55121910

55121990
55122100
55122910
55122990
55129100
55129910
55129990

Woven fabrics of synthetic staple fibres:

55131110
55131130
55131190
55131200
55131300
55131900
55132110
55132130
55132190
55132200
55132300
55132900
55133100
55133200
55133300
55133900
55134100
55134200
55134300
55134900

Woven fabrics of synthetic staple fibres:

55141100
55141200
55141300
55141900
55142100
55142200
55142300
55142900
55143100
55143200
55143300
55143900
55144100
55144200
55144300
55144900

Other woven fabrics of synthetic staple fibres:

55151110
55151130
55151190
55151210
55151230
55151290
55151311
55151319
55151391
55151399
55151910

55151930
55151990
55152110
55152130
55152190
55152211
55152219
55152291
55152299
55152910
55152930
55152990
55159110
55159130
55159190
55159211
55159219
55159291
55159299
55159910
55159930
55159990

Woven fabrics of artificial staple fibres:

55161100
55161200
55161300
55161400
55162100
55162200
55162310
55162390
55162400
55163100
55163200
55163300
55163400
55164100
55164200
55164300
55164400
55169100
55169200
55169300
55169400

Twine, cordage, ropes and cables:

56071000
56072100
56072910
56072990
56073000
56074100
56074911
56074919
56074990
56075011
56075019
56075030
56075090
56079000

Knotted netting of twine, cordage or rope:

56081111
56081119
56081191
56081199
56081911
56081919
56081931
56081939
56081991
56081999
56089000

Carpets and other textile floor coverings, woven:

57021000
57022000
57023110
57023130
57023190
57023210
57023290
57023910
57023990
57024110
57024190
57024210
57024290
57024910
57024990
57025100
57025200
57025900
57029100
57029200
57029900

Carpets and other textile floor coverings, tufted:

57031010
57031090
570320111
57032019
57032091
57032099
57033011
57033019
57033051
57033059
57033091
57033099
57039010
57039090

Carpets and other textile floor coverings, of felt:

57041000
57049000

Other carpets and other textile floor coverings:

57050010
57050031

57050039
57050090

Other knitted or crocheted fabrics:
60021010
60021090
60022010
60022031
60022039
60022050
60022070
60022090
60023010
60023090
60024100
60024210
60024230
60024250
60024290
60024311
60024319
60024331
60024333
60024335
60024339
60024350
60024391
60024393
60024395
60024399
60024900
60029100
60029210
60029230
60029250
60029290
60029310
60029331
60029333
60029335
60029339
60029391
60029399
60029900

Men's or boys' suits, ensembles, jackets, blazers:
61031100
61031200
61031900
61032100
61032200
61032300
61032900
61033100
61033200
61033300
61033900

Women's or girls' suits, ensembles, jackets, blazers:
61041100

61041200
61041300
61041900
61042100
61042200
61042300
61042900
61043100
61043200
61043300
61043900
61044100
61044200
61044300
61044400
61044900

Men's or boys' shirts, knitted or crocheted:
61051000
61052010
61052090
61059010
61059090

Women's or girls' blouses, shirts and shirt-blouses:
61061000
61062000
61069010
61069030
61069050
61069090

T-shirts, singlets and other vests, knitted or crocheted:
61099090

Jerseys, pullovers, cardigans, waistcoats and similar:
61101010
61101031
61101035
611010381
61101091
61101095
61101098
61102010
61102091
61102099
61103010
61103091
61103099
61109010
61109090

Babies' garments and clothing accessories, knitted:
61111010
61111090
61112010
61112090
61113010

61113090
61119000

Men's or boys' suits, ensembles, jackets, blazers:
62031100
62031200
62031910
62031930
62031990
62032100
62032210
62032280
62032310
62032380
62032911
62032918
62032990
62033100
62033210
62033290
62033310
62033390
62033911
62033919
62033990

Women's or girls' suits, ensembles, jackets, blazers:
62041100
62041200
62041300
62041910
62041990
62042100
62042210
62042280
62042310
62042380
62042911
62042918
62042990
62043100
62043210
62043290
62043310
62043390
62043911
62043919
62043990
62044100
62044200
62044300
62044400
62044910
62044990

Women's or girls' blouses, shirts and shirt-blouses:
62061000
62062000
62063000
62064000

62069010
62069090

Babies' garments and clothing accessories:
62091000
62092000
62093000
62099000

Garments, made up of fabrics of heading No 5602, 5:
62101010
62101091
62101099
62102000
62103000
62104000
62105000

Track suits, ski suits and swimwear; other garments:
62111100
62111200
62112000
62113100
62113210
62113231
62113241
62113242
62113290
62113310
62113331
62113341
62113342
62113390
62113900
62114100
62114210
62114231
62114241
62114242
62114290
62114310
62114331
62114341
62114342
62114390
62114900

Bed linen, table linen, toilet linen and kitchen linen:
63021010
63021090
63022100
63022210
63022290
63022910
63022990
63023110
63023190
63023210
63023290

63023910
63023930
63023990
63024000
63025110
63025190
63025200
63025310
63025390
63025900
63026000
63029110
63029190
63029200
63029310
63029390
63029900

Curtains (including drapes) and interior blinds:
63031100
63031200
63031900
63039100
63039210
63039290
63039910
63039990

Other furnishing articles:
63041100
63041910
63041930
63041990
63049100
63049200
63049300
63049900

Industrial Products (2)

Hydrogen, rare gases and other non-metals:
28046900

Colloidal precious metals; inorganic or organic:
28431090
28433000
28439090

Oxygen-function amino-compounds:
29224100

Pig iron and spiegeleisen in pigs, blocks or other:
72011011
72011019
72011030
72012000
72015090

Ferro-alloys:
72021120

72021180
72021900
72022110
72022190
72022900
72023000
72024110
72024191
72024199
72024910
72024950
72024990

Ferrous products obtained by direct reduction:
72039000

Ferrous waste and scrap; remelting scrap ingots:
72045090

Iron and non-alloy steel in ingots or other:
72061000
72069000

Semi-finished products of iron or non-alloy steel:
72071111
72071114
72071116
72071210
72071911
72071914
72071916
72071931
72072011
72072015
72072017
72072032
72072051
72072055
72072057
72072071

Flat-rolled products of iron or non-alloy steel:
72081000
72082500
72082600
72082700
72083600
72083710
72083790
72083810
72083890
72083910
72083990
72084010
72084090
72085110
72085130
72085150

72085191
72085199
72085210
72085291
72085299
72085310
72085390
72085410
72085490
72089010

Flat-rolled products of iron or non-alloy steel:
72091500
72091610
72091690
72091710
72091790
72091810
72091891
72091899
72092500
72092610
72092690
72092710
72092790
72092810
72092890
72099010

Flat-rolled products of iron or non-alloy steel:
72101110
72101211
72101219
72102010
72103010
72104110
72104910
72105010
72106110
72106910
72107031
72107039
72109031
72109033
72109038

Flat-rolled products of iron or non-alloy steel:
72111300
72111410
72111490
72111920
72111990
72112310
72112351
72112920
72119011

Flat-rolled products of iron or non-alloy steel:
72121010

72121091
72122011
72123011
72124010
72124091
72125031
72125051
72126011
72126091

Bars and rods, hot-rolled:
72131000
72132000
72139110
72139120
72139141
72139149
72139170
72139190
72139910
72139990

Other bars and rods of iron or non-alloy steel:
72142000
72143000
72149110
72149190
72149910
72149931
72149939
72149950
72149961
72149969
72149980
72149990

Other bars and rods of iron or non-alloy steel:
72159010

Angles, shapes and sections of iron or non-alloy steel:
72161000
72162100
72162200
72163111
72163119
72163191
72163199
72163211
72163219
72163291
72163299
72163310
72163390
72164010
72164090
72165010
72165091
72165099
72169910

Stainless steel in ingots or other primary forms:
72181000
72189111
72189119
72189911
72189920

Flat-rolled products of stainless steel:
72191100
72191210
72191290
72191310
72191390
72191410
72191490
72192110
72192190
72192210
72192290
72192300
72192400
72193100
72193210
72193290
72193310
72193390
72193410
72193490
72193510
72193590
72199010

Flat-rolled products of stainless steel:
72201100
72201200
72202010
72209011
72209031

Bars and rods, hot-rolled:
72210010
72210090

Other bars and rods of stainless steel:
72221111
72221119
72221121
72221129
72221191
72221199
72221910
72221990
72223010
72224010
72224030

Other alloy steel in ingots or other primary forms:
72241000

72249001
72249005
72249008
72249015
72249031
72249039

Flat-rolled products of other alloy steel:
72251100
72251910
72251990
72252020
72253000
72254020
72254050
72254080
72255000
72259110
72259210
72259910

Flat-rolled products of other alloy steel:
72261110
72261910
72261930
72262020
72269110
72269190
72269210
72269320
72269420
72269920

Bars and rods, hot-rolled:
72271000
72272000
72279010
72279050
72279095

Other bars and rods of other alloy steel:
72281010
72281030
72282011
72282019
72282030
72283020
72283041
72283049
72283061
72283069
72283070
72283089
72286010
72287010
72287031
72288010
72288090

Sheet piling of iron or steel:
73011000

Railway or tramway track construction material:
73021031
73021039
73021090
73022000
73024010
73029010

Tubes, pipes and hollow profiles, of cast iron:
73030010
73030090

Tube or pipe fittings (for example couplings):
73071110
73071190
73071910
73071990
73072100
73072210
73072290
73072310
73072390
73072910
73072930
73072990
73079100
73079210
73079290
73079311
73079319
73079391
73079399
73079910
73079930
73079990

Reservoirs, tanks, vats and similar containers:
73090010
73090030
73090051
73090059
73090090

Tanks, casks, drums, cans, boxes and similar containers:
73101000
73102110
73102191
73102199
73102910
73102990

Containers for compressed or liquefied gas:
73110010
73110091
73110099

Stranded wire, ropes, cables, plaited bands:
73121030
73121051
73121059
73121071
73121075
73121079
73121082
73121084
73121086
73121088
73121099
73129090

Barbed wire of iron or steel:
73130000

Chain and parts thereof, of iron or steel:
73151110
73151190
73151200
73151900
73152000
73158100
73158210
73158290
73158900
73159000

Screws, bolts, nuts, coach screws, screw hooks:
73181100
73181210
73181290
73181300
73181410
73181491
73181499
73181510
73181520
73181530
73181541
73181549
73181551
73181559
73181561
73181569
73181570
73181581
73181589
73181590
73181610
73181630
73181650
73181691
73181699
73181900
73182100
73182200
73182300

73182400
73182900

Sewing needles, knitting needles, bodkins, crochets:
73191000
73192000
73193000
73199000

Springs and leaves for springs, of iron or steel:
73201011
73201019
73201090
73202020
73202081
73202085
73202089
73209010
73209030
73209090

Stoves, ranges, grates, cookers:
73211110
73211190
73211200
73211300
73218110
73218190
73218210
73218290
73218300
73219000

Radiators for central heating:
73221100
73221900
73229090

Table, kitchen or other household articles:
73231000
73239100
73239200
73239310
73239390
73239410
73239490
73239910
73239991
73239999

Sanitary ware and parts thereof, of iron or steel:
73241090
73242100
73242900
73249090

Other cast articles of iron or steel:
73251020
73251050
73251091
73251099
73259100
73259910
73259991
73259999

Other articles of iron or steel:
73261100
73261910
73261990
73262030
73262050
73262090
73269010
73269030
73269040

73269050
73269060
73269070
73269080
73269091
73269093
73269095
73269097

Unwrought zinc:
79011100
79011210
79011230
79011290
79012000

Zinc dust, powders and flakes:
79031000
79039000

Motor vehicles for the transport of ten or more persons:
87021011
87021019
87029011
87029019

Motor vehicles for the transport of goods:
87042131
87042139
87042291
87042299
87042391
87042399
87043131
87043139
87043291
87043299

Annex 23

Products to Which Article 6(3) Shall Not Be Applicable

Industrial Products (1)

CN code 96

Motor cars and other motor vehicles:
87031010
87031090
87032110
87032190
87032211
87032219
87032290
87032311
87032319
87032390
87032410
87032490
87033110
87033190
87033211
87033219
87033290
87033311
87033319
87033390
87039010
87039090

Chassis fitted with engines:
87060011
87060019
87060091
87060099

Bodies (including cabs), for the motor vehicles:
87071010
87071090
87079010
87079090

Parts and accessories of the motor vehicles:
87081010
87081090
87082110
87082190
87082910
87082990
87083110
87083191
87083199
87083910
87083990
87084010

87084090
87085010
87085090
87086010
87086091
87086099
87087010
87087050
87087091
87087099
87088010
87088090
87089110
87089190
87089210
87089290
87089310
87089390
87089410
87089490
87089910
87089930
87089950
87089992
87089998

Industrial Products (2)

Unwrought aluminium:
76011000
76012010
76012091
76012099

Aluminium powders and flakes:
76031000
76032000

Agricultural Products (1)

Live horses, asses, mules and hinnies:
01012010

Milk and cream, not concentrated:
04011010
04011090
04012011
04012019
04012091
04012099
04013011
04013019
04013031
04013039

04013091
04013099

Buttermilk, curdled milk and cream, yogurt, kephir:
04031011
04031013
04031019
04031031
04031033
04031039

Potatoes, fresh or chilled:
07019051

Leguminous vegetables, shelled or unshelled, fresh or chilled:
07081020
07081095

Other vegetables, fresh or chilled:
07095190
07096010

Vegetables (uncooked or cooked by steaming or boiled):
07108095

Vegetables provisionally preserved:
07111000
07113000
07119060
07119070

Dates, figs, pineapples, avocados, guavas, mangoes:
08042090
08043000
08044020
08044090
08044095

Grapes, fresh or dried:
08061029 (3) (12)
08062011
08062012
08062018

Melons (including watermelons) and papaws (papayas):
08071100
08071900

Apricots, cherries, peaches (including nectarines):
08093011 (5) (12)
08093051 (6) (12)

Other fruit, fresh:
08109040
08109085

Fruit and nuts, provisionally preserved:
08121000
08122000
08129050
08129060
08129070
08129095

Fruit, dried:
08134010
08135015
08135019
08135039
08135091
08135099

Pepper of the genus Piper; dried or crushed:
09042010

Soya-bean oil and its fractions:
15071010
15071090
15079010
15079090

Sunflower-seed, safflower or cotton-seed oil:
15121110
15121191
15121199
15121910
15121991
15121999
15122110
15122190
15122910
15122990

Rape, colza or mustard oil and fractions thereof:
15141010
15141090
15149010
15149090

Fruit, nuts and other edible parts of plants:
20081959

Fruit juices (including grape must):
20092099
20094099
20098099

Unmanufactured tobacco; tobacco refuse:
24011010
24011020

24011041
24011049
24011060
24012010
24012020
24012041
24012060
24012070

Agricultural Products (2)

Cut flowers and flower buds:
06031055
06031061
06031069 (11)

Onions, shallots, garlic, leeks:
07031011
07031019
07031090
07039000

Cabbages, cauliflowers, kohlrabi, kale and similar:
07041005
07041010
07041080
07042000
07049010
07049090

Lettuce (Lactuca sativa) and chicory:
07051105
07051110
07051180
07051900
07052100
07052900

Carrots, turnips, salad beetroot, salsify, celeriac:
07061000
07069005
07069011
07069017
07069030
07069090

Leguminous vegetables, shelled or unshelled, fresh or chilled:
07081090
07082020
07082090
07082095
07089000

Other vegetables, fresh or chilled:
07091030 (12)
07093000
07094000
07095110
07095150

07097000
07099010
07099020
07099040
07099050
07099090

Vegetables (uncooked or cooked by steaming or boiled):
07101000
07102100
07102200
07102900
07103000
07108010
07108051
07108061
07108069
07108070
07108080
07108085
07109000

Vegetables provisionally preserved:
07112010
07114000
07119040
07119090

Dried vegetables, whole, cut, sliced, broken:
07122000
07123000
07129030
07129050
07129090

Manioc, arrowroot, salep, Jerusalem artichokes:
07149011
07149019

Other nuts, fresh or dried, whether or not shelled:
08021190
08022100
08022200
08024000

Bananas, including plantains, fresh or dried:
08030011
08030090

Dates, figs, pineapples, avocados, guavas, mangoes:
08042010

Citrus fruit, fresh or dried:
08052021 (1) (12)
08052023 (1) (12)
08052025 (1) (12)
08052027 (1) (12)

08052029 (1) (12)
08053090
08059000

Grapes, fresh or dried:
08061095
08061097

Apples, pears and quinces, fresh:
08081010 (12)
08082010 (12)
08082090

Apricots, cherries, peaches (including nectarines):
08091010 (12)
08091050 (12)
08092019 (12)
08092029 (12)
08093011 (7) (12)
08093019 (12)
08093051 (8) (12)
08093059 (12)
08094040 (12)

Other fruit, fresh:
08101005
08102090
08103010
08103030
08103090
08104090
08105000

Fruit and nuts, uncooked or cooked by steaming:
08112011
08112031
08112039
08112059
08119011
08119019
08119039
08119075
08119080
08119095

Fruit and nuts, provisionally preserved:
08129010
08129020

Fruit, dried:
08132000

Wheat and meslin:
10019010

Buckwheat, millet and canary seed; other cereals:
10081000
10082000
10089090

Flour, meal, powder, flakes, granules and pellets:
11051000
11052000

Flour, meal and powder of the dried leguminous vegetables:
11061000
11063010
11063090

Fats and oils and their fractions, of fish:
15043011

Other prepared or preserved meat, meat offal:
16022011
16022019
16023111
16023119
16023130
16023190
16023219
16023230
16023290
16023929
16023940
16023980
16024190
16024290
16029031
16029072
16029076

Vegetables, fruit, nuts and other edible parts:
20011000
20012000
20019050
20019065
20019096

Mushrooms and truffles, prepared or preserved:
20031020
20031030
20031080
20032000

Other vegetables prepared or preserved otherwise:
20041010
20041099
20049050
20049091
20049098

Other vegetables prepared or preserved otherwise:
20051000
20052020
20052080
20054000

20055100
20055900

Vegetables, fruit, nuts, fruit-peel:
20060031
20060035
20060038
20060099

Jams, fruit jellies, marmalades, fruit or nut puree:
20071091
20079993

Fruit, nuts and other edible parts of plants:
20081194
20081198
20081919
20081995
20081999
20082051
20082059
20082071
20082079
20082091
20082099
20083011
20083039
20083051
20083059
20084011
20084021
20084029
20084039
20086011
20086031
20086039
20086059
20086069
20086079
20086099
20087011
20087031
20087039
20087059
20088011
20088031
20088039
20088050
20088070
20088091
20088099
20089923
20089925
20089926
20089928
20089936
20089945
20089946
20089949
20089953
20089955

20089961
20089962
20089968
20089972
20089974
20089979
20089999

Fruit juices (including grape must):
20091119
20091191
20091919
20091991
20091999
20092019
20092091
20093019
20093031
20093039
20093051
20093055
20093091
20093095
20093099
20094019
20094091
20098019
20098050
20098061
20098063
20098073
20098079
20098083
20098084
20098086
20098097
20099019
20099029
20099039
20099041
20099051
20099059
20099073
20099079
20099092
20099094
20099095
20099096
20099097
20099098

Other fermented beverages (for example, cider):
22060010

Wine lees; argol:
23070019

Vegetable materials and vegetable waste:
23089019

Agricultural Products (3)

Live swine:
01039110
01039211
01039219

Live sheep and goats:
01041030
01041080
01042090

Live poultry, that is to say, fowls of the species:
01051111
01051119
01051191
01051199
01051200
01051920
01051990
01059200
01059300
01059910
01059920
01059930
01059950

Meat of swine, fresh, chilled or frozen:
02031110
02031211
02031219
02031911
02031913
02031915
02031955
02031959
02032110
02032211
02032219
02032911
02032913
02032915
02032955
02032959

Meat of sheep or goats, fresh, chilled or frozen:
02041000
02042100
02042210
02042230
02042250
02042290
02042300
02043000
02044100
02044210
02044230
02044250
02044290
02044310

02044390
02045011
02045013
02045015
02045019
02045031
02045039
02045051
02045053
02045055
02045059
02045071
02045079

Meat and edible offal:
02071110
02071130
02071190
02071210
02071290
02071310
02071320
02071330
02071340
02071350
02071360
02071370
02071399
02071410
02071420
02071430
02071440
02071450
02071460
02071470
02071499
02072410
02072490
02072510
02072590
02072610
02072620
02072630
02072640
02072650
02072660
02072670
02072680
02072699
02072710
02072720
02072730
02072740
02072750
02072760
02072770
02072780
02072799
02073211
02073215
02073219
02073251

02073259
02073290
02073311
02073319
02073351
02073359
02073390
02073511
02073515
02073521
02073523
02073525
02073531
02073541
02073551
02073553
02073561
02073563
02073571
02073579
02073599
02073611
02073615
02073621
02073623
02073625
02073631
02073641
02073651
02073653
02073661
02073663
02073671
02073679
02073690

Pig fat, free of lean meat, and poultry fat:
02090011
02090019
02090030
02090090

Meat and edible meat offal, salted, in brine:
02101111
02101119
02101131
02101139
02101190
02101211
02101219
02101290
02101910
02101920
02101930
02101940
02101951
02101959
02101960
02101970
02101981

02101989
02101990
02109011
02109019
02109021
02109029
02109031
02109039

Milk and cream, concentrated:
04029111
04029119
04029131
04029139
04029151
04029159
04029191
04029199
04029911
04029919
04029931
04029939
04029991
04029999

Buttermilk, curdled milk and cream, yogurt, kephir:
04039051
04039053
04039059
04039061
04039063
04039069

Whey, whether or not concentrated:
04041048
04041052
04041054
04041056
04041058
04041062
04041072
04041074
04041076
04041078
04041082
04041084

Cheese and curd:
04061020 (11)
04061080 (11)
04062090 (11)
04063010 (11)
04063031 (11)
04063039 (11)
04063090 (11)
04064090 (11)
04069001 (11)
04069021 (11)
04069050 (11)
04069069 (11)
04069078 (11)

04069086 (11)
04069087 (11)
04069088 (11)
04069093 (11)
04069099 (11)

Birds' eggs, in shell, fresh, preserved or cooked:
04070011
04070019
04070030

Birds' eggs, not in shell, and egg yolks, fresh:
04081180
04081981
04081989
04089180
04089980

Natural honey:
04090000

Tomatoes, fresh or chilled:
07020015 (12)
07020020 (12)
07020025 (12)
07020030 (12)
07020035 (12)
07020040 (12)
07020045 (12)
07020050 (12)

Cucumbers and gherkins, fresh or chilled:
07070010 (12)
07070015 (12)
07070020 (12)
07070025 (12)
07070030 (12)
07070035 (12)
07070040 (12)
07070090

Other vegetables, fresh or chilled:
07091010 (12)
07091020 (12)
07092000
07099039
07099075 (12)
07099077 (12)
07099079 (12)

Vegetables provisionally preserved:
07112090

Dried vegetables, whole, cut, sliced, broken:
07129019

Manioc, arrowroot, salep, Jerusalem artichokes:
07141010

07141091
07141099
07142090

Citrus fruit, fresh or dried:
08051037 (2) (12)
08051038 (2) (12)
08051039 (2) (12)
08051042 (2) (12)
08051046 (2) (12)
08051082
08051084
08051086
08052011 (12)
08052013 (12)
08052015 (12)
08052017 (12)
08052019 (12)
08052021 (10) (12)
08052023 (10) (12)
08052025 (10) (12)
08052027 (10) (12)
08052029 (10) (12)
08052031 (12)
08052033 (12)
08052035 (12)
08052037 (12)
08052039 (12)

Grapes, fresh or dried:
08061021 (12))
08061029 (4) (12)
08061030 (12)
08061050 (12)
08061061 (12)
08061069 (12)
08061093

Apricots, cherries, peaches (including nectarines):
08091020 (12)
08091030 (12)
08091040 (12)
08092011 (12)
08092021 (12)
08092031 (12)
08092039 (12)
08092041 (12)
08092049 (12)
08092051 (12)
08092059 (12)
08092061 (12)
08092069 (12)
08092071 (12)
08092079 (12)
08093021 (12)
08093029 (12)
08093031 (12)
08093039 (12)
08093041 (12)
08093049 (12)
08094020 (12)
08094030 (12)

Other fruit, fresh:
08101010
08101080
08102010

Fruit and nuts, uncooked or cooked by steaming:
08111011
08111019

Wheat and meslin:
10011000
10019091
10019099

Rye:
10020000

Barley:
10030010
10030090

Oats:
10040000

Buckwheat, millet and canary seed; other cereals:
10089010

Wheat or meslin flour:
11010011
11010015
11010090

Cereal flours other than of wheat or meslin:
11021000
11029010
11029030
11029090

Cereal groats, meal and pellets:
11031110
11031190
11031200
11031910
11031930
11031990
11032100
11032910
11032920
11032930
11032990

Cereal grains otherwise worked:
11041110
11041190
11041210
11041290
11041910
11041930
11041999
11042110
11042130
11042150

11042190
11042199
11042220
11042230
11042250
11042290
11042292
11042299
11042911
11042915
11042919
11042931
11042935
11042939
11042951
11042955
11042959
11042981
11042985
11042989
11043010

Flour, meal and powder of the dried leguminous vegetables:
11062010
11062090

Malt, whether or not roasted:
11071011
11071019
11071091
11071099
11072000

Locust beans, seaweeds and other algae, sugar beet:
12129120
12129180

Pig fat (including lard) and poultry fat:
15010019

Olive oil and its fractions, whether or not refined:
15091010
15091090
15099000

Other oils and their fractions:
15100010
15100090

Degras:
15220031
15220039

Sausages and similar products, of meat, meat offal:
16010091
16010099

Other prepared or preserved meat, meat offal:
16021000

16022090
16023211
16023921
16024110
16024210
16024911
16024913
16024915
16024919
16024930
16024950
16024990
16025031
16025039
16025080
16029010
16029041
16029051
16029069
16029074
16029078
16029098

Other sugars, including chemically pure lactose:
17021100
17021900

Pasta, whether or not cooked or stuffed:
19022030

Jams, fruit jellies, marmalades, fruit or nut puree:
20071099
20079190
20079991
20079998

Fruit, nuts and other edible parts of plants:
20082011
20082031
20083019
20083031
20083079
20083091
20083099
20084019
20084031
20085011
20085019
20085031
20085039
20085051
20085059
20086019
20086051
20086061
20086071
20086091
20087019
20087051

20088019
20089216
20089218
20089921
20089932
20089933
20089934
20089937
20089943

Fruit juices (including grape must):
20091111
20091911
20092011
20093011
20093059
20094011
20095010
20095090
20098011
20098032
20098033
20098035
20099011
20099021
20099031

Food preparations not elsewhere specified:
21069051

Wine of fresh grapes, including fortified wines:
22041019 (11)
22041099 (11)
22042110
22042181
22042182
22042198
22042199
22042910
22042958
22042975
22042998
22042999
22043010
22043092 (12)
22043094 (12)
22043096 (12)
22043098 (12)

Undenatured ethyl alcohol:
22082040

Bran, sharps and other residues:
23023010
23023090
23024010
23024090

Oil-cake and other solid residues:
23069019

Preparations of a kind used in animal feeding:
23091013
23091015
23091019
23091033
23091039
23091051
23091053
23091059
23091070
23099033
23099035
23099039
23099043
23099049
23099051
23099053
23099059
23099070

Albumins:
35021190
35021990
35022091
35022099

Agricultural Products (4)

Buttermilk, curdled milk and cream, yogurt, kephir:
04031051
04031053
04031059
04031091
04031093
04031099
04039071
04039073
04039079
04039091
04039093
04039099

Butter and other fats and oils derived from milk:
04052010
04052030

Vegetable saps and extracts; pectic substances:
13022010
13022090

Margarine:
15171010
15179010

Other sugars, including chemically pure lactose:
17025000
17029010

Sugar confectionery (including white chocolate):
17041011
17041019
17041091
17041099
17049010
17049030
17049051
17049055
17049061
17049065
17049071
17049075
17049081
17049099

Chocolate and other food preparations:
18061015
18061020
18061030
18061090
18062010
18062030
18062050
18062070
18062080
18062095
18063100
18063210
18063290
18069011
18069019
18069031
18069039
18069050
18069060
18069070
18069090

Malt extract; food preparations of flour, meal:
19011000
19012000
19019011
19019019
19019099

Pasta, whether or not cooked or stuffed:
19021100
19021910
19021990
19022091
19022099
19023010
19023090
19024010
19024090

Tapioca and substitutes:
19030000

Prepared foods:
19041010
19041030
19041090
19042010
19042091
19042095
19042099
19049010
19049090

Bread, pastry, cakes, biscuits:
19051000
19052010
19052030
19052090
19053011
19053019
19053030
19053051
19053059
19053091
19053099
19054010
19054090
19059010
19059020
19059030
19059040
19059045
19059055
19059060
19059090

Vegetables, fruit, nuts:
20019040

Other vegetables:
20041091

Other vegetables:
20052010

Fruit, nuts and other edible parts of plants:
20089985
20089991

Fruit juices (including grape must):
20098069

Extracts, essences and concentrates, of coffee:
21011111
21011119
21011292
21011298
21012098
21013011
21013019
21013091
21013099

Yeasts (active or inactive):
21021010
21021031
21021039
21021090
21022011

Sauces and preparations therefor; mixed condiments:
21032000

Ice cream and other edible ice:
21050010
21050091
21050099

Food preparations not elsewhere specified or included:
21061020
21061080
21069010
21069020
21069098

Waters, including mineral waters and aerated water:
22029091
22029095
22029099

Vinegar and substitutes for vinegar:
22090011
22090019
22090091
22090099

Acyclic alcohols and their halogenated derivatives:
29054300
29054411
29054419
29054491
29054499
29054500

Mixtures of odoriferous substances and mixtures:
33021010
33021021
33021029

Finishing agents, dye carriers:
38091010
38091030
38091050
38091090

Prepared binders for foundry moulds or cores:
38246011
38246019
38246091
38246099

Agricultural Products (5)

Cut flowers and flower buds:
06031015 (11)
06031029 (11)
06031051 (11)
06031065 (11)
06039000 (11)

Fruit and nuts, uncooked or cooked by steaming:
08111090 (11)

Fruit, nuts and other edible parts of plants:
20084051 (11)
20084059 (11)
20084071 (11)
20084079 (11)
20084091 (11)
20084099 (11)
20085061 (11)
20085069 (11)
20085071 (11)
20085079 (11)
20085092 (11)
20085094 (11)
20085099 (11)
20087061 (11)
20087069 (11)
20087071 (11)
20087079 (11)
20087092 (11)
20087094 (11)
20087099 (11)
20089259 (11)
20089272 (11)
20089274 (11)
20089278 (11)
20089298 (11)

Fruit juices (including grape must):
20091199 (11)
20094030 (11)
20097011 (11)
20097019 (11)
20097030 (11)
20097091 (11)
20097093 (11)
20097099 (11)

Wine of fresh grapes, including fortified wines:
22042179 (11)
22042180 (11)
22042183 (11)
22042184 (11)

Agricultural Products (6)

Live bovine animals:
01029005
01029021
01029029
01029041
01029049
01029051
01029059
01029061
01029069
01029071
01029079

Meat of bovine animals, fresh or chilled:
02011000
02012020
02012030
02012050
02012090
02013000

Meat of bovine animals, frozen:
02021000
02022010
02022030
02022050
02022090
02023010
02023050
02023090

Edible offal of bovine animals, swine, sheep, goats:
02061095
02062991
02062999

Meat and edible meat offal, salted, in brine:
02102010
02102090
02109041
02109049
02109090

Milk and cream, concentrated:
04021011
04021019
04021091
04021099
04022111
04022117
04022119
04022191
04022199
04022911
04022915
04022919
04022991
04022999

Buttermilk, curdled milk and cream, yogurt, kephir:
04039011
04039013
04039019
04039031
04039033
04039039

Whey, whether or not concentrated:
04041002
04041004
04041006
04041012
04041014
04041016
04041026
04041028
04041032
04041034
04041036
04041038
04049021
04049023
04049029
04049081
04049083
04049089

Butter and other fats and oils derived from milk:
04051011
04051030
04051050
04051090
04052090
04059010
04059090

Cut flowers and flower buds:
06031011
06031013
06031021
06031025
06031053

Other vegetables, fresh or chilled:
07099060

Vegetables (uncooked or cooked by steaming or boiling):
07104000

Vegetables provisionally preserved:
07119030

Bananas, including plantains, fresh or dried:
08030019

Citrus fruit, fresh or dried:
08051001 (12)
08051005 (12)
08051009 (12)
080510111 (12)
08051015 (2)

08051019 (2)
08051021 (2)
08051025 (12)
08051029 (12)
08051031 (12)
08051033 (12)
08051035 (12)
08051037 (9) (12)
08051038 (9) (12)
08051039 (9) (12)
08051042 (9) (12)
08051044 (12)
08051046 (9) (12)
08051051 (2)
08051055 (2)
08051059 (2)
08051061 (2)
08051065 (2)
08051069 (2)
08053020 (2)
08053030 (2)
08053040 (2)

Grapes, fresh or dried:
08061040 (12)

Apples, pears and quinces, fresh:
08081051 (12)
08081053 (12)
08081059 (12)
08081061 (12)
08081063 (12)
08081069 (12)
08081071 (12)
08081073 (12)
08081079 (12)
08081092 (12)
08081094 (12)
08081098 (12)
08082031 (12)
08082037 (12)
08082041 (12)
08082047 (12)
08082051 (12)
08082057 (12)
08082067 (12)

Maize (corn):
10051090
10059000

Rice:
10061010
10061021
10061023
10061025
10061027
10061092
10061094
10061096
10061098
10062011
10062013

10062015
10062017
10062092
10062094
10062096
10062098
10063021
10063023
10063025
10063027
10063042
10063044
10063046
10063048
10063061
10063063
10063065
10063067
10063092
10063094
10063096
10063098
10064000

Grain sorghum:
10070010
10070090

Cereal flours other than of wheat or meslin:
11022010
11022090
11023000

Cereal groats, meal and pellets:
11031310
11031390
11031400
11032940
11032950

Cereal grains otherwise worked:
11041950
11041991
11042310
11042330
11042390
11042399
11043090

Starches; inulin:
11081100
11081200
11081300
11081400
11081910
11081990
11082000

Wheat gluten, whether or not dried:
11090000

Other prepared or preserved meat, meat offal:
16025010
16029061

Cane or beet sugar and chemically pure sucrose:
17011110
17011190
17011210
17011290
17019100
17019910
17019990

Other sugars, including chemically pure lactose:
17022010
17022090
17023010
17023051
17023059
17023091
17023099
17024010
17024090
17026010
17026090
17029030
17029050
17029060
17029071
17029075
17029079
17029080
17029099

Vegetables, fruit, nuts and other edible parts:
20019030

Tomatoes prepared or preserved:
20021010
20021090
20029011
20029019
20029031
20029039
20029091
20029099

Other vegetables prepared or preserved:
20049010

Other vegetables prepared or preserved:
20056000
20058000

Jams, fruit jellies, marmalades, fruit or nut puree:
20071010
20079110

20079130
20079910
20079920
20079931
20079933
20079935
20079939
20079951
20079955
20079958

Fruit, nuts and other edible parts of plants:
20083055
20083075
20089251
20089276
20089292
20089293
20089294
20089296
20089297

Fruit juices (including grape must):
20094093
20096011 (12)
20096019 (12)
20096051 (12)
20096059 (12)
20096071 (12)
20096079 (12)
20096090 (12)
20098071
20099049
20099071

Food preparations not elsewhere specified or included:
21069030
21069055
21069059

Wine of fresh grapes, including fortified wines:
22042194
22042962
22042964
22042965
22042983
22042984
22042994

Vermouth and other wine of fresh grapes:
22051010
22051090
22059010
22059090

Undenatured ethyl alcohol:
22071000
22072000

Undenatured ethyl alcohol:
22084010
22084090
22089091
22089099

Bran, sharps and other residues:
23021010
23021090
23022010
23022090

Residues of starch manufacture and similar residues:
23031011

Dextrins and other modified starches:
35051010
35051090
35052010
35052030
35052050
35052090

Agricultural Products (7)

Cheese and curd:
04062010
04064010
04064050
04069002
04069003
04069004
04069005
04069006
04069007
04069008
04069009
04069012
04069014
04069016
04069018
04069019
04069023
04069025
04069027
04069029
04069031
04069033
04069035
04069037
04069039
04069061
04069063
04069073
04069075
04069076
04069079
04069081
04069082
04069084
04069085

Wine of fresh grapes, including fortified wines:
22041011
22041091
22042111
22042112
22042113
22042117
22042118
22042119
22042122
22042124
22042126
22042127
22042128
22042132
22042134
22042136
22042137
22042138
22042142
22042143
22042144
22042146
22042147
22042148
22042162
22042166
22042167
22042168
22042169
22042171
22042174
22042176
22042177
22042178
22042187
22042188
22042189
22042191
22042192
22042193
22042195
22042196
22042197
22042912
22042913
22042917
22042918
22042942
22042943
22042944
22042946
22042947
22042948
22042971
22042972
22042981
22042982
22042987
22042988

22042989	22082014	22083038
22042991	22082026	22083052
22042992	22082027	22083058
22042993	22082062	22083072
22042995	22082064	22083078
22042996	22082086	22089041
22042997	22082087	22089045
Undenatured ethyl alcohol:	22083011	22089052
22082012	22083019	
	22083032	

Footnotes

(1)   (16/5–15/9)
(2)   (1/6–15/10)
(3)   (1/1–31/5) Excluding Emperor variety
(4)   Emperor variety or (1/6–31/12)
(5)   (1/1–31/3)
(6)   (1/10–31/12)
(7)   (1/4–31/12)
(8)   (1/1–30/9)
(9)   (16/10–31/5)
(10) (16/9–15/5)
(11) Under the agreement on trade, development and co-operation between the European Community and the Republic of South Africa, the annual growth factor (agf) will be applied annually to the relevant basic quantities.
(12) Under the Agreement on Trade, Development and Co-operation between the European Community and the Republic of South Africa, the full specific duty is payable if the respective Entry Price is not reached.

Annex 24

Fishery Products to Which Article 6(3) Shall Temporarily Not Be Applicable

Fish Products (1)	Fish Products (2)	
		03037985
CN code 96	**Live fish:**	03037987
	03019110	03037992
Live fish:	03019300	03037993
03011090	03019919	03037994
03019200		03037996
03019911	**Fish, fresh or chilled, excluding fish fillets:**	03038000
Fish, fresh or chilled, excluding fish fillets	03021110	**Fish fillets and other fish meat:**
03021200	03021900	03041019
03023110	03022110	03041091
03023210	03022130	03042019
03023310	03022200	03042021
03023911	03026200	03042029
03023919	03026300	03042031
03026600	03026520	03042033
03026921	03026550	03042035
	03026590	03042037
Fish, frozen, excluding fish fillets:	03026911	03042041
03031000	03026919	03042043
03032200	03026931	03042061
03034111	03026933	03042069
03034113	03026941	03042071
03034119	03026945	03042073
03034212	03026951	03042087
03034218	03026985	03042091
03034232	03026986	03049010
03034238	03026992	03049031
03034252	03026999	03049039
03034258	03027000	03049041
03034311		03049045
03034313	**Fish, frozen, excluding fish fillets:**	03049057
03034319	03032110	03049059
03034921	03032900	03049097
03034923	03033110	
03034929	03033130	**Fish, dried, salted or in brine; smoked fish:**
03034941	03033300	03054200
03034943	03033910	03055950
03034949	03037200	03055970
03037600	03037300	03056300
03037921	03037520	03056930
03037923	03037550	03056950
03037929	03037590	03056990
	03037911	
Fish fillets and other fish meat	03037919	**Crustaceans, whether in shell or not, live, fresh:**
03041013	03037935	03061110
03042013	03037937	03061190
	03037945	03061210
Pasta, whether or not cooked or stuffed	03037951	03061290
19022010	03037960	03061310
	03037962	03061390
	03037983	

03061410
03061430
03061490
03061910
03061990
03062100
03062210
03062291
03062299
03062310
03062390
03062410
03062430
03062490
03062910
03062990

Molluscs, whether in shell or not, live, fresh:
03071090
03072100
03072910
03072990
03073110
03073190
03073910
03073990
03074110
03074191
03074199
03074901
03074911
03074918
03074931
03074933
03074935
03074938
03074951
03074959
03074971
03074991
03074999
03075100
03075910
03075990
03079100
03079911
03079913
03079915
03079918
03079990

Prepared or preserved fish; caviar and caviar substitutes:
16041100
16041390
16041511
16041519
16041590
16041910
16041950
16041991

16041992
16041993
16041994
16041995
16041998
16042005
16042010
16042030
16043010
16043090

Crustaceans, molluscs and other aquatic invertebra:
16051000
16052010
16052091
16052099
16053000
16054000
16059011
16059019
16059030
16059090

Fish Products (3)

Live fish:
03019190

Fish, fresh or chilled, excluding fish fillets:
03021190

Fish, frozen, excluding fish fillets:
03032190

Fish fillets and other fish meat:
03041011
03042011
03042057
03042059
03049047
03049049

Prepared or preserved fish; caviar and caviar substitutes:
16041311

Fish Products (4)

Live fish:
03019990

Fish, fresh or chilled, excluding fish fillets:
03022190
03022300
03022910
03022990
03023190
03023290
03023390
03023991
03023999

03024005
03024098
03025010
03025090
03026110
03026130
03026190
03026198
03026405
03026498
03026925
03026935
03026955
03026961
03026975
03026987
03026991
03026993
03026994
03026995

Fish, frozen, excluding fish fillets:
03033190
03033200
03033920
03033930
03033980
03034190
03034290
03034390
03034990
03035005
03035098
03036011
03036019
03036090
03037110
03037130
03037190
03037198
03037410
03037420
03037490
03037700
03037931
03037941
03037955
03037965
03037971
03037975
03037991
03037995

Fish fillets and other fish meat:
03041031
03041033
03041035
03041038
03041094
03041096
03041098
03042045

03042051	03054945	16041416
03042053	03054950	16041418
03042075	03054980	16041490
03042079	03055110	16041931
03042081	03055190	16041939
03042085	03055911	16042070
03042096	03055919	
03049005	03055930	
03049020	03055960	

Fish Products (5)

Fish, fresh or chilled, excluding fish fillets:

03049027	03055990
03049035	03056100
03049038	03056200
03049051	03056910
03049055	03056920

03026965
03026981

Fish, frozen, excluding fish fillets:

03037810
03037890
03037981

03049061	
03049065	

Crustaceans, whether in shell or not, live, fresh:

Fish, dried, salted or in brine; smoked fish:

	03061330
	03061930
	03062331
	03062339
	03062930

Fish fillets and other fish meat:

03042083

03051000
03052000
03053011
03053019

Prepared or preserved fish; caviar and caviar substitutes:

16041210
16041291
16041299
16041412
16041414

Prepared or preserved fish; caviar and caviar substitutes:

16041319
16041600
16042040
16042050
16042090

03053030
03053050
03053090
03054100
03054910
03054920
03054930

Annex 25

Form for Application for Derogation

ANNEX VIII TO PROTOCOL 1

1. Commercial description of the finished product 1.1 Customs classification (H.S. code)	2. Anticipated annual quantity of exports to the Community (weight, No of pieces, meters or other unit)
3. Commercial description of third country materials Customs classification (H. S. code)	4. Anticipated annual quantity of third country materials to be used
	5. Value of third country materials
	6. Value of finished products
7. Origin of third country materials	8. Reasons why the rule of origin for the finished product cannot be fulfilled
9. Commercial description of materials originating in the ACP States, EC or OCT to be used	10. Anticipated annual quantity of ACP, EC or OCT materials to be used
11. Value of ACP, EC or OCT materials 12. Working or processing carried out in the EC or OCT on third country materials without obtaining origin	13. Duration requested for derogation from.................... to........................... 14. Detailed description of working and processing in the ACP States 15. Capital structure of the firm concerned for a derogation
16. Amount of investments made/foreseen 17. Staff employed/expected 18. Value added by the working or processing in the ACP States: 18.1 Labour: 18.2 Overheads: 18.3 Others: 20. Possible developments to overcome the need for a derogation	19. Other possible sources of supply for materials 21. Observations

NOTES

1. If the boxes in the form are not sufficient to contain all relevant information, additional pages may be attached to the form. In this case, the mention 'see annex' shall be entered in the box concerned.

2. If possible, samples or other illustrative material (pictures, designs, catalogues, etc) of the final product and of the materials should accompany the form.

3. A form shall be completed for each product covered by the request.

Boxes 3, 4, 5, 7: 'third country' means any country which is not an ACP or Community State or OCT.

Box 12: If third country materials have been worked or processed in the Community or in the OCT without obtaining origin, before being further processed in the ACP State requesting the derogation, indicate the working or processing carried out in the Community or OCT.

Box 13: The dates to be indicated are the initial and final one for the period in which EUR 1 certificates may be issued under the derogation.

Box 18: Indicate either the percentage of added value in respect of the ex-works price of the product or the monetary amount of added-value for unit of product.

Box 19: If alternative sources of material exist, indicate here what they are and, if possible, the reasons of cost or other reasons why they are not used.

Box 20: Indicate possible further investments or suppliers' differentiation which make the derogation necessary for only a limited period of time.

Annex 26

EUR 1 Movement Certificate

1. Exporter *(name, full address, country)*	**EUR.** **No A** 000.000
	See notes overleaf before completing this form
	2. Certificate used in preferential trade between
	and
3. Consignee *(name, full address, country) (Optional)*	*(insert appropriate countries, groups of counries or territories)*

4. Country, group of countries or territory in which the products are considered as originating	5. Country, group of countries or territory of destination

6. Transport details *(Optional)*	7. Remarks

8. Item number; Marks and numbers; Number and kind of package (1); Description of goods	9. Gross mass (kg) or other measure (litres,m³,etc.)	10. Invoices *(Optional)*

11. CUSTOMS ENDORSEMENT		12. DECLARATION BY THE EXPORTER
Declaration certified Export document (2) Form .... No .... Customs office .... Issuing country or territory .... Date .... *(Signature)*	Stamp	I, the undersigned, declare that the goods described above meet the conditions required for the issue of this certificate. Place and date .... *(Signature)*

(1) If goods are not packed, indicate number of articles or state "In bulk" as appropriate
(2) Complete only where the regulations of the exporting country or territory require

13. Request for verification, to:	14. Result of verification
	Verification carried out shows that this certificate (*)
	  was issued by the customs office indicated and that the information contained therein is accurate. does not meet the requirements as to authenticity and accuracy (see remarks appended).
Verification of the authenticity and accurancy of this certificate is requested	
.... *(Place and date)*	.... *(Place and date)*
.... Stamp	.... Stamp
.... *(Signature)*	.... *(Signature)* (*) Insert X in the appropriate box.

NOTES

1. Certificates must not contain erasures or words written over one another. Any alterations must be made by deleting the incorrect particulars and adding any necessary corrections. Any such alteration must be initialled by the person who completed the certificate and endorsed by the customs authorities of the issuing country or territory.

2. No spaces must be left between the items entered on the certificate and each item must be preceded by an item number. A horizontal line must be drawn immediately below the last item. Any unused space must be struck through in such a manner as to make any later additions impossible.

3. Goods must be described in accordance with commercial practice and with sufficient detail to enable them to be identified.

Annex 27

Declaration by the Exporter

I, the undersigned, exporter of the goods described overleaf,

DECLARE   that the goods meet the conditions required for the issue of the attached
certificate;

SPECIFY   as follows the circumstances which have enabled these goods to meet the
above conditions:

. . . .

. . . .

. . . .

. . . .

SUBMIT   the following supporting documents (1):

. . . .

. . . .

. . . .

UNDERTAKE to submit, at the request of the appropriate authorities, any supporting
evidence which these authorities may require for the purpose of issuing the
attached certificate, and undertake, if required, to agree to any inspection of
my accounts and to any check on the processes of manufacture of the above
goods, carried out by the said authorities;

REQUEST   the issue of the attached certificate for these goods.

(Place and date)

(Signature)

Annex 28

Information Certificate

ANNEX VII TO PROTOCOL 1

1. The form of information certificate given in this Annex shall be used and be printed in one or more of the official languages in which the Agreement is drawn up and in accordance with the provisions of the domestic law of the exporting State. Information certificates shall be completed in one of those languages; if they are handwritten, they shall be completed in ink in capital letters. They shall bear a serial number, whether or not printed, by which they can be identified.

2. The information certificate shall measure 210 x 297mm, a tolerance of up to plus 8mm or minus 5mm in the length may be allowed. The paper must be white, sized for writing, not containing mechanical pulp and weighing not less than $25g/m^2$.

3. The national administrators may reserve the right to print the forms themselves or may have them printed by printers approved by them. In the latter case, each form must include a reference to such approval. The forms shall bear the name and address of the printer or a mark by which the printer can be identified.

European Communities

1. Supplier (1)	INFORMATION CERTIFICATE
	to facilitate the issue of a
2. Consignee (1)	**MOVEMENT CERTIFICATE**
	for preferential trade between the
	EUROPEAN COMMUNITY and THE ACP STATES

3. Processor (1)	4. State in which the working or processing has been carried out
6. Customs office of importation (1)	5. For official use
7. Import document (2) Form .... No .... Series.. Date ☐☐☐	

GOODS SENT TO THE MEMBER STATES OF DESTINATION

8. Marks, numbers, quantity and kind of package	9. Harmonised Commodity Description and Coding System heading/subheading number (HS code)	10. Quantity (1)
		11. Value (4)

IMPORTED GOODS USED

12. Harmonised Commodity Description and Coding System heading/subheading number (HS code)	13. Country of origin	14. Quantity (3)	15. Value (2)(5)

16. Nature of the working or processing carried out

17. Remarks

18. CUSTOMS ENDORSEMENT	19. DECLARATION BY THE SUPPLIER
Declaration certified: Document .... Form .... No......... Customs office .... Date: ☐☐☐ Official Stamp .... (Signature)	I, the undersigned, declare that the information on this certificate is accurate. .... ☐☐☐ (Place) (Date) .... (Signature)

(1)(2)(3)(4)(5) See footnotes on verso

REQUEST FOR VERIFICATION	RESULT OF VERIFICATION
The undersigned customs official requests verification of the authenticityand accuracy of this information certificate.	Verification carried out by the undersigned customs official shows that this information certificate: a) was issued by the customs office indicated and that the information contained therein is accurate (*) b) does not meet the requirements as to authenticity and accuracy (see notes appended) (*)
(Place and date) Official Stamp (Official's signature)	(Place and date) Official Stamp (Official's signature) (*)Delete where not applicable

CROSS REFERENCES

(1) Name of individual or business and full address.

(2) Optional information.

(3) Kg, hl, m^3 or other measure.

(4) Packaging shall be considered as forming a whole with the goods contained therein. However, this provision shall not apply to packaging which is not of the normal type for the article packed, and which has a lasting utility value of its own, apart from its function as packaging.

(5) The value must be indicated in accordance with the provisions on rules of origin.

Annex 29

Application for a Movement Certificate

1. Exporter *(name, full address, country) (Optional)*	EUR. No A 000.000
	See notes overleaf before completing this form
	2. Application for a certificate to be used in preferential trade between
3. Consignee *(name, full address, country) (Optional)*	and
	(insert appropriate countries or groups of counries or territories)

4. Country, group of countries or territory in which the products are considered as originating	5. Country, group of countries or territory of destination

6. Transport details *(Optional)*	7. Remarks

8. Item number; Marks and numbers; Number and kind of packages (1); Description of goods	9. Gross mass (kg) or other measure (litres,m³, etc.)	10. Invoices *(Optional)*

(1) If goods are not packed, indicate number of articles or state "In bulk" as appropriate